Foxfire 11

Foxfire 11

Wild Plant Uses, Gardening, Wit, Wisdom, Recipes, Beekeeping, Toolmaking, Fishing, and More Affairs of Plain Living

edited by KAYE CARVER COLLINS, LACY HUNTER, and FOXFIRE STUDENTS

ANCHOR BOOKS

A DIVISION OF RANDOM HOUSE, INC.

NEW YORK

Anchor Books First Edition, December 1999

Library of Congress Cataloging-in-Publication Data

Foxfire 11: wild plant uses, gardening, wit, wisdom, recipes, beekeeping, tool-
    making, fishing, and more affairs of plain living / edited by Kaye Carver
    Collins, Lacy Hunter, and Foxfire students.—1st ed.
        p.   cm.
    Includes bibliographical references and index.
    1. Rabun County (Ga.)—Social life and customs.   2. Appalachian
Region, Southern—Social life and customs.   3. Country life—
Georgia—Rabun County.   4. Country life—Appalachian Region,
Southern.   I. Collins, Kaye Carver.   II. Hunter, Lacy.   III. Title:
Foxfire eleven.
F292.R3F7   1999
975.8'123—dc21   99-27305
                                                              CIP

ISBN: 0-385-49461-0

www.randomhouse.com

Book layout by Bonni Leon-Berman

Printed in the United States of America

20 19 18 17 16 15

This book is dedicated to all the people still searching for their place in the world; to those who have found and cherish their sense of place; and to all the people here in these mountains who have helped us find our place.

CONTENTS

ACKNOWLEDGMENTS

With any Foxfire project, so many people contribute so much that it would be almost impossible to name and thank all of them individually. We owe so much gratitude to students who, over the years, have gathered the information for the books and made the program a success; to parents who often carry the students on the interviews; and to current teachers Angie Cheek and Joyce Green and Principal Matt Arthur at Rabun County High School, who provide a base of operations and unfailing support and guidance for the magazine program.

In particular, we owe a special thanks to the many people who helped us in the production of *Foxfire 11*. This book was edited entirely by former students who worked when they came home from college, when they had time off of their regular jobs, or around their other jobs. Without Teresia Gravley Thomason, Amy York, and Robbie Bailey, we could not have finished this book on schedule or with the diversity and perspective it managed to achieve. Teresia, while on summer vacation from her job with Pioneer RESA, produced both the "Wild Plant Uses" chapter and "Wit, Wisdom, and Remembrances," as well as looking at the rest of our sections for grammar and stylistic problems. Amy, who had just graduated from high school and was preparing to go to college, completed the "Hunting Stories" and "Farm Animals" chapters. Robbie, the three-time veteran of Foxfire book production, compiled the

"Fishing" and "The Old Homeplace" chapters and frequently told us what to expect next in the process of compiling the book.

Our help did not just come from former students. Many friends and family members of both the *Foxfire 11* crew and the Foxfire program also helped in the production of the book. Bill and Pat Gravley and Jane Thomason and Warren Thomason answered questions on everything from recipes to chickens on a regular basis throughout the summer. For a few weeks, we were at the house of J. C. Stubblefield and Bernice Taylor weekly, conducting interviews for nearly every section of the book. There were days when we called Jimmie and Juanita Kilby several times with questions to which they either had a cheerful answer or did their best to find out for us. Jimmy Hunter read and reread several sections, providing comments, insights, and corrections. Debbie Hunter, Bessie Ramey, and Al Durham gave last-minute advice and help with the recipe section. Former Foxfire students Allison Adams and Teresa Thurmond Gentry helped with final edits.

Various community members also provided needed support. Mildred Donaldson and Susie Smith graciously provided needed information for our "Gardens and Commercial Farms" chapter. Doug Adams, Kyle Burrell, and Perry Thompson provided needed advice and knowledge regarding the "Fishing" chapter. Marie Mellinger and Billy Joe Stiles gave invaluable assistance with wild plant names and uses. George and Howard Prater kindly helped us fill in missing information about beekeeping and then sent us away with a few bottles of delicious honey as gifts. Mary Elizabeth Law helped with our research of historical information.

The Foxfire staff, as always, helped when needed. Robert Murray, who could not come near the *Foxfire 11* crew without having several questions thrown at him, was always willing to assist. Lila Anna Hiers advertised the coming publication and took numerous pictures for us. Mary Lou Rich did a little of everything, from reading to ordering more supplies, to providing cheerful encouragement and moral support. Michael Buchholz acted as go-between with the Doubleday editors, kept us on task, and helped broaden our perception of what this book could be. Ann Moore read, reread, and read again every page of the book, never complaining, and often encouraging us with everything from words to kind notes left with our sections after she had finished reading them yet again. Bobby Starnes agreed the book should be done and allowed Kaye the time to work on it.

And finally, a heartfelt thanks to the members of our community who welcomed us into their homes and gave freely of their time, their knowledge, and themselves, and, most important, gave us love, friend-ship, and a sense of belonging. They are the everyday heroes upon which this book and all the others are based. We are indebted to them for raising us right; for supporting us; for showing us that no matter what changes our beloved mountains see, the values and ideas that make us Appalachian—the ones that tell us to be self-sufficient, yet remind us that ultimately we belong to our community and our Creator—will not change. Thank you.

Foxfire 11

INTRODUCTION

L ong before my father passed away in 1995 at the age of ninety, he used to boast that he had seen it all—from the stone age to the atomic age—from right there in our tall-grass prairie community on the southern plains where he was born, raised, and planned to meet his maker "walking out across the pasture." While his story may be unique, it is not out of character for many of America's elderly whose lives spanned most of the twentieth century. Born in Indian Territory (in Geronimo, no less) and raised among the Comanches, he survived boyhood by farming and hunting the hillsides and creek bottoms on the homeplace. Later he served as Indian agent for the government and, at one time or another after that, was the teacher in a one-room schoolhouse, a threshing crew boss, an oil field roughneck, a sharecropper, a cowboy, and a bulldozer driver. While he was the gentle family patriarch and "strongest man in the county" to his sons, he was "Uncle Cecil" to my buddies and cousins who would sit gaped-eyed while he enthralled them for hours with his tall tales of yesteryear. He taught us, among other things, to make our own bows and arrows out of the osage orange tree "just like the war chief Great Monsikay" taught him, how to predict exactly when a pregnant sow would have piglets, and how to hypnotize a chicken. What neater information could a twelve-year-old boy possibly possess in 1954! This was, of course, before we went forth to the big world and learned to hide our country ways and disguise our Okie accents so we, too, could sound like the man on the six o'clock news.

While rummaging through my father's possessions after the funeral, I discovered something that brought back a flood of memories. There among his few books—Bible, various Year Books of Agriculture, and a surveyor's handbook—was a water-stained, tattered, and duct-taped copy of the original 1972 Foxfire book. My brother George and his wife, Lynn, had given it to my dad for Christmas that year. As I flipped through the worn, consumed pages with carefully penciled-in personal observation notes in a distinguished handwriting of an earlier generation, I realized that he must have read this Christmas gift at least a hundred times. I remember coming home from Europe that winter to a country and its families torn apart by Vietnam and racial strife. We gathered around the fire on Christmas Eve to admire this most unusual gift—and how a high school English class way down in a faraway place called Rabun Gap, Georgia, decided to go out and interview the old people about their traditions as a project in cultural journalism. I now realize that this positive bridging of young and old by the Foxfire kids could not have been better timed for a troubled America. For my father and his generation, the simple fact that their knowledge was appreciated and recorded in black and white was a verification of a hard life well lived. For my part, I momentarily forgot about the generation gap and felt very grateful in being reminded that there was no need to feel shame in this family and rural place. It was one of the happiest Christmases of my life.

Exactly a quarter century later I took a personal pilgrimage to the little log cabin on the mountain above Mountain City, Georgia, where the very simple but beautiful and effective Foxfire philosophy of education through practice had been crafted and nurtured. Here, within hand-hewn heart pine walls, successive *Foxfire Magazine* classes, in pursuing what interested them in the local community, had created perhaps the world's richest archives of regional folk history. Engulfing me in the cabin were the results of more than three decades of premier oral history research—wall-to-wall catalogs and files containing over two thousand taped and transcribed interviews, twenty thousand black-and-white photos and slides, and hundreds of videos. Here was a scholars' paradise and a national treasure in need of immediate attention. I learned from Dr. Bobby Ann Starnes, the president of The Foxfire Fund, and Michael Buchholz, the resource director, and other dedicated staff members that for several years the archives had suffered benign neglect when the organization was going through changes in leadership. Dust, silverfish, dampness, and time were beginning to take their toll. I felt honored when the Foxfire folk asked me and Dr. Virginia Nazarea, my colleague in anthropology at the University of Georgia, to help them in their ongoing efforts to preserve the materials.

The first product of this revitalization effort is this wonderful new volume on Appalachian farm life prepared by present and past Foxfire students. The Foxfire archives, through voices of local people, document one of the greatest transformations of the American landscape since our country was founded: the decline of the American farm. The official statistics are brutally honest: between the 1960s when the Foxfire Approach was being conceived and today, the number of farm families has declined by over 50 percent. During this same period, the farm population dropped from 15 million to around 4 million. Accompanying this decline has been the physical abandonment of the countryside and the industrialization of farming. The culture has disappeared from agriculture. Most farmers today do not even grow their own food, preferring instead to purchase it at the supermarket. Simultaneously, the remaining farms are increasingly assaulted by an encroaching suburbia that is often spiritually and aesthetically bland. Much of rural America has become a "subdivided" landscape where every place is no place. Strip Mall, Georgia, looks the same as Strip Mall, Anywhere, USA. As we destroy the cultures of our rural past, to quote Kentucky author-poet Wendell Berry, "we did not know what we were doing because we did not know what we were undoing." And rural futurist Wes Jackson warns, "The loss of cultural information due to the depopulation of our rural areas is far greater than all the information accumulated by science and technology in the same period."

As we enter the twenty-first century, however, men and women much like my dad are still out there waiting to tell their stories of change and continuity. While the Southern Appalachian region has faced much the same fate as other rural areas, the ruggedness of terrain and the doggedness of the people have allowed a traditional world to linger on long after its disappearance in the flatter parts of the country. By tapping into these survivals, *Foxfire 11* offers a countervailing perspective to the assumed inevitable decline of regional character and rural traditions. Unlike those of us who waited too long to listen to the turn-of-the-last-century generation, the students of Foxfire have shown us how a sense of place still lives on in historically hardscrabble communities with names like Licklog, Turkey Cove, and Warwoman Creek. The homogenizing march of the interstate highways, fast food and motel chains, tourism, and land speculation may have altered the main thoroughfares over the mountains, but growth and "progress" have not stomped out either the memories or the desire to maintain the old mountain ways.

The pages of this book portray farm families who created and refined the practices associated with tilling the soil, tending the seed, harvesting the produce, and finally preparing it for consumption or storage for the next planting. In this system, tied closely to the changing seasons, an intimate and sacred connection prevailed between the people and the earth and between the society and the landscape. Children learned directly from their parents by observing and participating. A farm child never had to explain or hide what his father or mother did for a living. However poor the economy, the locally evolved foodways and survival tactics were part and parcel of a rich human culture that gave a special meaning to life.

I can hear some "growth without limits" proponents arguing "so what?" If the family farming way of life has virtually disappeared, then what value is bygone knowledge today? After all, aren't technology, information, and global markets supposed to work for a better future? And in this future, what use are bean stringings, pea thrashings, corn shuckings, and taffy pulls? I, for one, leap to disagree with this quick deterministic dismissal of the past. What was is just as good as what is. While specific knowledge, technology, or activity may sometimes seem like folkloric anachronisms acted out only in heritage fairs, the underlying principles of rural living can still serve as a moral and ethical compass in our individualistic, hypermodern world. Our citizenry has grown used to a society where children don't have any idea where their food comes from other than the supermarket and old folks die in heat waves because no one checks on them anymore. We are seeing a deterioration of our communities, our ecologies, and our physical and mental health. If an appreciation of the past helps us move forward and make better choices, then why not use it?

The student editors, writers, and compilers of *Foxfire 11*—Kaye Collins, Lacy Hunter, Amy York, Robbie Bailey, and Teresia Thomason—once gathered with me in the archival log cabin to educate me on what they learned from working on this volume about farm life. Although none of the students had ever lived on a farm, much less milked a cow by hand, they all said the exercise provided a powerful vehicle to reflect on the lives of the earlier generations who had sacrificed so much. Unanimously, they felt the lessons for living provided by the elders could guide us in the future. First, they were impressed by the brave self-sufficiency of their parents and grandparents who had no guaranteed nine-to-five job and no social security but survived nonetheless with pride and joy. Second, the simpler lifestyle of the old mountain way could teach us a few things about bringing balance back to our rush-about modern lifestyles. Third, the students yearned for a more personal world where neighbors supported each other, where resources were shared, and oral communication (talking, singing, storytelling, preaching) was a valued art form. Finally, they learned that the land from which they sprang helped pay for the prosperity of America and the education of its youth. They know that it is time now to repay the land through revival of an old-fashioned stewardship and reverence drawn from the inspiration of bygone generations of farmers. Sure, we cannot go back to an earlier life—even if we wanted to—but as we search for ways to cure our modern social ills, heal our land's wounds, and restore a balance between ourselves and our lost roots, there is much of value in these pages.

The first person I ever met at Foxfire was its conservator, Mr. Robert Murray, who can best be described as a modern-day Will Rogers. He kept me and my graduate students spellbound and in stitches as he gave us a knowledge-rich folk tour of the wild useful plants around the center's grounds. As we strolled back down a winding path to our car, he told me that when the Foxfire project started in the mid-1960s, the Appalachian hill people were experiencing a "period of shame" in which they believed their hand-me-down knowledge, hard won through everyday experience, had little value compared to the higher-status knowledge found in America's cities and flatlands. They thought that to be accepted they had to shed their "hillbilly" ways and adopt those of outsiders. Learning had to come from textbooks or other materials designed and produced by formally educated people who lived far from Rabun Gap. Highland culture had to be replaced by a national culture promoted by the mass media. Today, however, all over the United States and cultures beyond our borders where the Foxfire philosophy of experiential hands-on learning has taken root, students and teachers know better. As the world globalizes and regional identities disappear, a counterreaction emerges in villages, towns, and cities where people are actively seeking their roots—and listening to the aging guardians of indigenous knowledge—for inspiration in capturing lasting values of a community-based culture. This Foxfire volume, published on the dawn of a new millennium, not only continues the grand American tradition of the ten Foxfire books before but comes at a time when we as a people need more than ever such fine examples of how young and old can realistically anchor themselves in their communities. The timing of this Foxfire book is no less critical for our country than the original Foxfire book of 1972.

> —*Robert E. Rhoades*
> *Professor of Anthropology*
> *University of Georgia*
> *Athens, Georgia*

Being involved in *The Foxfire Magazine* class benefits everyone in one way or another. Of course, the obvious benefits are practical ones: computer skills, business skills, and proficiency in communication. These skills, however, seem unimportant when I think about what I really learned in my years spent working for Foxfire. I started out new to the program and painfully shy. I could not imagine how I would ever survive the first interview. I was quite sure, in fact, that the man I was interviewing was going to hate me. But I did survive (and he did not hate me). After a summer of interviewing people, arguing with other senior editors, and seeing articles I had written published in the magazine, I gained confidence that has impacted every part of my life.

Another aspect of the Foxfire experience, one that really did not become clear to me until I began working on this book, was the insight gained from working with Foxfire students of other generations. Kaye Carver Collins, who has been my adviser, mentor, and friend over the past four years, was a Foxfire student of the 1970s. When we first began putting the book together, I ran across a place in a transcript where a lady had made a comment concerning what she thought about men wearing mustaches. I laughed and turned around to tell Kaye, who surprised me by quoting the lady word for word. She had been on the interview and described it for me, talking about how she had laughed when this tiny, eighty-year-old lady had talked about men with mustaches. Experiences like that helped me to see all the interviewees, even the ones whom I had never met, as people, and not merely names. Furthermore, they helped me relate to Kaye as a former student just like me.

Working with former students from three different decades was an experience in itself. Of course, the technical aspects of producing a book have changed greatly: Kaye remembers using typewriters, Robbie and Teresia remember getting the first computers, and Amy and I are computer-dependent. However, some aspects of the Foxfire books have not changed and hopefully never will. Each of us has at least one or two people who stand out in our minds as having changed our perspectives.

The people I have been able to meet and interview are a large part of what has made my Foxfire experience so special. When I think about Mr. and Mrs. Hoyt Tench, the first people I interviewed, I still feel gratitude that borders on hero worship for them. I went to their house, terrified I would not be a good interviewer and that they wouldn't like me, and they took me in, patted my back, and talked to me as if they'd known me for years. Their kindness and warmth not only made me more comfortable as I was interviewing them but affected me later as I went on more interviews. I did not get nervous after that first experience—in fact, going on the interviews actually became my favorite part of the production of the magazine.

Mr. and Mrs. Tench are far from being my only memorable interviewees. As a seventeen-year-old high school student, I had the privilege of meeting and photographing the governor of Georgia, Zell Miller, when one of my friends interviewed him. What an inspiration to see a man who came from "just across the mountain" sitting in the governor's chair.

Perhaps the most influential interview I had, though, was with Mrs. Annie Chastain, my last interview as a high school student. Mrs. Chastain, whom you will meet later, took me under her wing, prayed for me, and showed me the kind of neighborly love you will read about throughout this book. Recently, she, her husband, and I were sitting on their front porch talking. (He was laughing and threatening to make me help him rob the bees.) When one of her cousins dropped by, Mrs. Chastain introduced me as her friend. I have never had a greater honor than to be called the friend of this wonderful woman.

This book and the others in this series are full of people like Mr. and Mrs. Tench and Mrs. Chastain. They have wisdom and experience, always beneficial, but they give us so much more. Perhaps the greatest gift they impart to us is love—love for family, friends, neighbors, and strangers; love learned from good parents, strict rearings, years of hard work, and years of sharing with those in need; love that their faith in God tells them they would be wrong not to share. We can learn so much from them because they have lived through hard times; seen enormous changes, both technological and social; and they have survived and are happy. They will tell you, in spite of whatever circumstances they may have lived through or overcome, that they have had a good life. We have more to learn from them than a lifetime could teach.

—*Lacy Hunter*

I consider myself a very fortunate person for several reasons. Two of these are that I have had the privilege of living in Rabun County, Georgia, all my life, and I have had the opportunity to be involved with Foxfire, in numerous capacities, for almost thirty years.

I'm proud of the fact that I am a lifelong resident of this community; I'm proud to come from a long line of Rabun Countians who survived adversities, cherished family, praised their Creator, and found contentment with their lives. Although I own a home here, home is much more than a house—it is this place and these people. I am not a landowner, for the land owns me. It is a part of who I am and what I hope to become. (All locations in *Foxfire 11*, unless noted otherwise, are in northeastern Georgia.)

I firmly believe that part of that strong sense of belonging comes from having been involved with Foxfire, in one way or another, since 1969. First, by being the kid who watched teenagers interview my parents, and later, as a Foxfire student; then as a Foxfire volunteer on their Community Board; and finally as a member of the Foxfire staff. One of the true pleasures of my job has been working with *The Foxfire Magazine* senior editors during the summer, and with them and their teachers, Angie Cheek and Joyce Green, during the school year. Together, the teachers and I see those students start to make connections with their community. As they explore and research their articles, they are also discovering more about themselves and how they fit in this community.

I hope that they, like I, get a tremendous sense of self-satisfaction knowing who they are and where they come from. I believe Foxfire plays a major role in that. Foxfire helped me see the elders of my community as friends and mentors—not as old people. The knowledge and friendship I acquired from them helped me develop my self-image and my appreciation of individualism.

The first interview I ever went on was with Aunt Arie Carpenter. She lived in a dilapidated log cabin, carried water from a well, walked wherever she needed to go, and had a heart full of love to share with everyone she met. She had no money, no car, no television, wasn't famous—but she had the gift of making a sixteen-year-old feel special, cared about, and valued. And she wasn't the only one. Minyard and Lessie Conner, Kenny Runion, Lawton Brooks, Clara Mae Ramey, Margaret and Max Woody, and many, many others, have all helped me, with their friendship, love, and patience, to develop my sense of belonging here. To me, there is no greater gift we can give ourselves and others.

My father died fourteen years ago, but I share him with my eight-year-old son, Alex, through Foxfire magazines, books, photos, and videos. As I show Alex the photos and read him the stories, I hope I will be able to give my son a sense of place and help him value his heritage. Eventually, I hope he will come to recognize and love his connection to these people and this place.

When the opportunity arose to write this book, and the suggestion was made that I and another former student would coedit it, I immediately wanted Lacy Hunter as my coeditor. I knew that with her English, writing, and organizational skills, she would be a real asset to the production of *Foxfire 11*. Lacy and I have worked together for the last four years. She came to Foxfire as a senior editor of *The Foxfire Magazine* in the summer of 1994. She didn't know the first thing about magazine production, but with the help of the more experienced senior editors, by the end of the summer, Lacy knew it all—how to operate the computer, use Pagemaker, take photographs, develop negatives, conduct an interview, and edit it. She worked with me for the next two summers, training new senior editors. This past year, she organized our archives for us. When she first came to work for us, she was extremely shy and wouldn't dare share an opinion; and while she excelled at many things, she was still searching for her place in the world.

Lacy and I have both come a long way from our days as Foxfire students. I think in one way this book is representative of our search for who we are. As you read the stories in this book, you will become acquainted with many of the people we have met throughout the years. Our hope is that each of you will gain some sense of connection from their stories. In a way, these people personify Foxfire. They worked together to better their lives. They shared what they had with others. They tried to find beauty in the simple things. They took the knowledge that had been given to them and improved it to fit their circumstances.

I also believe the work we have done on this book depicts what Foxfire stands for. First, it is the only book in this series coedited and written entirely by former *Foxfire Magazine* students. I think that is profound—that the ones who have learned over the years are now the experts. It is part of what the Foxfire teaching approach is all about; the learners naturally progress until they are skilled enough to begin teaching others.

It represents collaboration, which is also part of the teaching approach. One of my major concerns as we began working was that when a problem came up, Lacy might defer to my opinion because I have been her supervisor for so many summers. But I soon learned that along with her magazine production skills, Lacy had acquired many other skills in the Foxfire classroom. She wasn't afraid to speak her mind, wasn't influenced by my point of view, and often had much more creative contributions than I. I think we make a good team. We collaborate well together. We each have our strengths and weaknesses when it comes to producing a good article, but we work together to make it the best it can be.

It represents our commonality. Even though I'm a Foxfire student of the 1970s, Teresia Thomason and Robbie Bailey are students of the 1980s, and Lacy and Amy York are of the 1990s, I believe we share many common bonds. We care passionately about the people we interview; we know more about ourselves from having been in Foxfire; and we feel that, in some way, Foxfire will always be a part of us and us a part of it.

It represents our shared wisdoms. Just like the people featured in this volume, we each had knowledge to share with the others. We each drew on our own experiences in Foxfire to make this the best book we could produce.

And, finally, it represents the knowledge, skills, and wisdom of the people here and their willingness to share all that with teenagers toting microphones, tape recorders, and cameras. Out of that sharing develops ideas that those teenagers will carry into adulthood, and parent-hood, and the cycle goes on and on . . .

—*Kaye Carver Collins*

THE OLD HOMEPLACE

"... deep down in you, there is always a longing to get back home."

PLATE 1 A view of
J. C. Stubblefield's homeplace

When I started this chapter, it was called "Farm Buildings." After reading the various articles, people kept referring to the "old homeplace." With the help of Kaye Collins, I decided to change the name of the chapter because although the buildings themselves are important, the very essence of the "homeplace" is what ties this chapter together. When people talk about the homeplace, they're not just referring to the house or the farm buildings. They're referring to a piece of land—their land—that they've lived on and farmed, and hope to pass on to a new generation of the family to give it the same care that they and their ancestors have. It is a place where you spend numerous hours wondering if there is another place in the world that is as beautiful and majestic as it is. It is something you can call your own and be proud of. It is where you are from and where you always belong. In *The American Farm*, David Brown explains:

Home place. Sit a spell on the tailgate of a farmer's pickup. Tailgates were made for conversation. Soon enough, every farmer mentions "the home place." He'll give the words a slightly reverent tone, emphasizing them with a gesture. Your eyes follow his hand to a small collection of buildings at the end of a country lane where a red gambrel barn sits near a house dressed in white. You'll be forgiven for thinking the old-fashioned house is his home place. The farmer, however, means more than just a clutch of buildings. To him, the home place isn't boards held together by nails. It's the land, and not any land, mind you, but his family land. Only those particular acres—handed down through the generations—are the home place.

My grandmother grew up on the old Highlands Road at the Carver homeplace. The old house fell due to decay and eventually burned to the ground. Of course, the piece of land, covered in ivy and weeds, is still there, but there are no structures on the place. To an observer, it is simply an unkept piece of land, but to my grandmother, it is a place that will always be home to her, whether she lives there or not.

My grandfather was born in Carroll County, Georgia, on a farm. He left that area and moved to Rabun County when he and my grandmother married. He worked in various places, mostly in Oak Ridge, Tennessee, and Aiken, South Carolina, but they returned to Rabun County and bought a place. He had an original homeplace, but when they bought their house, they attained a new homeplace. They will always have fond memories and stories of that little piece of land they called home. That's what happens to many people today. My homeplace will always be in Mountain City, where my grandmother and grandfather lived, but I will start my homeplace for my family somewhere else. In the case of my grandfather, he would always tell you that he was from Carroll County but that Rabun County was his home.

Along with the appreciation of home comes a sense of responsibility, of hard work, dedication, and self-sufficiency. Self-sufficiency is the ability to support or maintain oneself without aid or cooperation from others. In the Appalachian Mountains, farming is, and has always been, a means of self-sufficiency. When one has a farm, it has to be carefully and diligently worked and harvested to ensure the proper growth and use of the crops. Farmers couldn't sleep in or take the day off. They had to get up every day and milk the cows, clean out the barn, feed the animals, mend a fence, plant or harvest crops, and cut hay. This just didn't happen every Tuesday or once a month; it happened every day of their lives, and if they didn't do it, life was at stake—an animal's, someone else's, or their own. In the past, there wasn't much money for people to go to the store and buy food. The only store available was a small country store, but many families were living in remote areas and sometimes couldn't get to it. That is why farming was a way of life.

The farm buildings were just as important as the soil the crops came up from. Not all homesteads were alike, but almost all included a chicken house, barn, smokehouse, springhouse, root cellar, and in some cases, a hog scalder and sorghum mill. Try to imagine the beautiful, rustic buildings that dotted the land as Sallie Beaty talks about the farm she grew up on in the Warwoman community.

"The old house we used to live in is still standing down at [her brother] Nathan's place. The wind blew it off its foundation. The smokehouse was just at the edge of the yard, and in it, we kept our meat and, I believe, our canned stuff. The crib was about seventy-five yards from the house, and in it was the corn that we used for meal and to feed [the cows and horses] with, and then it had a shed to it that we kept the wagon under. Back then, we didn't have no tractors. The crib would be left opened at the top so we could throw our corn in it. Our chicken house was up to the left of the house, between the barn and the crib, and the chickens stayed there. Back then, we'd turn them out [during the day], but they laid [eggs and slept] in this chicken house. [About] twenty-five feet from it was the barn where the livestock stayed. It was the biggest building on the farm. Mostly, at night, we'd fasten the livestock all up. We milked in the [barn] stalls back then. It had a loft to it where we kept the hay and the fodder [leaves of the cornstalk] and tops [upper part of the stalk] and stuff like that. I believe all of them had tin roofs, except the old house, which had boards made out of oak. All of the buildings were made of rough-cut lumber. Most all of it was cut off the farm. Daddy had somebody to move in down there with a sawmill, and they sawed it there on the place. In fact, they sawed what Nathan's house is built out of today."

These buildings served as a living area for the family and their animals, and for food storage and food preparation. Barns were used to hold livestock and store hay and corn. Smokehouses were used for storing and preserving meat. Springhouses and root cellars were used for the refrigeration of food, with water from springs or creeks for the springhouse and the natural temperature of the ground for root cellars. On some farms, the hog scalder and the sorghum mill were used for food preparation.

Additional information can be found in previous Foxfire books. For example, barn raisings can be found in *Foxfire 2*, springhouses in *Foxfire 4* and *Foxfire 9*, and smokehouses in *Foxfire 1*, *Foxfire 2*, and *Foxfire 9*.

—*Robbie Bailey*

CHICKEN HOUSE

PLATE 2 Nathan Bleckley's chicken house

The chicken house was not a specific size, and the location of it really didn't matter in reference to the house. Most of the time, though, the chicken house was built close to the house so it was easy to gather the eggs. These houses were not the industrial-sized chicken houses that most people are familiar with today. Their size really depended on how many chickens you owned and the amount of material you had to build it. Usually, it wasn't very fancy, just a building constructed out of rough lumber because in those days most of the lumber was cut rough. The chickens stayed in the chicken house at night and laid the eggs, and during the day they roamed around the pasture or yard.

Sallie Beaty recalled, "Our chicken house was made out of rough lumber or slabs of wood. It was square-shaped, about twelve by twelve [feet], with a roof and a door. [We kept our chickens here] when we didn't let them roam outside. We fed them corn outside."

SPRINGHOUSE

The springhouse was used to keep foods cold and preserved and was usually built over or near a spring. Cold water ran through the springhouse and kept the food cold. Most were constructed of wood, but many used rock because it was believed that the rock absorbed the natural coolness of the water. Wooden ones were quicker to build, but didn't last

PLATE 3 Rock springhouse at Hambidge Center for Creative Arts and Sciences, Inc.

as long as the rock buildings did. The decision to use wood or rock was based on the ability to obtain the material and the amount of time available to construct it. (See *Foxfire 4*, pages 347–61, for more information on springhouses.)

Oza Kilby shared, "We didn't have refrigerators or freezers. We had a spring and what we called a springhouse. We had water that would run into a trough. We built the little springhouse over that trough. That is where my mama stored her milk and butter. It was convenient, and

PLATE 4 Wooden springhouse from Aunt Arie Carpenter's homeplace

the milk would stay cold. She would put her butter in containers, in a bucket or something, where the water wouldn't get in it."

Others like J. C. Stubblefield and Bernice Taylor didn't have the actual structure—the spring was their springhouse. J. C. told us, "We didn't have a springhouse. There was just a branch. The temperature of that water was cold."

His sister Bernice added, "We had a concrete trough made in that little branch. There was a hole in each end for the water to run in and out of. It stayed going all the time."

THE ROOT CELLAR

The root cellar, or food storage cellar, was constructed of logs. It was called a root cellar because people stored crops such as potatoes and turnips in it. (The word "cellar" is derived from the Latin word *cella*, which means storeroom.)

The building shown in the photo is aboveground, but other root cellars were underground. The roof of most root cellars is aboveground, but

PLATE 5 The root cellar located at the Foxfire Center

covered with sod and dirt, and the rest of the structure is below the ground. This kept foods cool in the summer and above freezing in the winter. The underground cellars usually maintained a temperature of fifty degrees in the summer and about thirty-eight degrees in the winter.

J. C. Stubblefield described the root cellar that he still uses today. "[We had a root cellar] down in the basement of the house. Well, it's just a hole. Dirt floor and all. It's been dug out from under the house. [We put] canned stuff, sweet potatoes, Irish potatoes, onions, pumpkins, and acorn squash [in it]—whatever we had that had to be took care of during the wintertime—to keep it from freezing. I don't know [what the temperature was;] it was cool, though. [The fairly constant temperature] was created because of where it was, in the ground, and the house over the top of it and all, and not opening the door [to the outside] much."

PLATE 6 The Foxfire Center smokehouse

SMOKEHOUSE

A smokehouse was used for preserving meat and usually, like the other buildings, was constructed of rough lumber. The floors were dirt and served to keep the air inside the smokehouse cool. Usually, there was a roof on the building and it was kept tightly enclosed to keep out insects and animals. (See *Foxfire 3*, pages 354–60, on the construction of a smokehouse.)

Sallie Beaty told us, "Our smokehouse had a dirt floor—no ceiling, [just a roof]. It was made of rough-cut lumber and was about fourteen-by-sixteen feet. We hung the meat up in that smokehouse. Back then it was cold. On one side, [we had shelves]. We had a space and a rod across it [on the other side] that they hung the beef on and the same way with pork. [We'd hang it on this rod] until it drained some."

The animal was slaughtered and then carried to the smokehouse as soon as possible. Meat was always taken in the twenty-four hours after the animal was killed, to avoid spoilage. The best time to take the meat was while it was still warm. The most common meats cured were hams, shoulders, and middlin' meat (the side, between the shoulder and back, down the spine).

Meat was cured by mountain families in several ways. It might be thoroughly salted and then set up on waist-high shelves or down in boxes or barrels to "take the salt." Most people preferred the shelf system, as it allowed the meat to get the necessary ventilation easily. Meanwhile, the winter weather provided natural refrigeration while the meat was going through the curing process. When the weather began to get warm, the second phase of the operation began. The meat was taken out of the salt mix, washed, and then treated. (Cover the meat with a mixture of pepper and borax.)

Many people, however, preferred smoking the meat. Holes were poked in the middlin' meat, hams, and shoulders, white oak splits were run through the holes, and the meat was hung from the joists of the smokehouse. Then a fire was built inside the smokehouse. If it had a dirt floor, the fire could be built right on the ground. Otherwise, a washpot was set in the middle of the room and a fire built in that. The fuel for the fire was small green chips of hickory or oak, pieces of hickory bark, or even corncobs. Smoke from the fire was kept billowing for two to six days or until the meat took on the brown crust that was desired both for its flavor and for its ability to keep flies and other insects out of the meat.

There was no specific size for smokehouses. They were tailor-made to a family's needs. Sometimes they stood alone among a complex of outbuildings, but more often they were part of another building that had several uses.

Some smokehouses were relatively open, while others were sealed and tightly closed, to keep insects out. To keep flies out, aluminum screen wire was tacked to the inside of the logs and to the underside of the ceiling between the rafters. The salt would eventually eat holes in the wire, but it was easy enough to replace when that happened. To keep out rats, a trench could be dug six inches into the ground under the bottom logs, and cement poured in it to make a solid barrier that rats couldn't get through and wouldn't tunnel under. The door and walls would keep out dogs and other animals.

"We had a smokehouse out in the [backyard]," Amanda Turpin said. "The floor was the ground, just dirt. It would be so cool. We had a big wooden tub, and we would draw water to pour in that tub and set our milk and butter in it. It kept it so cool we didn't have to draw fresh water but about twice a day—in the morning and in the afternoon. [That well water] was just like ice water."

J. C. Stubblefield recalled, "We built that for a smokehouse way back then. When we was killing hogs, we put our meat up there in the wintertime. It's made out of oak lumber. It's got a tin roof. I believe it was a seven by eight [feet]. It's setting on big rocks. Back then you didn't know what a block was. It's just a junk house now. It's at least forty years old, and it may be older. I built it myself."

PLATE 7 J. C. Stubblefield's smokehouse, which was built in the 1950s

BARN

The barn stored corn and hay, usually in the loft, and housed animals, such as cows, horses, and mules. Built only a short distance from the house, the barn was usually the biggest building on the homestead, sometimes even bigger than the house itself. The loft was accessible by a ladder through a hole in the middle of the loft. The barn was covered with board shingles, and it was planked on the inside to close it in.

PLATE 8 The barn at J. C. Stubblefield's

J. C. Stubblefield explained his barn in the Wolf Creek community. "The barn is a log building, the bottom is. The top is lumber covered with metal roofing. I helped build it—me, my daddy, and somebody else built it in 1939. It is thirty by fifty [feet], I believe. The bottom part is where we kept the cattle, and the top part is where we kept the hay. You call it two stories. Go right straight up there through the hole to the loft. It's got a ladder. The outside door is where you haul your hay and throw it in the barn. You can throw it right from [the ground] because I built the ground up above the barn where you could back up level to it [in a truck or wagon]."

BARN RAISINGS

When people in a community were building a barn, all the families would gather at that homestead and have a barn raising. It was a time of fellowship and a time for others to pitch in and help out. It also showed the common bond that these people had with each other. One of Foxfire's most memorable times was when Millard Buchanan raised a barn at the Foxfire land. It was the first and only barn on the property. The following account of the actual barn raising and the historical background of the Ingram mule barn is given by Steve Smith, a former student.

Under the leadership of Millard Buchanan, the first barn was added to the reconstruction project on the Foxfire land. The barn was found abandoned in an adjacent county, bought from its owner, dismantled, and moved in on Millard's logging truck, "Big Red."

Putting the barn back up took approximately two weeks. It looked like one of the old-style barn raisings to people who dropped by to watch the Foxfire kids, Millard, and his crew of community men working hard to fit it back together on its new site. It was amazing to watch Millard cut and notch new replacement logs for ones that were rotted and sort through the piles of original logs for the good ones that could be used again.

And because he worked in the woods and with logs all his life, he knew hundreds of shortcuts and ways to make the job go faster and easier. When the gnats got too bad in the hot sun, for example, he built a small fire with green wood and leaves. The smoke almost choked everyone sometimes, but at least the gnats left them alone.

Now that the barn is finished, it (along with the other buildings that are being moved in and reconstructed) will be filled with all of the tools and materials that have been collected by Foxfire.

THE INGRAM MULE BARN

The Ingram mule barn was originally built by Nathaniel Ingram between the late 1800s and early 1900s, near Warne, North Carolina. The barn was used for housing animals and animal feed. Holes were drilled in some of the logs in the walls.

PLATE 9 Foxfire's Ingram mule barn

The original barn had pegs stuck in these holes to form a hay catch. This kept the hay off the ground so it wouldn't be trampled and spoiled. The barn now serves as storage space at the Foxfire Center.

OTHER BUILDINGS

On some farms in Rabun County, there were less commonly found buildings. These were a symbol of the ingenuity and practicality of these people. They made do with what they had, but if they had to develop new or different ways or structures that would help them tend the farm, they'd do it.

HOG SCALDER

Hog scalders were a rarity on Appalachian farms, unless the farm was big. They were usually made of rock, and in the center, a big pot held the water in which a hog's hair was singed off. A fire was built underneath the pot to heat the water.

The hog scalder at the Foxfire Center in Mountain City is a traditional design using an iron pot set in cemented rocks. This particular hog scalder would have been extravagant for the 1800s. A typical Appalachian family would not have been able to afford such a hog scalder unless they had a large farm, because the iron for such a large pot and the rock work would have been very expensive.

PLATE 10 The hog scalder at the Foxfire Center

The hog was rarely put in the pot itself but was laid close to it and the water dipped out of the pot and poured onto the hog. The hot water loosens the hair follicles so they can be easily removed. The hog scalding pot could also be used for washing clothes, making lye soap, rendering lard, and making cracklin's, or it could cook large amounts of soup. In the more southern regions of Georgia, a scalding pot might also be used for sorghum syrup production.

Other families used a more conventional way of cleaning the meat, as J. C. Stubblefield described. "We usually had a sled that we would drag the hog out on, and pour the boiling water on the hog and clean it off."

PLATE 11 A closer view of the hog scalder

CORNHOUSE

J. C. Stubblefield told us about a building he has on his farm called a cornhouse. "We built it to put soybeans in it because we used to grow soybeans to feed the milk cows in the wintertime. When we quit having milk cows, we used it to put corn in because we used to grow a lot of corn here. It's about fourteen or sixteen by twenty [feet]. We had it for a house for three months. We carried water to the old place way off over the hill, and it didn't have no kitchen or dining room. They built a small place just for the kitchen and dining room. Bernice, my daddy and mother lived in it for three months before they moved down here. It's [made of] logs. The rafters on it is poles about three to four inches [around]. Now, you know they use two-by-fours or two-by-sixes for rafters, and [the cornhouse has] poles. That's the little old building they lived in, and we moved down here and put soybeans inside of it. I took it apart and had to put it back together when I moved down here. [Bernice] was the only [child] then [in] 1912."

PLATE 12 The cornhouse at J. C. Stubblefield's homeplace

SORGHUM FURNACE

Another rarity on an Appalachian farm was the sorghum mill or furnace. In order to get sorghum, one had to grow sugarcane. Many people in the mountains didn't grow it, but there were some that did. The structure was made of stone and cement with some type of metal as the frame. It sits beneath the ground, and the dirt is used as the floor of the furnace.

Former student Preston McCracken said, "In *Foxfire 3* [pages 424–36], we published an article about making sorghum molasses. Shortly after the book came out, one of our readers contacted us saying that she was interested in making some sorghum herself, but she needed the dimensions so that she could build the furnace.

"Therefore, Margie Bennett, John Bowen, and I went up to Sylva, North Carolina, to Mrs. Varn Brooks's and Mrs. Myrtle McMahan's to get the requested measurements and take a series of photographs. At that time, the furnace was still covered over because the sorghum would not be cooked for another month or two, but the pictures will give you an idea of how the furnace looks when in use."

Jim Turpin reminisced, "Daddy always greased [the boiler pan] with burnt motor oil to keep it from rusting before he put it away each year. [The next fall,] it would take about two days to get it cleaned up before they could make the syrup. [To clean the pan,] they'd have to fill it full of water and take five or six boxes of soda and pour in it. Then they'd take the steel wool [and scrub it] 'til that boiler was perfectly shiny.

PLATE 13 The furnace is a simple stone and cement structure with pieces of angle iron used as a supporting frame

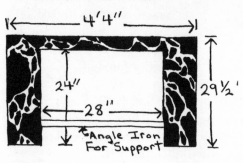

PLATE 14 Diagram of the front view of the furnace

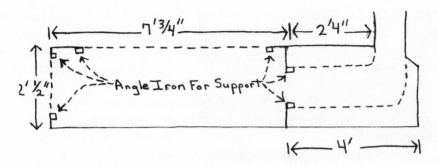

PLATE 15 Diagram of side view of the furnace

PLATE 16 This is a side view of the furnace. A fourteen-foot length of culvert is used as a smokestack.

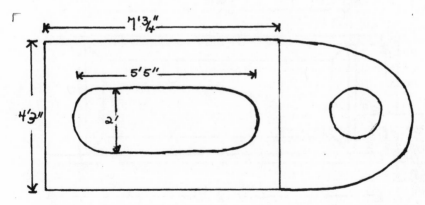

PLATE 17 The top view of the furnace. The pan sits over the oblong hole. The circle on the right indicates the placement of the smokestack.

PLATE 18 The sorghum pan is made by nailing together four two-by-eights covered with a sheet of tin to form the bottom and sides.

"The boiler sat right [over the furnace]. To keep from burning the woodwork on the boiler, they would paint it with mud and pack red clay [under the edge]. Finally, they'd pile the furnace full of wood slabs, ready to set it afire.

"There was a one-inch metal pipe that was screwed into the barrel [into which juice from the squeezed cane was caught]. It ran all the way down [to the boiler pan]. Daddy would whittle out a wooden peg to plug that pipe when he got his boiler full. That boiler would hold about twenty gallons of syrup. It was made of solid copper, because copper trays get the syrup the hottest. He had a plug in the lower end of the pan, also, and when the syrup was cooked, he'd pull that plug and sorghum would run out [into his barrels or syrup cans]. Nothing was added to the juice. Just the cane juice was cooked. When it came out, it looked like honey, clear and pretty.

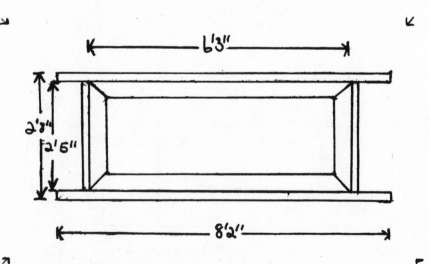

PLATE 19 Diagram of sorghum pan

"He'd make twenty-five or thirty gallons [of sorghum] a year and sometimes even fifty. It depended on the cane crop. We'd store it in gallon Mason jars. If we had enough, we'd sell it for seventy-five cents a gallon. A gallon of syrup wouldn't last long. Syrup and honey were the only sweeteners we had back then. We didn't have enough money to buy [sugar]. We had to either make our own stuff or do without.

"Boy, that was good stuff! It was good with hot biscuits. I wish I had some now."

THE OLD HOMEPLACE

When someone mentions homeplace, there is usually a name associated with it. If you buy a piece of land, that will be your homeplace, but to the many older people in the community, it is referred to as the "old Bleckley homeplace," or whoever owned that piece of land before you bought it.

Today a growing number of people are leaving Rabun County for better jobs, and the family homeplaces are being sold to outsiders, thus breaking the bond that was established in these families. In a sense, when the next generation in a family leaves the land, it's as if someone has torn away a piece of family history.

Land was once essential for a family's survival. It is now a commodity. Richard Norton recalled, "There is too much land growing up [being developed] and the population is gettin' bigger all the time. I don't know just how long it's gonna last. It is just a shame that the old people is a-lettin' the people talk 'em out of their land, sellin' it and all. We ain't going to on Betty's Creek. We are goin' to set down on it. I could have sold this place for a thousand dollars an acre [back in 1975], but I figure that such fellows as that right there [points to his grandson Tony] has got to have a place to live. And if we sell it, you can't get it back. It is gone."

Margaret Norton told us, "I've lived here on Betty's Creek all my life. I've seen all the changes as they come along up here. Course it just seemed like it didn't change all at once. Gradually came on.

"Before the pavin' of the road, this was just a small settlement and all the families and the farmers owned their land. Now lots of the land has been sold out, and now they have new families moved in here, or they are in the process of movin'. If people sell their land, the mountains might get overcrowded. They don't sell it for the money. They sell it because the tax is so high that they are not able to pay it. So many people are wanting land, I don't know why now.

"[Other] people are selling out their land even to where their children wouldn't have anywhere to live, but now not so up on Betty's Creek. People on Betty's Creek won't sell their land. Somebody comes [to my house] nearly every day to buy land, but we got four children and seven grandchildren. They all got to have a place to live. Richard won't sell an acre of land for two thousand dollars. What would he do with his money and his land gone? Well, it would soon be gone, and you wouldn't have nothin'.'."

Former Foxfire student Andrea Potts explained, "We were raised on Betty's Creek, and we kind of like to look back and remember it like it was. And I don't like the [development]. Because you think of it as a homeplace and not a vacation land. You hate to see the old people that have worked for their place and then lose it. If I was to get my hands on some land, it would not go unless it was a have-to case. I think in the next ten years, Betty's Creek will be chopped up and sold. All the old ones are dying and the middle-aged ones are selling it off now."

Coyle Justice stated, "Local people, people who were born and raised here, they don't leave because it is getting overcrowded. They might leave to make a better living somewhere else. But most people that leave, sometime or other they come back. Sooner or later, there won't be a place to come back to. That's why I wouldn't even think about selling. If I were to move, I'd still keep the house because if I sold it, somebody else would get it and make something else out of it. So I just wouldn't think about moving. That's a mistake. That's why we are in the predicament we are in now. Too much has been sold."

Ethel Corn said, "The biggest reason I moved back from Charlotte, North Carolina, was because I was born and raised here. It seems so much better here, and I feel the mountain people is a little better off than them people off down around the cities. The people here are friendlier. Some people like city life, but I don't, and I never did. But I'll tell you, you can wonder about a whole lot, but when you go to growing old, you want to get back to where you was born and raised. I wasn't one bit satisfied 'til I did get back."

Lassie Bradshaw observed, "We was born and raised here. I ain't nothing but a mountain woman. There is a song, you can take the girl out of the country, but you can't take the country out of the girl. I have to agree with that. When I got back, I felt like I was home. It's really hard, you know. When you live out in the country and you have to holler really loud to get your neighbor to hear you. [Living] up there [in Canton, Ohio], you can spit from one house to the other one. It's really different. I like to get out and hunt and fish. Up there, you had to go to a pool with hundreds of other people. Down here you can just jump in the river. I admit, I really miss the friends I had there. I could have stayed there. But I missed the people down here too. I love the country. There is no place like it!"

Beulah Perry exclaimed, "Clayton has always been my home. I hope to stay here the rest of my life. There is nothing more beautiful than to get up in the morning and look at the mountains. I love Clayton!"

J. C. Stubblefield summed up his feelings about home by saying, "Some of the folks in town asked me if I would like to have a new house, and I said, 'No, that won't be home to me.'"

Millard Buchanan commented, "I don't think there's anyplace in the world that can compare to this. You have a feeling for the place where you were born and raised. No matter where you've been or where you go, deep down in you, there is always a longing to get back home."

PLATE 20 "You have a feeling for the place where you were born and raised."—Millard Buchanan

The homeplace isn't something easily described. Sure, you can touch an old barn or grab a handful of dirt, but the homeplace is more than that. It is a feeling from deep inside that makes you swell with pride one minute and fill your eyes with tears the next. It is an emotion that only the people who toiled in sweat to create homeplaces, and their generations to come, can experience. I also found that even if you are not a farmer or don't live on the family homeplace, you are still a piece of the puzzle that fits together to form the old homeplace. Your ancestors did the work and you feel as if you, in a sense, did too. There is a personal bond between you and the people who spent the time to take care of the land. This book is dedicated to people who are trying to find their place. I would also like to make my own personal dedication to "the hands"—the hands that fixed the fence lines, plowed the fields, constructed the buildings, and brought new life from the ground. That is what made it possible for us, the next generation, to find our personal utopia, our place that we call home.

REFERENCES

Brown, David G. *The American Farm: A Vanishing Way of Life.* Toronto: Key Porter Books, 1998. The passage cited is on page 15.

Springhouse and Root Cellar

Irwin, John R. *The Museum of Appalachia Story.* West Chester, Pennsylvania: Schiffer Publishing, 1987.

Slone, Eric. *Eric Slone's Sketches of America Past.* New York: Promontory Press, 1986.

Smokehouse

Wigginton, Eliot, and students, eds. *The Foxfire Book.* New York: Anchor Books, 1972.

Wigginton, Eliot, and students, eds. *Foxfire 3.* New York: Anchor Books, 1975.

Page, Linda Garland, and Wigginton, Eliot, eds. *The Foxfire Book of Appalachian Cookery.* New York: E. P. Dutton, 1984.

WIT, WISDOM, AND REMEMBRANCES

"I've had a good life . . ."

The people of Southern Appalachia have always been generous in sharing their wisdom of things past. To fully experience Appalachian culture, one must indulge in a colorful story or two.

Southern Appalachian people are wonderful storytellers. Even the simplest incident or insight can be molded into a fascinating story. A fond memory triggers the beginning of a masterpiece. Whether witty, wise, sanguine, or sad, each story is a unique word sculpture of the personality, sufficiency, and resilience of the culture and its people. A deferential relationship with the land, the people, and the Creator is often a common thread in these stories where hard work, farming, faith, fun, and freedom abound. As Doug Sheppard said, "Having freedom is my idea of being rich." From living a simple life, these people have gained a foundation of wisdom upon which we and future generations can build. We must look back in order to move forward, for it is in the root of each living thing that strength is found.

Day-to-day life could often seem dismal when the hardships, mishaps, and personal tragedies of mere survival were constantly in focus. Thankfully, each day, though sometimes apparently endless, is but one piece of the giant puzzle of life. When the pieces are fit together, a beautiful picture emerges: a picture of a life fulfilled through heartaches and joys, mistakes and victories, foolhardiness and wisdom. Aunt Arie Carpenter, who lived in Macon County, North Carolina, all of her life, demonstrated the sentiment of life fulfillment when she said, "They want me t' sell and move away from here. But I won't do it. It's just home—'at's all. I spent my happiest days here."

Whether or not you reside in Southern Appalachia, you can, if but for a few moments, experience a culture that is truly unique simply by perusing this chapter. Herein is but a minute sampling of the flavor of the mountains. Enough said. Enjoy!

—*Teresia Gravley Thomason*

COMMUNITY

While there were some small townships and even a city or two, the vast majority of the Southern Appalachian people lived and worked in rural areas. A life filled with almost constant hard work is a trademark memory for this culture. Farming chores, home chores, and manual labor took up most of the day for people in this area. However, brotherly love and community support were a priority. Although hard work was a necessity of survival then, most people continue to express a strong appreciation and preference for the country and this often harsh way of life.

"The community was very cooperative. People were very helpful at

that time," Clive Smith told us. "If anybody needed something done, enough [people] would show up to do the job. You didn't expect any pay for doing that. Everybody did it. It was expected.

"I think a lot about Luther Stubblefield. When I was sixteen years old, I was sick and in the bed for a month. I believe Luther came every night to see how I was getting along. He'd come in and set and talk with me. I remember that. I think about that a lot. All the other neighbors would come by to see how I was too."

Susie Smith remembered, "The ladies would work in the kitchen fix-

PLATE 21 Susie Smith

ing dinner for the corn shuckings. We'd work one day here and one day down at the Stubblefields'—just different places. We'd help pull cane fodder and cut cane to make syrup. If anybody was sick, the neighbors would come and sit up with them at night."

Omie Gragg recalled, "I don't know [if we had money to get food]. I tell you, the ones that did have it would share with the ones that didn't have it. If we had it and someone else didn't, they'd come, and we'd share it with them. What you have now is yours, or what somebody else [has] got is theirs. They don't come now and expect you to share what they have with them like they did then.

"[We used to use a] five-gallon churn every day. Did you ever see people churn this way? Well, we churned five gallons of milk every day. And we could use all of that butter. It was hard times for people back then. Somebody would knock on your door in the morning, 'Have you got as much as one-half pound of butter I can have? We don't have any.' I [would] cut down until I would not have but one-half pound left for my family. We shared with everybody that wanted. If [a neighbor] ever got out of coffee, he'd peck on the door, and I'd have one-half cup of coffee for him. We'd share whatever we had with each other. Just good living!"

FARM LIFE

Rural farm life was the way of life for the majority of people in earlier times. Days were long, filled with chores inside and outside the home. None were excused from the work, for it was not done as excess but as necessity for survival. Harley Gragg recollected, "Back in those days, a main source of [income was the] farm. About the only thing there was to do was farm back then. Make what you lived on on the farm."

"I didn't have any specific jobs that I had to do. Everyone had to help out," Clara Mae Ramey told us. "You had to carry water, milk the cow, churn butter, cut the cane when it was ready to cut, cut cornstalks, cut wood, and to do all kinds of work.

PLATE 22 "We worked all day long. You get up early, and you just stay busy all day."—Clara Mae Ramey

"I was born at Glassy Mountain. We lived up there until I was four, and then we moved down to Liberty [community]. We had to move because my father worked in an orchard and the spray was getting to his lungs. One day my daddy told my mother, he said, 'We'll just move and not look back.' My daddy bought the one hundred and forty acres down there [in Tiger], and we moved to Liberty.

"At first, in Liberty, we lived in a log house. It did not have partitions in it, but it was home. We hung up quilts and bedspreads and different things for the bedrooms. It was great living there.

"My family and I made big fields of about three acres of green beans. We grew our own corn so we could carry corn to the mill and have it ground for cornmeal. We had a cow for the milk. We made butter and grew cane so we could have homemade syrup. We also had all kinds of fruits and eggs. It was great. For our water, we carried it from half a mile over the hill from the spring. Every morning we got up at four o'clock and put fire in the woodstove, no matter how cold. When I got old enough, it was my turn to build a fire in the fireplace. We worked all day long. You get up early, and you just stay busy all day.

"We were not allowed to eat between meals. At twelve o'clock my mother would quit and go build a fire in the woodstove to fix lunch. Then we'd all go in and sit down together and eat. We would leave the dishes and go right back. After the sun went down, we would go back in and have cornbread and milk. That's what we had most of the time for supper."

Esco Pitts thought back upon his life in rural Appalachia. He said, "Just as soon as we got big enough to work, we all had a job. We had to work because that's how we made our living. Everybody had to work. They didn't know anything else. You see, there wasn't any TV or radio or telephone. All the heat we had was one big old fireplace. You could lay a three-foot log in there, and that's how we kept warm in the wintertime. We cooked on it. Oh, I reckon I was fourteen years old before we even had a cookstove. We cooked on the fireplace in the old black pot. Your cornbread and biscuits baked in the oven in front of the fire. There is nothing to compare with it. I wish I had it today.

"We had to do chores. We knew to do it and do it right! My daddy'd go before us when we were little and show us how, and then we were depended on to do it—whatever it was. We had to get all of our chores done before we could do any playing. We had to cut our own wood and bring it in from the mountains. And then we had stock. The first thing I had to do in the mornings after I got big enough was to drive the cattle to our pasture about a mile and a half and come back and then go to school. Then I'd have to go get the cattle and bring them in for the night—do the milking and the feeding of the stock, taking care of them. That was about the last thing before we had our evening meal. And we didn't have any light but a little brass lamp—a kerosene lamp—and it furnished the light. Of course, we'd go to the woods and get a lot of lighter pine knots and bring them in, and we'd use that for light to study by. And that's the way I learned all my first studying. Get our lessons right there in front of the fire—be ready for the next day at school to recite.

"I worked for my neighbors, on the farm or wherever I could get something to do, and whatever I made I had to give to my daddy. Yes, I helped my daddy instead of him helping me, because we were raised poor—but we didn't suffer. We had plenty to eat and plenty to wear, but that was about it. No extras. We never went to town, I don't guess, more than three times in a year for anything out of the store. We had a good apple orchard, and my daddy'd gather his apples and take potatoes and cabbage and apples and chestnuts (there was plenty of chestnuts in the world those days) and put them in his wagon and go down in the country and swap them for groceries. [Sometimes] he'd sell them for money, but most of the time he'd swap them for groceries because there wasn't any money much. He'd bring back a hundred pounds of sugar and maybe fifty pounds of coffee and a whole barrel of flour; and that provided us for a long time. That's about all we had to buy. We raised all the other stuff we needed—plenty of beans, corn, potatoes, and cabbage.

"We didn't use any fertilizer in those days. The ground was fertile, and it grew good crops—produced well. It won't do it today. This old world is getting older, and erosion has taken off a lot of the good topsoil—put it down in the valley and washed it into the ocean. I don't know why it is, but it's that way. You can go into the mountains and clear up a brand-new ground—cut all the trees, dig up all the stumps, and plant stuff where nothing has ever been planted before—and it won't produce like it used to. We didn't have any insects back then. Nothing to bother anything. You didn't have to spray your apple trees. You didn't have to spray your beans or corn, nothing like that. It all grew and produced good, big, heavy crops.

"Well, I'll tell you, we didn't have much free time in those days because we had to work to make a living, and we lived on a farm. We had about twenty acres in the farm that we had to work. During the growing season, we were busy all the time. Of course, in the wintertime, we had to get wood to build fires. We did that in all kinds of weather—get out and cut wood—and we didn't have power saws. We'd have to chop it with an ax. We'd cut wood and snake it down off a mountain with a horse to a woodyard. Then we'd chop it or saw it up with a crosscut saw. It just about kept us busy to keep stovewood to cook with and fireplace wood to keep us warm."

Oliver Meyers's parents were farmers when he was growing up in the mountains. He recalled, "We had about sixty acres, more or less. My daddy had a syrup mill and made syrup. I never saw a fodder pack. Where I was raised, [we] didn't pull fodder and cut tops like they do in Georgia.

"I ate real good when I was at home with Daddy and Mother [when I was a child]. We had a bunch of corn, and we canned everything we could get hold of. We had a big dugout where we'd put our cans. We'd go up the steps [from there], and we had a big smokehouse. Then we climbed up a ladder up to a table, [and this was] where we put our onions. We didn't have any money, but as far as having something to eat, we had plenty.

"[We lived in] some bad [houses]. We lived in some houses that had big cracks in them, and you could see the chickens down under the floor. When we moved to Fontana [North Carolina], we lived in this little house that just had lumber laid in for the ceiling and had a big old fire-place. [In the winter] it was the coldest, snowiest time you ever saw. The house didn't leak when it rained, but that round hominy-sized snow cov-ered the boards and [came through]. We got the children and put them on the bed. We took quilts and made a tent-like thing, and that snow was blowing all over the floor. I knew we had [the children] all snuggled in there really good. We had a big old fire going, and we walked back up there. I [sang to the children] 'Wait now 'til the sun shines down.' Those old spring boards would leak. Boy, was that a cold house!"

Susie Smith thought back to her childhood days of working in the garden. "I did a lot of daydreaming in the cornfield, parked on top of my hoe handle, about what I wanted to do when I finished school. My main thing was a schoolteacher. That was all I could think of. That's about the only thing I remember dreaming and wondering about. We had a lot of time to think with that hoe handle. In the long, hot sum-mer days, you had a lot of time to dream."

Edith Cannon shared, "We were farmers, and we would take all our vegetables, except what we canned, to the market to get enough money for us to buy material so Mama could sew our clothes. We raised our own sheep also. We did not waste anything. Now I don't think anything about throwing away a piece of material eight to ten inches long, but back in those days we would use the very last stitch.

"When I got big enough, I would plow. I also ran the planter my daddy had. We planted the soybeans so we would have something to feed the cattle with. We always killed two or three hogs and a steer every winter so we could have our own meat. We did not buy anything except material. We had our own ducks, and Mama would pluck their feathers to make our feather beds with. She would make our own pillows too. We sold apples. We had apple trees, so we would take our apples to town and sell them to buy sugar and coffee.

"We canned the foods we needed for winter. We didn't have pressure cookers back then. We had a big washpot that we used. My daddy made a rack to sit down in the washpot so Mama could set seven or eight half-gallon jars in it. We would keep the fire under it and boil them three hours. For tomatoes and berries, we would use the open kettle method—just heated it on the stove, sterilized our jars, and put it in."

PLATE 23 Edith Cannon

DISCIPLINE

Good behavior, respect for elders, and a disciplined work ethic were essential to Southern Appalachian child-rearing. Clear guidelines and consistent correction helped many generations of Appalachian children grow into fine, honest adults. Threats of physical punishment were used when necessary, but most people remember obeying the wishes of their parents out of respect and love.

"We had a pretty strict rearing—not hard, but we had rules and regulations that we would abide by," Winnie Lovell remembered. "We shucked and shelled corn, helped feed the chickens and the cows, and got the wood in at night for the fire the next morning. If it was your job to get the wood and the kin'lin' in, and you didn't get it, you had to get up the next morning and get it then. You soon learned to do what you're supposed to do."

PLATE 24 "You soon learned to do what you're supposed to do."—Winnie Lovell

Jesse Ray Owens shared, "My parents were strict. If they told you something to do, then you knew to do it. You couldn't just wait around and try to get out of doing it. You had to do it right away. You didn't back-talk 'em or nothing. They was good to us and all that, but when they told us something, they meant it, and I say that was good."

Clara Mae Ramey revealed, "You didn't stand around and whine, boy, uh-uh. If you ever gave one excuse [for not doing your chores], you got whipped with a razor strap. I did not like that."

HARD TIMES

At one time or another, almost all of the people of the Southern Appalachians saw difficult days. Money was scarce, and every basic need was provided through backbreaking labor and pioneer persistence.

"We [have been] through some pretty tough times," Oliver Meyers declared. "We lived over in Clay County [North Carolina] after the Depression hit, and we got down to where I couldn't [find] any job. [We didn't have much to eat.] We just had cornmeal. We got it ground, and then [we] had to sift it out. We made coffee, and a lot of times we wouldn't have anything but onions and cornbread and that coffee made out of grain. It was pretty good.

"[One of the hardest times of my life] was in 1932, when we had just recently been married, and we were staying across the mountain from Tate City. It was during the Depression, and we couldn't get a job anywhere. I built a scaffold to dry apples, and they were what we lived on— dried fruit and groundhogs. I'd catch every [groundhog] I'd come to. That's [all we] had to eat [besides cornbread].

"It [really] pleased [my wife] to see me coming [home] with a big woodchuck. We'd cook that rascal, [and] I'd dress him. [After I cleaned out parts of the woodchuck] I'd dress that thing good, and then I'd go and cut some spicewood and break it up and put it in [the big old iron pot] with the woodchuck. [My wife would] cook it until it was real good and tender, then take it out and put it in the stove and brown it. Boy, was it good!"

Adam Foster's recollection also revealed hard but happy times. "[When we were living at home with our parents,] we had to get out here and hoe corn, cut wood, plow the mules, and build fences. I'd rabbit hunt when I had the time and Daddy didn't have something for us to do. If it was drizzling rain or something, us boys would get out and hunt or fish. We didn't get much time off, I'll tell you, on account of we had to work every day to live back in that time. We had our farm and all like that, but that wasn't saying we had any money.

"Back then you couldn't get a dollar. Money was hard to get. Yeah, things are a lot different than they was when I come along through the world. And I'm still here horse-trading. I've worked a many a day for fifty cents after me and my wife were married and were raising our children. Of course, I've always had land and a place, and I didn't have to get out and pay rent. I always had a farm to work on, but I couldn't get no money, no job. I'd go out there and work for fifty cents a day, and I thought I done pretty good. That was pretty hard times back then, but we lived good, I guess—had plenty to eat and enough to wear to keep us warm, but it wasn't the finest like people want now. I don't know how people ever made it."

RELIGION

Hard work and a strong faith went hand in hand for most families in earlier times. Belief in God and church attendance were foundations for enduring hardships. Many people with whom we spoke shared heartfelt testimonies and endearing memories of church life.

Bernice Taylor recalled the importance of going to church. "We had a [church] meeting every fourth Saturday and every fourth Sunday. That was all the meetings we had unless it was revival. Then we had Sunday school every Sunday. We'd go over there, and they'd sing, and have Sunday school, and then sing some more. We'd leave here about a quarter 'til ten or twenty minutes 'til [and] we wouldn't get back home 'til one o'clock, and they'd have to cook dinner for forty. They didn't hurry up. They just took their time and sung several songs before and after Sunday school.

"[We] always had a big crowd. Back when you had revivals, all the churches watched out and didn't have [their] revivals when [the other churches] were having it. Everybody [would] come to Wolf Creek, and then they had [revival] the next week somewhere else, and everybody went there. We've walked many a time from here to Lakemont church and here to Camp Creek. Sometimes we didn't get home 'til twelve at night. [We] didn't get in bed 'til one or two o'clock. [Then] we got up about five o'clock. We had to get our farming done and get ready to go to church at eleven when a revival was going on.

"[Back then we] just [had] the Baptist [denomination]. One time, we was over there, and I don't remember whether it was revival or just regular Sunday service, [but] a funny-type man said 'Amen' [big and loud] when somebody was praying, and they churched him 'cause he said 'Amen.' He might have not meant for it to have been like that, but they still churched him. [They] kicked him out of the church. [They] sure did that!

"[That] didn't happen often, but you didn't dance or play cards; [if] church members found out about it, [there would be trouble.] I remember when Papa wouldn't even let a stack of cards come in the house. The boys would slip around and play them, but they didn't bring them things in the house. Times are a lot different now than what they used to be."

Aunt Addie Norton told us, "I sit here and study by myself when I have a lot of time, and I think about things. I've got so I can't read my Bible much because I can't see to read for long at a time. I think how thankful people ought to be that they're living in this beautiful world, and I wonder how they can ever think that there is not a higher power. Who makes all these pretty flowers? We can make artificial flowers, but they don't smell and are not as pretty as the flowers that we pick out there. We can't make flowers like the Almighty."

Esco Pitts said, "I advise you not to be carried away with the ways of the world. The Bible says love God and love your neighbor. That's the commandment that Jesus gave. Love God and love your neighbor. In order to do that, you've got to study the Bible a whole lot, and you've got to go to church and hear the gospel preached. You've got to mix and mingle with Christian people, and you've got to worship your Maker. We were put here for a purpose. This world was made for man's enjoyment—for man's use. Man was put in charge of the world and everything that's in it. We don't realize it, but the Spirit of the Lord is present at any time. You can call on it any time. If you call on it in faith, you'll get an answer."

Ethel Corn had this to say about luck. "I heard of people taking a rabbit's foot for good luck. I don't see where that can bring you any good luck. I have learned through life that the only place you're going to get luck is by serving God and being close to Him. Good things will come your way. But if you're serving the devil, all of the clover leaves and rabbit's feet aren't going to help you any."

PRANKS AND JOKES

Although much time was consumed with work and chores, everyone found time for socialization and recreation. In the face of adversity, these people were still able to laugh and live life to the fullest. Most of the fun was homemade and relished by the whole family. Several contacts shared memories of playing as children and how they entertained themselves as adults.

Pulling pranks and jokes on friends and neighbors was a common source of fun. Wholesome diversions were a priority at home, at church, at work, and at school. Many pranks were pulled around the holidays, especially Halloween and Christmas. Aunt Arie Carpenter said, "I don't reckon the devil'll get me fer laughin', but if he does, he'll shore get me 'cause I've always done more'n my share of the laughin' in the world."

Many people took the pranks well, while others got mad. Ethel Corn said, "They felt sorta like they do now—some took it in fun, and some'd get awful mad about it. Some people could take a joke, and some couldn't. You find it the same way today. People were just out to have a bunch of fun—they didn't usually pick one person or family to play pranks on because they didn't like them. It didn't make no difference who they done it to, just any house they come to. They was just out for a bunch of fun, and they had their fun. And they got bawled out over it."

PRANKS AT SCHOOL

Some of the pranks played at school were pulled on fellow students, but many were played on the teachers.

Clive Smith recalled a joke he and the principal pulled on one of the teachers. "One thing that happened in high school [was that] the French teacher seemed to go out of her way to try to make things harder for [us kids]. She was [always] real fussy. One day in class, there were several kids that were talking to each other. She jumped up from her desk and shouted, 'Shut up! I'm tired of tellin' you! I've told you two hundred times to stop talking in class!'

"Well, I couldn't help it and I said, 'Two hundred!?' [I said that] because it sounded ridiculous that she'd told us two hundred times not to talk. Boy, she jumped on me and said that I was gonna get what I deserved. She took me to the principal's office and told him [what happened].

"So the principal said that he'd handle it and told her to go back to keep order in the class. She went out and closed the door, and he asked me what happened. I told him. So he signaled for me to be quiet and he said, 'I'm gonna have to punish you now, so you won't do that again.' He said it real loud [because] the teacher was standing outside the door [listening]. He told me to stand up. He went to slapping down on top of his desk to make it sound like he was whacking me with his yardstick. He hit [the desk] about eight or ten times and [then he] went over and cracked the door. The teacher was going down the hall a-gigglin'. She thought that he'd really plastered me! Things like that is what I remember about school."

Minyard Conner reminisced, "When I was in school in the fifth grade, it was in a one-room schoolhouse with one teacher. Along in the early fall, we was all playin' Anty Over over at the schoolhouse, havin' a cuttin'-up time. The teacher rang the bell for us to come in. All the students on the back side of the house just stepped in through a low window instead of going around front. Me and a husky boy was the last two steppin' in [the window], and the teacher turned around from the door and seen us, and then he really gave us a licking. He didn't say nothin' to the rest of the students. Well, me and him [the other boy] got together an' talked a little about it; the teacher was a grown man about forty-four years old. We had to walk back an' forth to school, and he'd always wait 'til we'd all left school before he left, and he'd come on later. There was a big hornets' nest beside the road—great big hornets' nest. We decided to stir up that nest for the teacher when he come by. One of us stayed at the hornets' nest, and the other got up on the hill to watch for the teacher. When he come around the bend, the one on the hill signaled to the one by the hornets' nest. Well, the one at the nest hit the nest and ran. He ran as fast as he could. Then we both got up on the hill behind some bushes where we could see. The teacher come walkin' up with his head down, and them hornets all just *zzzzzzzz* in his face. God! That hat went up in the air, and he went to stompin' his big feet—he had about number twelve shoes—and then he run just as hard as he could go.

"Next day he come to school, and he could just see a little out of one of his eyes, and he had big lips; they was just turned wrong side out. He said he'd give five dollars to find out the one who stirred up that hornets' nest. Dollars looked awful big then, but me an' that other feller didn't say nothing to nobody. He'd a beat us up again. We got even with 'im."

Buck Carver told us about a prank played on him one day. "I got one pulled on me one time at the two-room schoolhouse. Ralph Burrell had been a-cutting match heads off and sticking them in his knife. He would pull the blade down just a little and stick them in. When the blade was pulled back and hit that match head, it would pop like a cap pistol. One day I leaned over and told him I wanted to borrow his knife to sharpen my pencil. I flipped the blade back—everything was quiet in the room—and it went off. It sounded like a twelve-gauge shotgun. The teacher didn't give me time to explain that I didn't know it was loaded. She whopped the heck out of me."

Harry Brown related, "A couple of the boys was out a-possum huntin', and they caught a little small civet cat [according to Mr. Brown, a small striped skunk-like animal with an odor stronger but similar to that of a skunk]. The schoolteacher had a big table with a drawer in it, and they took that small civet cat, put it in the drawer, and when the teacher opened the drawer, she got sprayed. Oh, we had a nice time in the schoolhouse there for a while!"

PRANKS AT HOME

Homesteads were the site of numerous pranks. Family members played pranks on one another, neighbors good-naturedly tricked neighbors, and strangers had fun with homeowners while passing through.

"We used to do everything, we boys did. Guess we did everything there was to be done," Lawton Brooks remembered. "Anything mean, and get by with it. We didn't hurt anybody, just did things we oughtn't to do. We didn't have things to do like other people, you know, no cars to ride in. We just did something to pass the time.

"We'd do things to people like taking their wagon apart and put it together up on top of their barn astraddle of the roof, and they'd have to take them down a piece at a time.

"We'd run off, and then we'd laugh at them when they'd go to tearing them down, and they'd rare and growl, 'cause the only way they could

PLATE 25 Lawton Brooks

get their wagon down was to do like we done, get up on the barn and take it down a piece at a time. He'd have to take every piece loose to get it down off the roof of the barn.

"When men come to get their corn ground, we'd put cockleburs under their saddles [and we'd] be upstairs looking out the window. One mule threw a fellow off and went off and left the old man.

"He lived up on Shooting Creek [North Carolina], and that mule had to go back across that creek. When the mule went out of sight, he was flying. The old man waited there 'til a man that lived about two miles away from him happened to come to the mill in a wagon. He hauled the old man back as far as his house, and that old man carried his meal the other two miles home. He said he knew the mule had gone back home. He said he couldn't figure what was wrong. That mule had always been gentle.

"We'd go by people's houses and get their ax and hide it in the wood-pile and they'd have to hunt their axes out. They knowed somebody had done it, though, because it was a custom, people going around and hiding people's things like that. They'd keep a-hunting. We'd hide it where they'd find it, but they'd have to hunt for it to find it. I've took the horses outta the stable and put their cows in a different stable where their horses was, and they'd go to milk and find their horses, instead of cows, and that'd make them mad, and they'd growl about that. We oughta been killed, but we weren't. They ought to beat the devil out of us for doing such things as that."

Buck Carver reminisced, "Bill Martin was all the time pulling pranks on Uncle George Grist. George was married to Bill's sister. There was panthers there where they lived. Old man Grist had a mare that had a young colt. Bill Martin slipped over there after George was in bed. He took a stick and was a-tickling that old mare's heels. The mare was a-kickin' the walls and a-raising Cain. George was afraid to go over there. He was afraid it was that panther. He'd get out in the yard and holler, 'Hey, Bill!' He wanted Bill to come over there. Uncle Bill was right there, but he just laid quiet while George was hollering. The mare would quiet down, and George would go back in and go to bed. Bill would give him enough time to get in the bed and get straightened out good; then he'd start tickling the mare again. He done that two or three times. The last time, when the light come on in George's house, Bill throwed his pole down and run down to the branch near the house. George started hollering, 'Hey, Bill! Hey, Bill!' Bill raised up out of the branch and said, 'What did you want, George?' Old man Grist offered Bill a heifer if he wouldn't tell that tale on him. But Uncle Bill would get about half drunk, and he had to tell it every time.

"When I was about fifteen, I was going to Dillard one day, and when I passed by the early harvest tree, there was my brother Bill and my sister Mabel. Bill was in the tree, shaking off apples, and Mabel was on the ground picking them up. I hid good behind the trunk of another tree. I changed my voice to sound just like old man Grist and I said, 'Hey there, boys. Get out of my apple tree.'

"Mabel said, 'Bill, there's Mr. Grist! Get down from there!'

"Bill nearly fell out of that tree. When he got down, I walked out and showed them who it was. It made them about half mad.

"Daddy pulled one on me one time. He told me to roll him a cigarette, but he only smoked a pipe. Boy, I rolled him one just as pretty and smooth as you ever seen. I wasn't a-thinking that he was trying to trap me. I licked it and sealed it and handed it to him. He looked that cigarette over good and close, and then he said, 'Now, by josh, that likes a whole lot of being the first one you ever rolled.'

"My brother Pritch would tie a string to his pocketbook, throw it in the road, and hide in a thicket. When a car would come by and stop to get the wallet, he'd pull it back down into the thicket. One or two boys wised up to it, and they'd run over the string, slam on their brakes, get the pocketbook, and take it on with them."

Kimsey Hampton told us, "When I was a little feller and just big enough to start a-courting, I was afraid of the dark. I'd see something along the road and think it was a booger and I'd run. So one night I was a-taking this girl home, and this bunch of boys decided they'd give me a scare. They took some old chicken wire and kinda doubled it up around a great big thing and put a sheet over it and tied a wire to it and put the wire across the road up in the forks of a bush. Up above this, they put two sacks of leaves, one on each side of the road, and put a wire from one over to the other. Well, I looked, and I could see that thing, and every time I would look at that thing, it would weave. They'd pull that wire up on the hill, and I didn't know it.

"So after a while that white thing crawled up the bank of the road and across the road and on up the other bank and climbed a tree. I seen that thing, and I just knowed it was a booger. So I was ashamed to go back to my girlfriend's house, and I knowed good and well if I could get even with it, I could outrun it. I got up just about even with that thing, and I broke to run just as hard as I could go. 'Bout the time I made two or three big steps, my big toe got hung in that wire and both sacks of leaves hit me right in the face. I hollered 'til you could hear me for two miles. I just knowed that thing had me!"

Harry Brown told us about a prank played on newlyweds. "When old Diamond got married, some of his friends sneaked into his and his wife's house before they got home and tied a bell to their bedpost. They stuffed some rags in the bell so it wouldn't ring when they got into bed, and had a string rigged up and attached to the rags and pulled it out after they got into bed. Then, while the couple was asleep, one of 'em sneaked in, grabbed their clothes, and sewed them up—sewed up his pants and coat and shirt and her dress—sewed 'em together just like quilting all over. They like to never got their clothes on the next morning!"

PRANKS AT CHURCH

Oftentimes the church was the center of the community. Almost everyone attended because it was a way of life. It was also an opportunity to see friends and neighbors and catch up on the news. Children and teenagers took advantage of this gathering to pull pranks on the church family.

"Mel Lamb and a bunch of others were bad to turn the saddles around on people's horses while they were at the night services at church," Buck Carver recalled. "The people didn't know nothing about it, and they'd start to [mount] their horses and find out. They'd have to turn the saddles around."

Kimsey Hampton remembered, "Me and some boys went to church one time up at Inman Hill in North Carolina. There was a woman and her husband that went to church all the time, and her husband was church superintendent. She decided one time that she owned the church. She got her a tablet and pencil and got next to the window in church, and she was going to see all the boys on the outside who were skipping church and take their names down. She was gonna see them in the courthouse in Waynesville.

"I was kind of a mean boy and didn't care hardly what I done. I told a buddy of mine to get down there below the church a piece, and to turn his cap the wrong way and kinda pull his coat up around his neck. When I motioned for him, he was to come by the window. So he got down a little below the end of the church. It was after dark, and this woman was sitting right next to the window. I went down below the church and cut me a limb looked like a fishing pole about eight feet long and trimmed it up right real good. I got right behind the window where I knowed she'd stick her head out, so I motioned for that old boy to come. He come a-running as hard as he could run. That old woman stuck her head out the window, and she had on a little ol' stylish hat that looked like a hornets' nest on one side of her head. Just as she stuck her head out the window looking up the way he was running, so she could see who it was to take his name down, I cut down on her neck with that fishing pole, and it popped kinda like a whip. That little hat flew right straight up and rolled down the hill. Me and her husband went the next day looking for it and found it way down the hill from the church, and from that day on she would never set next to the window anymore.

"Another time me and some boys were around the church in back (the church was kinda rounded behind), and the pulpit where the preacher stood was kinda rounded. The people that sung set on that bench that circled around in the back end of the church. The church was made out of old-time pine lumber and had a big old pine knot out of it, and it left a hole in there under that bench. Me and some boys were looking through that knothole one time, and I see'd a woman's leg right down in front of that knothole. I just reached through it and got ahold of her leg, and she got up and screamed, and my daddy was the preacher, and he jumped up and hollered 'Amen' and grabbed her and thought she was shouting, and it was me that had ahold of her leg.

"When I was a little boy about seven year old, they was having meetin' in a church up here, and there was about four or five steps from the ground you had to go up into the church. Uncle Hamstalk had a apple orchard up the road above the church, and I went up there an' got me some apples an' come back down, and was standing in front of the church door eatin'. Uncle Hamstalk had a long white beard come down him nearly a foot. Looked kinda like Santa Claus. He was in the church a-preachin'. I decided I'd throw one of his own apples at him. I rared back and throwed one apple in there and hit him right in the mouth with it. I see'd what I'd done, and I run into the church door lookin' back out. Ever'body jumped up, broke up the meetin', and they wanted to know where that apple come from, and I told 'em they's some boys on the outside throwin' apples at me. We got out there and got to huntin', and I helped hunt like everybody, and it was me the one that throwed the apple."

HOLIDAY PRANKS

Several people remember pranks and jokes that were played around various holidays. Because tangible gifts were often scarce, having a good laugh was an inexpensive treat that everyone could enjoy together.

Roy Mize told us, "One time we tied up the

PLATE 26 Roy Mize

heads of a bunch of a man's cattle [with old rags]. The family who owned the cattle had about four growed-up children, and they's all the time some of 'em havin' the headache. They'd go around with something tied around their heads. We tied up a bunch of their cattle's heads one night at Halloween [to make fun of them], and they got sorta sore about it."

Ethel Corn recalled, "On Halloween, they just went around to the houses an' done meanness. They slipped around and didn't make no racket. They'd wire their doors shut from the outside, put their buggies on their porches, fill the buggy up with cabbage. I never did get into that. Poppy'd have skinned me alive! I was afraid to! But I knowed a lot of 'em that did. It didn't ruin the cabbage; it was the time o' year cabbage should be took up. They'd pull 'em up by the roots, so then all the people had to do to store their cabbage was to bury 'em.

"On Halloween people'd also take soap an' go around to the stores an' other places of business and soap them good. Just wet the soap and rub it all over the windows. Some people have put paint around on windows. They just messed up the windows of stores and such. They never did people's houses—they's afraid they'd get caught and get shot!"

MORE PRANKS

Pulling pranks wasn't limited to any one environment, as you will see in the following stories. Anyone and any subject were fair game. All it took was imagination, mischief, and in some cases, a touch of bravery.

"We used to go snipe hunting," said Florence Brooks. "You take somebody snipe hunting and put them at the end of a ditch holding a bag. Tell them you're gonna scare the snipes in. You go back home and leave them there holding the bag. Some of 'em will stay nearly all night. There ain't no such thing as a bunch of snipes. You won't get it on nobody but one time."

Ada Kelly shared, "I had a date with a young man who lived four or five miles from me. He came Sunday morning to spend the day. He had a brand-new buggy that he had driven over in. I had a brother about eleven or twelve, and he had a friend visiting him. While we ate dinner, they filled the back of my date's buggy with pumpkins and switched his front and back wheels. (My brother and his friend didn't eat.) He didn't know about it 'til time to leave that afternoon. (The pumpkins were in the space where the top folded down.) He saw the boys watching him from a hill, and he drove off as if nothing had happened. When he got out of sight, he changed the wheels again. But he didn't find the pump-

PLATE 27 Lelia Gibson

kins until a good while later. They were hidden under the folded-down buggy top and started to rot."

Lelia Gibson remembered, "When we lived in Burning Town [North Carolina], we lived near an uncle of mine [by marriage] who was a strong Democrat. You couldn't name a Republican in his presence. He was out on the porch at his house and these two men came along. Just for meanness, they sang as they went up the road across from where my uncle lived. The two men running for the presidency were William Bryan and William McKinley. The men sang:

> 'McKinley rides on a big white horse,
> Bryan rides the roan.
> McKinley stays at the big White House,
> Bryan stays at home.'

It made my uncle so mad he said he was going to go out and whip 'em!"

Minyard Conner told us, "There was a coon hunter who was out hunting all the time. He had a good coon dog, but another feller was catching all the coons, and he wasn't catching none. So he asked the other feller why. This other feller had a little monkey along with him. That feller said his monkey helped him. He said that he put him down in the swamp where the moss is on the tree, and you couldn't see him.

"Well, this feller would tree a coon or his dog would. He had a little .22 pistol, and when his dog would tree one, he would give his monkey the pistol and tell him to go up the tree and find the coon. The monkey would go up there and hunt around, find the coon, shoot him out, and come on down.

"Now this [first] feller got so interested in it, he wanted to buy the monkey. The other man said he'd sell him the monkey. He took the monkey and went off hunting with him. His dogs treed a coon, but moss was hanging down from the tree, and he couldn't see the coon. He gave the monkey the pistol and told him to go up and find the coon, and he was gone and gone and gone. He couldn't find the coon. He come back down to the foot of the tree and shot the dog.

"The next time he saw that other feller, he said, 'Your monkey killed my dog.'

PLATE 28 Ethel Corn

"The other feller said, 'I forgot to tell you about that monkey. He hates a lying dog.' "

Ethel Corn said, "One time we was sleddin' out tanbark, me an' Mel an' Poppy an' Bill. Mel had some little ol' hound pups, and it was hot. We'd have to go up places as steep as a horse's face nearly, and that'd just tickle Bill to death. He'd let 'em get way up there [near the top], then he'd jerk their feet from under 'em, and those poor little ol' pups would go just scootin' back down the hill. I watched him do that, and I thought how funny it'd be to do him that way. So I let him get to the top, and I jerked his feet from under him, an' boy, down on his belly and down the hill he went slidin'. I took around the hill. I was afraid to stay around him. I got my distance and begged him to not do nothing to me. He said, 'I won't this time, but if you ever do it again, I'll whip ya.'

"I said, 'Now, Bill, you know how them poor little pups felt.' "

ENTERTAINMENT

Toys were not in abundant supply and recreational time was sparse in earlier times. Most children used common objects touched with a little imagination to create toys and games, and children and adults alike were more than happy to play with anything available.

"Sunday was about the only time us girls had any time to do anything," Susie Smith told us. "Most of the time, we'd either be at our neighbors' or they would come and visit us. We'd go out here in the woods and find big fluffy moss and sweep a place out here in the yard to make us a dollhouse. We just had all kinds of dollhouses and furniture made out of moss. We didn't have the yard then that we've got now. We had apple, peach, and plum trees out here in the yard [then]. We would [also] go out and hunt the trailing arbutus when they would start blooming. We thought they smelled so good and were so pretty. We would [also] go visiting on Sundays to our neighbors, the McKays, the Williamses, and the Stubblefields. The Stubblefields and us are about the only ones that's in the same place."

Clive Smith recalled, "At school and on weekends is where I remember [doing] most of the ball playing [as well as other games]. Somebody always had a sponge [or string] ball. We'd choose up sides and play. We called it town ball, but it was like baseball. We had three bases, a pitcher, and a catcher for each side. We [also] played marbles. In the late twenties, rolling a hoop was [popular]. We'd get ahold of a metal hoop and take a strip of wood and nail a T-bar across it. [We would] get out there and see who could roll that hoop the furthest without letting it fall over. Back then we got to where we could roll one for miles and turn it around and come back. I've spent hours doing that.

"Another thing the boys did [was to] make a sled and get out in the woods and find a steep place to slide down the hill. If your sled is made out of oak, after you've used it a few times, the bottom of the sled runner will get just as slick as glass. We'd take our sleds and go out and slide down all the steep hills around here to see who could go the furthest before we hit a bush or smacked a tree. It's amazing that none of us got killed.

"And a lot of times, us boys would get out in a thicket and climb one tree and see who could go the furthest swinging from one tree over to where we could cross over to another tree and then to another one. [We would] see who could go the furthest without having to come down. Like I said, it's amazing that none of us were killed."

M. S. York shared this story about candy pullings. "Over on Liberty, around Tiger, the

PLATE 29 M. S. York

young people would go over there, and I would walk the girls home and
stay over there on Sunday. There were lots of young people over on
Liberty. They would gather up there on Sunday and there would be
twenty-five and thirty. I would run around with my nephews mostly and
cousins. That was about all there was on the creek here. We had to walk
everywhere, and we would have parties and play games. We'd all gather
up at one of the neighbors' houses.

"We'd have a candy pulling every once in a while. You'd pull it until
it would change color, and it would get to where you could twist it up.
It would get hard. It took a lot of pulling!

"Mrs. Dickerson would get us to her house, and it was supposed to be
a sangin' but it wasn't. They wouldn't let the girls go if they were goin'
to a party. But if they were goin' to a sangin' [a singing in the commu-
nity], their parents would let 'em go. We would get up there and there
wasn't no sangin'! She looked after us. We didn't get in any trouble."

Omie Gragg reminisced, "We enjoyed growing up and being
teenagers. The boys and girls all got out and entertained each other
together. They didn't go off two and two; they stayed in a crowd. We
played ball and hide-and-go-seek.

"The first person I ever dated was Harley [her husband]. I'd say I
was about fifteen years old. We went to school together. We didn't go
off nowhere or nothing. He'd come up to the house. We [were] just all
like a family. When we dated, we'd date just like a family thing. We
never did go off and do things by ourselves. People just didn't do that.
We just always got out, a crowd of us all together, and just entertained
each other. Like y'all have a party, we just got together and had a good
time. Maybe we would all eat at one home one day; maybe, the next
Sunday, we would eat at another home. The children and adults in the
community all shared alike."

Winnie Lovell told us, "I spent a lot of time with my brothers and sister. We played football and baseball, and we used to slide on the pine hill.
Our favorite thing to do was to slide down that hill. Those pine needles
would get slick 'til you couldn't even walk back up. Every Thanksgiving,
if it wasn't raining, we raked leaves. Everybody was in charge of their
own little pile. We had to clean up our own area. If somebody left a leaf,
one of us would say, 'Oh, you left a leaf!' We liked to play in them. I'd
get a big pile and then somebody'd run and jump in it and scatter it, and
I'd fuss. Sometimes I'd jump in their piles. That's kids!"

Dorothy Kilby lightheartedly exclaimed, "I love for it to snow! The
kids and I used to get on the hill and make us a homemade sled, get on
there, and go through the hallway of the barn. We had some fun! I still
love for it to snow. I might try it again sometime!"

STORIES

Remembering past adventures and retelling fictional tales is a fond pastime for the older generation. Vivid stories bring smiles and laughter to those who take the time to listen. The following stories are just a sampling of those shared by the generous people of Southern Appalachia.

"I was going down the railroad one night, and there was an old store that set down below the road, a big old store," recalled Kimsey Hampton. "The windows were all broke out of it, and there was nothing in it. There was a screech owl flew up on the railing right in front of me, and I just tried to pick it up. It would fly on down the road five or six feet in front of me, and I just kept trying to pick it up, and every time I would bend over to get it, it would fly a little further. It flew off the railroad down in that old store. I went down there, and it was setting in the window, and I tried to catch it. It flew inside that old store onto one of the counters. I walked in the door. The moon was shining in one of the windows. It was setting on the counter, and I just decided I was gonna catch it. When I reached to get it, it went to crying just like a baby. You talk about somebody getting out of there in high gear! Brother, I got out of there. As far as I know, that owl is still there.

"One time up in North Carolina, a feller by the name of Rube Mull had a old shepherd dog, and you could throw a stick in the creek, and that old dog'd jump in, get it, swim back out with it, and lay it down right at your feet. So Rube and another feller went one time to dynamite the creek and get 'em some fish. The old dog tagged along behind, and they didn't know he was with 'em. Rube got his dynamite fixed and put the fuse in it and lit it and throwed it out in the creek. Just about the time the dynamite hit the creek, the old shepherd dog jumped in. Went and got that stick of ol' dynamite, come swimmin' back to Rube, an' Rube started runnin' out through an old broomsage field, and that old shepherd dog right behind him. He'd look back over his shoulder every once in a while an' say, 'Lay it down, Shep, lay it down!'

"After a while, the stick of ol' dynamite went off, and the ol' dog went up about two foot high and just flew all to pieces. The feller asked Rube, 'Why didn't you climb a bush an' get out of his way?'

"Rube said, 'I did think about it, and I was 'fraid the dog'd lay the dynamite down at the foot of a bush and blow us all up!' "

Another vital part of Southern Appalachian storytelling is the Jack Tale. Jack Tales are fictional stories, told to entertain and occasionally teach a lesson, about a cantankerous fellow named Jack.

PLATE 30 Pat Cotter with his wife, Lonna

Pat Cotter uses Jack Tales to bring the pumpkins he carves to life. He states, "This is a Jack Tale that my grandfather told me about how the jack-o'-lantern got its name:

"There was an old Irish farmer who lived pretty close to him, and he was very, very mean. He didn't go to church on Sunday. He didn't go to PTA meetings. He didn't pay his paperboy. He was just all in all a bad character. He did have one attribute that made him famous in East Tennessee. He grew some of the best apples in the state. On his farm there, he had fine apple trees, and he grew the best, biggest, and sweetest apples in the state. Even the governor would come in and buy his apples. They were just great.

"The devil heard about Jack's apples. It don't happen so often now, but the devil used to drop in and see people every now and then. So the devil dropped in at Jack's house one day and said, 'Jack, I hear you've got the best apples in the state.'

"And Jack said, 'I have. I've probably got the best apples in the eastern United States.'

"And the devil said, 'Well, I'd like to have some of 'em.'

"And Jack said, 'Well, you'll have to go to the very back part of my farm on the highest hill, in the tallest tree on the very top limb. That's where you'll find the sweetest apples.'

"So the devil said, 'Well, I think I'll go get some of 'em.'

"So he left and started to the apple tree. Jack followed him with a hatchet. And the devil clumb to the top limb. He set down, picked an apple, and sure enough, it was the sweetest, best-tasting apple he'd ever eaten. While he was up there partaking of the apples, Jack took his hatchet and carved a cross on the bottom of the apple tree. I don't know if you know about devils and crosses, but the devil couldn't get by the cross, because it was on the tree trunk. So he was stuck up there for something like forty-three years. He couldn't get down, and, of course, he was hopping mad all this time.

"Well, Jack eventually died of meanness and old age.

"His first stop was heaven and St. Peter said, 'You've been so mean and bad, you can't stay here.' He said, 'You'll have to go to hell.'

"When Jack died, the spell was broken, so the devil came down out of the apple tree and had to walk all the way back to hell. He was mad and thirsty. He'd been up there for a long time with nothing to drink. He and Jack got to hell about the same time, and they had an awful fight. The devil was mad, and he was ripped, and Jack was ripped because he'd gotten kicked out of heaven. The devil said, 'You can't stay here in hell, after what you've done to me.'

"And Jack said, 'I've got to. I hadn't got any other place to go.'

"And the devil said, 'No, you can't,' and they fought some more.

"The devil gets the best of a lot of us from time to time, you know. Well, the devil started getting the best of Jack, and Jack lit out running. The devil hadn't had enough, so he picked up a hot coal out of hell and flung it at Jack. It come bouncing along, and Jack saw it, and he said, 'You know, I've been condemned to wander through eternity in darkness. I can't go to heaven, and I can't go to hell; I might be able to use that coal.' He started to reach down and pick it up to use it for a light, and he realized it was hot, so he looked over in a field and sure enough, there was a pumpkin. He took his pocketknife out, and he hollowed out the pumpkin, cut a hole in it, and put the hot coal in there. Halloween night now, you can still see him going up through Union County and some of the other places with his light. That's how my grandfather told me the jack-o'-lantern got its name."

WISDOM AND VALUABLE LESSONS LEARNED

Age often claims many things. Skin wrinkles, eyes dim, and steps slow. While age takes away many obvious things, it gives one valuable gift: wisdom. Lessons are learned through hardships. These people have certainly seen their share and are stronger in body, better in heart, and wiser in mind because of them. Wisdom is the gem given in the eve of life. In the following passages, several people share their pearls with us.

"We didn't have a lot of fancy things, but we had all the necessaries," Clive Smith stated. "I've had a good life. I'll soon be seventy-one years old. I still live near the house that I was born in, and I sincerely hope that I never have to go north of Clayton or south of Tallulah Falls again in my life. There's nothing out there that I want."

Dorothy Kilby reminisced, "My marriage to Delo Kilby has been a challenge, to say the least. A lot of hard work, but we were both young, and we learned to do things together. We had to learn to get along together and how to make it work. One didn't always get their way; nei-

PLATE 31 "My life has been complete, and I'm happy with what I got, and I'm blessed." —Dorothy Kilby

ther did the other one. It was fun, and at times it was hard.

"When we were first married, we didn't have things that newlyweds have today. That didn't bother us. We had each other, and as long as we had each other, we could make anything work.

"I think that I am fairly self-sufficient. I can do just about anything. I can do things that a lot of women have never done. As I get older, I might not be able to do them, but right now I figure I can do just about anything to survive.

"I can't think of anything that I would have liked to have changed about my life. My life has been complete, and I'm happy with what I got, and I'm blessed. I wouldn't change anything. I'm not rich as far as moneywise, but Delo and I have everything I reckon we need. We've our children, our grandchildren; we have each other, so I guess we are contented and happy and hope to live a long life together."

Ernest J. Henning recalled, "It was a good life, but, on the other hand, it was a hard life. We all had chores and work to do, but we all got together and enjoyed ourselves on the weekend. We had the old parties with a fiddle and guitar. That's the way life was. It was simple but good.

"The thing about it was everybody trusted each other. There was never any stealing going on or things like that. If one of your neighbors got sick, the neighbors took his farm on and worked it just like part of the family. In fact, the whole neighborhood was one big family. We all looked after each other, which, in a way, was good."

Omie Gragg said, "We had very little trouble [raising our children]. We didn't have to sit and worry where the children were at, what they were doing, and never worried about them getting into any kind of trouble. Back then you just didn't worry. The children in the community would get out there and play sort of like you guys get out there and play ball now. Everybody had a good time. There weren't any bad kids.

There wasn't any trouble. They didn't fuss. They didn't fight. Everybody shared with each other. Whatever they had, they shared with each other. It was a good life to live. It was hard, but it was good."

CHANGING TIMES

Time has brought many changes to the Southern Appalachian region. Some of these changes are considered improvements, while others are thought of as hindrances. Many of the changes noted are in the relationships between people.

"People were more honest back then," M. S. York declared. "They didn't work on Sunday either when I was growing up unless the ox fell in the ditch, and they had to pull it out. You didn't hear any weed eaters. Of course they didn't have 'em back then, but people wouldn't do that sort of thing on Sunday. I've heard a lot of people talk about cooking their Sunday dinner on Saturday. They wouldn't even cook on Sunday. I heard some of the old people talk about it. People worked hard back then. With all the things they had to do, they had to work harder than they do now. Everything was manual labor. They didn't have no machinery. People don't do like they used to. They used to help one another."

Dorothy Kilby said, "The differences in kids these days is that they don't have any responsibility. They don't seem to have as many chores to do like I had. Nowadays they have a lot of free time on their hands. They go places where we didn't get to go. We never went anywhere, and when it came dark, you went to bed. When it got daylight, you got up; you did your chores before you went to school. The kids nowadays just don't have that responsibility. They don't have the chores to do, so they have a lot of free time to do whatever they want to do."

Esco Pitts told us, "I believe people lived closer to the Lord then than they do now, simply because there wasn't so many distractions to get your mind. [There're] so many things to occupy your mind this day in time. You see, back yonder, if a family in the community couldn't cultivate the crop, why, the people in the community would gather in and take care of their crops. Or if it was in the wintertime when there was cold [weather], and they didn't have wood to keep warm, people in the community'd go and cut and pile wood on their porch where they could get it.

"Times are just changed. People just don't do that anymore. Back yonder when I was young, our neighbors would come in on Saturday and spend the night. Next day all would get in a wagon and go to church. But this day in time, they don't do that. They visited their neighbors in those days.

"People live faster this day in time. They don't have time for anybody but themselves. People used to have time for anything they wanted to do. It seemed they had more time than they do today. Of course, we have the same amount of time. But today they just have so many things on their minds—so many things to look after and to do and to think about—until they don't have time for their neighbor. A lot of them don't even have time to go to church.

"Back yonder you never saw anybody working on Sunday. If you did see a person working on Sunday, people in the community were astonished about it. But the way things are today, there's people that just have to work on Sunday because there's so many others that depend on what he's a-doing—for whatever he produces. If he's running the store or a gasoline station or whatever, there's so many that demand his service that he has to work. Especially the filling station has to [be open] on Sunday because that's when people are out joyriding. They're bumper-to-bumper out on the highway, and they've got to have gas to run on."

Clive Smith said, "The biggest changes here [in the Wolf Creek community] are the roads, and the improvement of the fields and farming areas. We used to have red clay roads. Many times, the [school] bus would get stuck, and we'd have to walk on to school. That was long before the road was even graveled.

"Electricity and telephones made a big difference [too]. Back then, we had to draw water from about an eighty-foot-deep well. We'd draw up a two-gallon bucketful at a time. You'd just have to keep repeating that to get the amount of water you was gonna need.

"Back then you didn't consider going to Clayton just for some minor object. You had to need something before you'd start planning the trip.

"We don't have to cut wood and build fires [now either]. There's a lot of people that still heat with wood, but it's because they want to more than anything else. I like the wood heat and [the woodstove] cooking, myself. It just seems better."

PLATE 32 "I think people were happier then than they are now. They appreciated what they did get."—Belle Dryman

Belle Dryman stated, "Most people now has got jobs, and they don't help out like they did back then. And people don't go see the sick like they use t' either. They don't have time, I reckon.

"People used to stay at home and work. Made what they had, and done without what they didn't make.

"Well, if people would raise them something to eat, they wouldn't need as much money. People have to have some kind of work to live. Country people have to work to keep the city people something to eat. And in the country, well, people can get fresh air. People can get out and walk places. People used to walk places, and I believe they were healthier. I don't believe people gets enough exercise. I think people were happier then than they are now. They appreciated what they did get."

Claude Darnell said, "People used to go see one another, and they didn't have no way to go but walk or ride a horse. Now they're livin' a lot faster than we did back then. Nowadays they ain't got no time to go see anybody. They're going all the time, and they don't go nowhere either."

Roberta Hicks shared, "Most people these days have to work harder for the modern things that are wanted and do not really have time to spend with their children."

Hazel Killebrew believes, "Life today is a lot different than when I was a child. It is much easier in some ways. Living was hard back then. We didn't have washing machines or electric stoves or those kind of things. It is a much more convenient world now, but on the other hand, the world seemed to have had much more time then than it does now."

Jesse Ray Owens stated, "The new ways is easiest, but I wouldn't say they're the best. Well, I know the young people were happier

PLATE 33 "It is a much more convenient world now, but on the other hand, the world seemed to have had much more time then than it does now."—Hazel Killebrew

back then because they would always play outside instead of in the house watching TV. We were raised in the mountains. I'd say we always had a great time, especially on Saturdays and Sundays when we didn't have to work.

"I seen the old-time way, and that's the way I was brought up. I never did see any modern methods 'til I went into service [the U.S. Armed Forces]. I didn't know what the outside world was about. We was living from day to day and happy. We wasn't hungry. I reckon that was what life was about. It would be nice if it was that simple again, because it was a simple life."

GARDENS AND COMMERCIAL FARMS

"I like to see anything grow."

Today, most people plant gardens for one basic reason: they want to. Planting and harvesting is a choice they make, not something necessary for their survival. Many people, however, can still remember a time when having a garden was one of the few ways a family could get fruits and vegetables, which they canned and preserved to help them survive the winter.

Not too long ago, families in Southern Appalachia had few options for making a living, and money was scarce no matter what they chose to do. Even if money had been plentiful, it would have mattered little, as stores did not ship in produce from other parts of the country or world as they do today. In order to have food, families had to grow nearly all of their fruits and vegetables on their own farms.

Adding to the precariousness of the situation was that the success of the family's crops depended not only on their abilities as gardeners but also on factors beyond the farmers' control like the weather, the amount of rainfall, and the abundance or lack of pests. It is no wonder, then, that many families religiously followed superstitions when conducting the everyday affairs of farm life.

The self-sufficiency and independence that people developed from having to produce nearly all of their own food is still an important characteristic of Appalachian life and culture. However, the mountaineers who grew up knowing they had to produce their own food also grew up knowing how important their community was. There was no question, therefore, about what to do when a neighbor became ill or when his crops failed. Everyone in the community simply came together to help him, knowing the same would be done for them should they ever face a time of severe misfortune or need.

Many common aspects of life in those days seem so unreal to us that they are almost like legend now: watching the [zodiac] signs to know when to plant; inspecting the harvest to find the best plants to save for seed; gathering with others to shuck, string, or thrash the harvested plants; and traveling, by covered wagon, to the market to peddle the excess.

This chapter focuses on remembrances of old-time gardening and farm life; of planting by the signs; of life on the farm; of gathering as a community to bring in the harvest; of saving seeds; of going to the market; and of the few commercial farms in the area.

The people featured in this section represent years of knowledge and experience passed down from generation to generation. Most of them learned to garden out of necessity, and many of them still have bountiful gardens that produce delicious vegetables. There are many lessons to be learned from these men and women beyond how to make a good garden.

—*Lacy Hunter*

GARDENING

PLANTING BY THE SIGNS*

At one time, not only was planting by the signs a fairly common practice, it was regarded by many as absolutely necessary to ensure a successful crop, and thus survival. This region of God-fearing people often refer to the Bible as the source of this practice.

Furthermore, experience seemed to prove to many the necessity of planting by the signs, even when reasons as to why the practice worked were not obvious.

Mrs. Leona Carver discovered, as a small child, the consequences of

*Planting and harvesting by the signs of the zodiac. For more information on planting by the signs, see *The Foxfire Book*, pages 212–37.

not planting in the correct sign: "One time, the signs were in the heart, and us children were going to plant pole beans for sale. We had our ground ready, and we could not wait to plant them. Dad said, 'You better wait because the signs are in the heart.' We went on and planted them, and not one bean came up. We had to plant them over." As Oakley Justice said, "I plant by the signs. I don't know what, but there

PLATE 34 Leona Carver with Kari Hughes

is something about it that makes crops grow better."

Never plant when the signs are in the heart. Leona Carver emphatically stated, "You do not want to plant anything in the seasons when the signs are in the heart because they will rot in the ground." Eva Vinson backs her up with a story about a man who planted when the signs were in the heart, and his crop failed. "The lion's in the heart, and you know, I want to tell you, when we was a-farmin', a man sowed a cabbage bed when the signs was in the heart and I told him, I said, 'Watch 'em rot.' And you know, they set out that, and they didn't get one cabbage out of that patch. They all rotted."

If crops can't be planted when the signs are in the heart, then when should they be planted? Well, according to the Vinsons, beans, at least, should be planted when the signs are in the arms. As Eva said, "They have more beans on 'em. The vines, they spread out. We had 'em down there, this summer was a year ago, and you never saw as pretty a beans. We didn't have many rows, and we had more beans than we could use. And it's just wonderful just to see 'em how pretty they are." She goes on to list other plants that should be planted when the signs are in the arms. "Anything that runs—a vine—plant when the signs is in the arms. Pumpkins, tomatoes, cucumbers, just anything." According to Leona Carver, "You should plant in the arms or the feet. Those are good times to plant things."

For plants that grow underground, however, the arms do not seem to be an auspicious time for planting. When planted on the "dark nights" of the moon (the three nights in the last quarter of the moon before it reaches the new moon), underground plants such as potatoes seem to fare the best. According to Oakley Justice, "Irish potatoes—you plant them on dark nights of the old of the moon. [If you plant them] on the new of the moon, they grow vines and no potatoes much." Eva Vinson agreed, saying, "Stuff that bears underground, now, that's another thing. My uncle's always said that he didn't plant potaters in the moon. He planted 'em in the ground. And he had a bunch of vines and no potaters, you see. They make vines if you don't plant 'em when you're supposed to. That's on the dark moon and not in the heart or in the bowels. Now, in the heart or in the bowels, like them cabbage, they'll rot."

Corn also seems to fare better when planted on the dark nights.

Eva's husband, Frank Vinson, told us, "You want to plant corn on the dark moon. When you plant it on the new moon, that stuff'll grow

fifteen feet high and the ears [will stick] right straight up. The shuck won't come over the end of it and then water gets in there and, why, it rots! And on the dark moon, [the ears will] grow out there and hang right over. Now, there was a feller down here at Otto [North Carolina] years ago when I lived down there, [and] he had ten acres of corn to plant. He didn't believe in the moon, and he planted half of it on the new moon, and it done just like I told you about that new moon stuff. He waited about ten days (it had rained and got the ground wet), and he planted on the dark of the moon, and them ears just hung over [like they were supposed to]. He said he'd never plant no more on the new moon!"

PLATE 35 Frank Vinson

Not only do the signs appear to affect the success of crops, they also seem to hold the fate of other activities as well. Pickling, for instance, is not done when the signs are in the bowels. As Leona Carver said, "When the signs is in the bowels, then you better not pickle anything from the garden because it would smell real bad."

The signs don't just affect planting and pickling. As Eva Vinson told us, mothers watched the signs when weaning their babies. "Now, people used to, when a baby was on the breast, they would start weaning that baby when the signs was in the knees, and [when the signs would] go out the foot, the baby was weaned. That's right."

The heart seems to be a bad time not only for planting but also for activities that might cause bleeding. Frank Vinson illustrated this point. "I know about that heart business. They's a woman down here had her tooth pulled when the signs was in the heart, and it liked to bled her to death. She sent for my uncle to stop the blood, and whenever they told him, why it stopped. [He knew how to stop bleeding.] [But] it liked to [have] killed her." (For faith healing, see *The Fox-fire Book*, pages 346–68.)

Times are changing, and fewer people strictly follow the signs when planting. Most families do not depend on the signs, but rather on the weather, the time of year, and when time permits. But when we asked Jimmie and Juanita Kilby, they told us that there was truth to what the old-timers said, and both

PLATE 36 Jimmie and Juanita Kilby

remembered their parents planting by the signs. However, they couldn't really remember which signs were favorable for planting what, and their garden has been beautiful every year for as long as can be remembered. Still, Eva Vinson gives a compelling argument for planting by the signs. "That's God's work. The Bible says the moon's for signs and seasons. And that's the handiwork of God, that moon business, and these signs and all that. People's just follered it up, you know, all the way 'til they just know it works."

BEAN STRINGINGS, PEA THRASHINGS, AND CORN SHUCKINGS

Once the plants in the garden had matured, the hard work had just begun. Even today, the gathering, stringing, shucking, and shelling of various garden vegetables to be frozen or canned for the winter is a summertime ritual for many families. Although the task is often tedious, the friendly, ever-inventive mountaineers find it a good excuse for a social gathering.

PLATE 37 Mr. and Mrs. Adam
Foster

Adam Foster told us about bean stringings and pea thrashings. "When I was growin' up, we'd have old-timey bean stringings. When we had a lot of beans, we'd get out and pick fifteen to twenty bushels, bring 'em in, and throw 'em down in the middle of the floor. Put sheets or quilts on the floor to keep from getting dirty. We'd ask all our neighbors in to help string them beans. So they'd come in and string beans and throw beans at one another, the boys and girls would. Yeah, we had lots of good times back then. Just enjoyed ourselves.

"We growed corn and wheat and stuff like that. Corn, wheat, and Irish potatoes, peas, rye, and sweet potatoes. That was the stuff we had to eat here on the farm. The year me and my wife was married, we growed sixty-five bushels of old clay peas. You've heard tell of them. [We] picked that many peas right up there on the pasture ground. We didn't pick 'em all, though. We had two acres in peas, and we let other people pick on the halves. They'd give us half of what they picked. So that's how come us to have sixty-five bushels. We wouldn't never [have] gotten so many. We had to thrash 'em. They was dry peas. We thrashed 'em with big poles—just let the peas lay out in the sun a day or two, then lay them peas on a sheet. We'd take the poles and beat the peas out. Get a bucket and pour them into it."

Bernice Taylor recalled times when all the neighbors would gather to help shuck corn and then share a big meal afterward as a reward for an evening of hard work. "We had corn shuckings, but not barn dances. Back then they would church you if you danced. When we had our corn shuckings, the whole community would come help us gather our corn and haul it up. They would come back the next day and go to another house and do the same thing. We had a good time. When we had them shuckings, everybody would come in, both the women and the men. But the women didn't go to the shucking business until after dinner. Everybody that came brought a dish of something. Then Mama would cook what she was gonna cook, and we had plenty to eat."

Esco Pitts also remembered corn shuckings and told us about how the teenagers in the community would use those times as an opportunity for courting and flirting. "We had corn shuckings. People farmed in those days, and they lived on the farm. They'd gather their corn in the fall of the year and pile it under the shed in the crib. Then they'd go out in the community and invite all their neighbors to come in and help husk the corn. They'd come in, and the womenfolks, a lot of them would help at the corn pile, and a lot of the older women would gather in and prepare the meal for the people. Have a big dinner. They'd have a great spread of something to eat. So they did that, and they had a good time. After the corn shucking was over in the evening (if they got it all shucked and put up in the barn and had everything cleaned up), lots of times there was plenty left over from the midday meal for the evening meal. After they'd eat supper, they'd have a party, and we'd have a candy drawing [candy pulling].

"Sometimes they'd have a box supper—a cake sale—and the young folks would bring in cakes, and they would auction them off. Whoever bought this cake got to court the girl that made it. That's the way they got their money out of it. The money was taken up for different purposes. They had different interests that they wanted to raise a little money for. I think most of it went to the church. They'd say, 'Now, here's a cake baked by a certain young girl in the audience.' And the young men would go to bidding on that, and if [a girl] had a special friend there, he'd bid just as long as he had any money. And the other boys tried to keep him from winning it because they wanted to make him pay for it. They did too!"

SEED SAVING

Almost every aspect of the old ways of life points to a time of self-sufficiency and independence. Just as most of the food, clothing, and other necessities were made on the farm, so were the seeds needed for planting. Today when a farmer plants his garden, he goes to the feed-store and buys hybrid seeds that produce a slightly better yield. Every year he repeats the process for three reasons: because the hybrid plants don't reproduce their own seeds; because he can afford to do so; and because it is easier than saving seeds. Many years ago, however, not only were hybrid crops that didn't produce seeds unheard-of, money was so rare that when families had some, they used it for necessities that couldn't be grown on the farm. Because seeds could be gathered from the crop, families simply made a habit of saving seeds from year to year, thus ensuring the success of their gardens and their survival. Although the practice is slowly dying out, a few people do still save their seeds. One of them is Numerous Marcus. Here he tells about what he grows and how he saves his seed from year to year.

PLATE 38 Numerous Marcus

"I try to make a garden every year. We grow most of our vegetables like tomatoes, potatoes, and cabbage. I save most of my seeds, all I can of them. I've got some old-fashioned seed corn, field corn. I pick out the biggest, prettiest ears and save the best I've got for my seeds. You have to let the kernels get hard on the darned things or they'll mold up on you. You can take the kernels off the cob if you want to, but I usually just rub the tip end off and get the faulty grains out and save the center of it—keep it in a box or something where it can get plenty of air. You could tie a string around it and hang it up if you wanted to. If it's good and dry, it won't freeze and bust.

"We'd save our tomato seeds too. We'd put the tomatoes on a paper and let the tomatoes dry up, and the seeds would be left. Let them dry real good. Don't let them get too hot or get wet. If they get damp, they'll mold and rot. When you get them good and dry, you can put them in a container of some kind with holes in it so they can get plenty of air. They've got to have a little air or by gosh, they'll mold over on you. If you leave the tomatoes on the vine and let them rot, then you could have volunteers [plants that come back on their own] the next year.

"You could take a cabbage and grow them up good and mature and leave them over 'til next year and set them out again, and they'll grow up and make seed. Collards are the same way. You could set collards out again, and they'll bloom and form a head. They'll make seeds, and turnips are the same way. Just one cabbage head or one collard green would make all the seeds you would want. You could put the cabbage seed in a paper sack or something just so it could get air. To store the cabbage head until you get ready to set it back out, you can dig a hole out in the ground where the land drains good. Turn the cabbage upside down so the root is pointing up to the sky. This way the water will drain off. The other way, it would catch the water, and [the] cabbage would rot. Then you put tarpaper over the cabbage and cover it up with a bit of dirt so it won't freeze too bad."

Billy Long elaborated on how his father picked which plants to use for seed and which to eat. "We always saved different kinds of seeds— bean seeds, potatoes, and corn. You wanted to kinda pick the [best]. In corn, you always picked a good straight grain. You could see it when you shucked it. My daddy always wanted to plant that kind. When he was shuckin', he would lay them out.

"[With beans] he'd let some of them go to seed. They'd turn yellow, then he'd pick 'em, let 'em dry, and hull them out. We used to make all of our soup beans that way.

"With sweet potatoes you usually just take so many, bed them down in a tub or something, and they'd sprout out and get big enough to set out. We'd slip them eyes off and reset them."

GOING TO THE MARKET

Most of what farm families grew went toward family needs. The few surplus crops that were grown, however, along with the occasional chicken or eggs, were taken to market to provide money, one of the few items that could not be grown or raised.

Amanda Turpin described the reasons for this practice. "We didn't have any crops for sale much. We just grew enough stuff for ourselves—corn, beans, other vegetables like that. We would keep a few chickens and have a few eggs to sell. We'd get a little money that way, but we didn't have much money.

"In the fall, my daddy would haul produce to sell down in Royston or Athens. We called it 'going down in

PLATE 39 "We'd get a little money that way, but we didn't have much money." —Amanda Turpin

the country.' He'd take apples and chestnuts and cabbages, mostly. We didn't have too much way to haul produce in and out. People would have to go in wagons and bring it up here. The train just came to Tallulah Falls, and there wasn't too much shipped up here, just things people had to have like flour, sugar, and coffee. We mostly had to grow what we ate."

Adam Foster gave a touching account of taking produce to the market with his father when he was a child, and later, as a teenager by himself for his ailing father.

"When I was a kid, me and my daddy went to Clarkesville with a load of Irish potatoes, and we were gone three days from Tiger to Clarkesville. I was four years old, and I can remember that trip. We started, and my mother went with us. She had a sister that lived over there in Habersham County. The first day, she rode with us over there, and she stayed all night, and we did too.

"The next night me and my daddy started, and my mother stayed there with her sister. Well, I was just a four-year-old kid. We got a way down there next to Clarkesville—five miles from Clarkesville—and it was getting dark. There was a camp alongside the road there where people camped with their wagons. [Daddy] said, 'We'll stop right here and stay all night.' I can remember that just as well if you'd told me five minutes ago. Said, 'We'll stay all night right here.' Well, it was comin' up a storm. I never have heard better in my life. Thunder and lightnin', but he got his mules tied to the wagon, and he just left me a-sittin' up in it—an old covered wagon. We had our taters back in the back. I was sittin' there and went to sleep 'fore the rain ever come—the storm. And them mules got scared, and they got to jumpin' and surging about there, and they broke loose from the wagon, and they was just backwards and forwards, up and down that road. Them mules would run five hundred yards that way, and then here they'd go back the other way that far. They wouldn't leave. So it was just back and forth nearly all night. They didn't even take time to eat hardly.

"So next mornin' Daddy got up and them mules was standin' right there at the back of the wagon. He just walked up, tied 'em, and fed 'em. They wouldn't leave a wagon. They thought that was home. They was trained mules. They knowed just as well what to do as I did.

"I was fifteen years old when me and my father started off to Athens with a load of apples—dried fruit. We got down to Cornelia, and my oldest brother lived there. So we drove in there and stayed all night with him, and we was a-goin' the next mornin'. Another one of my brothers was goin' with us. Next mornin' my daddy was sick with a cold, the flu, you know. He wasn't able to get out and go on. I was fifteen years old, and he said, 'Adam, I reckon you can go. Take this load on to Athens with the wagon.'

"I said, 'Well, yes, Dad. I'll try it.' So I went on with that load of apples. I had a brother and a brother-in-law with me. They had a wagon apiece. So we went on down.

"They told me, said, 'Now, you can go any way you want to. We'll go one way, and you go the other.' I started off, got a head start, [and we got to Athens separately and didn't find each other right away]. I was so interested in selling apples, workin' away, I didn't notice it was coming dark. And I kept sellin'—they was just a-buyin' 'em good. I like to have sold the whole wagonload that evening. It was nine o'clock, and I was tryin' to get to the center of town. I was lookin' for my brother and lookin' for camp. I had a little feller workin' for me, said he didn't know how to get back to the center of town. I told him that either he was gonna take me to the center of town, or I wasn't gonna let him loose. He was a little feller, just about twelve years old. I kept holdin' him, and then I happened on Main Street and still didn't know where I was. As it turned out, I was goin' toward where the wagonyard was. My brother and brother-in-law had just started to camp, and I just run into them. They said they'd kept lookin' for me—they'd pulled in the center of town there in Athens, thought I'd come through there.

"They had regular places for people to camp—called 'em wagonyards. We'd just go there, pay fifty cents or something for a night's camping. Inside the building, there'd be fifteen or twenty wagons in there. Had a place to cook—a fireplace. We'd fry sausage and stuff like that—done our own cookin'.

"After that first trip I always went from then on [with] that wagonload of apples. From then on I done the wagon trips. There'd always be somebody else, neighbors or relatives who'd want me to take a load. I'd just fill up with a load and go on. Wouldn't make my daddy go—he never was stout. I just said, 'Daddy, I can take care of it from now on.' And I did. I took care of things from the time I was fifteen 'til the time I was twenty-three. He died when I was twenty-three."

COMMERCIAL FARMS

Not so many years ago, although most families farmed, few were involved in commercial endeavors. Farmers occasionally took a few of their surplus crops to market, but those were often used to trade for supplies that could not be grown on the farm. The earlier necessity of growing crops to feed one's family, however, eventually gave way to the modern world, as farm families began to be aware of the marketability of their crops and thus became connected to an economic system beyond their own families and community. One such entrepreneur was J. C. Stubblefield. Mr. Stubblefield ran a sweet potato seedling business for many years and supplied most of the Rabun County area with sweet potato slips.

"We did [sweet potato slips] for years and years. I don't know when we started 'cause I wasn't big enough to know. [Daddy] started it. It's a lot of work. When you first start, you dig a hole about eighteen inches in the ground, and you put on some pine tops. Just cut off a sprig of pine and put it in the bottom [of the hole]. That's to help heat it. Then you get about twelve inches of barnyard manure and put in there. That's for heat [too]. Then you lay the potatoes and put about an inch of dirt on them. Then you put [three or four sweet potato sprouts on top of that to ensure the plant "takes"]. Put dirt on top of that. Then, when you get that done, you take old tarpaper or tin—we've used both—and cover it to keep the water out of it. They'll come up in about a month. [Then] you take the cover off of it, and you water it a little, and they start growin'. Whenever they get [six or seven inches tall], you start pullin' [the sprouts]. When they get ready to pull, you've gotta pull 'em, and you've gotta have a market for them or somebody to come get them. Then you start again in about two or three days. We have had as high as sixty bushel in the ground. Our beds was four and one-half or five feet wide, and we had one about four feet long and one about six feet long. When they'd get started good, it took two hands to keep them plants pulled, and I mean [it took] all day!

"Then you've got to count 'em. When you're selling 'em to the public, you get instructions [from the state] on how to do things, and the instructions say you must count 'em. There must be a hundred in the bunch."

Bernice Taylor, J. C.'s sister, remembered her mother giving them instructions to always err on the side of having too many potato slips in the bunches. "[It'd] take about two days to pull 'em and tie 'em. Mama said, 'Count them things now. You got a hundred?'

" 'Yeah.'

PLATE 40 Bernice Taylor   " 'Put three more slips in.' "

J. C. continued, "Yeah, we always put two or three extras in there. They'd send you tape to tie [the slips] with. The rules and regulations say they must be a hundred in a bunch. [The tape is] about twelve inches long and it's got 'Certified Sweet Potatoes' with the year [printed on it]. That tape was supposed to tie that bunch of potato [slips]. [We'd sell them] anywhere in the county. We could have took a third inspection and sold 'em anywhere in the state, but we didn't fool with that, because we could get shed of 'em here.

"[After you count them] you've got to put 'em in the shade and set 'em in some water or something where they'll be a little wet to keep 'em alive.

"Plantin' season went from about the first of May to about July. You've gotta get 'em in between the last week of March and the first week of April to have 'em up big enough to sell by May. You'd get about three thousand [sprouts] to a bushel of sweet potatoes. I remember selling a lot of [the potato slips] for ten cents a hundred. That was one dollar a thousand. Now they bring about seven dollars a hundred, but money went a lot further then than it does now.

"We planted down in the lower field. We had some good land down there. It was red clay. We planted there because the potatoes seemed to do better. There was four or five terraces, and we'd have sweet potatoes in every one of 'em.

"The state inspector would come and check [the potatoes]. He'd watch and see if they had any diseases or anything. They won't let you sell 'em if they've got a disease.

"The mail carrier carried a lot of 'em to town to the co-op store, and they'd sell 'em there. A lot of times, they'd want plants, and we didn't have 'em because they's takin' 'em as fast as we could raise 'em. A lot of folks would come after 'em [too].

"[In] 1957 was when we done away with the sweet potatoes because we didn't have no help, and it took a lot of help. Sometimes you'd have to hire some help to help get 'em in. [Hired help] worked for ten or twenty cents an hour. You didn't make a whole lot. You just made barely enough to live."

APPLE GROWING

Perhaps the most prominent type of commercial farming was apple growing. Just before the turn of the twentieth century, John P. Fort discovered that Rabun County and the surrounding area were especially suited to growing apples. In the following sections from his pamphlets and his personal journal, John Fort tells why he chose this part of the country for his fruit-growing activities and his observations of how weather and topographic conditions affected the fruit. Mr. Fort wrote extensively concerning fruit growing in northeastern Georgia. The following excerpts, which focus on apple growing, are taken from *John Porter Fort: A Memorial and Personal Reminiscences,* published by the Knickerbocker Press (New York) in 1918.

"I now come to what I consider the most successful undertaking of the latter part of my life—the growing of apples in Rabun County.

"Through Demorest there used to pass covered wagons full of apples on their way from the mountains to Athens. I was struck with the beauty of these apples, especially with an apple called the 'Mother' apple, which was capable of a very high polish and was very free from blemish. On talking to the wagoneers, I found that they came down from Rabun County and near Shooting Creek, North Carolina, and that they grew their apples with very little care or cultivation. I was so interested that I went up to Rabun to study the apple question. I applied for the government meteorological maps of this section. I was struck by its heavy rainfall. An area of about thirty miles square with the center at Clayton, Rabun County, and extending into North Carolina, has the largest rainfall of any part of the United States, except Puget Sound on the Pacific Coast—a rainfall averaging from seventy to one hundred inches per annum. This does not come in floods, but all through the year in continual showers. I have often stood in Rabun Gap and been struck with wonder at the mist being drawn through Rabun, Hiawassee, and Crow's Gap, forming clouds laden with moisture to be deposited upon the mountains and vales of this favored country. They often present scenes of sunshine and clouds so inspiring and grand that they seem to encircle us with the majesty of Almighty Power. This rain upon a well-drained soil is very adaptable to the growth of splendid apples.

"On seeing what fine apples could be grown without cultivation, one naturally asked what could not be done with modern scientific culture. I wished very much to plant an orchard in that favored section. At first I tried to interest persons with capital in this enterprise, which I felt confident would be a profitable investment. I met with no success so, in spite of my limited resources, I determined to make the venture myself."

In *The Story of an Apple,* published by Cornelia Enterprise Press in Cornelia, Mr. Fort documents his apple-growing experiment and successes in Rabun County.

"In pursuance of a long contemplated desire, I purchased, in 1906, fifty acres of land near Rabun Gap, in Northeast Georgia, for the purpose of planting an apple orchard.

"The position chosen was within a mile and one-half of Rabun Gap, on the Tallulah Falls railroad. The place was known as Turkey Cove, on Black's Creek, forming the headwaters of the Tennessee River. [Editor's note: Black's Creek runs into, rather than forms, the headwaters of the Tennessee River.]

"There was upon the place about fifty apple trees that had been planted fifteen or twenty years previous. They were over-grown with wild vines, and presented a very neglected appearance. I had the old trees cared for, and I planted a young orchard of twelve hundred trees on the place, of approved varieties of apples.

"The young apple trees I planted grew, and the old trees responded to the care given them. After the first year's care and cultivation, there appeared among the old trees in the orchard four trees that produced a red apple that surprised me with its splendid appearance. They ripened about the first of November, 1908.

"About this time, I received by mail a pamphlet showing that there was to be held at Spokane, Washington, the first national apple show. A prize was offered for the best two barrels or six boxes of apples grown in the sixteen Southern states. This

PLATE 41 Alvin Alexander and Chet Welch surveying the ruins of the orchard foreman's home in Turkey Cove

prize was called the Southern States Special and was divided into first, second, and third prizes. I conceived the idea of sending six boxes of my apples to the contest for the Southern States Special. I had about twenty-five bushels from the four trees. I shipped six boxes by express to the secretary of the national apple show to enter for the premium. In return, I received a check for $50 for the second best apples. North Carolina received first prize, my apples from Georgia the second, and apples from Oklahoma the third prize.

"Being elated with my success, I had my four apple trees specially cared for. November 1, 1909, they presented an appearance superior to any similar sight I ever beheld. The National Apple Show was again held in Spokane in November, 1909. I again contended for the first prize above all competitors. The chairman of the committee making the award was the most renowned pomologist in our country—Mr. H. E. Van Demar of Washington, D.C. Besides, I obtained a diploma for the best new variety of apples.

"This apple, having been pronounced a new variety and worthy of being put upon the pomological books at Washington, was listed and given the name of Fort's Prize.

"The apple having demonstrated those qualities that make a financial success, such as appearance, color, taste, and above all, keeping without decay until the spring time, I at once proceeded to investigate its origin. I was fortunate in finding the man who had grafted and planted the four apple trees whose products had made so much commotion among the apple growers. The originator of this apple is named Kell. He lives near Clayton in Rabun County. His story is this: About sixteen years prior to 1908, he lived at Turkey Cove. At this time, while on a visit to his uncle near the source of Warwoman's Creek in Rabun County, he noticed an apple tree growing from beside the chimney of his uncle's cabin, upon which was a beautiful red apple. His uncle informed him that the tree was a seedling, and that he had named it after his niece, Mollie. From this tree Mr. Kell cut a switch, and from a graft made upon young trees, planted the four trees in Turkey Cove.

"Anticipating that an orchard of this new variety of apple will be valuable, I have obtained grafts from the old trees and have put out an orchard of three hundred of them."

Recently, interest has been rekindled in the Fort's Prize apple. Some

people claim that it is actually the Jim Kell Thin Skin that Mr. Fort named after himself when the apple won first prize in the National Apple Show in 1909, and even Mr. Fort stated that the apple was originally grafted by a man named Kell. Be that as it may, the trees from which the apple grew have apparently been "lost" as houses deteriorated and burned or collapsed and orchards were overtaken by the surrounding forests.

Ross Brown also remembered growing apples commercially. However, unlike John Fort, who came into the area because of its favorable apple-growing climate, Mr. Brown inherited his first apple orchard from his father.

PLATE 42 "I like to see anything grow."—Ross Brown

"We came down here and began to clear our land because it was all timberland. Then we began to plant the orchards. When my family started growing apples, there were no orchards around here [Hiawassee] except just home orchards, you know, just a few trees for home use. Everybody said that Brown was as crazy as a lunatic to put an orchard in this region here because there was no railroad, no market. There were lots of orchards over in Habersham County in that region around Clarkesville, but none closer.

"My dad grew apples commercially. He grew Winesap, Arkansas Black, Yates, and the Terry Winter. Yates is just a small red apple, and it and the Terry Winter will keep all winter. He ran both a nursery and an orchard in here above Hiawassee. There was six of us kids and he worked all of us. He had no other help. He had about a hundred-acre orchard, and he kept adding younger trees on up until he died in 1928 of a stroke. That was around the Fourth of July. He didn't last but just for a few hours after he got sick. I stayed on and ran the nursery for a while longer.

"All they knew back in those days was standard-sized trees, so that's what we had. They made a big tree, and [the trees were] set approximately thirty feet apart, each direction. That would figure out around between thirty and forty trees per acre.

"Then we began to get some diseases in our section of the country. We had apple worm. I know you've bit into an apple, maybe bit a worm half in two. I don't think they'd hurt you, though. Had a lot of protein in those worms that you ate. There were the worms, and then the blight, the scab, and the ground rot, belly rot, and what they called the apple blotch. You've seen an apple with black spots on it? That's what they call the blotch.

"So in 1917 we bought the first spray pump that ever come in this county. We always bought our sprayers, didn't try to make them ourselves, and Hardie Pump was the best pump that was made. We had to spray the whole tree. Our main spray was lime-sulfur. We boiled fifty pounds of lime and one hundred pounds of sulfur for about one hour. It would be real strong, and that controlled most of the diseases. When we first started spraying, people wouldn't even buy our apples. They claimed the apples were poisoned.

"We had two large storage houses dug out in the side of the mountain. They were square and had dirt floors and walls, hard sandrock, you know. It wouldn't cave in. The walls were straight up and down, and we could stand up in there. One was about thirty by fifty feet and the other about twenty by twelve or fourteen feet. I don't remember exactly, but they'd hold a bunch of apples. We had double doors on them and had it real tight. We had slatted bins in there made out of one-by-fours, and the air would circulate through them. There were overhead ventilators bringing air in. Of course, we didn't have electricity, and there weren't any fans in there. We'd just cut a hole right up through the roof and run a pipe through. The air would just circulate through, forming a suction.

"We'd let the apples get almost ripe, and then we picked them. That way, they'd stay real juicy and crisp all winter long in storage. When it was real cold on the outside, below zero, it was warm in there. And when the weather began to warm up, it still stayed cool in there. The apples would be real juicy, and they would have a real good flavor. Those apples had a better flavor than any cold-storage apple you eat now. The bugs wouldn't get in them after they got ripe in the storage houses.

"Years ago, we took apples to the fair, and they always got prizes. It was probably good advertisement. We sold our apples at Young Harris, Georgia, and Murphy, North Carolina.

"During World War I, good apples would bring around four and five dollars a bushel. Most everybody had enough money. People would come in wagons and buy a wagonload of apples. There wasn't but just a few trucks, one just once in a while.

"My dad bought a Ford truck in 1922. After that, he would haul apples to Athens and Gainesville. They'd take maybe some dried fruits and chestnuts and Irish potatoes, maybe a jug of moonshine, you know, to sell it. They'd be gone about ten days or two weeks.

"In 1929 it was rough going! Apple growing was just like everything else. It was hard to make a go at it during the Depression. We had a real fine apple. We sold some of 'em three bushels for a dollar, but a whole lot of 'em we couldn't even sell. So, still your labor and your spray and fertilizer had to go on just the same.

"I sold my dad's nursery sometime in the 1930s and moved up east of Hiawassee on Route 76 and lived there from about 1934 up to 1960. I went up there and set out a small orchard. It was just for a pastime, a hobby of mine. That's one of my main weaknesses. I like to see anything grow.

"Even now, apples from Rabun County, Towns County, and all those orchards back in towards Waynesville, North Carolina, have got the best flavor of any apples. A mountain apple will sell. If people ever eat any of them, they'll always prefer to buy them.

"In these mountains, your orchards should face the north, northwest, or due west. You do not want to set out fruit trees in these mountains that are facing due east or south or southeast. If the trees are in bloom and there's a big frost, when the sun comes up in the morning, it'll bake that frost right into the bloom. It'll kill the bloom. If they're facing west or northwest, the frost will gradually thaw out as the sun is coming up. My orchard faces west, and I've never failed to have a crop there either. I've seen a few light crops, but we've always had a crop of apples.

"It's better, if you can, to plant above the frost line. There can be frost, you know, lower down, but after you get above there, there won't be any frost! The north wind, during the winter, won't affect the trees very much.

"This day and time, they use different root systems to what they used to. Years ago, all people knew was old-time seedling rootstock, which they called a standard-sized tree. They made a great big tree. There are so many different rootstocks now that you graft onto. You've got 106, 111, and 7M. With the 7M rootstock, you have to tie the tree to a post. They won't produce maybe over a peck of apples, but you know, they're a real small dwarf tree. Semi-dwarf makes a medium-sized tree.

"Semi-dwarf rootstock doesn't make such a large tree or take as long to come into production as a standard-sized tree. They're more compact, you see, and don't take as much spraying material and as much labor. Picking the apples is not a problem because the tree is smaller. Yet, you pretty well get the same amount of apples as you do with standard-sized trees. Of course, semi-dwarf and dwarf are going to bear young, but naturally, you don't pick a whole lot of apples off them at first because you ain't got very much bearing surface, you see. When they begin to get up pretty good size, I'd say around eight years, they'll begin to pay you right along, and then by twelve years, you'll begin to get a pretty good crop.

"I prune pretty well the same way as we did when I was young, but spray material and fertilizer have changed a great deal. All we could buy back then came in two-hundred-pound sacks. We got a 10-2-2 guana, and then we got a 20 percent acid phosphate. Eventually, we began to get nitrogen soda. And that's what we fertilized with back when I was a kid. Me and my brother, we'd throw a two-hundred-pound sack on our back an' carry it up in the orchard. We'd pour it in a bucket and spread it in a big band around the tree. I couldn't even roll one of them big sacks up on my knee today.

"I fertilize about the middle of March. And then again around the first day of June. You don't want to fertilize in the fall because, if it turns warm, you're liable to stimulate the growth. That would injure the tree. If a tree set too heavy, grows too fast, you should go in about the middle of May and use some calcium nitrate. That way, you're feeding the calcium and the nitrate at the very same time. Nitrogen soda and ammonium nitrate don't have any calcium in them, and a tree needs the calcium. Use just a good-grade, completely balanced fertilizer. You've got to have your potash, phosphates, and nitrogen and your calcium-magnesium. I use a 8-24-24. I won't go higher than a 8 percent nitrogen this spring, because in my experience, if you use too much plain nitrogen soda, it encourages fire blight to go to working on your fruit trees. You've seen fruit trees, especially pear trees, with dead twigs, dead limbs? That's fire blight. You've got to fertilize the trees; you've got to take good care of them or you don't get any returns off of them. An apple tree, if pruned and cared for, will last on and on.

"I'd advise anyone that's going into the orchard business to start out with a few trees and just grow into it. You will learn by experience, by trial and error, and there's a whole lot of errors in lots of things to do with apple growing.

"The main drawback is real estate. It's getting so high that people just can't go out here and buy up enough land for a big orchard. You've

got to put in a right smart of time before you begin to get any returns out of it. It's regular work, all right. There's so much to orchard work! That's the reason most people don't stay in it very long. The younger generations are just not interested in all that work. They can go to work for wages and punch a time clock and draw a check every week. There's a lot of difference in that and

PLATE 43 Ross Brown's apple orchard

living up here on a farm and starting a orchard. There are no returns for a long time, and they're liable to throw up their hands and leave out.

"Now, I think apple growing is worth it. I don't make a decent living at it. If I'd a-took [to] making a living at it, I'd have starved to death. I just grow apples for a hobby. I have apples for a lot of my friends. I give a lot of apples away, and I make some cider and a little vinegar. I just enjoy working at it."

The love Ross Brown has for apple growing is undoubtedly a large part of what made him a successful orchard owner. Another such man, one who is respected and successful because he not only loves his business but is very educated in his field, is Bob Massee. The youngest child of a farm family who lived through several disasters, Mr. Massee is familiar with the hazards of commercial farming and knows how to start over. In fact, his family came to Rabun County to grow apples because of a disaster in Florida just before he was born.

"In 1929, one year before I was born, the Massee family moved here. My mother and daddy were farmers in South Florida in 1926, and a hurricane wiped out everything they had. So they went back, rebuilt, farmed, and were doing great in 1927. In 1928 a hurricane blew them away. They got on a barge, barely, with their lives and their children. I wasn't born, but twelve hundred people were killed in the 1928 hurricane. My dad decided to go back and help bury the dead—which he did—and then came back to get my mother to go back and rebuild. She said, 'Not with me.' She said, 'I'm not going back.' My uncle [who was a doctor] had a patient who was president of the Southern Bell Telephone Company, and he said, 'By the way, I just bought a farm in Tiger, and I need somebody to go in with me—to run it.' And my dad said, 'I believe I'll take that.' So that's how I got here; that's how they got here.

"When my family got started in the apple business, the apples were already here. The orchard started with my dad and a man named Ben Read in 1929. There was a small orchard here then. My dad bought another orchard in 1933 on Glassy Mountain. He bought one hundred thirty acres there, and then, in 1939, we bought an orchard on Seed Tick Road."

After graduating from high school, Mr. Massee attended Clemson College and Virginia Polytechnic Institute and later served in the Army during the Korean War. "[In college, I was a] horticulture major. Horticulture consists of a lot of things; I'm a pomology major. Horticulture covers leafy culture, which is vegetable production; food processing, which is canning; landscaping, which I'm not; and pomology, which is fruit production. I basically took pomology, but I had to take all those other courses, and, amazingly, I took a lot of chemistry.

"I was born in the apple business. I didn't know anything else, and I love it! I've got a son right up there who's just as bad as I am; he loves it too. I've got lots of children—Jim, Gigi, Emme, Robin, Melody, and Sterling. Sterling is thirty years old and runs the apple business. He is the manager and my partner.

"We have about seventy-five acres now. We're down to about seventy-five. I think you can get too big. At one time, I bought one hundred fifty acres and that was just too much. It's down to where my son and I can handle most of it ourselves except during harvest. We've got a couple of boys working for us right now. They just came and started helping us last week. I try to keep [it] just down to family business. When you hire a lot of labor, you're getting in trouble right then.

"I also produce raspberries, blackberries, grapes, tomatoes, and sweet corn. We ship apples primarily. We don't do much shipping of those others—we don't really have enough production. We may this year. We're getting kind of heavy in the grapes; we may ship some of those. Commercially, we do apples; we do have peaches, nectarines, and sweet cherries too, but it's mostly a small operation.

"A lot of this is pick-your-own. It's people who come in, and they pick. We just leave a money box down there with a sign that says this pint is so much or a quarter of a gallon is so much. We don't see a lot of these people. They just come, pick their stuff, and leave. What they don't pick, we pick and put in the freezer. I have a lady in Highlands, North Carolina, who buys all the frozen fruit.

"The amount we ship out per year is very variable. Like this year, I doubt we'll ship—at least I won't ship—two thousand bushels. Normally, we'll ship anywhere from ten to fifteen thousand bushels, and years ago you shipped thirty to thirty-five thousand bushels. That's been a long time ago.

"We used to have a big packing house. There was a big packing shed there in 1962. I was living in the brick house right here that I built, and we heard all kinds of commotion at two o'clock in the morning. The packing house was on fire. Now, you don't think that's a frightening feeling? You know, I could just see all our boxes, all our equipment, everything we had, going up in flames. We didn't have much insurance on it. My dad and I were still in business together then. He said, 'Okay, we've got fifteen thousand dollars.' He said, 'Build us a new packing house and put some equipment in it.' Fifteen thousand. Well, I built the packing house down here for five thousand, started on the Fourth of July, and had it ready to go by picking time in August. I spent ten thousand on the equipment, and that's how we got back in business. It was cheap equipment and a cheap-built packing house, but it got us back in there.

"It is very interesting to see the bins being dumped up, twenty bushels a lick, and the machine polishing them, taking out the little apples; then the graders take out the defects. Then I have a machine that takes out a certain size that goes in the plastic bags and go to the supermarket. Then I have another machine that the rest of the apples run down, and it weighs each one. It has eight different sizes. In other words, one size would have one hundred thirty-eight apples in the box, in another would be one hundred twenty-five in a box, and on down to one hundred thirteen, one hundred, eighty-eight, eighty, seventy-two, and sixty-four in a box. Each bin has that particular size; it'll put them in trays and put them in a bushel box and mark them. It's an interesting operation. Everybody is more than welcome to come and see us. This year we'll probably work a little bit at night, and that's about all. So we don't have enough to really warrant hiring a lot of people.

"I don't do any canning or processing. I'll tell you what we do. We have a lot of processing and canning apples—normally, mostly juice apples, which go to the processor for juice. We load them and send them to Lincoln, North Carolina, or to Hendersonville, North Carolina, or Seneca, South Carolina; sometimes they go to another outfit up in Pennsylvania. Last year I sent some up to Newcomerstown, Ohio—all for juice. We load them in twenty-two-bushel bins, so we put about one thousand bushels on a truck just in open bins. We get very little for them. We might get two dollars a bushel, something like that. It will cost you about a dollar to get them picked. So you're losing money. On anything, if you can make at least eight dollars on about a bushel of apples, that's about a break-even price. That's about all we've been doing the last few years.

"One struggle of being self-employed is we don't have any income except, you know, that period of time when we sell. I enjoy being self-employed, but there are a lot of pitfalls, a lot of hard things. When you come home at night, you're not through with your work. If you're working on a public job, you try to forget that job when you get home at night. We never forget it. It's twenty-four hours with me. But I like it, you know. That's okay.

"One risk is, if you're in the apple business and the fruit business, you risk getting hit by spring frost. Then if you make it through spring frost, hail can wipe you out, and right now the drought is hurting us real bad, the dry weather. Then you have a disease problem, insect problems, labor problems, getting it picked, and wind. A strong wind can blow them off about the time you get ready to pick them. Hail is the most damaging. There are a lot of bad things that can happen.

"To handle spring frost, what you really need to do is plant up on the side of a hill high enough so that the cold air always flows to the bottom. If you go to school some morning, look down in the pastures. You know when you see all the frost down in the bottomland? Now, what happens, during the day all the hot air is being formed down in the bottom, but at night it reverses, and the warm air moves from the bottom beside the hill because of the specific density of air. Cold air is heavier than hot air. It's like water. If you leave water in the bathtub a long time, you can put a thermometer down in it, and you can feel it's cooler, or you've been swimming in the lake or something—you feel the water's

colder down below. It's the same way with air. Cold air will shove down
to the bottom, displace the hot air, and push it up the side of the hill. A
year ago, right over here at the orchard, we checked the thermometer,
and we lost a lot of apples. It got down to twenty-seven degrees, twenty-
six degrees in places. In one place, it got down to twenty-five degrees.
Up on this hill right here, I had a couple hundred trees up on top of the
mountain. I went up there to check the temperature; it was forty-two
degrees. So you can see, there's fifteen degrees difference in about three
hundred feet elevation. So plant up on the side of a hill. If you'll notice
most orchards, all of them are planted on a hillside for that reason.

"I can't protect them from the frost. They do have wind machines. I
used to have an oil system. I had one hundred sixty smoke heaters,
smudge pots that were pressurized and used fuel oil. I had it rigged so
I could just drive by and throw a match at them, and finally I had it
rigged on the front bumper of a truck so I could put a torch out there
and drive by them and they'd light. But fuel oil costs over a dollar a gallon. When I put my system in in the 1960s, it was fifteen cents a gallon,
and I would burn something like five or six hundred gallons of fuel a
night, which, you know, wasn't bad; it was less than a hundred bucks.
Now you burn seven or eight hours, and you've burned a thousand dollars' worth. If you do that two or three nights, the apples aren't worth
it. So we just took it out. I let the junkman haul it away.

"A real cold winter normally is good. What happened this year was it
got real warm for a few days in February, and then it got down to four
degrees—in some places zero. The trees and the plants and things (the
chemical makeup is such that everything is weather-related), as the temperature goes up, they start getting ready for spring. Well, then, the shock
of that four degrees put them out of business just about, and it did kill.
Normally, it doesn't hurt apples, but this year it was a little freak thing.
What happens with apples is they put out in the spring, and normally
they get blooms and then it gets cold. They get killed during the bloom.
They can't stand it—just before opening, the bloom can stand about
twenty-five degrees or twenty-four degrees. As they skip into pink, they
can stand about twenty-six and twenty-seven degrees, but when they get
wide-open blooms, they're exposed to the world during about twenty-
eight degrees for an extended period. They can stand a tornado for two
or three hours, but they can't stand twenty-eight degrees from eleven
o'clock at night to seven the next morning. It's timewise.

"It's also related to the amount of moisture in that tree. Most people
think, well, the wind's blowing; it has dried them out. They won't
freeze. That's wrong. The wetter the apple, the wetter the bloom is, the
harder it is for the bloom to freeze. In physics, there's a thing called

kinetic energy, and it takes more kinetic energy to convert water to ice. The drier that fruit is, the easier it freezes. The wetter it is, the harder it is for it to freeze. With that in mind, a lot of people—I'm not able to do it, couldn't afford to—have overhead sprinkler systems that mist the trees during the spring of the year if it starts to freeze. They know that thirty-two degrees does not hurt that apple. So they mist it over, and when it freezes, it protects them; it's just like a blanket, a blanket of ice. They look like Christmas trees covered with ice, and they keep that sprinkler system going until the weather warms back up above thirty-two degrees. So ice, amazingly, protects them from freezing.

"During the winter, we prune, basically. We spend most of the winter pruning, getting our orchard ready for the spring, spraying, and getting it cleaned up. Pruning is an all-winter job; we never get through.

"We don't sell anything during the winter. Our income is limited just to summer and fall months, mostly just in the months of August, September, and early October. I don't have any income except for a few weeks. All the rest of the time, it's outgo.

"Primarily, I grow Red Delicious and Golden Delicious apples. We also have Fuji, Gala, Jonigo, Arkansas Black, Yates, Ginger Gold, and I can go on and on. We have about twenty different varieties. There are just a lot of different varieties that we carry, but basically Red and Golden Delicious. That's our 'bread and butter.'

"There are something like six thousand known varieties of apples. Only about fifteen or twenty are really grown commercially. There are a lot of old apples that if people knew about them, we'd still be planting them probably.

"[The looks are] what sells Red Delicious. [Some of them are just beautiful and taste awful.] I like the Red Delicious that I grow or that somebody else grows in the East that are at just the right stage. I don't like them mealy; I don't like them green. I like them just right."

In response to a comment made by Lacy Hunter that she liked Granny Smith apples, Mr. Massee jokingly said, "I worry about anybody that likes Granny Smith. That's the worst apple I ever put in my mouth. It's so sour, you know. It's just awful sour. You'd probably like the Lodi apple if you like Granny Smith.

"The price of apples has not changed a whole lot, but the price of labor and spray material and the cost of land and everything's gone up. In 1945 my daddy sold a crop of apples for five dollars a bushel. And in 1990 I sold a crop of apples for about five or six dollars a bushel. He was paying fifteen cents an hour for labor, and I pay a minimum of five dollars an hour for labor. That's probably going to change now that minimum wage is going up.

"There are anywhere from sixty-four to one hundred thirty-eight apples in a bushel. If it's sixty-four, they're big; if it's one hundred thirty-eight, they're medium. Then the ones that go in the bags, it takes about one hundred fifty of them to make a bushel. It's all related to size. The bigger the apple, the smaller the number. The average-sized apple is three inches in diameter.

"I would only recommend going into the apple business if you were a rich man, had a lot of money, or a rich lady, and could withstand several years of getting into it 'cause it's real expensive to get started. If you were going to go out, buy the land, get the right site, buy the trees, it costs about fifty dollars per tree to get into production. So if you're putting one hundred trees per acre, that's five thousand dollars per acre trying to get into production. You're going to pay another five thousand to buy the rest; then you've got ten thousand dollars in it without any work involved. You've got another four or five years, a lot of the time, before that tree comes in. So it takes a lot of investment, and there's not a banker in the world that's going to bankroll somebody to do that unless they've got a lot of collateral."

Another facet of the apple-growing industry in this region is the work it provided for those who did not necessarily own the orchards, but tended them. Alvin Alexander recalled working for John P. Fort as a foreman.

"I worked in an orchard all my life—ever since I was a kid. I went up there when they was grafting. I told 'em I hadn't never done that before, but I was gonna give it a try. I watched how they done it, and I got me a knife and a saw and grafted 'em just like they did. Every cherry tree I grafted up there lived, and they didn't lose a tree.

"I didn't make much in the orchard. About a dollar a day. Finally got to a dollar and a half, and we thought we was getting rich. I was a foreman for the Forts for

PLATE 44 "I didn't make much in the orchard. About a dollar a day. Finally got to be a dollar and a half, and we thought we was getting rich."—Alvin Alexander years and years—six dollars a week. Paid two dollars of it a week for boarding. Then I had four dollars left. I thought I was doing well. Bet I could take that four dollars and buy more than you can with twenty-five now.

"I worked for Mr. Fort about thirty years. He hired me for a foreman when I was twenty years old. I was a foreman for the Forts for years and years.

"Mr. Fort was one of the smartest men that was ever in this country. He was just born for apple growin'. He was always experimenting on everything he growed, but his main business was growin' 'em to sell. He used to ship 'em on the Tallulah Falls Railroad. I used to load eight and ten cars from Baldwin to Cornelia.

"He was a great orchard man. He came to this area from Athens. He set out the first peach trees that was ever set out in Habersham County. He also had several apple orchards between here and Cornelia, and he had every orchard named. The one in Cornelia on that high hill was Clearview, and the one in Mount Airy was Bright Hope, and he had one between Mount Airy and Cornelia called Esco. Now, the Turkey Cove orchard in Rabun County was about fifty or sixty acres. He named it Turkey Cove because when he first bought it, he seen a bunch of turkeys.

"He set this orchard out way back years ago. Two men come with him from Cornelia. They thought he was going crazy. They got suspicious of him and were about to slip off and go back to Cornelia. He'd stop all along, put his ear to the ground, and listen. He was listenin' to air breezes. If the wind blows, it won't frost. Turkey Cove's up on a high mountain in a gap that comes across there. He went on up there, and the air come through that gap all the time. You hardly ever go up there but what the wind's not blowin' right in your face. I don't think it's ever failed havin' a crop of apples because of that.

"That Fort's Prize apple was just a big ol' red apple up here in the country somewhere. He pulled up some sprouts where they'd come up and set 'em out, and they made big red apples. They was having a big state fair for apples, and he carried some of those apples to the fair and took the prize for the whole state of Georgia. That's why he called 'em Fort's Prize.

"I never was the foreman at Turkey Cove. I was a foreman between Cornelia and Baldwin. But one year, when the foreman at Turkey Cove died, I took a crew of men and gathered the Turkey Cove crop for Mr. Fort. I think we gathered almost fifty hundred [five thousand] bushels there that year. That's a lot of apples.

"I stayed with 'em till all of 'em went away, and that left me settin' out in the cold, because they finally let somebody else have the orchard. So then I came to work in Rabun County for the Catheys in 1934.

"The Catheys had a large operation for growing apples. Over at Mr. Cathey's, we grafted several hundred trees at one time for his great big orchard. We'd go over there and graft trees of a night 'til ten or eleven o'clock. Then just lay off some rows in the garden, heave 'em out, and throw a little loose dirt over 'em. Then let 'em go for about a year, take 'em up, and set 'em out.

"When they first got ready to spray the trees, they had a pump house that contained large cement vats in which they mixed water and chemicals together to spray on the apples. Then they pumped the mixture out through a three-quarter-inch pipe that run underground all over the orchard. Every two-hundred-foot section of hose was hooked for spraying the trees. The first spray was when the trees first bloomed and then one more time in the middle of the year."

Another veteran of the apple orchards is Hugh Holcomb. Mr. Holcomb pointed out some of the changes that took place while he worked in the apple orchards and some of the changes since he left.

"Back in the early twenties, Mr. [Julian] Roberts came here from Florida and bought Glassy Mountain. He set out an apple orchard, but he knew very little about growing apples. My dad, Jeff Holcomb, took it over and looked after it for him.

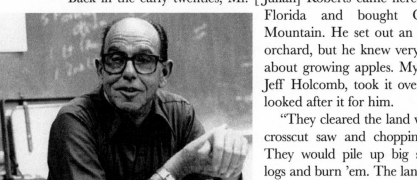

PLATE 45 Hugh Holcomb

"They cleared the land with a crosscut saw and chopping ax. They would pile up big sawed logs and burn 'em. The land was steep and hard to work on. They went with a wagon anywhere they could and used a sled anywhere else. In later years, they built roads with picks, shovels, and a drag scoop pulled by a mule.

"We used a pick and shovel and a crowbar and a mattock up there to plant the trees. It was so rocky you had to shovel the dirt. There wasn't no such thing as an auger to bore the holes with, so you had to go in there with just a shovel and mattock and dig your holes. And it was so rocky that sometimes you had to pry big rocks out of the holes and then get dirt to fill it back up.

"We'd dig a hole about eighteen inches around, and [the depth was] according to your tree. Some would be a lot deeper than the others on account of the rocks. And sometimes you'd have to plant 'em between rocks—anywhere that you could find to get a place to put it. You couldn't keep direct rows like you can now where there aren't so many rocks.

"There wasn't many apples made while Mr. Roberts had the orchard because he had nothing but Stark's Delicious, and they would not pollinize theirselves. You know Stark's Delicious apple trees have to have a pollinator, something like a Grime's Golden or Arkansas Black or Yates to make them bear. In the spring of the year, when it'd come time for the apple trees to bloom, we would go over at the Tiger orchards here and cut blooms off the Winesap trees and Yates trees and all the trees that were pollinizers and haul them to Glassy [Mountain]. We'd nail buckets up in the trees and also set big barrels full of water around in the orchard and put those blooms in those buckets and barrels. That's the way he got his apples to bearing at Glassy, until he had time to get some trees planted for pollinizers.

"Wild bees came off of the mountain, and they did the pollinizing. Bees was all over the mountain. The wind might carry some pollen, but bees was the biggest pollination that's done. The wind might blow some from tree to tree, but it wouldn't blow it very far.

"The high elevations in Rabun County make this good apple-growing country. We plant at elevations above the frost line. If you go up there at Glassy, they had a frost line, and you could almost tell, after the summertime come, where this had hit. Your trees would have more apples on 'em after the orchard got up to a certain height on the mountain. And the higher the elevation, the better the apples grew.

"Sometimes the frost would maybe kill one out of ten or maybe two out of five or something like that, and you'd still have plenty of apples on your tree for a good crop of apples. Sometimes the frost would help you thin your apples if there was too heavy a bloom. We never used a heater of any kind to keep frost or freeze down, but in later years, we'd go build fires in the orchard, and the smoke from the fires sometimes would keep the frost off if it didn't get down too cold.

"Robert Massee, who owns that orchard now, [used] gas when it [got] cold. He [had] gas burners which [would] blow the heat and would keep the moisture in the air stirring and keep the frost from getting on the trees. Ice, just like frost, would freeze your buds, freeze your little apples.

"It does make a difference which side of the mountain the apples are planted on, because of the frost. The north side doesn't have as much frost as the south side of the hills. That's the reason your north side of your hills was better than the south side to grow apples—on account of frost and weather in the spring of the year. You'd have an earlier frost on the south side and it would cause your apples to get killed during blooming. Down low in the valleys, your trees would get bigger, but you'd only get a good crop of apples maybe every three or four years. The frost'd come and kill the ones that was low down, although they was bigger trees.

"Too much rainfall could hurt if you couldn't spray insecticide. Insects cause scab and bitter rot and stuff like that on your apples. It would cause your apples to get infected if you had too much rain. That was the only time rain would hurt. The more rain you have during the growing season, the better the apples are. Then you need a lot of sunshine to make 'em color when they start ripening.

"We grafted all over the orchard on all those Delicious trees with different kinds of apples. Arkansas Black was a good one, and Black Twig and Yates were good grafting trees. We had one old-timey tree there, Streak o' June, on the branch right down in the middle of the orchard, and you could see where that tree was because it was a good pollinizer when it bloomed. There would be apples for about four or five trees out from it—just loaded—and the trees out from that didn't have as many.

"We pruned in the winter, the dormant season, and it was awful cold up there on Glassy Mountain. We depended on a pair of straight pruners and a saw. We would prune the trees, but the orchard owners back then wouldn't let us do nothing but cut the water sprouts out. The higher the trees got, the better they like it. There was no spreading of the limbs, they wanted 'em to grow straight up. And they didn't thin 'em out none; they just let the trees grow straight up. Therefore, the sun didn't get in much on the trees, on the apples on the inside.

"We'd go up there on Glassy with big mowing blades, sickles they called 'em, and mow the weeds down to where we could get through it two or three times a year. There was snakes everywhere you went up at Glassy. We'd kill a rattlesnake or two or three pilots [copperheads] every day when we was mowing. I remember one time I was mowing and a big rattlesnake struck where I'd stepped and went between my legs, and the man below me slapped his mower on it. I think it had eight rattlers. It struck at me and just barely went by my leg as I stepped. They was every day killing a rattlesnake or a pilot one. But nobody never got bit. We was always lucky.

"When I came back from the CCC's, I went to workin' up at Glassy for Mr. Massee all the time, and we set out another orchard about like that first one I was telling you about. After we got this one started, we set out about thirty or forty acres of Red Delicious and some Golden

Delicious, Yates, Arkansas Black, and several other kinds of apples that would pollinize the Red Delicious. We didn't put in any kind of fertilizer at the time we planted them. After a year, then we just put regular commercial fertilizer on 'em, lime and some ammonia nitrate, but not very much. Back then they didn't put as much fertilizer as they do today. We never did put ashes around them. We'd haul manure out of cow barns or horse barns and put that around 'em when we could find it.

"In the summertime, when we weren't mowing, we were spraying. When Mr. Roberts owned the orchard, we used a barrel spray pulled by mules on an old sled, and I remember I'd ride on that sled and pump it. You pumped it like an old water pump, and that sprayed. My dad sprayed the trees, and one of my brothers would drive the mule, and I'd stand on that spray and ride and pump that thing.

"They didn't spray but two or three times during the whole season, and the biggest thing they used back then was lime and sulfur and arsenic of lead. They started off spraying with lime barrels. That was for your wood, to coat the back and kill insects' eggs, same as the oil is used today. That was for your first spray, to protect the wood. I don't remember what proportions it came in, but it was strong. It'd eat you up. A many a time my fingers'd be eaten around my fingernails, and it'd be round my eyes where it'd get on them, and I'd come home and have to scrub half the night to get it off my face and hands before I could eat supper. It wouldn't come off very easy. You've smelt sulfur, and you know what sulfur smells like. And we used arsenic of lead mostly spraying for insects.

"They didn't use too many fungicides then. They used arsenic of lead, and then they had a Black Flag stuff they mixed with that to kill the insects. It was very poison, and it'd kill all the birds.

"The chemicals was worse then than they are today. They're outlawed today. They won't let 'em use that kind of stuff today in the orchards. Lead and stuff like that is against the law to use. They've got new chemicals, which I don't know about. They've come out since I quit working. I haven't worked much in apple orchards in thirty years.

"Sometimes it'd be two or three weeks or longer after the last spray before you started picking. You had to let that stuff get off of the apples.

"After Mr. Massee took the orchard over, he put a pump house at the upper end of the orchard and run a pipeline, a three-quarter-inch galvanized pipe, all the way down the mountain. Every two hundred foot, he'd put a standpipe, and we had a spray gun with just one nozzle on it and a big two-hundred-foot-long black hose. One man'd use the spray gun, and two of us'd pull that hose around all them rocks and bushes. He had the pipes about every three to four hundred foot apart so we could hook on from one to the other. The pipes'd go out, and then down the line. He would have 'em about a hundred foot apart where we could spray and reach further in and could go around the orchard. One team would go two hundred foot, and then the other two men on your other line would come the other way and meet you coming down the mountain. Be three or four crews a-spraying.

"It did better than the hand pump. You could get the tops of the trees. After Mr. Massee took it over, he cut some of the trees back, cut the tops off.

"There was a natural spring coming off of Glassy Mountain, and he had a big reservoir there that he held his water in. He didn't put any chemicals in that reservoir. He had a tank sitting there with his pump. I think it was about a five-hundred-gallon tank. It was made of wood. Then he had a pump gasoline engine settin' on the end of it. No electricity. You'd crank that engine and run your pump. You'd get about three hundred pound pressure on the pump, and that would spray it into the lines. The spray nozzles were in a cone shape—nozzles were like the same guns they use today. They didn't have the pressure they have now, and it came out in a heavier mist.

"They didn't spray much 'til after the apples bloomed and started shedding. Then's when you put on your spray, because if you put on this poison spray during the blooming season, you'd kill all your bees, and then you wouldn't have anything to set your pollen.

"To irrigate, there was two or three branches coming off the mountain, and when it got dry, Mr. Massee would turn that water down into his reservoir and open it up through his spray pipes and let it run out over his orchard down through there. Just gravity flow. It wasn't run by no pump or anything, just gravity force would force it down into the orchard. You could see a lot of difference if it was real dry. Where the water went around the trees, your apples would be bigger than the ones you couldn't get water to. It'd run around the hill and then seep down to maybe two or three trees. You couldn't get all over your orchard 'cause there wasn't enough water coming through this three-quarter-inch pipe to do much except right down the line where the trees run.

"We thinned all the time by hand. We'd climb up into the trees and pick off some of the green apples and throw 'em down so there wouldn't be so many apples that the limbs would break off. We'd cut poles and nail 'em together to make a brace or cut a fork in the pole and prop up the limbs to keep 'em from splittin' the trees. You couldn't hardly get through the orchard with a sled or a wagon or anything else when there were so many props under the trees. If you had a big crop, props were standin' thick under the trees. You couldn't ever get enough

PLATE 46 Bob Massee's apple orchard

thinned off these big long limbs, if you had a big bumper crop, to what they'd bust off or break if you didn't put a prop under 'em. You could thin half of 'em off, and then there'd be sometimes more than the trees could hold after the apples got up a big size. If you had too heavy a crop on your trees, and you didn't thin them out well, you wouldn't have a productive crop the next year. You usually had all the apples that a tree would stand to hold, if the frost didn't get 'em, even when you thinned them out a lot.

"They had the trees a lot farther apart than they have them today. They had 'em about thirty foot apart; you wouldn't get but about half the trees you get today on a acre of land. So where they get three hundred today, you got a hundred trees on a acre of land back then. They let their trees grow up so big! They didn't have none of these dwarf trees. There were only big trees, so you'd have to set 'em far apart to get through 'em. They didn't keep 'em cut back. They thought the more limbs you left on 'em, the more apples you had.

"I've seen some that'd have fifty or sixty bushels to a tree and some ten or fifteen bushels, but the apples wasn't no size; they was so little. You'd have a lot of small apples.

"When Mr. Roberts owned the orchard, and we went to gather the apples—there was about four or five or six of us boys—we would gather around the tree with a big sheet and hold it, and my father would climb the tree and shake the apples in that hole right in the middle of that sheet and the apples would roll down and roll out through that hole onto the ground. Then we'd pick 'em up and put 'em on the

sled and take 'em down to an old house he had down there where he
stored his apples.

"After Mr. Massee took over, we started picking about the middle of
August—first picking Red Delicious and then finishing up with the winter apples, which sometimes lasted on up into October before you got
all the Yates and Arkansas Blacks and Black Twigs and other winter
apples picked. We used pick sacks, and we'd haul the apples to Tiger to
the packing house in a truck. We'd fill up the pick sacks and haul 'em
down on the sled and set 'em out to the place where the truck could get
'em, and then the truck would haul 'em to Tiger to the packing house.

"I've seen apples three and four inches in diameter that came from
Glassy. We'd make a bushel pack with thirty-six apples of those Stark's
Delicious, the old-timey Stark's. It usually takes anywhere from fifty to
sixty-five apples to make a bushel. Biggest thing was Stark's Delicious
up there. There were a few trees of a big old yellow sweet apple and
then an apple they called Early Harvest scattered around in orchards,
but as pollinizers only.

"Those apples wouldn't keep too good. They wouldn't pack 'em.
They just had to be sold locally or to peddlers that'd come in and buy
'em off the trucks or wagons and haul 'em off to market and sell 'em.
That's where all the culls went.

"Another good pollinizer was the Black Ben. But they never packed
them either. It was just used solely for a canning apple and a cooking
apple. It was one of the best apples you could find for drying and making dried fruit.

"We picked all the apples. Back then they cleaned 'em up. When
we'd pick a tree, we'd go back and pick every one of them up. We'd take
them to the packing house, and they would be sorted and graded and
sold as culls. Some would be used for cider or vinegar, and the others
they'd sell to truckers that'd come in and buy 'em by the bulk and take
'em off and peddle them.

"Utility-grade apples were packed in baskets or ring packs. The only
thing Mr. Massee ever sold at a high price was little, round, half-bushel
baskets. Those were called ring packs. He sold them for three dollars for
a half a bushel there at the shed. The tourists would come in and buy
them, and those ring packs would bring more money than any other
apples he sold. The others didn't bring very much. Two or three dollars
a bushel was all you could get for them. [We] hauled 'em to the Atlanta
Farmers' Market.

"When trucker peddlers picked apples up at the packing house, he'd
get anywhere from seventy-five cents to a dollar a bushel, sometimes
fifty cents. It was according to the grade of the apple and how many

they bought. We just sold apples at the packing house, no roadside stands. I stayed at the packing house six days a week during the packing season, and then if anybody come and wanted a load of apples on Sunday, I'd open up and sell 'em to 'em. There was no cooler back then. You just had to move 'em out. They had a contract with a man at the Atlanta Farmers' Market, and he had storage where, if they couldn't sell 'em, he'd take 'em down there and store 'em for 'em and sell 'em later at a discount price. He had to have his cut out of 'em for storing 'em and takin' care of 'em.

"We used culls to make vinegar and cider. We'd make the barrels of cider, and we had to do that at night. We had no way to keep the bees off of us. They was so bad that we had to make our cider at night with just a old-type cider mill with a press. And we'd grind the apples at night and pour the cider in big fifty-gallon wooden barrels and let it set and make vinegar; and then they'd sell the vinegar to people for use in their cooking and pickling in their homes."

Bob Massee summarized the feelings of many growers when he stated, "I've gone to apple meetings all my life. When I started, there were a lot of young people. Georgia used to have an apple meeting; we'd get two or three hundred people. South Carolina and North Carolina were [the] same way. Now they have five states that all have the same meeting, and there's less people who go to that meeting than used to go to any one of those state meetings. There are no young people at the meeting. Sterling, my son, has about three or four people that he sees at these meetings that are about his age, and Sterling is thirty years old. There are very few young people that show up at this meeting, which makes me think the apple business is going to phase out if something doesn't change."

PLATE 47 Bob Massee

PRESERVING AND COOKING FOOD

"Then y' had some good eatin'."

I make my sauerkraut by the full of the moon because my mother and grandmother made it that way and their mothers before them made it that way." That's what Lizzie Moore told Russell Bauman, a Foxfire student, when he interviewed her. She also told him, "When you learn something in the family, it goes right down the family with you." Lizzie Moore's words, however, don't just apply to sauerkraut. They apply to a whole way of life, one that is disappearing in some places, changing in others, but still occasionally appearing when we least expect it. After having worked with Foxfire for several years, while in high school and now in college, I know that we are trying hard to preserve the old Appalachian customs and ways of life—our heritage. What I didn't realize is that some parts of it are still very much present.

While working on this section, I called my grandmother daily for help in editing the recipes. Not only did she not mind, she was thrilled. She doesn't care how I learn to cook or what my motivations are just as long as I eventually learn. I was proud to announce to my grandmother that I knew how to make sauerkraut and that the recipe I was using was similar to my great-grandmother's.

I was at home one night with my mother, who was trying to teach me how to make slaw. I remembered Lizzie Moore's comments about learning to make sauerkraut from her mother. That's when I realized that this chapter is about family traditions, and one of those traditions is taking the time, each and every day, to sit together over a meal and discuss family life. The importance of dinner cannot be stressed enough. Mealtimes were among the few occasions when the whole family sat in the same room, did no work, and simply enjoyed each other's company. Important decisions were made as steaming bowls of corn and potatoes were passed around the table. News about engagements and births, local gossip, and news from far away were shared as families gathered together for the evening meal. And when the community lost a member, people gathered at the home of the bereaved family, bringing every kind of good food imaginable so that the family wouldn't have to worry about cooking.

Although our lifestyle is quite different today, the dinner meal is still one of the most important parts of the day. In spite of the fact that meals where the whole family eats at the same table and at the same time now seem to occur less frequently, the times when families do eat together still bear resemblance to those of years ago. Who's getting married, who's having kids, and who's moving in or out of the community are still favorite subjects. Other matters often discussed are who makes better biscuits or when the next fishing trip will be. And neighbors still take food to those who've lost a loved one, knowing that the food is not as important as the concern behind it.

I will be the first to admit that my motivation for putting together this section on recipes was that, first and foremost, I love to eat, and much of what I love to eat is discussed in the following pages.

The words on these pages represent a collection of recipes, hints, and cooking stories, knowledge that has been passed down for generations, mother to daughter (or perhaps father to son), about how to care for a family in the form of fixing them what they like to eat. Here you have time-tested and well-loved recipes from families throughout the region. Many directions are not precise, as the women learned to add "a little bit" of this and "a dab" of that from their mothers, who did it that way because that's the way *their* mothers did it.

—*Lacy Hunter*

PRESERVING, CANNING, AND PICKLING

Before the era of deep freezes, store-bought fruits and vegetables, and restaurants, not only did people depend on their ability to grow food on the farm, they also depended on saving what they had grown. To provide fruits and vegetables year-round, methods of preservation such as canning and pickling were devised. Even today many families prefer the vegetables they can "put up" themselves to those bought from the store. Thus, canning and making jams and jellies are still late-summer rituals in many families, including my own. Though the actual work is occasionally tedious, the results are always worth the effort.

PRESERVING FRUIT

PLATE 48 Lessie Conner

Lessie Conner remembered her family's methods for preserving fruits and vegetables. "Before we bought our deep freeze—people ain't had deep freezes so long, you know—in the fall of the year, we'd put up a big barrel of bleached fruit, apples. (Just peel 'em and bleach 'em in sulfur.) We'd have a barrel of bleached fruit, and we'd have a barrel of kraut, and that's the way we spent the winter—with stuff like that to eat."

As Mrs. Conner mentioned, one of the methods of preserving fruit was bleaching it. Several people told us that unless the fruit was prepared with too much water when it was later cooked, they could not taste the sulfur used in the process, and the bleached fruit was actually quite good. As Susie Smith said, "That fruit was just as pretty and white [as it could be]."

Her brother Clive Smith also remembers bleached fruits. "My mother, aunts, and sisters would cut up apples to smoke them in the fall. They'd cut 'em up and put 'em in a basket with an iron pan. Then sprinkle a little sulfur in it to preserve the apples. They'd store 'em in a churn. We had fresh fruit all winter. You don't hear of smoked fruit anymore."

Furman Arvey spoke of what his family did with the fruit after it was bleached. "Applesauce and stuff like that, they usually made it out of bleached fruit. They take it and get a big barrel and put a run of that in there, and they'd get sulfur or brimstone—that brimstone was hard, and it'd burn—and they'd cover that [barrel] up and let it smoke. That's what cured it. Turned it real white. And give it a good taste. Then they put it in jars. It stayed soft. It wouldn't dry out. It'd keep. If they wanted to, they could just leave it in the barrel and use it out of the barrel. It'd keep right in that barrel. Be big oak barrels, you know, back then."

Susie Smith graciously gave us specific directions for bleaching apples. She said that the first step is to find an airtight container or box approximately thirty-six inches deep. She remembers her family using an old cement box with a quilt draped over the top of it. They placed a hot stove eye from the top of their wood-stove in the bottom of the box on which they placed one teaspoon of sulfur and one teaspoon of cream of tartar. The sliced apples should be placed in a bas-ket—she used an old market basket—and suspended from the top of the box and covered with a quilt. The sulfur and cream of tartar will burn on the hot plate, producing smoke, which will, in turn, bleach the fruit. (If the stove plate

PLATE 49 Furman Arvey

wasn't hot enough to burn the sulfur and cream of tartar, they were lit with a match to make them burn.) The bleaching process takes about forty-five minutes to one hour.

DRYING APPLES

Another commonly used method of fruit preservation was drying. Ruby Eller recalled how people found a way to make the chore of peeling the apples to be dried a social event. "There were candy drawings, corn shuckings, apple peelings [for social get-togethers]. In the summer when the apples would get ripe, people dried a lot of them. They'd meet at somebody's home one night to peel a bunch of apples and have them ready to set out in the sun to dry the next day. They'd go to a different house each night and help each other."

PLATE 50 Ruby Eller

PLATE 51 Lucy York

Lucy York found a slightly more convenient way to dry apples, especially in times of rainy or bad weather. "I would peel my apples and slice them and put them in the oven when I finished cooking a meal. I'd slip the trays in there and leave the oven door open. It would take several days for them to dry because I would leave them in there only until the oven cooled down.

"Now I dry them over my hot water heater because it's a low heat yet it dries the apples out. I can stack three trays of apples up on the heater by putting pieces of wood across and separating the trays."

Lettie Chastain told us how she stores her apples once they are dried. "I've always dried apples out in the sunshine. Then I put them in the stove and heat them, get them hot all the way through. I pack them in gallon jugs while they're real hot, and they just keep real good. We didn't have gallon jugs years back, and we used large crocks."

Furman Arvey summarized the whole process. "We didn't have refrigerators or freezers. Had to dry most of our food to keep it. We had one kiln. That old kiln—I can't recollect when it was built. The sides were four feet wide by eight feet long by two feet high built of rock. Then there was rock over the top of it. They tried to make it about four inches thick. That's what you laid your fruit on. They didn't burn their fruit that a-way. See, they just got that rock over the top of the fire hot, and it stayed a certain temperature. Then they took flour back then and made a paste out of it and stuck old newspapers—all kinds of papers— to the rock cover. It was clean, you know, about layin' your apple on. I recollect that. Then they'd peel 'em and just cut 'em wide open and quarter 'em, you know, and took the cores out. They'd dry better and dry even that way. It'd take about twenty-four hours to dry a run, and then they'd put a new run in. It wouldn't be over a couple of layers thick on the [furnace]. Stir it up ever' three or four hours. Just go in and stir it, you know.

"Then they'd take it off and put it in sacks, and on them good sunny days, they'd take that sack and lay it out on the porch where the sun could hit it, and they'd go and turn it over ever' once in a while so it'd dry out good, keep good. I seen a room one time—a little old pantry they called it—and I seen it stacked full of sacks of dried fruit."

BURYING APPLES, BEETS, CABBAGE, POTATOES, AND TURNIPS

Although drying was a common method of preservation, it was by no means the only one used. Burying fruits and vegetables was both an excellent means of preserving food and a testament to the ingenuity of the mountaineers. In order for the food to keep, the hole had to be well drained and insulated to prevent water accumulation and freezing. Sallie Beaty remembered well her family's potato hole. "Another way we kept our food was by putting it in a hole in the ground. We did our potatoes like this. [After] we dug up our potatoes in the fall, we would dig a hole [in the ground and put them in it]. We put straw or whatever we could find around them. Then we'd hill them up. [Next we] put dirt on top of them to keep 'em from freezing. Then we took an old piece of board or tin and put over the—we called it a hill—so it wouldn't get so wet. You could do turnips and cabbage the same way. Then, as you wanted a mess, you would go out there and get whatever you wanted at a time."

Ada Kelly also recalled her family's hole. "They'd dig a hole to put the apples in, put some hay, straw, or something in there, and just pour them in that hole. They they covered it over with leaves or straw and then heavy soil. Turnips, apples, and potatoes are all buried that way."

The logical question of how the fruits and vegetables were removed from the hole during the winter was answered by Roberta Hicks. "You would hoe up the potatoes in the garden, then put them in a hole, then put hay in the hole, and place your potatoes in the hole. Then you leave a place to where you can reach in and get them out."

Gertrude Mull also told us about storing fruits and vegetables in this manner. She felt, however, that perhaps due to changing weather patterns, burying fruits and vegetables would not be as effective today as it was years ago. "Back in them days, they just dried fruit and holed up their taters— get 'em off the trees and carry them to the cellar. We packed leaves in there and put the apples down in them. Then we'd cover the apples over with more leaves. They kept all winter. Nowadays they wouldn't

PLATE 52 Gertrude Mull

keep over a week. They'd be rotten. [Apples] don't keep like they used to. I don't know why. It's just the weather changing."

Mrs. Mull recalled that beets were also stored in a hole before canning became common. "We buried our beets [to keep them through the winter]. We never canned beets. We didn't know nothing about canning beets then. [When we cooked them,] we fixed them up with a lot of syrup."

In spite of the skepticism about their effectiveness today, holes for fruits and vegetables were an excellent method of preservation, especially in this climate where the winters are cool, but not too cold. As Roberta Hicks noted, the fruits and vegetables "would stay good all winter if it did not get too cold."

CANNING

"Back then there wasn't no money, much, and we had to grow what we had to eat. We grew beans, cabbage, tomatoes, everything like that [in our garden]. We canned everything we grew. We dried fruit too. My mother dried blackberries. She just put 'em on a cloth and let 'em dry. After she dried 'em, she cooked 'em with a little water. Then she'd sweeten 'em. You could make pies out of 'em or anything you wanted to. Why, they was good! They aren't as good dried as they was canned, but back then they didn't have too many cans to can in."

PLATE 53 "Back then, there wasn't no money, much, and we had to grow what we had to eat."—Minnie Dailey

This quote from Minnie Dailey summarizes one of the changes in food preservation that have taken place in the past century in the mountains—the advent of canning. Although definitely one of the better means of keeping food, canning could not be used until glass jars became common and cheap enough for the average family to afford.

By the 1930s, when glass jars became readily available, canning quickly became widespread and is still very common today. Roberta Hicks said, "I grew corn, green beans, taters, okra, and tomatoes in my garden. In those days, you had to can everything. I canned beans in half-gallon jars and jelly in quart jars. I canned a lot of tomatoes. One year I canned a thousand jars. I had eighteen different kinds of jams and jellies. I had seven or eight dozen jars of applesauce, and a hundred and fifty cans of green beans, and about a hundred and something quarts of peaches. We also had cows and pigs. We raised most of our own meat, but I say most of our food was from things that I had canned."

Over the years, the process of canning has changed. Now we have pressure cookers and stove timers to help us can. However, years ago, food had to be canned by the open-kettle method. Lola Cannon said, "I learned to can by the open-kettle method. That was where you cooked your food in an open kettle and had your jars sterilized and standing right there. You put your hot food in the jars and sealed them from the heat in the food. It was hard to keep. You

PLATE 54 Lola Cannon

pretty well have to process your jars after they're sealed. Later on, several different types of canners came along. We had a pressure canner."

Bessie Underwood also remembered canning in an open washtub. "I

PLATE 55 Bessie Underwood

have canned beans on the woodstove in a washtub. I boiled them three hours."

Sallie Beaty gave a detailed account of this method of canning. "[When] we canned our beans, we would pick them, string them, and then break them up. Then we would cook them outside for three hours in a big old wash-tub [over a] fire. This would [help the beans] keep [longer]. Most of our vegetables we did like this. We put

tomatoes, corn, and okra in our homemade soup. We scalded our tomatoes and pulled the skin off them. Then we cut our corn and our okra up and mixed [the corn, okra, tomatoes, and one teaspoon of salt] up. Then we either cooked it in a hot water bath on top of the stove or outside in a washtub with a fire around it."

These days the process of canning is much simpler, although it still involves hard work, and an afternoon of canning can turn even a well air-conditioned house into a sauna. The method of canning used today that utilizes pressure cookers is much easier than it was years ago. This change can be seen in Gladys Nichols's description of how she cans now. "I boil my tomatoes real good around thirty minutes and put them in a can and seal them. I process the cans about ten to fifteen minutes. I hardly ever lose any canned stuff."

PICKLING

Although bleaching, drying, burying, and canning were all excellent methods of preserving food, they did not give much variety to the diet. Another means of keeping food was pickling. Many foods, from beans to beets and cabbage to cucumbers, could be pickled. Not only did pickling preserve the food, it also provided a different taste and texture. Margaret Norton remembered pickled foods. "People grew and preserved everything for the winter to come. They had huge wooden barrels they used for kraut, pickled beans, and different types of pickles. They were all made with salt. They'd keep through the winter. I don't make sour pickles. They don't like me, and I don't like them."

Eva Vinson also recalled pickling as an effective means of food preservation even before canning became common. "People would think it was funny now to see a fifty- or sixty-gallon barrel of kraut or pickled beans. But they made 'em back then! And they kept all winter. And I don't know how they did because you can make a churn jar full now and seem like it won't last. They didn't put anything but salt [in with it], and as you chop it in the barrel, it makes its own juice. And salt it, you see, to taste—not so it won't work. It has to work. [Let stand ten days, or as long as needed in order to pickle.] And then they put boards over that. They had 'em special, you know, that they'd had hewed out. Then put rocks on top of [the boards] to hold them down, white flint rocks. They didn't have any way to can anything."

JELLY AND PRESERVES

Making jellies and preserves was yet another way of keeping fruits. Daisy Justice told us, "We canned berries, peaches, and apples. For instance, with blackberries, we'd put them in a big aluminum dishpan, and when they come to a boil, you started dipping them into your jars that you've already washed and scalded and sterilized. We'd seal them as we went."

Sallie Beaty gave specific directions for making jellies and preserves. "[To make our jellies,] we would boil our fruit peelings. We would boil 'em half an hour to one hour and then strain [the] juice out. [We] used [the juice] to make our jelly. [Then] we would use one cup of sugar to one cup of juice and boil it down on top of the stove till it was thick like we wanted it."

BLACKBERRY JELLY

1 quart of Blackberries to make 3¾ cups juice
1 box Sure-Jell (or pectin)
4½ cups sugar

Boil blackberries with ½ cup water to make a juice. Mash berries to see when they are done. Strain berries and place juice and Sure-Jell in pot. Stir while cooking. Let boil and then add sugar. Stir and cook until mixture jells.
—*Leona Carver*

PRESERVES

Lettie Chastain shared her mother's method for making preserves. "My mother made fruit preserves by putting whatever fruit she was using, pears or figs or whatever, into a pot on the stove. She'd add her sugar and a little water and any spices she might like, and let the mixture boil while she was cooking breakfast. Then, when she finished the meal and the fire was beginning to go out, she'd cover her pan up. Then the next time she started the fire in the stove up, she'd let the fruit get to boiling again. Sometimes it'd take her a couple of days to get the preserves ready, but they'd sure be good. They were better than any I've ever made."

SORGHUM

Years ago, when sugar was hard to get, sorghum and honey were often the only sweeteners available to farm families. So, in typical mountain fashion, families grew sorghum cane; usually one or two families in the community had a sorghum mill; and neighbors helped neighbors harvest and produce sorghum, sharing the final product. Minyard Conner remembered fondly the times his family worked together with his neighbor Bill Lamb at sorghum-harvesting time. "We growed sorghum cane here, and [Lessie, his wife] and the young'uns hauled it in a one-horse wagon [over to Bill Lamb's farm]. Bill had one horse over there, and we'd use his'n when we had to double up. Bill had a big ol' syrup mill over there, and Lessie and the boys would strip the cane here and carry it over there on our wagon. [They'd help Bill make his syrup, and he'd help them.] We'd get a barrel of syrup, you know. Just living at home, wasn't we!"

We wanted to mention sorghum because of its importance to the diet of most mountaineers. However, for in-depth information on sorghum making and diagrams, please refer to *Foxfire 3*.

APPLES

Although frequently used in desserts, apples are also cooked and quite often served on the dinner table with the vegetables and meat. The following recipes are just a few of the many ways apples can be prepared to go with a meal.

APPLESAUCE
Peel your apples but leave the core in them, because there's something around the core that makes the applesauce thicken. Use about 12 apples and cut them up into 4 or 5 pieces each. Put about 1 cup of water in a large pot and put your apples in there. Put them on top of the stove and cook until the apples are done, very soft. Run the apples through an applesauce grinder or ricer. Sugar may be added, but it's not necessary.
—*Margaret Norton*

COOKED APPLES

Peel and core your apples and slice them. Put them in a pan, add sugar and butter to taste, and cook them until they're tender and the

syrup thickens. I usually add cinnamon, but you can add whatever spices suit you. These are good served with baked ham and sauerkraut.
    —*Bessie Underwood*

SCALLOPED APPLES

6 tart cooking apples
¾ cup sugar
⅛ teaspoon cinnamon
Graham crackers to make 1 cup crumbs
Margarine
Water

Pare, core, and slice apples. Mix sugar and cinnamon. Roll out crackers and add sugar-cinnamon mixture. Arrange apples in baking dish in layers, covering each layer with crumbs and dotting with margarine. Add hot water to moisten. Bake in oven at 350°F for 45 minutes to 1 hour or until apples are well cooked and the crumbs browned.

SOFT-BAKED APPLES

Peel and core 12 apples. Cut each into 8 or 10 pieces. Place in a shallow baking pan and sprinkle with sugar. Add a small amount of water and cook on top of the stove until apples are tender. Put the pan inside the oven and bake a while longer.
    Serve the apples as is, although the guests usually will mash them, as they are very soft.
    —*Addie Norton*

PLATE 56 Addie Norton

VEGETABLES

The following recipes for fresh or canned vegetables come from interviewees who used them to feed their own families for many years. Many of these recipes were passed down from mother to daughter for generations and still frequently grace the kitchen tables of grateful families throughout northeastern Georgia.

BAKED BEANS

Pick [white half-runner] beans when they turn yellow. Shell them out. Place the beans in a pot and cook in water until they're tender. Drain water and put some onions in them, then add bacon, salt, tomato catsup, and a little vinegar. Pour them into pint canning jars and let them come to a boil, in a pan on the stove, to seal them.

—*Margaret Norton*

BEETS

Choose small beets and wash them with the skins on. Then cut the tops off, leaving about an inch of the top on the beets so they won't bleed. Then you boil them until they're tender with the skin still on. When they are done boiling, cool and just slip the skins off with your hands and slice the beets up. For buttered beets, add enough water to cover them, salt and butter to taste, and simmer for around 10 minutes. For pickled beets, instead of adding butter and salt, you add, again, enough water to cover them, and then vinegar and sugar to taste, and simmer for 10 minutes.

—*Juanita Kilby*

CABBAGE

For fried cabbage, you wash and coarsely chop a head of cabbage. Then you cook it in about a cup of salt water with streak o' lean drippings [streak o' lean is pork meat that is salt-cured and has one streak of lean meat running through fat meat] and about a teaspoon of sugar until it is tender.

—*Juanita Kilby*

CORN

Select about 6 ripe ears of corn and shuck, wash, and silk them. Then cut the corn off the cob and scrape the cob. Combine this with ½ cup of water and ¼ stick of margarine in a black skillet and cook in the oven, stirring it every now and then. It needs to cook approximately 30 minutes.

—*Juanita Kilby*

GREEN BEANS

Pick the green beans from the garden. Wash them and string them. Put them in

PLATE 57 Bertha Waldroop

a pot and cover them with water. I add Wesson oil, but you can put a piece of fatback [a piece of fat pork meat] in them too. Add salt to taste. Let them cook down until they're tender and almost dry.

—*Bertha Waldroop*

HOMINY

The various methods of preservation lent different tastes and textures to ordinary garden vegetables. These methods helped women provide many tasty and interesting meals for their families with a small number of vegetable choices.

Certain vegetables seem to have been more versatile than others. Corn, for example, had many uses, from vegetable to meal for bread, from snack to decoration of the family Christmas tree. Another use for corn was making hominy. Served as a starch, hominy is a delicious variation of a very prevalent vegetable in the mountains.

Although the making of hominy is generations old, the method has changed little through the years. In fact, Belle Wilburn Henslee, who learned how to make hominy from her mother, told us, "The process of makin' it hasn't changed any except according to what you lye it with. I used soda to lye mine, but old people used to use lye off of ashes, corncob ashes or hickory wood ashes."

For those who don't use "bought lye," making the lye with which to make the hominy is the first step in the process. To make the lye, water is dripped through oak or hickory ashes that have been saved from the fireplace. The ashes are placed in a metal barrel (which may be made of iron, plastic, or porcelain, but not aluminum, as it corrodes in the presence of the lye) with a spouted hole in its bottom. A few gallons of water are slowly poured over the ashes and allowed to drip into another bucket beneath the metal barrel, yielding the lye. The lye-making process should take about two hours.

Once the lye is made, approximately a peck [¼ bushel] of dried corn is shucked, silked, and, according to Mrs. Algie Norton, shelled by hand "so y' could get all the sorry grains and things out of it" and placed in a large washpot along with one part lye and two parts water to cook over a fire. After several hours of boiling, the skins and shells of the corn should begin to come off, at which point the pot is taken off the fire, and the corn is removed. The next step is to thoroughly wash the lye off the corn. Belle Henslee stated that "you wash it an' wash it—I don't know, about a dozen times or more!" Mrs. Norton agreed with her, saying that "you'd have t' wash it through maybe a dozen waters and rub it t' get all that skin off."

After being washed to remove all the lye, the corn is placed in a pot and put back on to boil until it is tender. Once the corn is tender, it is ready to be consumed by those eager for the rewards of their hard work, fried with bacon grease, or "put up" by either freezing or canning it. According to Mrs. Norton, once the corn has been cooked, "y' take it out when it's good and tender and done. Then y' had some good eatin'."

Granny Carrie McCurry told us her method of making lye. "For hominy, I always take hickory wood and burn it and take them ashes and put it up and drip the lye to use. Or you can keep the hot ashes and tie 'em up in a rag and do it. Fill your pot with water and put the corn in and the lye in and boil that until the skin [of the corn] comes off, and then you take the corn out and wash it, parboil it, soak it, and get the lye out of it." If you're doing it with a bag of ashes instead of lye, she adds, just get a handful and tie it up in a rag, stick it down in the pot, and boil it with the corn.

The best place to cook hominy, Mrs. Norton and Belle Henslee agree, is in a big, black iron washpot. Belle Henslee suggests waiting for a clear day in order to get a good fire and to make washing the hominy numerous times much more pleasant. Mrs. Norton added that "y' always make it in the winter-

PLATE 58 Granny Carrie McCurry

time. Houses were open enough 'til y' had plenty of ice, and anything y' had froze in it. Out somewhere away from the chimney or fireplace, it'd keep for a week."

MUSTARD GREENS

Pick a mess of greens and wash them at least 4 or 5 times until the water is clear. Then take out the stem and boil the greens in salt water until they are tender. This takes about 1 hour. Then take them out of the water and place them in a skillet with streak o' lean drippings, add about a teaspoon of sugar, and fry them for about 10 minutes.

—*Juanita Kilby*

PARCHING PEANUTS

Preheat your oven to a moderate temperature. Be careful not to let the stove get too hot. Put the raw, dried peanuts in a shallow pan and place in the oven. Test them every few minutes to see if they are

parched to your satisfaction. It will
usually take 15 to 20 minutes.
—*Ruth Cabe*

COOKING PICKLED BEANS

Wash pickled beans once to get the
salt and vinegar taste out. Then cook
in a small amount of water with 1
tablespoon bacon grease for 15 to 20
minutes, just long enough to heat
them throughout and to cook the
water out.
—*Lucy York*

PLATE 59 Ruth Cabe

POTATO SALAD

For 6 to 8 servings of potato salad, peel, wash, and dice 6 Irish potatoes. Then boil and drain them. Add about ¼ cup cubed pickles or rel-
ish, a tablespoon of mayonnaise, a teaspoon of mustard, 3 chopped
boiled eggs, and salt to taste, and mix.
—*Juanita Kilby*

RUTABAGAS

Peel them and slice them, and cook them in salt water to cover with
approximately ¼ cup of brown sugar and drippings of streak o' lean.
They should be cooked until they are tender and almost dry.
—*Juanita Kilby*

SAUERKRAUT

Another vegetable that was transformed by good cooks into many
different, tasty dishes is cabbage. Aside from the obvious slaw and fried
or boiled cabbage, sauerkraut is an ingenious way of both preserving an
easily grown vegetable and providing more variety at the dinner table.

Lizzie Moore gave Russell Bauman instructions on how she makes
sauerkraut—a favorite use of cabbage in northeastern Georgia. "I
make my sauerkraut by the full of the moon because my mother and
grandmother made it that way, and their mothers before them made it
that way. I always make my kraut on the full of the moon 'cause it's
always harder and firmer then than it is at any other time. I like my
kraut hard and firm. I don't like soft kraut. Other people may have different times of the moon when they make theirs—I don't know about
that. As far as my pickled beans and kraut go, I have always made mine
on the full of the moon.

"Don't put the kraut in a tin barrel. Put it in a wooden barrel. A tin barrel'll rust, and you can't eat your kraut. To make kraut in the barrel—now, this is an all-day job—you take your cabbage, trim the outside leaves off, and save them for later. Wash and chop up your cabbage in a washtub. I got a number two washtub, and I just wash mine in that. If you want to make chopped kraut, you chop 'em up as fine as you want it. If you want to make shredded kraut, you can just take your cabbage, cut it into quarters, and slice it just as thin as you can make in those little strips—either way. I don't make the shredded 'cause I like chopped the best. Just take it, chop it up, and put it in your barrel.

"When you get your cabbage chopped up, put it all into that fifty-gallon barrel. Take those green leaves that you trimmed off the outside of your cabbage, wash 'em, and put 'em over the top of your barrel. Just take those leaves and lay 'em agin' your barrel so that none of your chopped kraut is showing. Get a big ol' flat rock and lay it down on top of your cabbage. That weights it down. It keeps the cabbage down in the bottom of the barrel instead of coming up when it starts working. With a fifty-gallon barrel, I'd say you'd have to get two pretty good-sized rocks to go across it and weigh it down. You don't pack it in the barrel. These rocks pack it for you. Pack your cabbage in there 'til it comes up six or eight inches from the top. I forgot how much salt you put into a fifty-gallon barrel, but the way I do when I make it is I'll take my water and taste of it and get it as salty as I want it. Pour your salt water in that barrel and put it away to set for a while.

"It'll take anywhere from two to three weeks for a fifty-gallon barrel of kraut to work off and get sour. After it gets sour, you have to take it out of the barrel. Take your hands and squeeze all of the water out of it and put it in a cooker or a dishpan. Run cold water over it, wash it, and take your hands and squeeze all of the water you can get out of it again. Put it in another pan, put water over the top of it, and put it on the stove. Don't let it come to a boil. Just let it get ready to come to a boil. Stir it so the heat can get all the way through. Pack it in your cans and don't put no more salt or nothin' in it. Pack it in your cans, seal it up, and set it away.

"You can eat kraut with just about anything. You can make kraut with weenies. You can make fried kraut. If you want to, you can always put pepper in your kraut. Now, a lot of people don't like pepper in their kraut. I do, but now, a lot of people don't. I like hot pepper in my cabbage. You can eat it out of the can. I usually just get me some out in a bowl and eat it raw. To me, beef's not good in kraut like pork is. You can also eat kraut with cracklin' bread.

"Another thing you can do with your cabbage is to take your stalks that are left over and pickle them. Take the stalk, peel it off, and drop it down in your kraut. It'll sour and be good too. When you get ready to eat it, put 'em in a pan of grease from bacon or fried meats. If you ain't got that, just put your Crisco or lard in a pan, let it get hot, and eat it. That's all there is to makin' kraut. Of course, when you're makin' it, it takes longer than it does to tell about it. When you make it in a fifty-gallon barrel, oh, my goodness, that takes fifty pounds of cabbage!"

Lola Cannon told us how she judges the correct amount of salt to put into the barrel of cabbage and how she knows when the kraut is through "making." "I've always judged how much salt to put in by the size of the container I'm using. If it's a gallon container, I put two table-spoons of salt, fill the container with water, and weight the top down carefully. Then I watch till it ferments. You can tell by the bubbles coming up in the jar. The time it takes to ferment depends on the heat. In cool weather, it will take quite a bit of time. I just have to watch it."

SQUASH CASSEROLE

I make a casserole out of squash, and the Florida people say I'm the only person they know that knows how to cook squash to eat. I take real small squash, and I always scrape them and cut them up in thin pieces. I put them in a pan and put onions and crumbled-up Ritz crackers on top. Then sprinkle a tiny bit of water and some grated cheese and dots of butter over the crackers. Then I put aluminum foil over it and put it in the oven to cook.

—*Mrs. Effie Lord, Proprietor of Lord's Cafe, Clayton*

PLATE 60 Effie Lord

SWEET POTATOES

For candied sweet potatoes, I peel and quarter about 4 large sweet potatoes, put them in a pot with enough water to cover them, a cup of sugar, a dash of cinnamon and butter, and I let them boil until they're tender and the juice is syrupy.

—*Bessie Ramey*

TOMATO SOUP

For tomato soup, take the juice from 1 quart of home-canned toma-toes. Stir 2 tablespoons flour into a small teacup of milk. Pour tomato juice into the flour-milk mixture and heat. Add ½ teaspoon sugar to taste.

BREADS

Few Southern Appalachian families consider a meal complete unless it contains at least one type of bread. Cornbread is always a favorite in mountain homes, as are freshly baked "from scratch" biscuits.

BISCUITS

>   2 cups plain flour
>   1 level teaspoon baking soda
>   ½ teaspoon salt
>   2 or 3 tablespoons shortening or lard
>   1 cup water or buttermilk

Sift flour with soda and salt into large bowl. Mix in shortening or lard until flour is crumbly or in little balls. Add enough water [or buttermilk] to dampen dough. Mix well. Pour out onto floured board. Roll out with rolling pin or press out thin with hands. Cut into circles with biscuit cutter or top edge of water glass. Put biscuits onto greased pan and bake in hot oven (425°F) 10 to 20 minutes, depending on thickness of biscuits.

—*Margaret Norton*

CORNBREAD

There's one thing we did that was really good. Make up cornbread and make it to where the dough was hard-like, you know, so it'd hold together. And rake them coals out on that hearth, and my mother'd just throw one of them patties in there on that hearth and rake some ashes back over it and let that cook. And it'd brown and that's the best bread I've ever eat! Ash cake I believe they called it.

But anyway, when they got that to where it was done, they just washed it off with water, washed all that ashes and coals and stuff off. Well, now, that's really good. You just don't know without you've lived back then!

I went to spend some days with my grandmother on my mother's side, and she'd have me to cook, and I was just a small girl. I must have been about eleven or twelve years old. And Grandpa, he wouldn't eat anything in his bread, only just water. He wouldn't have a thing in his cornbread. No salt nor soda, nor nothing but just water. Well, she'd tell me to cook him a little cake like that and put me and her one with buttermilk and salt and soda in it.

—*Eva Vinson*

2 cups ground cornmeal
2 tablespoons baking powder
1 teaspoon salt
½ cup flour
1 cup buttermilk

Use water to thin to consistency of pancake mix. Cook at 400°F for about 30 minutes.

—*Jo Ann Chastain*

HAPPY ROLLS

1 cup warm mashed Irish potato
⅔ cup shortening
2 teaspoons salt
½ cup sugar
1 cup hot scalded milk
1 yeast cake
2 eggs, well beaten
Flour to make a medium dough—not stiff
Melted butter

Put mashed potato in bowl. Add shortening, salt, sugar, and milk. Let stand until cool. Add yeast, which has been dissolved in ½ cup warm water. Add eggs and flour. Knead slightly until smooth. Set aside in warm kitchen and let rise 1 hour or so before putting in refrigerator. About 3 hours before serving, take dough from refrigerator and, using as little flour as possible, make into rolls. Dip each one in melted butter and let rise. Bake in hot oven (425°F) and serve at once.

Rolls are lighter if made up and put in the refrigerator the day before you want them.

HUSH PUPPIES

A long time ago, when people used to go out on picnics or camping trips out on the creek banks, their dogs always went with them, of course. When they got their fish fried, they couldn't keep their dogs out of their supper. They had the grease where they had fried their fish and they had cornmeal they had rolled the fish in. So they'd stir the hot grease and cornmeal up together with some water or milk and salt and put that back in the pan. They'd cook that and throw it to the dogs. The dogs would hush and get off to the side. That's how hush puppies got their name.

—*Margaret Norton*

DESSERTS

Although today desserts are one of the staples of the mountain menu, years ago they were a rare treat. Sugar was expensive and occasionally unattainable, and as a result, dessert foods were saved for special occasions such as Christmas, all-day singings, and dinner-on-the-grounds at church.

APPLE PIE

Place several cups of bleached apple pieces in an uncooked piecrust and add butter, sugar, and cinnamon to taste. The pie can be covered with pastry strips or a second crust if preferred. Bake in a preheated oven at 350°F for 30 to 35 minutes or until the crust is a golden brown. The Parker family enjoys the apple pies made from bleached apples because they taste so much like fresh apples.
—*Edith Parker*

APPLESAUCE CAKE

2 teaspoons baking soda
2 cups applesauce
2 cups sugar
1½ sticks butter
2 eggs
3 cups plain flour
1 teaspoon baking powder
1 teaspoon ground cloves
½ teaspoon salt
1½ teaspoons nutmeg
1 tablespoon cinnamon
1 cup chopped pecans
1 cup raisins

Preheat oven to 300°F. Add soda to applesauce and set aside. Combine sugar, butter, and eggs and mix well. Beat in dry ingredients. Add applesauce, nuts, and raisins and mix well. Pour into tube pan and bake at 300°F an hour and a half. Cool before removing from pan.
—*Arizona Dickerson*

BAKING HINTS FOR PIES

Mix all the ingredients for your pie together and put them in a pan on top of the stove. Bring them to a boil. Place dough on top of pie

ingredients, then put the pan into the oven to finish cooking, and it won't take so long because it's already hot.
—*Lola Cannon*

You put your pies on the top rack in the oven to bake them. If you take your pie out and it isn't done, set it on top of the woodstove and let it boil. When you're baking pies, you can boil them on top of the stove and then put them in the oven on the top rack, and that bakes them.
—*Ruth Holcomb*

BLACKBERRY PUDDING

2 cups blackberries
1 cup water
1 cup sugar
1 cup cornmeal
Pinch of salt

Wash freshly picked blackberries. Put them in pan on top of the stove and add water and sugar. Heat to boiling. Stir in cornmeal and continue cooking until the pudding is as thick as you want it. Add salt and continue stirring. Put it over a low heat and continue cooking until the cornmeal is cooked through.
—*Ruth Holcomb*

COBBLERS
Put your fruit [about 2 cups] in a pan with a little juice or water. Get it to boiling on top of the stove. Add sugar and butter. I like to use a biscuit dough, but some people use pie pastry just as well. Just roll it out good and thin, and make enough for 2 layers. Dip half of your fruit and juice out and save. Put a layer of the dough on the fruit remaining in the pan and boil that a few minutes. Pour the reserved fruit and juice back in and place the second layer of dough in the pan. Let this boil up. Then put it in the oven (350°F) to brown.
—*Bessie Underwood*

FRIED APPLE PIES
Make a biscuit dough. Roll the dough out on your dough board and cut into saucer-size circles. Cook dried apples in small amount of water until soft. Mash and add sugar to taste. Place several spoonfuls on one half of each dough circle. Fold over the other half and seal the edges with a fork. Fry in a pan on top of the stove in a small amount of grease.
—*Addie Norton*

Use 1 quart dried apples cooked in a little water until tender. Add ½ cup sugar and a little allspice. The dough for 2 large pies requires 4 cups self-rising flour, lots of lard, and a little water. Knead the dough and roll it out thin. Put the cooked apples on the dough, fold over, and fry in an iron skillet in lard until brown.

—*Bertha Waldroop*

HONEY SWEET BREAD

2 eggs
½ cup butter
1 cup strained honey
2 cups self-rising flour

Follow the directions used for Syrup Sweet Bread on page 118.

—*Ruth Holcomb*

ICE CREAM

We had a lot of milk and cream. Our daddy or one of the men in the community would go into Dillard and get some ice. We had a grinder that you turn. You put your ice and your salt around the churn on the inside of the grinder. Then in the churn you put your milk and sugar and whatever flavor you want to make your ice cream: peaches or vanilla or strawberry. You turn the crank on the grinder, and when it gets to where it won't turn anymore, your ice cream's made.

—*Margaret Norton*

PUMPKIN BREAD

4 cups sugar (all white or equal parts white and brown sugar)
4 cups cooked pumpkin
1 cup vegetable oil
1 cup chopped nuts
1 teaspoon ground cloves
4 teaspoons baking soda
2 teaspoons cinnamon
1 teaspoon vanilla
1 teaspoon salt
Chopped dates or raisins
5 cups flour

Mix all ingredients together. Bake in 4 tall 1-pound coffee cans, filling each about ⅔ full. Bake at 350°F for 1 hour or a little longer. Bread will shake out of cans freely when cool. Store in refrigerator or other cool place.

—*Arizona Dickerson*

OLD-FASHIONED TEA CAKES

1 stick butter or margarine
1 egg
1 cup sugar
2 tablespoons milk
½ teaspoon vanilla
1¾ cup flour (omit salt and baking powder if self-rising flour is used)
½ teaspoon salt
2 teaspoons baking powder

PLATE 61 Arizona Dickerson

Cream butter, egg, sugar, milk, and vanilla. Sift flour, salt, and baking powder. Add to creamed mixture and blend well. Chill the dough for several hours. Remove from refrigerator and roll out into half-inch thickness. Cut out with a biscuit or cookie cutter. Bake in 375°F oven for 8 to 10 minutes. Note: More flour may be added to make the dough stiffer, and cookies may be cut out immediately instead of waiting for the dough to cool.

—*Bertha Waldroop*

QUICK MIX TWO-EGG CAKE

2¼ cups sifted cake flour
3 teaspoons baking powder
1 teaspoon salt
1½ cups sugar
1 cup milk
½ cup shortening
1 teaspoon vanilla
2 eggs

Sift together flour, baking powder, salt, and sugar. Add shortening and milk. Blend together. Beat by hand 300 strokes. Add vanilla and eggs. Blend together and beat an additional 2 minutes. Pour into 2

greased 9-inch-layer cake pans and bake in moderate oven (350°F) about 30 minutes.
—*Bertha Waldroop*

SYRUP SWEET BREAD

2 eggs
3 tablespoons butter
1 cup syrup or molasses
2 cups self-rising flour

Preheat oven to 350°F. Cream eggs and butter. Add syrup. Fold in flour and mix good. Bake in lightly greased pan until brown. This usually takes about 20 minutes.
—*Ruth Holcomb*

SWEET POTATO PIES

I used to make the best sweet potato pie you ever put your tooth on. Sweet potato pie is wonderful! You just peel your potatoes and cut them up raw. Cook them 'til tender. Add a teaspoonful of cinnamon. I don't want but a dash of nutmeg, quarter of a teaspoonful, in mine. Put a tablespoon of butter and a cup of cream and a cup of sugar in your pan. The sweeter you make your sweet potato pie, the better it is.
—*Addie Norton*

2 sweet potatoes, about fist-size
2 teacups milk, about 12 ounces
½ stick butter
2 cups sugar
½ teaspoon cinnamon
Dash of salt

Peel sweet potatoes, slice, and put them in a pan of water. Boil until tender. Leave the water in them. Add milk, butter, and sugar to the potatoes. Heat to boiling. Add cinnamon and salt.

Roll out a thin biscuit dough and place on top of the sweet potato mixture. Allow juice to boil through dough until dough is thoroughly cooked. Sprinkle sugar on top of the pie and set the pan under the broiler to brown on top.
—*Ruth Holcomb*

BEVERAGES

Although in recent years the traditional drink of southerners has been sweetened, iced tea, years ago all teas came not from tea bags bought at the grocery store, but from herbs in the woods. Because teas were used primarily as tonics and remedies, they will be discussed in the next chapter, "Wild Plant Uses."

The drinks preferred by the mountaineers of that bygone era tended to be coffee and milk, although some did make and keep wine both for a beverage and for medicinal purposes.

COFFEE

Spread out green coffee beans on a biscuit pan. Cook slowly in a moderate oven until they turn brown. It takes less than an hour.

—*Lucy York*

I have parched coffee, way back years ago, in a pan in the fireplace. I put my coffee in a pan, then set it on some coals, and let them get good and hot. I'd keep stirring it 'til it got good and brown. Then take it off, let it cool, and grind it. We used to have coffee mills that you put the coffee in and turned it with a crank to grind your coffee.

—*Granny Mary Cabe*

GRAPE JUICE

Use 2 cups grapes and 1 cup sugar for each gallon of juice. Put washed grapes in a gallon jar and fill with boiling water. Seal jars, place upright in kettle of boiling water with jars submerged completely, and boil for 30 minutes.

PLATE 62 Granny Cabe

WILD PLANT USES

"I used to go to the mountains and dig up herbs."

Society has long had a fascination with natural things, and wild plants are no exception. Currently, there is a strong trend toward the use of herbal or other medicines as opposed to laboratory-produced drugs. Many of the people of Southern Appalachia continue to use wild plants—found in blessed abundance in the woods—not in response to trend, but because this has always been a way of life.

The fact that plants were a necessity of life is evident in the following recipe for a remedy for dropsy, or edema, an excess accumulation of fluid caused by, among other things, chronic heart failure. It is presented here exactly as it was written in a book belonging to Mrs. Zada Fowler, the grandmother of Dr. John Ed Fowler of Clayton, Georgia:

> *A receipt for the dropsy 3 qts. of apple vinegar nine bunches of black snake root three bunches of sinaker snaker root three handful of stare root three handfuls of cammil flours too handfuls of worm wood forty five new nails put them all in a iron oven set them in the coroner by the fier let it stand nine days till it works then rige out (Ed. note: "rige" is sometimes spelled "rench" and means strain—or remove foreign matter) and in the same oven add one bottle of rum one pound of sugar then set on a slow fier simer it down four days to too bottles full one spoonfull at a dose eat no fat meat and no sweat milk keep out of the rain and dew.*

Dr. Fowler noted that the remedy probably did have some medicinal value, for a person suffering from dropsy would most likely need an iron supplement. The rust from the nails would add this in the form of ferrous oxide, and it would not be harmful but would be "clean rust." The reason that we are normally so concerned about wounds caused by rusty objects is that dirt, germs, and bacteria collect on the rough surface of these objects, and it is these substances, and not the actual rust, that cause the infection.

As an afterthought, Dr. Fowler added, "By the way, my grandmother did not die of dropsy, so . . ."

The Foxfire Book and *Foxfire 9* contain sections devoted to home remedies. Many of these involve natural or wild ingredients. *Foxfire 2* and *Foxfire 3* include chapters about wild plant foods. Since these books were published, much more has been collected concerning the use of wild plants for nourishment and medicinal purposes. We have attempted to compile these here. Due to limited space, we refer readers, where possible, to photos or drawings in previous Foxfire books in hopes of aiding them in the identification process.

Some of the plants listed here are very rare, and some are even on the endangered species list. Please be respectful of future generations and use a conservative approach when you "go a-gatherin'," as Charles Thurmond does. "I prefer to go out and get my own herbs. When I go gather the herbs, I use the old Cherokee way of being conservative. I make sure that I find four of the plants before I'll take one. This way I know that I will leave three plants to reproduce. You can take part of the root of most of the plants and leave part, and it will continue to grow. Always put something back."

This reverent relationship with the land and the belief that God owns and provides all continue to be integral parts of the simple lifestyle of the people of the rural Appalachians. Having knowledge of the land and the wild plants available for consumption is still a source of pride for the mountain people, who strive to live simple, self-sufficient lives. While some cultures or geographical areas attempt to shelter their resources, the Southern Appalachian people have always been willing to share their wisdom and skill in the old ways with anyone eager to learn.

Charles Thurmond demonstrated this willingness through a recent interview. Much of his knowledge came from ancestors who shared with him. "My grandmother was a midwife and had at least one herbal cure for everything. Her having a good bit of Cherokee blood in her caused her to know a lot of the herbs. Grandma used to take me out to show me things in the woods and tell me what they were good for.

"My grandma taught me some of her herbal cures, but most of it I've picked up since then. When you are a child, you don't listen enough. I remember some of what Grandma taught me. My father and uncles have supplemented my herbal education. I go to the doctor occasionally, but I like doctors that don't go overboard with antibiotics and things like that. I don't medically treat people, but I talk about herbs with 'em. I teach people about herbs so they can learn for themselves.

"My grandma had numerous cures for everything, usually two or three. There are many ways to prepare various herbs. Whether you want it prepared cold, warm, or hot depends on what you are treating. If it is cold, it takes longer to work, but it will work longer in your system. Most herbs can be boiled. You soak some herbs. Alcohol will take the chemicals and things inside the herbs out. It depends on how you fix them and, most importantly, how you use them."

While the knowledge of those who graciously contributed information to this section is not questioned, we must caution readers that these are personal uses and experiences with wild plants, and we in no way guarantee accuracy, effectiveness, or safety in the identification or use of these plants. Charles Thurmond agreed, saying, "When people learn about these herbs, they must be careful. If you use them improperly, they can be really dangerous."

Wild plants that have at least one medicinal or edible claim to fame are listed here alphabetically by the common Southern Appalachian name. The genus and, usually, species names follow.

—*Teresia Gravley Thomason*

WILD PLANT MEDICINAL USES

Alumroot *(Heuchera)* typically grows on rocks in open woodland areas and reaches a height of one to two feet. The leaves are usually parted into three or five divisions and are cleft and toothed. Flowers from this plant are small and white or green. Roots are usually thick and two to four inches long with several stem scars on the root showing old stem growth. The plant is gathered for the roots, which should be used before the spring flowering time of April through June. As the leaves get older, they are often spotted.

Alumroot has several uses as medicine. A tea brewed from the leaves is used for dysentery. A mixture made from the root is used for sore throats. Powdered root is also used on wounds to stop bleeding.

Clarence Lusk shared his experience with this root. "The alumroot is a very spindly little ol' stem that runs up out of the ground. It comes up very early in the spring, pretty much the first thing that comes up. That's when I generally gather it. All it takes is two or three little ol' roots as long as your finger to cure you usually. I've got up in the morning, especially when I was working in the woods in the forestry business, and I'd be sick with dysentery. I'd just say, 'Well, I just ain't gonna get to work today. That's all there is to it!' While my wife was getting breakfast, I'd go out and dig up some of them herbs and make a cupful of tea and drink it. Then I'd eat a pretty good breakfast and go right on to work, and that was the end of my sickness.

"Now, my granddaughter up here calls alumroot pig medicine because we used to use it for the pigs. Pigs is bad to take dysentery. If you feed 'em too much, they'll get

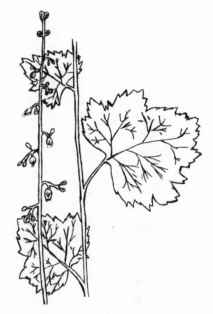

PLATE 63 Alumroot

sick. And calves too! Even the old cattle. In the spring of the year when grass shoots come up, gets so pretty and green, and then comes a freeze and that grass freezes, if you turn your cattle out right then and let them eat a bit of that frozen grass, it'll just nearly kill 'em. I come in one evening from work, and one of the cows was just the awfullest mess of sick you ever seen from eating that ol' frozen grass. At that time, I had a big bunch of alumroot from working in the woods and finding it, just digging along as I passed by it. I made about a quart of tea and put it in a five-gallon bucket. Then I put the cow in the barn. She didn't like it, but since that was all the water she got, she'd come to it and drink it. The next day, she was well."

Balm-of-Gilead (*Populus candicans*) can be found on roadsides and small waterways. The trunk of this tree can reach six and a half feet in diameter and a height of one hundred feet. Young branches are resinous and hairy with pleasantly scented buds. Leaves can be up to six inches long, are hairy when young, and are dark green on the top side and lighter green on the underside. This tree is sought for its buds.

As a remedy for erysipelas, a feverish infectious disease characterized by deep red, spreading inflammation of the skin, make a salve of "bamagilion" buds fried in mutton tallow. Add petroleum jelly if you wish.

As an all-purpose salve, boil the buds of the "bamagilion" in water and skim the wax from the buds off the top. Mix this wax with pine resin and good mutton tallow. Keep in a container for use whenever needed. Some people like to make a large amount of the salve each year and store it in small tins to have on hand.

"I used to go to the mountains and dig up herbs," Numerous Marcus explained. "We would get roots and plants and make herb medicines out of them. There are a lot of herbs in the woods if a feller knowed what they was. We used to get heart leaves [wild ginger] and Balm-of-Gilead buds and some hog lard and put all this together. We'd melt it down and make a salve out of it. It's good for sores. Rub it on them and it would clear them right up. It was good for cuts too."

Black-Eyed Susan *(Rudbeckia hirta)* is well known to everyone. With yellow flower heads and a black center, it is a biennial that grows to a height of one to three feet and blooms in summer. It was used to treat skin infections and does contain antibodies. Native Americans used its root for tea for worms and colds.

PLATE 64 Black-eyed Susan

Black Walnut *(Juglans nigra)* is often a signature tree of the Southern Appalachian homeplace; a black walnut cake is a regional favorite. Charles Thurmond thought that "the black walnut is good to eat, and the bark is good for dye and rubbing on the skin for any kind of skin ailment or disease. The juice from the husk of the black walnut was very good for ringworm." (See *Foxfire 3*, page 345.)

PLATE 65 Black walnut tree (top)

PLATE 66 Black walnut hull and bark off the tree (left)

Bloodroot *(Sanguinaria)* can be found in rich soil. It has a white flower that shows itself in early spring. One leaf with five to nine lobes and one flower are produced for each root. The leaves grow from approximately four inches to as much as twelve inches wide after the flowering period. The roots of this plant are collected in the fall and dried before using.

Marie Mellinger wrote, "Bloodroot is possibly the most common of the sang-sign plants, [plants that grow in the same area as ginseng], still found growing in many areas where ginseng, golden seal, and ladyslippers have been eradicated. This pretty springling has white, star-like blossoms before the scalloped leaves appear. The stems and roots contain an orange juice. This is the 'red-coonroot' of the mountains, and juice on a lump of sugar was a cough drop. Known as 'tetterwort' or 'sweet slumber' or

PLATE 67 Bloodroot

'she-roots,' the dried rootstocks were ground and used in an infusion to relieve pains of burns, or for coughs and colds and chest ailments. As 'she-roots,' bloodroot was a remedy for female complaints."

Charles Thurmond offered this wisdom: "Bloodroot is a neat little plant that grows in the woods. When you first break the roots, they look like they are bleeding blood-red. It is very, very bitter. If you know someone who's got asthma, you might want to give them bloodroot. If you break those roots and touch that juice to your tongue, it opens your sinus areas. It can be fixed in teas or other fluids. It can be used on the skin sometimes. Bloodroot can also be used for bronchial problems and stimulating your circulation and appetite. [It causes] you to sweat."

Blue Cohosh *(Caulophyllum)* grows to be one to three feet tall and is generally found in rich, loamy soil in the shade of the woods. Marie Mellinger told us, "Blue cohosh is often found growing with ginseng and goldenseal. This plant stands stiffly erect, with many small scalloped leaves. The leaves and stems have a frosted appearance, and the yellow flowers are followed by dark blue berries. The stocky roots are collected in autumn and have some market value. The plant is sometimes collected

as 'blueberry root' or 'blue ginseng' or 'yellow ginseng.' In home medicine, the mountain healers used the roots as medicine for lung troubles, or to stop the flow of blood. The roots contain an alkaloid, methylcytisine."

PLATE 68 Blue Cohosh

Boneset *(Eupatorium perfoliatum)* is usually found in wet ground near swamps or streams. The unusual leaf configuration makes this plant an easy one to spot. The leaves grow on a rough, hairy stem of one to five feet in height. They are joined at the base and sit opposite one another along the stem. Small white summer flowers are produced at the heads of each stem. Boneset is gathered in the summer for the flowers and leaves, which are stripped from the stalk. The flowers turn grayish white in late summer. This plant is closely related to the joe-pye weed and grows to about four feet tall. It was used to poultice broken bones.

As a remedy for colds, make a tea from the leaves of boneset. Boil three or four leaves in a cup of water, strain, and sweeten. Drink the tea when it has cooled because it will make you sick if taken hot. Leaves of this plant may also be cured and saved for use in teas during the winter months.

Varina Ritchie recalled, "Mother doctored with boneset tea and castor oil and turpentine. You'd drink a glass of boneset tea if you had a cold before you went to bed. It would help you to sleep. We raised it in our garden. It would grow to about two and one-half or three feet. Mother always had a patch of it in her garden. It was kinda like a weed that growed. You could take it, and even when it dried it would make good tea."

Mrs. Laura Patton remembered that boneset was a popular plant for making remedies. She'd put pieces of the plant in a cup and pour boiling water over them and let them steep. Then she'd strain the tea into another cup, let it cool, and then use it. She said it was especially good for flu and colds. In fact, in the winter of 1976 when the drugstore medicine wasn't helping one of her grown sons who had the flu, he used boneset instead and claims that it helped. He went to bed right after he took it, and it made him rest all night. In the morning, he was well.

One of Charles Thurmond's memories of his grandmother involved boneset. "My grandma had numerous cures for everything, usually two or three. One of her favorites was boneset. Boneset plants grow around waterways, swamps, creeks, lakes, and whatever. It is good for fevers. It cures about twenty-five different illnesses, but it's a natural quinine. Quinine is a medicine made from a tree in South America that kills fevers from malaria. During the Civil War, the South didn't have quinine because of the Northern blockade, so they used boneset. It works quite well. Boneset will kill a fever in ten to twenty minutes. This year I had a cold and a fever. I took some boneset, which killed the fever immediately. I had quite a bit of it left over, and I didn't want to waste it, so I drank it. Well, in half an hour my feet were cold and wouldn't get warm!"

Butterfly Weed (*Asclepias tuberosa*) is a variety of milkweed that grows well in dry, sandy, or rocky soil. It is found in the open, in open forest, or near the banks of streams. It has hairy stems and rough leaves with a large, white, meaty root and blooms in the summer. Butterfly weed is gathered in the fall for the roots. This plant is a perennial that grows to a height of one to two feet. Its bright orange flowers make it easy to identify. Early settlers thought the root cured pleurisy and called it pleurisy root. The plant attracts several types of butterflies. It can be toxic in large quantities. Monarch butterflies get their protective poison from this plant.

Of butterfly weed, Charles Thurmond said, "Some people call it chiggerweed. It has little orange blooms on the top of it, and butterflies go berserk over them. It has a root called the pleurisy root, which is good for anything to do with your chest or aching muscles. You must chip this root up to make it into a tea."

Catnip *(Nepeta cataria)* is strongly scented, grows in height to two or three feet, and has fine white hairs on the stems, giving it a white appearance. The almost heart-shaped leaves are also covered with fine white hairs on the underside and are about two inches long. Summer brings flowering spikes of white flowers that are dotted with purple. (For a photo and a drawing of catnip, see *Foxfire 3*, page 334.)

Catnip is gathered during the spring and summer for the leaves and flowered tops. This common plant is not native to the region but was introduced here by colonists. It grows well in dry soil.

One of Mrs. Laura Patton's favorite home remedies was catnip tea (made from the leaves), which she used when her children had the flu or were teething. She said it was good for helping them sleep.

Numerous Marcus told us, "Catnip tea is good for breaking up colds. It'll break out the hives too. You don't need to take but just a teacup at a time. I use the leaves on catnip. I don't use the root. I'd take the leaves and put them in a pot, then pour boiling water over them and let them set for a few minutes. Take the leaves out and pour the tea in your cup, sweeten it with sugar or honey, either one. Little fellers would smack their mouths on that. To keep catnip up through the winter, I gather the leaves, dry them out, and put them in a container where they can get a lot of air. They'll keep a long time."

Catnip tea is made by pouring about a pint of boiling water over a half cup of broken leaves and stems. Let this mixture stand for several minutes and then strain it.

PLATE 69 Christmas Fern

Christmas Fern *(Polystichum)* is an evergreen that got its name because of its generous use as a decoration at Christmastime. It was used in the winter for ills caused by cold and wet. Root tea was used for fever and chills. The toxicity of this plant is unknown.

Colic Root *(Aletris)* is found in dry, sandy soil and is gathered in the fall for the roots. This herb can be one to three feet tall with grass-like base leaves only. The leaves surround the stem in the form of a star. A white-yellow spike of flowers is produced from May through August. A concoction made

PLATE 70 Colic Root

from the root was used for diarrhea, rheumatism, and jaundice. It was also used for colic.

Colt's Foot *(Tussilago farfara)* grows along streams in wet, clay soil and has yellow spring blooms, which are seen before the leaves. This plant has many stalks, with each producing a yellow disc-shaped flower that only opens to the sun. The leaves, shaped like horses' hooves, arrive from the roots and can be as large as seven inches wide. They are covered on the underside by thick, woolly hairs.

Colt's foot, which is not native to Southern Appalachia, is gathered for the roots and the leaves. Leaves are usually taken near full-growth size. Gertrude Mull shared that colt's foot is good for coughing. "Just take [the leaves] of colt's foot and make tea out of it."

Comfrey *(Symphytum officinale)* is found in wasteland and has rough, thick leaves in branch fashion. The plant, which was introduced to the Southern Appalachian region, stands up to three feet tall and has large lower leaves and smaller, stemless upper leaves. Summer flowers are clustered, green, and four-petaled. Comfrey is collected in early spring

PLATE 71 Comfrey

or fall for the root. This plant can be dangerous if overused; therefore, readers should be cautious if they attempt to gather and use it.

Of comfrey, Numerous Marcus said, "I've got some comfrey root growing in the garden. It's good for arthritis and for when you get the gout in your foot. It's good for your blood. It helps keep it purified. You have to boil the root and make a tea out of it. You put it in alcohol so it won't sour. Most herbs you can use the roots. There's not many that you can use the leaves off of. But you can take comfrey root and use the roots and leaves, either that you wish."

Dogwood *(Coruns florida)* is found in well-drained soil throughout the Southern Appalachian Mountains and is used in the fall for bark from the root. This spring bloomer displays numerous showy white petals on delicate branches, followed by small leaves that turn red in the fall.

"Dogwood is easy to get," according to Charles Thurmond. "It's a stimulant; it picks you up. If you have got circulatory problems, it's supposed to be good for them. The dogwood bark and flowers are tonics."

Elderberry *(Sambucus canadensis)* likes damp, rich soil and can grow to ten feet in height. It possesses many smooth, light gray stems and large leaves on short stalks. Flowers are fragrant, five-lobed, and wheel-shaped, followed by clusters of juicy, small, round fruit. This shrub is gathered in June and July for the flowers and then from July to September for the berries, which are purplish black in color. The flowers are dried quickly. Berries must be carefully dried to avoid mold. Native Americans used a poultice of elderberry on cuts, sore limbs, and headaches. The bark, roots, leaves, and unripe berries are toxic, but the flowers and ripe berries are edible.

Ginseng *(Panax quinquefolia)* grows well in moist, rich soil in the mountains. It is usually about one foot tall and has three larger leaves at the top with thin leaflets. As many as twenty small greenish white flowers bloom in a cluster from May through August, and crimson berries appear in July and August. The root is thick and can be three inches long and one inch thick. (For a photo of ginseng, see *The Foxfire Book*, page 235.)

This increasingly rare plant is gathered in fall for the root. It is important to gather the root in the fall only, because roots gathered at other times shrink more during the drying process. But because this plant is rare and endangered, readers are asked to refrain from gathering it.

Ginseng's root is revered for its strong medicinal properties. It has been used for an aphrodisiac, for coughs, and as a heart stimulant. Because it is so popular, regulations have been placed on digging it.

Numerous Marcus believed that "ginseng is good for arthritis and for sick stomachs. To use it for arthritis, you can make a tea and drink it. Just take the roots and boil them, get the strength out of them. Or you could take the liquid and rub it on your joints, and it would have the same effect. I've got ginseng growing right there in the garden. It takes ginseng about two years to come up."

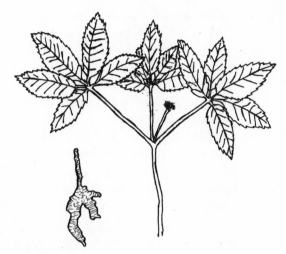

PLATE 72 Ginseng root and plant

Charles Thurmond said, "Another thing that is used around here [Southern Appalachians] a lot, but is very scarce, is ginseng. It is good for your stomach and has a calming effect on your nerves."

Goat's Beard *(Aruncus dioicus)* resembles a shrub and sometimes reaches a height of six feet. It has tiny, yellowish white flowers that bloom March through May. It was also called ghost breath. If you had a bad dream, you made a tea from the roots of ghost breath. Tea was also used to bathe swollen feet. The Cherokee Indians made a poultice of its root to treat bee stings.

Golden Ragwort *(Senecio)* is found in swampy areas and damp meadows. A perennial plant reaching two to four feet in height, this herb has smooth, slender stems approximately two feet long. It has two leaf types—heart-shaped or rounded and lance-shaped—which grow from the base of the plant and can be tinted purple on the underside. The flowers are yellow and found in clusters at the top of the plant. They bloom from March through July. The root and leaves of ragwort were made into a tea traditionally used by Native Americans and settlers for childbirth complications; it was also used for lung ailments, dysentery, and difficult urination. It is primarily gathered for the entire herb and the root.

Goldenseal *(Hydrastis canadensis)* is an increasingly scarce plant found in the open woods on hillsides, where soil drainage is good. It grows in patches and has a thick yellow root. Hairy stems come directly from the root and are about one foot tall with branches near the top. Each branch houses one small leaf, one large leaf, and a flower. Leaves can reach eight inches in diameter and have five to nine lobes. In spring, an unusual flower blooms, which is greenish white in color. Flowers are followed by large heads that turn red in the fall and resemble raspberries. Fresh roots are bright yellow throughout and become brittle when dry. Goldenseal is gathered in the fall after the heads are ripe for the root and in late summer for the leaves.

Marie Mellinger wrote, "Best known as sang-sign is the 'little brother of the ginseng': the goldenseal." Other names for *Hydrastis* include turmeric-root, tonic-root, ohio cucuma, orange-root, and jaundice-root. Its use as an eyewash gives it such names as eye-root and eye-balls.

"Goldenseal has two divided green leaves topped by a whitish fuzzy flower in early spring. The blossoms have an oddly aromatic odor that attracts small bees and the bee-like flower flies. The single fruit resembles a red raspberry, but is poisonous if eaten. The medicinal part is the thick yellow rootstock collected in the autumn. The roots are a bitter demulcent and contain three strong alkaloids: berberine, canadine, and hydrastine. They were used in medicines called 'bitters.' In 1856, S. G. Goodrich wrote, 'Bitters are esteemed as a sort of panacea, moral as well as physical, for even then morning prayer went heavily without it.' *The Herbalist* states that goldenseal is 'one of the most agreeable and expensive stomachics of the botanical kingdom, recommended for and esteemed as tonic for the liver and stomach. Weakened stomachs with enfeebled digestive powers are greatly benefited by its use. Goldenseal was used to stimulate circulation when hands and feet were cold, and the skin turned blue. It is also a fine herb to use on exzema or minor skin irritations.'

"Any plant with yellow roots or strong yellow coloring matter was, according to the doctrine of signatures [if the plant was shaped like, or resembled, a human organ or disease characteristic, then that plant was useful for that organ or ailment], a remedy for yellow jaundice. *Hydrastis* was sometimes called yellowroot when used as jaundice medicine."

Numerous Marcus stated, "I've got some goldenseal planted up there above the barn. I ordered it. There is some of it in this country around here, but it's a very scattered plant. You find it mostly back in North Carolina. It just grows in little patches around here. You can make a tea out of the roots of goldenseal. Take a little wad of the roots and put them down in a quart or a half gallon of liquor and let that set a while. Drink a little of that at a time. You don't want to drink too much of that 'cause it'll make you tired as the dickens. I never make too much of it at a time, because I've got friends who come in to see me that like it too!"

"Take the powder out of goldenseal flowers. It's good for cuts, keeps down infection. You just break [the blossoms] off, put 'em over paper, and let 'em drop. Sift that to get all the crumbs out of it to where it'll just be pure stuff, the powder out of the blossoms," Gertrude Mull added.

Charles Thurmond said, "A true yellowroot is goldenseal. [It] has a very toxic effect if you overdose on it. [It] is good for colds and the croup."

Hemlock *(Tsuga canadensis)* grows well in moist earth and is a common sight in the mountainous areas. This tree has short needles and small cones. The needles were brewed to make a tea for coughs and colds.

PLATE 73 Hemlock tree

Horseradish *(Cochleria armoracia)* enjoys rich soil and can reach heights of over two feet. (For a drawing of it, see *Foxfire 2,* page 77.) It is gathered and used for the root, which has a burning taste. As a blood builder, use the red part of the roots of the horseradish plant and drink as a tea. It was used to aid digestion.

Indian Root *(Aralia racemosa)* is gathered in the fall for the root. The stems have many branches and can be six feet tall with very large leaves. Flowers appear in late summer to early fall and are produced in clusters. It likes moist, rich soil.

PLATE 74 Horseradish

Marie Mellinger said, "*Aralia racemosa,* called spignet, false-sarsaparilla, spiceberry, shot-bush, or Indian root, is a tall, dramatic plant with huge dried leaves and a very showy panicle of fragrant flowers. Later the *Aralia* bears an abundance of juicy, garnet-red berries. The strong-smelling roots are dug in autumn. *Aralia* is a 'cure-all.' Sarsaparilla compound has been sold as 'Nature's best tonic of certain organic hormones.' With ginseng it 'eases ills of old age and prolongs life,' but only for men, giving it such names as 'life-of-man' and 'old man's roots.' The cooked roots have an agreeable aromatic smell and flavor and are sometimes used as food."

PLATE 75 Ironweed

Ironweed *(Vernonia or Verbena hastata)* likes moist, open places and is gathered for using the entire herb. The stem is rough, straight, and covered with fine hairs. It can stand seven feet tall and branches out above the leaves, which are broad, toothy, and lance-shaped. This herb produces small blue flowers in clustered spikes that can be six inches long.

Charles Thurmond told us, "Ironweed is very gentle. You don't really realize it's working. You make a concoction and use it on the surface of the skin for skin diseases and things like that."

Jack-in-the-Pulpit *(Arisaema)* grows well in shady, moist, wooded areas. It has smooth leaves that can be six inches long and three inches wide. The flower, which appears from April to early July, is shaped much like a calla lily and is green or green with eggplant-colored stripes. Fall brings a cluster of shiny deep red berries. The root (or corm) is turnip-shaped and has a strong burning taste. This plant is gathered in the summer for the root. The root is cut crosswise and dried to lessen the strong taste. Native Americans used the dried root for colds and coughs and to build the blood. Dried root poultices were used externally for rheumatism, boils, and swelling from snakebites.

Jerusalem Oak Seed *(Chenopodium anthelminticum)* is a naturalized, strongly-odored weed that grows in open places and is gathered for using either the entire plant or the fruit only. It is a common plant. It has a stem of two to three feet with many branches and several lance-shaped leaves. The lower leaves are much larger than the upper leaves. In summer, flower spikes mixed with leaves appear. These are followed by small round berries that contain a small black seed. The strong odor comes from the potent oil contained in the plant. This oil is distilled from the berries alone or from the entire plant.

Gertrude Mull told a story about using this plant. "One time, my brother got sick. Just looked like he had the nervous croup [not real croup, but the symptoms are similar]. We called the doctor, and the doctor gave him shots for the nervous croup, but [it turned out] he didn't have it. There was an old neighbor woman come, and she said, 'I believe he's wormy.' So she went out and got some peach tree bark and leaves and poured boiling water over that and made a poultice. She put that right across his belly. 'Now,' she says, 'go to the store and bring some of this Jerusalem oak seed medicine, and we'll try that on him.'

"The doctor said he was too weak to do that. He said, 'Maybe you'd better wait.'

"That woman said, 'I'm gonna put this poultice on him, and I'm going to the store and bring a bottle of worm medicine up here to give him.' She went up there [and got the medicine]. She give him a dose of that and told my mother, 'Tomorrow, you give him another'un. And you give him some castor oil after that and see.'

"So she did, and they got sixty-some big round worms out of that little-bitty boy. He was only about three or four years old. And that boy got well. He always was a little ol' weaselly-looking thing, and he seemed like he come out then [started growing].

"From then on, she always give us kids that medicine about twice a year. She got worms from some of 'em but never did get none from me. I'd take it, but boy! I'd go through that stuff. Nobody knows. [Mama would make us] candy out of syrup and that Jerusalem oak seed. Boil the syrup, put a little sodie in it, and stir it. Cook it just like candy. Twist it just like tobacco. Then she'd break that all up in big pieces and pass it around for us to eat. We'd eat it that a-way. And you can feed that to your chickens or anything that'd get worms."

Jewelweed *(Impatiens capensis)* grows well in wet places where shade is abundant. Stems are brown, can reach two feet tall, and hold variably sized, soft-green leaves. Charles Thurmond said, "Jewelweed grows all around the Foxfire office in Mountain City. The juice inside the jewelweed is a natural cortisone that is good for bee stings, poison oak, and poison ivy."

Joe-Pye Weed *(Eupatorium maculatum)* may grow as tall as six feet. Its cluster of several small pink flowers is slightly fragrant. Although there are several stories as to who Joe Pye really was, there is a general con-

PLATE 76 Joe-Pye Weed

sensus that he was an Abenaki Indian medicine man who lived in colonial New England. He earned his fame by "curing" typhoid fever and several other diseases by using concoctions made from this plant. In the Southern Appalachian Mountains, this plant is called queen of the meadow, a fitting name for this stately herb. It blooms August through September.

Native Americans had several uses for this plant. The one we found most interesting: a brave who was courting a young woman was assured of success if he stuck a wad of this plant in his mouth before he went visiting.

Charles Thurmond described his experience with this plant by saying, "Joe-Pye weed is very close to boneset, and because of this, it can be used for fevers and such. I have found that a tablespoon for a child and two tablespoons for an adult is usually enough. Once, my grandmother saved one of my older uncles' lives by breaking his fever."

Lily-of-the-Valley *(Convallaria majalis)* grows in clumps in wooded, damp places. Now rare, this plant was used for headaches—you could sniff it or put it on the back of your neck. It has two green leaves with a white stalk of bell-shaped flowers. The flowers are very fragrant. This plant is dangerous and should not be used internally.

PLATE 77 Lily-of-the-Valley

Linden Tree *(Tilia americana)* enjoys rich forestland in the mountains. It can grow to 125 feet tall, with a trunk diameter of 5 feet. Leathery leaves are pointed, toothy, and have one- or two-inch stems. Spring brings abundant flowers, which are yellowish in color, clustered, and fragrant. Collected from this tree are the bark and the flowers, which should be dried in the shade.

As a remedy for "risings" [boils], use the inside surface of the bark to draw them to a head. A tea made from the flowers is used as a remedy for a stomachache.

Liverwort *(Hepatica americana)* likes wooded areas and blooms in early spring. Its flowers, which arrive in April, stand on stems four to six inches tall. There are no petals, only five to nine sepals that protect the reproductive parts of the plant. The sepals of the *Hepatica* are delicate and usually pink, white, or lilac. Hairy, soft stalks of the plant spread along the ground. The leaves are leathery, thick, and round or kidney-shaped.

Liverwort is gathered in April for the leaves. It is believed to be medicine for the liver.

Maidenhair Fern *(Adiantum pedatum)* has wiry black stems with light green foliage and reaches a height of two feet. It is rarely found in poor soil. It was used mainly as a medicine for women.

Marie Mellinger wrote, "The soft fern is maidenhair. This dainty wildling is found growing near mountain trees and waterfalls with slender black stems and horseshoe-shaped fronds of palest green. Maidenhair has been a fever medicine, and the shiny black roots are sold under the name 'Capillaire.' It was also used for rheumatism. With agrimony and broomstraw *(Andropogon)* and ground ivy, maidenhair could give one vision to see witches. Called 'dudder-grass,' this fern made a mucilage for stiffening hair—or, as Gerard, an English botanist, said, 'It maketh the hairs of the head to grow that is fallen or pulled off.' "

Mustard *(Brassica)* has several different plants in the mustard family. Although not native to the Southern Appalachian region, some of those that grow in the area are winter cress, spring cress, tansy, black mustard, field mustard, and charlock. Some varieties enjoy damp areas, while others like drier soil. Most have clusters of green leaves near the base of the plant with a single, long stem rising to two feet in height. Most varieties have small flowers in varying shades of yellow. (For photos of this plant, see *Foxfire 2*, pages 74 and 80, and *Foxfire 3*, page 344.)

As a remedy for headache, pour hot water over mustard leaves to arouse their odor and strength. Bind these leaves in a cheesecloth poultice to the head.

New Jersey Tea *(Ceanothus)* reaches two feet in height. The flowers are showy, puffy clusters. A tea made from the leaves was once a popular beverage. Native Americans used the root tea for colds, fevers, snakebites, stomachaches, and lung ailments.

PLATE 78 New Jersey Tea

PLATE 79 Partridgeberry

Partridgeberry *(Mitchella repens)* enjoys damp, cool woods and sandy soil. The small branches produced from a tender underground stem are usually no taller than six inches. Leaves are near the top of the branch and are evergreen and leathery. The partridgeberry blooms May through July. The flowers, which occur in pairs, are followed by berries that are red in the fall and can stay on the plant until the next blooming season. The flowers are united at the base and smell a bit like lilac. After the blossoms wilt, the two flowers fuse together to form one berry.

This aromatic evergreen is gathered for the entire herb or for the leaves in fall. Cherokee Indian women made a tea from this plant and drank it for weeks before having a baby. It was believed to make childbirth much easier. The tea was also used to treat coughs and colds.

Pennyroyal *(Hedeoma pulegioides)* is very aromatic and enjoys dry soil. Its height is usually only one foot, and it possesses a slim, hairy stem with several branches. In summer, pale blue flowers among small narrow leaves appear in clusters. The entire plant has a strong minty odor and taste. (For a drawing of pennyroyal, see *Foxfire 3*, page 337.)

This cultivated herb is gathered in summer for the leaves and flowers. Gertrude Mull said that pennyroyal's leaves are really good for treating a cold and that it's prepared in the same way as boneset tea.

Persimmon *(Diospyros virginiana)* has gray bark and leaves that are ovate and multiveined. Fruits arrive after the flowers and ripen to an orange color. The fruits are generally sweeter after the first frost of the season. (For a drawing of persimmon fruit, see *Foxfire 3,* page 320.)

Clarence Lusk told us, "Sometimes, persimmon bark's good for that sore mouth. Just chew it, get the juice out of it. You'll get it all in your mouth, and it's just about [as bitter as yellowroot], but not quite." Minnie Dailey recalled, "Sometimes we'd put a persimmon stick in the fire and let it get hot enough for the sap [or juice] to run out. It looks like soapsuds. We'd catch that in a spoon and pour it in the ear for earaches."

Pine *(Pinus)* is abundant throughout the Southern Appalachian region. Most common are the white pine, the yellow pine, and the Virginia pine.

These evergreen trees are large and have horizontal branches. They can grow to two hundred feet tall and have slender green needles that can be up to five inches long. The white pine has cones that are one inch thick and five inches long. In fall, seeds fall from the mature cones. The Virginia pine has three to five needles in a cluster and can live about fifty years.

Information was not available concerning the type or types of pine trees that were used for the remedies below. A few people felt that any of these three—white, yellow, and Virginia—could be used, but this has not been confirmed.

Pine bark—A cough medicine can be concocted using pine bark and wild cherry bark.

Pine bud—Clarence Lusk said, "Pine bud tea's what you use for a bad cold. Go around and pick the little buds in the pine bushes that you can reach the tops of. Just pull that little ol' bud off the top of the little twig. We'd break the little buds out and make a tea out of that for a bad cold."

Pine oil—As a remedy for a nail puncture, pour pine oil over the wound.

Pine needles—As a remedy for colds, boil pine needles to make a strong tea.

Pine resin—Pine resin can be used as a remedy for cuts and bleeding.

Pink Lady Slipper *(Cypripedium acaule)* blooms from May through June. It is very rare. This plant was widely used in nineteenth-century America as a sedative for nervous headaches, hysteria, insomnia, and nervous irritability. Because this plant is rare and endangered, readers are asked to refrain from gathering it.

Poke *(Phytolacca americana)* is dangerous and can be toxic. It is advisable to read the material on poke on page 155.

As a remedy for rheumatism, roast a poke root in ashes in the same manner as you would roast a potato. While it is still hot, apply it to the inflamed joint. This eases the pain and reduces the swelling. You may choose to drink a mixture of pokeberry wine and whiskey instead. The leaves are also said to be good blood builders. Take the young leaves of the poke plant, parboil them, season, fry, and then eat several helpings.

Purple Coneflower *(Echinacea)* grows in patches in rich or sandy soil. It has a coarse, hairy stem and thick hairy leaves that can be eight inches long. The root, which is thick and black, is gathered in the fall. This perennial herb grows from three to five feet tall. The center of the flower head is cone-shaped. It flowers from June to September. Its extracts are used to stimulate the body's defense to infections and chronic inflammations.

Puttyroot *(Aplectrum)* has yellow to greenish white flowers that bloom from May until June. Also known as Adam-and-Eve root, the roots of this orchid were used by Native Americans to make a poultice for boils. Root tea was used for bronchial troubles. A preparation of the root was also used to mend broken dishes, hence the name. Because this plant is rare and endangered, readers are asked to refrain from gathering it.

Quince *(Prunus)* is used by many in the Southern Appalachian region. It is a shrubby bush that can reach approximately eight feet in height and five feet in width. This bush is thorny and has solitary leaves. It blooms in early spring with reddish flowers that resemble old-fashioned roses. The fruits are a little larger than a nectarine and have a hard core. This fruit was often used for making jelly, while the entire shrub itself was planted in rows and used as a fence line.

Of quince, Clarence Lusk recalled, "Another thing that we keep all the time is quince jelly. It's good for hiccups. I was told to put quince in regular sweet jelly. I don't know whether the sweet has something to do with it or not, but it stops the hiccups, even in the hospital. My mother-in-law sent some to a friend of hers in the hospital with stomach trouble because he had the hiccups. He took some of that jelly, and the hiccups went away. The doctor hadn't been able to stop those hiccups!"

Ratsbane *(Chimaphila umbellata)* enjoys shady, wooded areas of pine forests in dry soil. It gets no taller than one foot and has dark evergreen leaves that are positioned close to the top of the stem. In summer, sweet-smelling white to pink flowers arrive in clusters. It is gathered for the leaves only or for the entire plant.

Also called rat's vein, a tea could be made from it for coughs, backaches, bladder, kidney, and stomach problems. To make this remedy, boil two or three whole plants for several minutes in about a pint of water. Strain and sweeten.

Rattlesnake Fern *(Botrychium virginianum)*. Marie Mellinger wrote, "Two ferns mark the site of ginseng and are found in close association with the other sang-sign plants. The rattlesnake fern is known as the 'hope of ginseng.' This is a lacy-leaved fern with spikes of yellow-brown spore cases in early spring. These supposedly resemble the rattles of a rattlesnake. The bright yellow spore powder is applied to insect bites or snakebites. It may be called rattlesnake fern because it grows in the often rocky woods that are the haunt of the timbler rattler. Gerard wrote of this plant, 'Of the colonies, [North America] has berries given for twenty days against poison, or administered with great success unto such as are become peevish.' "

Rattlesnake Master *(Eryngium yucci-folium)* likes swampy, wet ground in low areas. The leaves are like thick grass and can be two feet in length. A stout two- to six-foot stem remains unbranched until it nears the top. It bears dense small flowers in summer and has a thick knobby to straight rootstock. This rootstock is the reason for fall gathering of the plant. This perennial grows from one and one-half to four feet tall. Its flowers are white and appear in September. Native Americans used the root as a poultice for snakebites.

PLATE 80 Rattlesnake Master

Redbud *(Cercis canadensis)* is a small tree with a rounded crown that reaches heights of forty feet. The flowers are red-purple, pea-like, and on long stalks. They bloom from March through May. The inner-bark tea is highly astringent, and Native Americans ate the edible flowers like candy. In order for the flowers to be edible, they must be picked from green stems.

Red Clover *(Trifolium pratense)* grows wild in most open places and along roadsides. It has a hairy stem and narrow, pointed leaves with a white mark near the fullest part of the leaf. This thriving plant is not native to the region. (For a photo of this clover, see *Foxfire 3*, page 332.)

Charles Thurmond said to "use the blossoms and leaves from clover. Not only does clover have a lot of vitamins and things like that, but it is a sedative. If you have trouble sleeping at night, get some clover tea. It improves your circulation and digestion. It helps thicken or thin your blood, depending on which way it is used. If you use too much to thicken or thin your blood, a good tonic of boneset will get it straight. Clover can also be used for bronchial problems and stimulating your circulation and appetite."

PLATE 81 Red Trillium

Red Trillium *(Trillium erectum)* likes damp, shady woods with rich soil. This low-growing plant has a stout stem with three stemless leaves (three to seven inches long and wide), arranged in a circular pattern at the top. In spring, a single flower, with petals arranged in threes, is produced. This foul-smelling flower is dull red and blooms from April to June. It is followed by a red berry. The plant is gathered at the end of the summer for its root. Native Americans used the root tea for menstrual disorders, to induce childbirth, to aid in labor, and for the "change of life." Because this plant is rare and endangered, readers are asked to refrain from gathering it.

Sassafras *(Sassafras albidum)* grows in wooded areas with rich soil and can reach one hundred feet in height. The leaves, which can have three different shapes, are long, toothless, and ovate. They can be oval, three-lobed, or mitten-shaped. In early spring, fragrant yellow-green flowers appear in clusters. The fruit, which is pea-sized and dark blue, ripens in September on a red stalk. (For a photo of sassafras, see *Foxfire 2*, page 49.)

This tree's inner root bark layer is used and gathered in spring or fall. Its roots are used to make tea and was a favorite spring tonic of settlers and Native Americans. As a blood builder, make sassafras tea using the roots of the plant.

"Sassafras is not real strong if the sap's not up," Charles Thurmond told us. "It's an ointment. It stimulates your system like a tonic, but it makes you sweat. If you've got something in your system, and you want to sweat it out, this is a good herb to take."

To make sassafras tea, gather the roots and tender twigs of red sassafras in the spring. Pound the roots to a pulp if they are very big, and wash them with the twigs. Boil them, strain, and sweeten.

Smooth Sumac *(Rhus hirta)* is most likely found in dry soil and open areas. It usually ranges from three to twenty feet in height with a smooth brown-gray bark. Leaves can be up to three feet long with as many as thirty-one pointed leaflets. Clusters of green-yellow flowers arrive in summer and are followed in the winter by large cone-shaped, crimson-haired berries. (For a photo of this shrub, see *Foxfire 3*, page 286.)

Smooth sumac is used for the berries, bark, and leaves. Berries are gathered while the hair is on them to produce a sour taste. The juice was supposed to be good for you because it contained malic acid. Native Americans used the bark to make a tea as a wash for blisters. The berries were chewed to treat bed-wetting. It was also used as a wash for poison ivy. Charles Thurmond said, "Sumac is a plant you must be careful with. If you get it at the wrong time, you have problems. Most sumacs are not poisonous. It is an astringent, so it'll cleanse the skin."

Snakeroot *(Prenanthes)* likes rich soil and can be found along riverbanks or in richly wooded areas. It has a slender wavy stem and grows six to eighteen inches high. It has heart-shaped base leaves that end in a point. Brown flowers bear near the base from May until July and are followed by a round, seedy berry. Roots are thin and fibrous and possess a camphor-like taste and smell.

Snakeroot is gathered in fall for the root. It was used as an expectorant and diuretic, for snakebites, and for swelling. As a remedy for colic, drink Sampson snakeroot tea.

Sourwood *(Oxydendrum arboreum)* is easily found in wooded areas, can be sixty feet tall, has a trunk diameter of up to fifteen inches, and has

PLATE 82 Sourwood tree

smooth bark. Its leaves are up to six inches long, three inches wide, and toothed. In early summer, small waxy white flower clusters appear. The inner wood of the tree is hard, heavy, and red-brown in color. The leaves can be chewed to quench thirst. It is also used as a diuretic.

Spicebush *(Lindera)* grows four to fifteen feet high. It produces aromatic leaves and tiny yellow flowers from March to April. Its red berries are also aromatic. (For a drawing of this plant, see *Foxfire 2*, page 50.)

Spicebush is gathered for the twigs and berries. The twigs are used for tea and the berries for seasoning. Native Americans used the berry tea for coughs, croup, and measles. Pioneers used the berry as a substitute for allspice. They also used it for colic, fevers, worms, and gas.

Star Chickweed *(Silene stellata)* reaches six to fifteen inches in height. The leaves are oval and smooth, and the flowers are small and white. It blooms from March through September. (For a drawing of this plant, see *Foxfire 2*, page 70.)

Tea from this common herb is traditionally used as an expectorant for coughs and for skin diseases. Star chickweed was said to be planted by the Cherokee Moon and Star Maiden. It was sacred to the Cherokee women.

Stonecrop *(Sedum ternatum)* has many thick, waxy leaves with a dense stem and can grow with almost no water. Stems are long and can be erect to prone. The young leaves were used in salads and as a poultice for wounds.

PLATE 83 Stonecrop

Sweet Birch or Spicewood *(Betula lenta)* enjoys rich wooded areas and grows along branch banks. This aromatic tree can reach eighty feet in height and has red-brown bark on the young branches and a thick, rough trunk. Male and female flowers are borne in April and May. (For a drawing of sweet birch, see *Foxfire 2*, page 52.)

This tree is sought for its bark because it contains oils that are similar to wintergreen oil. It is sometimes also called spicewood, and the bark was used as a substitute for chewing gum.

Spicewood tea is said to be good as a blood builder. To make it, gather the twigs in early spring when the bark "slips" or peels off easily. Break the twigs, place them in a pot, cover with water, and boil until the water is dark. Strain and sweeten. You can also use the bark, as Mrs. Laura Patton recalled. "The bark from the [birch] spicewood tree is good to drink as a tea. It is good for the whole system. Use about a half cup bark to a quart of water. Boil about twenty minutes, let cool, and drink three times a day for good health."

Mrs. Hershel Keener claimed the tea is especially good with pork and cracklin' bread.

Sweet Fern *(Comptonia peregrina)* grows two to five feet high on dry hillsides and has red-brown bark and spreading branches. The thin leaves of this deciduous shrub are three or more inches long and are shaped much like the leaves of a fern. Its flowers do not attract attention. It produces burr-like berries from September through October. The entire plant has a spicy scent that

PLATE 84 Sweet Fern

heightens when the leaves are scarred.

Sweet fern is gathered for the entire leaves and tops. It was used as a remedy for vomiting, diarrhea, and rheumatism. It was also used for Cherokee Indian ceremonies and medicinal tea.

Sweet Gum *(Liquidambar styraciflua)* is commonly found in low areas near waterways. The leaves are pointed, serrated, and smooth, and the fruits are round, prickly balls. The bark of this tree was used to make a sedative. Gertrude Mull said, "You get sweet gum bark for nerve trouble."

Trailing Arbutus *(Epigaea repens)* spreads along the ground in sandy soil and has stems of more than six inches. Leaves are evergreen and stem from rusty, hairy twigs. Flowers are pink, waxy, and fragrant and bloom in the spring. This plant is gathered during spring for its leaves.

"This trailing arbutus is the best [medicine] I've ever seen for [treating] kidney stones," Clarence Lusk recalled. "Trailing arbutus is a little vine that grows right on the ground. Just pull it up and wash it and take enough leaves and roots [about a handful] to make a half gallon of tea. Boil it at least an hour [in water]. Then drink about two or three cups a day if you have a kidney stone bothering you. If

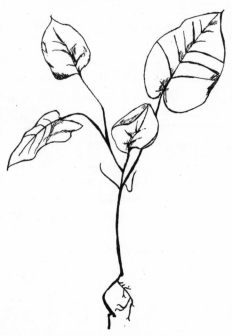

PLATE 85 Trailing Arbutus

you have had them and are afraid you might have 'em again— Well, me and my boy—we've both had kidney stones—make tea about once a month, and he'll take a quart, and I'll take a quart, and we'll drink that up. Maybe in about a month, I'll make another half a gallon. We ain't never had no more kidney stones since we've been doing that.

"The [tea from trailing arbutus] enlarges the tubes from your kidney to the bladder. It lets those little ol' stones pass through. I don't reckon there's anything that dissolves one of 'em totally. But a [stone] you can hardly see will just nearly kill you. I don't know how many people I've recommended that to [who] stayed out of the hospital. They said they was gonna have to go in [the hospital and have the stones surgically removed], and when they drank that tea, they didn't have to go. It's a herb that I [really believe in] as a medicine.

"It grows wild in the woods. You could find it right now [in December], but a little later on when the leaves settle down in the winter, it'll be hard to find. Next spring, it'll have a sweet-smelling flower on it, and that's a good time to gather it. I can find it, break the leaves off, and pull it out of the ground. I can get plenty of it up on the mountain. It looks different from most other plants. Anybody that's seen it [would know it]. It has green leaves, and it's very easy [to get confused] with poison ivy. You want to be very careful when you're gathering it to not get ivy."

Turtlehead *(Chelone)* grows in swampy areas and along water banks. It can grow up to four feet tall and has a stem that is angled four ways at the base. Toothy leaves are about four or five inches long with flower clusters that bloom in late summer to early fall. Rarely do more than two or three flowers open at once. The blooms are almost always white, very rarely pink. It gets the name "turtlehead" from the shape of its flower.

This herb is gathered either in its entirety or for the leaves while flowering. If a turtle bit you, you used this plant for a poultice.

Umbrella Leaf *(Diphylleia cymosa)* grows from eight to thirty-six inches tall. Its leaves are umbrella-like. A perennial, it produces white flowers, followed by blue berries, from May through August.

The Cherokees used the root of this plant to induce sweating. It was also considered useful for smallpox.

PLATE 86 Umbrella Leaf

Violet *(Viola)* plants come in many varieties of violets. Some of these are the common blue violet, the bird's-foot violet, the eastern dog violet, the downy yellow violet, and the green violet. These small plants have flowers that are singular and symmetrical. Most grow well in moist, shady places and bloom in the spring and summer. Flowers have five petals and are bearded. (For a drawing of the violet, see *Foxfire 2*, page 82.)

Ada Crone says, "And when we had a fever back then, they'd go out and get blue violet roots and make a tea out of that, and that'd take your fever down."

White Ash *(Fraxinus americanus)* often grows to one hundred feet tall in rich wooded areas. It flowers from April until June. The seeds are winged, flat, and about two inches long.

This tree is used for the bark from the root and the trunk. Native

Americans used inner-bark tea as a strong laxative. The seeds are thought to be an aphrodisiac.

White Baneberry *(Actaea)* "is another sang-sign plant of the rich, humusy mountain slopes, the 'doll's-eyes' of the mountain healers," according to Marie Mellinger. "This is a handsome plant with finely cut foliage and aromatic yellow-green flowers, followed by a cluster of waxy-white berries with red eyes and pink stems. The berries are very poisonous. The roots are potent and dangerous if used in quantity as they contain a substance that can cause marked irritation to the stomach and intestines. It is a violent purgative. It can affect the heart or increase the pulse rate. The roots have a strong aromatic odor, and a small pinch of *Actaea* supposedly adds potency to other medicines. It is also called the 'herb Christopher,' and the ground-up roots are used to poultice snakebite."

Wild Garlic *(Allium canadense)* is not native to the Southern Appalachian region. It grows well in sheltered meadows and wooded areas. The leaves resemble blades of grass. The flowers are small and sit on green stems above several small bulbs. (For a drawing of wild garlic, see *Foxfire 2*, page 57.) The entire plant has the smell and taste of onion. Numerous Marcus said, "Garlic is good to eat. It's similar to an onion. You can eat it raw if you want to or you can fry it. It's good to put on your chest if you've got a bad cold or are choked up with the croup. That'll break it up."

Wild garlic can be used fresh. It is sliced and put in with food, especially meats, while they are cooking. To preserve it for later use, just dry it, powder it, and store it in a closed container.

Wild Geranium *(Geranium maculatum)* blooms from April through June. The stem is hairy and grows one to two feet tall. The flowers have five pink or purplish petals. As the leaves get older they are often spotted with white.

The wild geranium was much treasured for its medicinal values. A treatment for sore throats and mouth ulcers was made from the boiled roots. A tea made from the leaves was used as a treatment for dysentery. Native Americans used it as a tonic and as an astringent.

Wild Ginger *(Asarum canadense)* is found in rich soil in wooded areas and reaches a height of four to five inches. It creeps along the ground. It has only two kidney-shaped leaves on soft hairy stems. The leaves are dark green on top and lighter green underneath. A single brown flower is produced between the leaves. The root is yellow and has a spicy taste and scent. The entire plant, especially the root, smells like ginger.

In fall, the root is gathered. People make an aromatic tea from it for crying babies and for stomachaches. As a remedy for colds, make a tea from powdered ginger or ground-up

PLATE 87 Wild Ginger

ginger roots. Do not boil the tea, but add the powdered root to a cup of hot water and drink. Add honey and whiskey if desired.

Wild Hydrangea *(Hydrangea arborescens)* is a shrub reaching up to five feet in height and has green-white flowers in round flat clusters in summer. Its common name is sevenbark, and it grows in rocky areas and valleys. It has slim stems and heart-shaped, toothy leaves. The bark sometimes peels back several times to reveal different colors. Native Americans chewed the bark for stomach problems or heart trouble. However, this plant has caused painful gas-

PLATE 88 Wild Hydrangea

troenteritis and cyanide-like poisoning. Because this plant is dangerous, readers are asked not to gather it.

The fresh root is juicy, yet very tough when dry. This shrub is collected for the root which can be used as a diuretic, for kidney stones, or for bladder problems. It is cut into small pieces before drying.

Witch-Hazel *(Hamamelis)* grows in damp, woody areas and can be twenty-five feet tall. It has smooth brown bark and produces four-inch leaves. The yellow thready flowers do not bloom until late fall or early

PLATE 89 Witch-Hazel

winter. The seed nut does not mature and open until the next season.

This shrub is gathered in the fall for the leaves, sticks, and bark, which contain a potent oil. Native Americans took leaf tea for colds and sore throats. Twig tea was rubbed on athletes' legs to keep muscles limber and relieve lameness. The twigs were favored for dowsing—searching with a divining rod—for water.

Yarrow *(Achillea)* is common to the Appalachians and is easily found in open areas such as fields, pastures, roadsides, and meadows. It can be almost two feet tall. Yarrow is a soft, fragrant perennial with lacy leaves. The flowers are white or, less frequently, pink. Flat clusters bloom from May through October. (For a photo of yarrow, see *Foxfire 3,* page 341.)

This naturalized weed is gathered in summer for its flowering tops. Herbal tea from this plant was used for colds, fevers, indigestion, anorexia, and internal bleeding.

Yellow Buckeye *(Aesculus octandra)* is not edible, but carrying the fruit, or buckeye, of this poisonous tree was thought to be good luck. Buckeyes were also thought to keep rheumatism away.

PLATE 90 Buckeye tree with fruit

Yellow Lady Slipper *(Cypripedium calceolarus)* grows well in wet, shady places deep in wooded areas. It is easily identified by the showy flower, which looks like a small air-filled bag. It blooms in the spring, and the flowers can be varying shades of yellow to striped or grossly spotted with shades of purple. This plant grows to two feet in height and can have leaves as large as six inches in length. The root runs horizontal and is fleshy with a foul odor and bittersweet taste. This unusual flower is gathered in the fall for its root.

Marie Mellinger wrote, "The yellow ladyslipper is a rare beauty of the mountains that once grew with ginseng but has been gathered too extensively by both herbalists and 'flower lovers.' The yellow blossoms appear only after the plants are seven years old, and digging the roots destroys the plants. Ladyslipper roots were used by pioneer doctors such as Samuel Thomson and Dr. Hales of Troy, New York, and Dr. Tully of Albany. It was sold under the name 'nervine-root' or 'umbil-root,' and roots were gathered in late autumn. The roots have a barbiturate effect, and powdered root was used in a teaspoon of sugar-water or added to chamomile or basswood blossom tea. The roots were also a favorite medicine for female troubles."

You can make a tea from the leaves as a remedy for headache, and Gertrude Mull told us to use the root for "nerve trouble," but we ask readers not to gather this plant due to its rarity.

Yellowroot *(Xanthorhiza simplicissima)* grows well in wooded areas in the mountains. It is usually between one foot and two feet tall with a short basal stem topped with a cluster of slender leaves approximately six inches in length. These leaves have five sharp, unevenly toothed leaflets. In spring, purple to brown flowers grow either individually or in small clusters. The roots, which are fairly long, and the bark are bright yellow and are bitter to the taste. This plant is gathered for its roots.

PLATE 91 Yellowroot

Marie Mellinger wrote, "True yellowroot, or shrub yellowroot, was also a jaundice medicine and a sang-sign plant. This is a small shrubby plant growing in colonies along streams—usually in valleys or coves. It was grown for medicine. It has finely divided leaves, and lacy racemes of yellow or pinkish-purple flowers in early spring. (For a photo of yellowroot, see *The Foxfire Book,* page 233.) The long, stringy yellow roots are very bitter tasting. These roots are used in a strong tea for sore throats or stomach disorders, or to lower high blood pressure. It is a favorite mouthwash said to cure sores or cankers of the mouth."

Ada Crone recalled, "For kidney ailments we'd go out and get rattleroot or yellowroot. Sometimes they'd be mixed up together or sometimes they'd make just a yellowroot tea. They'd make you drink that instead of water. Whenever you drank anything, it had to be that tea."

Gertrude Mull told us, "Yellowroot is good for infection too. That's the best thing in the world for ulcerated stomach. A lot of people used to come to Grandpa, wanted him to fix them up a tea [of yellowroot]."

Clarence Lusk said, "I can go down here on the creek and hunt me up some yellowroot. I use it when I get a little ol' ulcer on my tongue or on my lips sometimes. I generally just chew it. It's bitter! It's got the right name—it's yellow."

Charles Thurmond added, "The yellowroot here has roots that are really good for dyeing things. It is also good for any kind of sores."

WILD PLANT FOOD USES

American Beech *(Fagus grandifolia)* is a tall tree with smooth gray bark and coarse-toothed leaves. (For a photo of it, see *Foxfire 3,* page 350.) It produces small triangular edible nuts in a burr-like husk. These are good to eat if you can get to them before the animals do. It bears fruit in September and October.

Bilberry *(Vaccinium corymbosum)* is a shrub that can be one foot to seven feet tall and grows in wet, shaded areas. Leaves are small, ovate, serrated, and veined. The berries resemble small blueberries or huckleberries, but they have white specks. (More information concerning this berry, including a drawing of the plant, can be found in *Foxfire 3,* pages 291–92.)

Canada Violet *(Viola canadensis)* is found in bloom from April to July in rich deciduous woods. Its white petals, tinted purple on the back, are among the loveliest of spring flowers. The leaves can be eaten raw in salads, fried in butter, chopped for an omelet, or put in consommé. However, violet leaves should be used sparingly.

Creases or Winter Cress *(Barbarea Vulgaris)* is a damp-soil lover, often growing in old cornfields, lowlands, and bottoms. Also called wild turnip greens, creases have lacy leaves and tiny yellow flowers when older. The root is a tiny bulb. (For a photo of creases, see *Foxfire 2*, page 78.)

Pick the leaves when young, parboil them for about ten minutes, and then boil with a piece of fatback until tender. They can also be eaten fried. Chop them up fine, drop in hot lard, cover, and cook slowly until tender. They can be used raw in salads. They are much stronger than turnips.

Dandelion *(Taraxacum officinale)* can be found almost anywhere, but especially in lawns, fields, and most other open places. It produces a bright yellow flower followed by a fluffy, white ball of seeds. The entire plant is filled with a milky juice and has a large, deep-running root. (For photos of the dandelion, see *Foxfire 2*, pages 55 and 89.)

In the spring, a dandelion's young leaves are eaten uncooked in salads. The greens can be boiled about twenty minutes in water with fatback added, or they can be fried in grease until tender. Season with salt and pepper. In summer and fall, the root is used. At this time, the milky juice thickens and becomes bitter. After drying, the root should be used soon because age causes it to lose its medicinal potency. The root of the dandelion could be used as a substitute for coffee. To accomplish this, the roots were roasted until crisp and dark brown inside and then ground.

Elderberry *(Sambucus canadensis)* grows in rich, damp ground in low areas. It can reach ten feet tall and produces many light gray branches. Large leaves have as many as eleven leaflets and can be five inches long. Its fragrant white flowers grow in June and July. It also has purplish black fruit from July to September that is round and juicy. (For photos of this shrub, see *Foxfire 3*, pages 293–94.)

Elderberry is gathered in summer for the fully bloomed flowers, which are dried, and for the ripe berries. The berries can also be dried if caution is used to avoid mold. The bark, roots, leaves, and unripe berries are toxic, but the flowers and ripe berries are edible. The older mountain people used to make fritters out of the blooms by dipping them in a thin batter and frying in grease. The berries are eaten plain or used for jelly, pie, and wine.

Hawthorn *(Crataegus)* can reach thirty feet in height. Its flowers are white or pale pink. Some hawthorns have small edible fruits, or haws, that taste like apples and are used to make jam, jelly, and tea.

Honey Locust *(Gleditsia triacanthos)* is a small thorny tree with green flower spikes. Fall brings long, flat seedpods that are dark brown and rich when ripe. The seedpods may be eaten raw, used in making persimmon beer, or broken up and put into bread. The wood is often used for fence posts.

Huckleberry *(Gaylussacia)* is a small shrub, usually only about a foot high, and bears round, blue berries. Leaves are leathery. (For a photo of this shrub, see *Foxfire 3*, page 288.)

Huckleberries, also called wild blueberries or buckberries, enjoy mountainous areas and are sought for the ripe berries produced in late spring to early summer. They are very similar to tame blueberries, but they are a little larger, darker, and more sour. They are eaten plain, with cream and sugar, or used in pie, preserves, jelly, or wine.

Mayapple *(Podophyllum peltatum)* is the fruit of a low, umbrella-shaped plant that grows on the forest floor in the Southern Appalachians. It has smooth, dark green leaves and stands about one foot high. The single flower, which appears in spring, is white and is followed by a lemon-shaped fruit. The fruit is yellow-orange in color when ripe, and it is about three-fourths of an inch in diameter. (For a photo of the mayapple, see *Foxfire 3*, page 298.)

This plant is gathered for the ripe fruit. It tastes a little like an orange and is eaten plain. It can also be made into a delicious jam.

Mint comes in many different varieties. These are some of the most common:

Spearmint *(Mentha spicata)* grows in moist open places and has lance-shaped leaves with narrow flower spikes. It is gathered for the dried leaves and flower tops. Flowers are gathered before reaching full bloom. (For a drawing of spearmint, see *Foxfire 3*, page 339.)

Peppermint *(Mentha piperita)* grows in damp places and can reach three feet in height. It has long roots and pointed leaves of lengths up to two inches. In summer, purple blossoms appear in a circular pattern in thick spikes. (For a photo of peppermint, see *Foxfire 3*, page 339.) This plant is gathered for the leaves and tops just as the flowers start to open. In the summer or fall, gather the stems and leaves of peppermint, pour boiling water over them, and let stand for several minutes. Strain and sweeten with sugar or syrup.

White Horse Mint *(Monarda punctata)* enjoys dry soil in open areas and has several brown stems topped with light yellow flower clusters. Leaves are narrow and are positioned at the base and the midpoint of each stem. (For a drawing and a photo of white horse mint, see *Foxfire 3*, pages 335–36.) Gather mint leaves in the summer when the plant is young, just before or just after blooming. Boil the leaves in water, strain, and sweeten with honey. It is used for an exceptionally pleasant tea and as a cold remedy. (More information on mints can be found in *Foxfire 3*, pages 333–42.)

Mulberry *(Morus rubra)* is a small tree that enjoys fertile, well-drained soil. The leaves are hairy and ovate, and the female flowers become the fruits, which are commonly called berries. (For a photo of this tree, see *Foxfire 3*, page 277.)

The berries of the mulberry tree were very popular in Southern Appalachia for pie, jam, jelly, and wine. Lawton Brooks said, "They's a black old berry 'bout an inch and a half long, and they grow on a big ol' tree. Best berry I ever eat cold."

Mustard *(Brassica)* is described on page 137. The variety called turkey mustard is small and grows mainly along creek banks. The leaves are dark green on top and purplish underneath, and they taste very much like tame mustard. People eat the leaves raw, or they pour hot grease and a little vinegar over them. (For a photo of turkey mustard, see *Foxfire 2*, page 81.)

New Jersey Tea *(Ceanothus)* reaches two feet in height and blooms in late spring to early summer. The flowers are showy, puffy clusters and are followed by triangular seedpods. The bark is brittle and dark-colored and the roots are red. A tea made from the leaves was once a popular beverage. During the Boston Tea Party era, when imported tea was not available, Martha Washington made tea from this plant for the soldiers. It is also called Revolutionary tea.

Peppergrass *(Lepidium virginicum)* is also known as poor man's pepper and can be found in open areas and along roadways. It can reach two feet in height and has an erect stem among leaves that are clumped at the base. It produces white flowers, which are followed by round, flat, top-notched fruit. (For a photo of peppergrass, see *Foxfire 2*, page 71.)

Young peppergrass is usually used raw in a tossed salad along with lettuce, dandelions, or other greens. Just wash, cut up, and use. The green seeds of the peppergrass make a good pepper substitute.

Poke *(Phytolacca americana)* is found in moist, rich soil in fields, off the banks of creeks, and in other uncultivated areas. Also called pokeweed, it has a very large root that produces smooth stems of up to nine feet in height. These stems are branched and turn from green to reddish purple. The leaves are smooth and can be five inches long and three inches wide. Flowers arrive in summer in stalked whitish clusters on red stems. Berries follow the flowers and mature to a deep purple color. (For photos of poke, see *Foxfire 2,* pages 55 and 68.)

Pokeweed's root is poisonous. The plant must be picked in the early spring when the leaves are still yellow-green and the asparagus-like stalks are no longer than four to six inches. This plant is most often gathered for its leaves.

Bernice Taylor warned, "You've got to gather the leaves before they get about six inches high. Don't mess with them after that. When we was little and comin' up on hard times, the kids, we'd all gather us up some berries and mash 'em up and use 'em for ink."

The greens are usually washed well, parboiled for about ten minutes, rinsed three or four times, and then fried in plenty of fatback grease until tender. They can then be seasoned with salt and pepper. Some people scramble eggs in the pan along with the greens just before the greens are done. One woman said she served the greens with sliced hard-boiled eggs and chopped onions. Pepper sauce or apple vinegar also adds a nice flavor.

The stalks can also be eaten, and the best flavor comes when the plant is young. The stalks can be sliced (peeled first if desired), rolled in cornmeal or flour, and fried until tender. To pickle the stalks, slice and scald until tender and then add warm vinegar and spices.

Fried poke is believed to be a fine spring tonic. Old stalks, leaves, berries, and the white root should be avoided, as they can be harmful.

Rabbit Tobacco *(Gnaphalium obtusifolium)* grows in open areas with dry soil. It grows to three feet in height and is woolly. Narrow leaves are woolly on the underside and dark green on

PLATE 92 Rabbit Tobacco

top. In summer, flower heads appear. Caution should be taken when using this plant, because it is not edible. This fragrant herb is gathered in its entirety for chewing only. Be careful not to swallow the juice.

Rabbit tobacco was often used just like regular chewing tobacco when the latter was not available or was too expensive. Lawton Brooks said of it, however, "It'll make your mouth so sore. I've blistered my mouth on it many a time."

Ramp *(Allium tricoccum)* is a form of wild onion. It grows on the mountains in Southern Appalachia, in dark coves and mossy spots. There are two varieties: red and white. The white ones are supposed to be better than the red. This herb can reach three feet in height, is covered with white hairs, has ovate leaves, and blooms in summer. Its flowers can be white to red-purple. (For a photo of ramp, see *Foxfire 2*, page 58.)

It is best to gather this herb in its entirety in the very early spring. When the leaves are young and tender, they can be eaten raw, cooked with meat, or chopped fine and fried in grease until tender. They can be sprinkled with vinegar when ready to eat.

Serviceberry *(Amelanchier)* is one of the first plants with white blossoms in early spring. It was often the only thing in bloom at Eastertime. People would carry the blooms to church for Easter services. That is why it is called serviceberry.

The red edible berries produced after the flowers are one of the first berries to ripen. They are usually eaten plain and were often used for decoration in churches at Easter.

Smooth Sumac *(Rhus hirta)* is discussed on page 143. This shrub is used for its berries, which are gathered while the hair is on them, which produces a sour taste. The berries can be used for jelly or a lemonade-type drink.

Solomon's-Seal *(Polygonatum)* likes shady areas in light soil and has fragrant, greenish white bell flowers. It is closely related to Lily-of-the-Valley and grows to a height of eight

PLATE 93 Smooth Sumac

PLATE 94 Solomon's Seal

to thirty-six inches. The leaves are oval, pale green, and downy underneath. It has thick running roots, and after it flowers in May and June, it produces black-blue berries. This plant is gathered for the root in fall. The name "Solomon's-Seal" comes from the scars on the rootstock, which resemble a royal seal. "Solomon" is for King Solomon, the tenth-century-B.C. king of Israel who was famed for his wisdom.

While this plant is not edible in its raw form, Native Americans crushed the roots of Solomon's-Seal to make flour. They also used sections of the root for pickles.

Spring Beauty *(Claytonia)* enjoys light but rich soil. It gets about six inches tall and has dark green, wedge-shaped leaves. The flowers are white with deep pink veins or are all pink. This plant is gathered for its tasty, edible root and leaves. They have a sharp taste of radishes when raw, and when boiled or baked, they have the taste and texture of baked potatoes.

Sugar Maple *(Acer saccharum)* likes the rich soil of the mountainous areas, valleys, and hills. Its leaves are long, wide, and lobed with many veins. The leaves turn a brilliant red-orange in the fall of the year. This tree was a wonderful source of sweet syrup. To obtain the sap, bore a hole in a sugar maple tree in the fall, insert a small pipe, and hang a bucket from the pipe. Each time the sap freezes and thaws, it pours into the bucket. It is then boiled down into a thick syrup and used for sweetening as a sugar substitute.

Toothwort *(Dentaria diphylla)* is also known as crinkleroot, cut leaf, pepperwort, and pepperroot. This plant blooms from March through June. The root, which has a peppery flavor, can be eaten as a woodland nibble, or it can be diced and put into salads. It got its common name from the tooth-like projections on the roots. Some people believed that this plant would relieve toothaches because of its resemblance to teeth.

Watercress *(Nasturtium officinale)* thrives in most cold springs and streams in the mountains and has shiny, ovate leaves. Its flowers are small and white. The seeds were often used in making pickles, using two to three seeds per jar. The dark green leaves are used in salads to lend a spicy, tangy flavor.

White and Speckled Dock *(Rumex)* grows in fields, yards, and around barns, is about knee-high, and has leaves six to eight inches long, which resemble spinach in appearance. (For photos of dock, see *Foxfire 2*, pages 55 and 62.)

The leaves were sometimes cooked and eaten by themselves, but more often, they were eaten in combination with other greens such as horseradish leaves. To prepare, parboil until tender, rinse well, and fry in grease.

White Walnut *(Juglans cinerea)* grows well in rich wooded areas of the Southern Appalachians. Also called butternut, it can reach a height of fifty feet and is covered with rough, wrinkled bark. When young, all parts of the tree are covered with sticky hairs. Leaves consist of as many as seventeen leaflets that are about three inches long. Spring brings both the flowers and the leaves. The nuts ripen in fall and are encased in a hard, wrinkled shell within a sticky husk. This tree is sought for its nuts, which can be eaten alone or used in cookies and cakes.

Wild Blackberry *(Rubus allegheniensis)* can get up to nine feet tall. It grows on roadsides, in the woods, and along old fence lines and the edges of fields. It produces white flowers in summer, followed by juicy, black, seedy fruits. (For photos of the blackberry, see *Foxfire 3*, pages 283 and 285.)

Blackberries are a favorite of mountain people. They're eaten plain, used for pie, jelly, preserves, cobbler, juice, wine, cake, and bread.

Wild Cherry *(Prunus serotina)* can be found in both open and wooded areas. It can grow to be ninety feet tall with a trunk of four feet in diameter. Its bark is rough and black; its young limbs are smooth and red. In spring, smooth leaves and clusters of drooping white flowers appear. (For a photo of this tree, see *Foxfire 3*, page 305.)

The fruit ripens in summer, is round, purple to black in color, and has a sweet taste. The bark, stems, and leaves of this tree are poisonous; do not ingest them. The ripe cherries must be picked from green stems, and they must be carefully watched, as the birds often get to them before they are ripe. They are used for jelly, cobbler, and wine.

To make wine: Crush the cherries, put them in a large crock, and cover with boiling water. Cover the crock and let it sit fermenting and bubbling until the juice stops working. Then strain through a cloth, squeezing out all the juice. Put the juice back in the crock, add three cups of sugar to the gallon, cover, and let sit for nine or ten days or until it stops working. Put in bottles, but don't seal too tightly until it has stopped fermenting completely. The wine is supposed to be very potent.

Wild Grape *(Vitis)* comes in a tremendous variety in the mountains: possum, river, summer, fall, muscadine, scuppernong, and fox. (For drawings and a photo of the wild grape plant, see *Foxfire 3*, pages 316 and 318.) They are usually eaten plain or made into jelly, juice, or wine. The leaves can be used in making cucumber pickles. Place them between the layers of cucumbers in a crock. They add a nice flavor to, and help pickle, the cucumbers. Do not eat them.

To make grape juice: Pick and wash wild grapes (any kind), place in a large pan, add enough water to cover, and cook until soft, stirring occasionally. Strain through cheesecloth, heat to a boil, and add sugar to taste. Pour into jars and seal.

To make grape jelly: Pick about a gallon of wild grapes and wash, removing the stems. Crush in a large pan, add a pint of apple vinegar and, if you wish, some cinnamon. Cook for about fifteen minutes slowly, strain through cheesecloth, and boil for about twenty minutes. Add three pounds of sugar and cook until it starts to jell. Put into jars.

Wild Horseradish *(Cochleria armoracia)* should be picked in the early spring. According to Mrs. Selvin Hopper, "It looks quite a bit like mustard, but the roots are as hot as any red pepper you ever saw." They can be eaten plain or sliced and added to salad. To pickle them, peel, grate, or slice; cover with vinegar; and add a little salt and pepper. (For a drawing of wild horseradish, see *Foxfire 2*, page 72.)

Wild Sage *(Salvia lyrata)* gets to be about a foot high. Its leaves are oblong and wrinkled with strong veins; they are gray-green and covered with soft hairs. The plant's flowers arrive in summer. Wild sage is odorous and has a bitter taste. It flourishes in mountainous areas and is gathered for the whole herb or for the leaves only. The leaves are good for flavoring when cooking ham and sausage.

Wild Strawberry *(Fragaria virginiana)* likes dry soil. It is small, dark green, and has a thick root with hardy runners. The leaves are thick and toothy and grow on six-inch-tall stems. (For a photo of the wild straw-berry plant, see *Foxfire 2*, page 93.)

Wild strawberries are very much like the domestic ones, but they tend to be smaller and have a stronger flavor. This herb is gathered for its leaves and for the small berries in late spring. They make delicious jam, preserves, and pie.

To make jam: Put a quart of berries in a pot and add about a cup of sugar. Bring to a boil, stirring gently. Boil for three minutes, add another cup of sugar, and boil three more minutes. Add a final cup of sugar and boil three more minutes. Skim off any foam, put into jars, and seal. Makes about two pints.

The leaves of this plant were sometimes eaten along with blackberry leaves. They were fried in grease or boiled with fatback in water.

Wild Sweet Potato *(Dioscorea villosa)* is a vine that looks like a regular sweet potato vine. This vine grows well in damp thickets of other shrubs and bushes. It has a smooth stem that reaches fifteen feet. Leaves are heart-shaped and hairy underneath. In early summer, green to yellow flowers appear in drooping clusters and spiked heads. The fruit is a three-lobed capsule that is similar in color to the flowers and stays on the vine into winter. This fruit ripens in fall. Roots are small and run horizontally under the ground.

This plant is sought in the fall for its roots, or "potatoes," which are also called wild yam roots or wild yams. To prepare these roots, roast

PLATE 95
Wild Sage

them in ashes or peel, slice, and boil in salted water [so they won't turn dark]. They can also be fried in grease with brown sugar, salt, and pepper.

Wintergreen *(Gaultheria procumbens)* grows well in damp, cool, woody

areas with sandy soil. It is often found near or under evergreen trees. Usually growing to no more than six inches, the stems are smooth and bare to the tops, where leathery leaves proliferate. It spreads from creeping root stalks and has evergreen leaves, which turn dull red when mature. White, bell-shaped flowers appear in early spring and are followed by bright red, flat, round berries, which ripen in fall and have a spicy taste. Berries can stay on the plant until spring. This herb can be gathered in the fall in its entirety or for the leaves alone. Steam distillation produces fragrant oils. The leaves can be used to make wintergreen tea.

PLATE 96 Wintergreen

Other contributors: Dean Beasley, Gail Beck, Clyde Burrell, Lessie Conner, Nora Garland, Mary Claire Heffington, Margaret Norton, Bill Patton, Billy Joe Stiles, Mr. and Mrs. Marvin Watts

BIBLIOGRAPHY

Coker, William Chambers, Ph.D., LL.D., and Henry Roland Totten, Ph.D. *Trees of the Southeastern States.* Chapel Hill, N.C.: University of North Carolina Press, 1934; 3rd ed., 1945.

Duncan, Wilbur H., and Leonard E. Foote. *Wildflowers of the Southeastern United States.* Athens, Ga.: University of Georgia Press, 1975.

Forey, Pamela. *Wild Flowers of North America.* New York: W. H. Smith Publications, 1991.

Grieve, M. *A Modern Herbal in Two Volumes.* New York: Dover Publications, 1971.

Mellinger, Marie. "Sang-sign." *Foxfire,* vol. 2, no. 2 (June 1968), pp. 15, 47–52.

United States Department of Agriculture. *The Herb Hunter's Guide.* Beaumont, Calif.: Trinity Center Press, 1975.

BEEKEEPING

"There ain't no bees around much now."

As recently as the 1940s, almost every family in Southern Appalachia had a stand of bees. Rather than having to purchase sugar, honey was used as a sweetener in recipes. Howard Prater stated, "My son George is a third-generation beekeeper. My father had bees. I learned about bees from my daddy, and then I passed it on to George."

Jesse Ray Owens also told us that beekeeping is a family tradition. "My family has always had bees and hives as far back as I can remember. My dad told me when he got married that he got his bees from his dad. The old-timers thought that it was bad luck to give bees away, so they'd sell them for a penny or a nickel maybe.

"Some families had more bees than others, but every family seemed to have a few stands of bees. At one time, that honey was the only thing we had to sweeten with. Back during the Depression, we had a big family to feed. We used honey three meals a day—sweetened berries with it, made gingerbread with it."

Today honey is grown to sell, and honeybees are almost nonexistent in the wild. Predators and diseases have virtually wiped them out. And you find few, if any, bee gums anymore. It is easier, and probably more productive, to use commercial hive bodies. The following accounts range from the basic to very modern. But each adds to the history and how-tos of beekeeping.

—*Kaye Carver Collins*

BEE GUMS

A bee gum is a hollowed-out section of a log, usually black gum, used for the bees to make their hive in. The old-timers preferred black gum because it lasted longer, but they would use other types of wood if they had to. Once they burned the wood out of the center of the log, they attached handles and would cover the top with boards that fit tightly over the gum. Then holes were drilled in the handle so a stick could run through the handles and help hold the top boards in place.

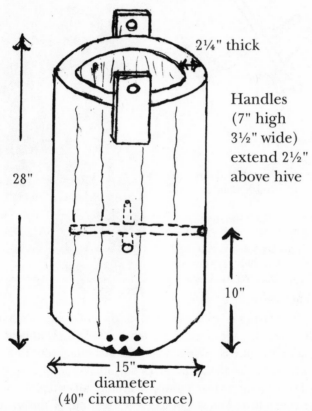

2¼" thick

Handles
(7" high
3½" wide)
extend 2½"
above hive

28"

10"

15"
diameter
(40" circumference)

PLATE 97 A close-up illustration of one of Jesse Ray Owens' bee gums made out of a black gum log. The top is covered with boards which fit tightly over the gum, and the holes [with stick running through] are drilled after the boards are fitted onto the gum. Bees will begin building their honeycomb at the top of the gum, attaching it in orderly cells to the underside of the board cover. (Diagram by Brant Sturgill)

Small notches were made on the lower edge of the bee gum for the bees to exit and enter. The gum was set on a large flat surface, either a rock or a board, so the bees would have a landing place.

Cross-section sticks were placed midway down the gum to support the honeycomb, which was built at the top of the gum. Two holes were drilled through the gum, and a stick was pushed all the way through from one side of the gum to the other. A third hole was drilled ninety degrees from the other two and slightly higher. The second stick pushed through the third hole and rested on the other stick.

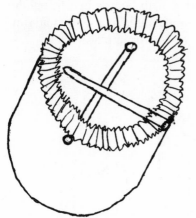

PLATES 98, 99 Holes are drilled through the gum, and a stick is pushed all the way through from one side of the gum to the other. A third hole is drilled ninety degrees from those two and slightly higher, so that a second stick pushed through this hole will rest on the other stick, as illustrated in the diagram and photo. (Diagram by Brant Sturgill)

Jesse Ray Owens's father gave him his own bee gum when he was ten years old. Jesse Ray recalled, "I first started helping Dad burn the gums out. He gave me one hive then, and that was mine from then on. Black gum's [what I like to make my hives out of]. We have used maple, but it don't last as long as black gum. It usually takes about two or three days to make a hive. You've got to get [a tree] out of the woods and up to the house. It takes all day to burn [the logs] out. When you start burning them, you have to put them up off the ground about three or four inches. You put your dry wood down in the little hollow [of the log]. You get the fire started in it and keep it burning, and the hole will get bigger and bigger. You let it get just as big as you want it, and then you turn it upside down and dump all the coals out. When it gets cold, you just scrape it out smooth with a dull hoe.

"I prefer the round hives, but the square ones are good too. I don't think there is any difference between a round gum and a flat gum. The

PLATE 100 Jesse Ray Owens with his bee gums

honey is all the same color. I had bees in round hives [made from hollow trees] for twenty years before the bees died out. If you'll keep the honeycomb cut out where there is a fresh comb in there, they'll stay in the hive a long time.

"You've got to keep that comb cut out, or it'll get tough and black. We always cut it out in March. We don't put any [paraffin] in the round hives. We don't put a thing in there but the cross sticks. [The bees] always go to the board [covering the top of the bee gum] and start pieces of comb. They fasten it to that board and go all the way down to the bottom of the gum with the comb. They've got to hang [their honeycomb] from somewhere, so that's why they start at the board [at the top of the gum]. The cross sticks are in there just to keep the comb from collapsing. I've seen one gum that collapsed and drowned all the bees. The comb was too big around and got too much weight in it.

"I never put in new queens at all. I just let the bees handle that [make a new queen] themselves."

PATENTED GUMS

Patented gums are rectangular boxes consisting of a hive body or brood [egg] chamber on the bottom with supers added, as needed, to collect honey. Supers are rectangular boxes about five inches tall. They hold nine frames in which the bees store honey. The first super above the brood chamber is left on the hive to give the bees a food source and additional room.

Patented gums can be handmade or purchased and have been used by beekeepers for over one hundred years.

Glen J. Taylor explained, "The first thing you got to do is get your hive bodies ready. The hive body is the lowest chamber of the hive, where the bees live and reproduce. These bodies consist of ten frames. Then get all your starter combs and everything in there. I build most of them, and I buy some; I use white pine to build my hives. Then you put your bees in there. To start with, you've got to give them sugar water to help boost them up where they'll go comb faster and build up faster. After you get that hive body full, then you put a super on there and let 'em fill it up. The super just goes on top of the hive body, and then after they get the hive body and super filled up, you can put another super on so you can get some honey for yourself."

PLATE 101 Glen J. Taylor examining one of the frames that make up the super

"The hive bodies we use now have been in use for over one hundred years. And they have really changed very little," according to George Prater. "The guy who designed the modern beehive's name was Langstrom. He came up with the principle called the bee space. He found out with his experiments that if you have a space inside a hive which is the same as the space between these frames, the size of a bee, they will leave that alone. Anything smaller than a bee space, they will take their bee glue, called propolis, and glue it up, fill it up. Anything wider than a bee space, they will build a comb in. But a bee space, they will leave it alone. That is why you can have a hive like this and have the frames where you can take

them out. They don't glue them to the sides and build combs from one
to the other.

"I run nine frames in my supers, but ten in my hive body. But a lot
of the old mountain beekeepers used board gums, which is four wide
boards nailed together, and I guess they did that so they didn't have to
buy all the equipment.

"This equipment is real easy to
make. Anybody with any kind of carpentry skill can make a hive themselves. But these frames, this is how
they come from the factory. It is in
pieces. You can see that that is pretty
precision stuff. You just stick the
pieces of wood together, then you
have got to nail it in several places.
Your brood [eggs] would be down in
the bottom. When you start out a
hive, you just start them with a brood
chamber, and then after they get that
filled up, then you put a super on top.
I usually don't even take the lower
super off. I'll pick it up to check the
frames underneath it.

"You can see the different divisions
of the hive. The bottom part is the
brood chamber [or hive body], where
they have their eggs mainly. Gener-

PLATE 102 A view of Glen J. Taylor's
bee gums

ally, the outside frames just have honey and pollen, and the eggs will be
in the center. The next one up—well, the next two up are the supers,
where they make their excess honey. Occasionally, the queen will actually move up into the super and lay some eggs up in there. In the summertime, you can have as many as four more supers on top of those,
just depending on how well the hive is doing.

"The way I put the supers on is I will have one above the brood, and
I'll stick another one on. If I need to put another one on top, I'll raise
the last one I put on up and stick the new one underneath it. The theory is that it encourages them to go up through this one to finish what
they were doing up there, and it will get them to working in the new
super faster.

"You don't take one super off and sling the honey [extract honey
from the frames], because when you get into the summer and they are
in full production, they need the extra room for the bees. Also, you need

to add a new super when the one on top is probably two-thirds full. So when you are putting a new one on, the old one is not ready to be taken off yet. If you try to extract honey before they get it all sealed up [before it is capped by the bees with wax], it will be too watery. If you eat it, it will give you dysentery.

"Mainly, you mess with the bees for six months out of the year. In the wintertime, you don't really do anything. When I close them up in the fall—around October—I probably won't look at them again until March. The springtime is when you have to keep an eye on them and make sure they have enough to eat.

"After you start getting frost and very cold weather, you put the entrance reducers on to help them hold the heat in the hive. [An entrance reducer is a small handmade block of wood placed over the entrance to the hive.] It just makes the hole a little bit smaller and makes it easier for the bees to be able to protect the hive. In the wintertime, all the bees will cluster with the queen right in the middle. If they don't cluster, a lot of the bees will die off. If the hive gets too cold, the brood will die."

ROBBING THE BEES

In order to obtain the honey, beekeepers have to "rob" the bees. Equipment used to rob the bees varies from beekeeper to beekeeper. All the beekeepers we interviewed used a smoker—a funnel-topped can with a small bellows attached—a veil, and a hive tool or pry tool. Some use gloves, bee brushes, and protective clothing.

George Prater told us he robbed the bees when the hive was ready. "I've never gone by the signs. When you pull the frame out and all the comb is sealed over, they are ready to be robbed. I look in there once a week or so. They can fill up a super, if there is a real good honey flow, in about a week.

"A lot of the old-time beekeepers don't even wear veils or gloves or anything. When I rob the bees, I use the smoker, and I have a set of coveralls; then I put a veil on that zips down to the coveralls and gloves. Now, Daddy didn't used to use anything but a veil and some gloves. A lot of beekeepers don't use gloves, but I find that they sting me on the hands worse than anywhere else. They are all the time stinging me on the hands; I don't know how people stand it, really! I get stung almost every time I mess with the bees. They can sting you right through your coveralls, gloves, or veil. If there is a way for them to get at you to sting you, they will try.

"Generally, the hives that are under stress are more likely to be mean. Stressed hives could be hives that are queenless, or if the weather is too hot or too cold, it stresses the bees. Also, if there is nothing in bloom for the bees to make honey out of, they're more likely to be mean. They will be more gentle if you work them regularly. If you check them once a week or so, they will kind of get used to it.

"Smokers distract the bees, generally, and it makes them calmer. The theory is that when you smoke them, they think their hive is on fire. They claim they will rush in there and go eat a bunch of honey. Then they are too fat to bend their tail down to sting you good! When you open up the hive and you start smoking them, you see them stick their little heads in there and start eating the honey. But they'll still sting you!

"My bees are pretty good-natured; the last few times I was taking off honey I hardly got stung at all. Usually, that is the worst time to get stung, because you are really disrupting them. You have to brush off the bees that are on the frames, because you don't want to take any bees in the house with you.

"I usually use hay in my smoker. That is generally all I use. Sometimes I use hay baling twine or newspaper to get it started. It takes a little practice to get a smoker going. This is the one I use now, and you can see it is the same thing as my daddy used. You take a handful of whatever you are burning, and you light it. Then stick it down in there. You give it a few puffs and try to get it started smoking. So what you have got is a smoldering fire. You don't really have any flames. Somebody explained it to me that the best way to do it is like you are smoking a pipe. The way people that smoke a pipe do it is they put tobacco in there three different times. Each time they put it in there, they put it in firmer. The first you put in there real loose and get it going; then put a little more in, and the third time, tap it down good.

"I have a little pry bar to get the lid off the hive with. It is a flat pry bar, and you just stick it underneath the edge. One end is crooked, so you can get in there and pry up one frame or another. It is called a hive tool. It just takes a little practice to learn how to use it. I also use a bee brush. It is soft and allows you to brush the bees out of your way."

According to Jesse Ray Owens, "I reckon, as you grow up, you just grow into [handling] them. When I'm putting a hive on the stands for the bees, I usually put a bee veil over my head. That's all I need. I never rob a new swarm at all the year I put it in [a hive]. We could rob 'em, but we don't. They might need the honey.

"We rob the hives on the new moon in March. If they make enough honey, we'll cut the hives again in June. Our ancestors always done it this way. They always went by the moon for everything. If the bees have lots of honey, we'll go in there and cut it all out, plumb to the cross sticks.

"A big swarm can fill up a gum in about four or five weeks. I figure a big swarm is about a gallon of bees, a little swarm about a half gallon. I don't know how many that'd be in number. I'd say [the number of bees in a hive] varies every year. Some years [there are a lot more bees in a hive] than in others. It depends on the honey flow. But once in a while you'll get a lazy stand of bees. They just barely will survive. I had two hives that made just enough to live on. Then they'd quit. They were just lazy bees."

Glen J. Taylor explained, "To rob the bees, you get you a pair of gloves, a veil, a hive tool, and a bee brush so that you can brush the bees off. The brush is soft, and it won't hurt the bees to brush them off. Now, you've got your smoker; put your smoking paper, which is newspaper soaked in saltpeter, so it will smoke, not burn, and light it and put it in the smoker. With one piece of paper, you can do eight or ten hive bodies. Whenever you take the lid and the inner cover off the hive, you just kind of smoke the bees down a little bit and get them out of your way. You can get the bees out so that you won't be killing none of them or nothing like that. You can smoke them down in the bottom, in the hive body. Then you take the super off and take the frames out with a hive tool so that you can check them. The hive tool is what you use to pry the super off.

"Daddy used to have bees all the time. If he had a hive that was real mean and he couldn't rob them and do anything with them, he would take some tobacco and use it on them. He would roll it up, put it in the

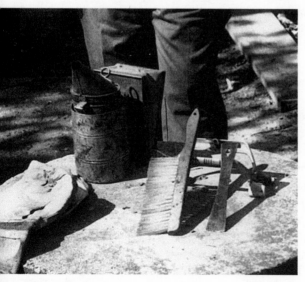

stove, and get it good and dry and brick-like, and then he would roll it up in an old club. He would light that and stand over the bees and blow, and that is the way he'd smoke the bees. He didn't have veils. He just robbed them without any gloves and without any veils."

PLATE 103 The hive tools used to rob the bees

PROCESSING HONEY

"Whenever they get the super filled up and get it capped over, that's when you sling the honey out, strain the honey, and jar it up," according to Glen J. Taylor. "It don't take long to harvest the honey. You can uncap it [with a knife] and sling a comb out in about an hour. I generally sling it out with a honey slinger and let it sit out 'til the next day. All that fine comb and stuff will come to the top, and you can kind of rake the top of it off and get that comb off of it. Then you can strain what you got left. You can get the rest of the comb out of it and have pretty clear honey whenever you strain it and jar it up.

"I don't know how many jars I get from a hive. Some years I make a lot. And, then again, some years I don't make too much. About three years ago, I didn't make but very little because we had a lot of rain that summer."

George Prater uses newer methods for extracting his honey. He uses an electric uncapping knife, rather than a butcher knife, to cut the caps off. He also uses an electric extractor. He told us, "I think an extractor is the best investment you can make if you are keeping bees, because you can double your honey production."

He also told us, "If you let the honey settle overnight [so small pieces of the comb come to the surface to be skimmed off], you should stir it up, because the heavier honey will settle to the bottom and lighter honey to the top. I have got ten hives right now. If a hive is doing a little better than average, it will produce three supers of honey a year. Each super will have about eight quarts of honey in it."

While some of his methods are newer, many are the same as what Glen Taylor described. As George finished describing his method of processing honey, he told us, "One of the things I like to advertise about my honey is that I don't heat it or treat it or do anything to it. It is just raw honey. This honey that has been in contact with the electric knife I consider heated. So a lot of this I will use to feed back to the bees in the springtime when they need feeding. The main thing with honey is to be clean with it. You have to be really clean, because it is food."

SWARMS

A swarm is a group of honeybees that fly off together, accompanied by a queen, to start a new hive. George Prater explained swarms to us. "Swarming is their natural way of reproducing. That is the way they reproduce. What we try to do as beekeepers is just inhibit that if we can. Because a lot of times, if a hive swarms, then they may not have enough bees to make any excess honey for that year. So you try to keep them from swarming if you can. One thing you will do during the swarming season, which is May and June, is take the hive apart once a week. Take out every frame where the eggs are to see if there are any queen cells in there and cut them out.

"When they are ready to swarm, they will build a special cell, and the queen will lay an egg in it. And they will feed the egg a special preparation called royal jelly that, I guess, has some type of hormone in it; it will make it into a queen bee. Then, when they get ready to swarm, generally what happens is the old queen will fly off, and half the bees will go with her. The new queen will stay there with the hive. But sometimes the queen will fly off before the egg hatches. Then hopefully, that queen will hatch out, and it will be all right. If the queen doesn't hatch out, if it is a bad egg, then you have got a queenless hive; and if you don't do something pretty quick, the hive dies.

"You may have been told how gentle swarms are. There is a lot of people will tell you swarms are gentle; they won't sting you. That is not exactly true. One time Daddy and I were hiving a swarm. Somebody had called us. We were both in the insurance business at that time. I think I had my suit in the truck. But I didn't have my boots with me. We went out to this guy's house, and the swarm had clustered on this little apple tree. It was on the main trunk of the tree, so we couldn't cut it off. So we put the hive underneath it. I was holding the hive, and Daddy was going to hit the tree to try to dislodge the bees. I had my coveralls on and my gloves and veil, but I didn't have my boots on. So Daddy hit the tree and all these bees went all over the hive and bunches of them just went right down on my feet, right on my ankles. I got stung about twenty times, through my socks. Swarms are fairly gentle. But if you start messing with them, they will sting you!"

Howard Prater recalled, "They are hard to do anything with; I tried to get a swarm of wild bees one day down in Hartwell. They were in a tree. I cut into it with a saw, and I smoked them down into my hive, had my hive down at the bottom of the tree. I tried to run them down in it; before I could get the lid on, they'd go out again. I worked and I worked down there and it was hot, but I didn't get stung a bit while I was working on them. So I finally just gave up and went out there and got a paper and set down out there near the tree. I was sitting there reading the paper and one of those bees jumped down *z-z-z*, bit me right here on the neck, and I slapped at it, and it was just like a hypodermic needle shot all that stuff in there. In a few minutes, I ran in there and got a bath, and I was white with red spots all over. I had to go to the doctor and get a shot. And I still didn't get the bees and didn't get but one sting. But I've been stung lots of times by bees. I didn't have any reactions after that."

DISEASES AND ENEMIES

Jesse Ray Owens had this to share with us about enemies of the bees. "I've noticed for the last few years, them Japanese hornets have been killing the bees. They'll go and set in front of the gum and catch [the bees] as they fly out and cut their heads off and eat 'em.

"We had some apple peelings in a bucket out here in the yard last summer, and there was Japanese hornets and honeybees flying around it. The Japanese hornets would catch [the bees] and eat 'em. They'd just fly off with 'em."

Glen Taylor declared, "These big Japanese hornets will tote your bees off. They brought them things over here to the U.S., as they said, to get rid of the wasps, hornets, and yellow jackets, but they tote our bees off and destroy a lot of bees. They will tear up a yellow jacket's nest and a wasp's nest. The stingers are about an inch and a half long on them big old yellow hornets. I used to stand in front of mine and kill the hornets with a board. I got to where I couldn't hit them, so I got a tennis racket, and I'd knock them down, and then I'd stomp them. I killed a lot of them like that in front of my beehives, catching my bees.

"We lost a lot of bees to them old mites, destroying them, killing them, getting in them. That is what has got rid of so many bees up here. Some of them mites gives the bees a breathing problem, and they suffocate the bees. You have to get Apistan strips for the mites. The strips are put in the combs at certain times to kill the mites."

George Prater told us more about controlling the mites. "We use Apistan strips to treat them for the mites. The state had been recommending that you treat them twice a year. I had already treated mine this spring. I went to a beekeeping meeting in Clarkesville about a month ago, and they had done some recent research, and they found that they do better to treat them once in August. They used to recommend treating them in April and October. The chemical is impregnated in the plastic, and you hang two of these [strips] in the hive where the eggs are. You leave them in there for six weeks and then take them out. Now, you can't have these in there when they are making honey. The insecticide will get in the honey.

"In the United States, you just assume that your hives have mites. The Apistan strips will control the mites; they won't eradicate them.

Even if it got rid of all of them, they could get reinfected. There is a lot of concern right now because there are areas of Florida that some of the mites are becoming resistant to this chemical. This is the only chemical in the United States that is approved to treat the bees for the mites. So if we lose that chemical, we are going to be in big trouble."

According to Glen J. Taylor, foulbrood, a bacterial disease of honeybee larvae, is another disease to watch for in your hives. "We have to put up with the old foulbrood. Foulbrood is a disease that kills the bees. I guess it came from Germany, with all the shipping they did. We treat them with a mixture of Terramycin and powdered sugar. That is what you use to doctor the bees with when you have a foulbrood. Put it in there, and it will kind of treat them; it kind of holds that foulbrood down. All you can do to bees that have foulbrood is pile them up and burn them and hope that they don't get to the rest of them."

Howard Prater added, "Foulbrood ruins your beehive. You can walk by it and smell it. It is just decayed in there. I have forgotten now what it was we treated that with. We treated it with Terramycin once a year. It comes in a granulated form and you sprinkle that on the top of the planks and mix it with powdered sugar. It is an antibiotic that has been in use for thirty or forty years. They have not found any kind of resistance to it."

PLATE 104 George (left) and Howard Prater examining the hive body

George Prater continued, "The mites make the foulbrood problem worse. They have got a thing called parasitic mite syndrome, which when your bees get the mites, it makes them more susceptible to getting foulbrood, and so the two compound each other. The year that all mine died, they had some foulbrood in them too. Foulbrood is extremely infectious. I took all my frames and burned them. I saved the hive bodies by taking a blowtorch and scorching the inside of them. But they say that just about the size of a head of a pin contains about a million spores of the foulbrood. It is extremely contagious. If your neighbor has bees that have foulbrood, then your bees can get it very easily. So you are supposed to treat them with the

Terramycin and powdered sugar as a preventative measure twice a year, in the spring and the fall."

Glen Taylor said bears are a common problem. "Sometimes bears come right out there to the hives. I had six hives down here, and they got into them. A fellow comes down here with dogs, and they run [the bear] off, but they never did tree the bear or catch him. I had them bears coming out here, and I had them coming up on the grave hill. They tore up a bunch of hives up there."

George Prater recalled, "I had a problem with bears last year. I had moved my bees when I had my trouble with the mites and the foulbrood. I moved them down to the other end of my property down there. Then I had a bear start getting into them. It was a very polite bear. It got into them four times and only on the very last time did he actually ruin the hive. Actually, he didn't even tear up the equipment; he ate all the bees and wax and everything and didn't even break a single frame. I had moved all my hives back over here except one. We had a bear up here a few weeks ago, but he has not got into my hives. I've got an electric fence around it.

"Right now the mites and the foulbrood are the main problems. There are people that will tell you that the wax moth and worms are a problem. But they are only a problem if you have a weak hive. If you have got a hive that the bees are dying off, then there is a moth that will fly in, in the middle of the night, three or four in the morning, and lay eggs; and if the hives are weak, these little worms will hatch out, and there will be too many for the bees to take care of them. They go in there and start burrowing little tunnels around, and they will even eat into the wood. They will just ruin the whole hive and make a complete mess out of it before you know it.

"There is another condition called chalkbrood. I have seen that some. That is another condition that can come up because of the parasitic mites. The eggs will just kind of wither and die. They will look like a little mummy in there.

PLATE 105 A view of the damage the wax moth inflicts on a hive

They will be all white. If the hive is very healthy, the bees will go ahead and pull those out of there and take them and throw them out of the hive. There is no treatment for it. It is generally not a problem. If the hive is healthy, they will take care of it."

TYPES OF HONEY

Jesse Ray Owens informed us, "I've heard of sourwood honey all my life, but I never believed they made a honey with sourwood. I've got sourwood [trees] growing right here in the yard, and I've watched them for years. I've never seen bees work in one yet. I don't say that they don't make honey [out of sourwood blossoms]. They *could* make it in the evening.

"[The color of the honey] depends on what your honey flow is. Most of the time I get light red or real light-colored honey. I have got about a pound of pink honey, but there's usually just a little of it."

J. C. Stubblefield said, "The dark honey is just any kind of flower, just anything they get. Some folks says corn tassels is in the light honey. Some of them calls it sourwood honey. Ain't a thing but corn tassel honey. I ain't never seen no bees on sourwood."

Glen Taylor told us, "I generally put a new super on when the sourwood starts blooming. I put new ones on the hive; then the honey is mostly sourwood. The first honey flow that comes on, I generally always take it off and put my supers on to catch the sourwood. Of course, bees get other nectar besides sourwood and put it in the hive. There's a lot of that sourwood in it. There is bees that is going to go out here on other flowers and bring something in besides sourwood. There ain't no such thing as pure sourwood. After they get the super filled up, you can check your bees to see how they got the hive body filled up. Then you can put another super on; the third super you put on, you can take off and sling the honey out, and then you can put that super back on, and they'll fill it up again."

George Prater acknowledged, "You get all different kinds of honey; it just depends on what is blooming. A lot of times they will work on clover; they will work on corn; they will work on sourwood. One time, Daddy took some honey off of the hive that was just as black as it could be. Black as night. We thought they might have gotten it off mountain laurel. We tried eating it—it was bitter. Daddy tried to feed it back to the bees, and they wouldn't eat it!

"Bees fly as far as they need to get nectar and pollen. They say they will fly up to two or three miles. They are going to go to the closest

nectar source, whatever is the closest thing. When things are blooming, they will generally work on whatever is the predominate nectar
source at that time and just not mess with anything else. When the
sourwood is blooming, that is why you get just sourwood honey at that
time.

"A lot of the beekeepers in the mountains will just label anything
they've got as sourwood. It sells better. What is funny is when you drive
down the road the first of June and you see these roadside stands that
will have these signs out, 'new crop of sourwood honey,' when the sourwood hasn't even started blooming yet that year. But you tell the honey
by the color. Sourwood is the lightest color. A pure, or almost pure,
sourwood is going to be almost as clear as water.

"I believe you are supposed to label it 'sourwood' or 'wildflower.'
And it is supposed to be over a certain percentage of whatever you
name as the dominant pollen source or nectar source; it should be over
a third that.

"I sent some in [to the state to be analyzed]; Robert Mitcham sent
some in for me about ten years ago. I sent a sample of my sourwood,
and I had a sample of my wildflower. And my wildflower had enough
sourwood in it that I could legally, by state law, label it sourwood."

THE FINISHED PRODUCT

"I usually get about three dollars a jar for my honey—that is a big
pint. I usually get about five dollars for a quart. It depends on the
honey," said Glen J. Taylor. "That sourwood honey is higher than wildflower honey. There are a lot of people who like the wildflower. There
are a lot of them who think the clear honey is the best. There are a lot
of them that like the dark honey because they get better medicine out
of the dark honey than they do out of the light honey. A lot of them
take dark honey and take apple cider, lemon juice, and vinegar to make
them some arthritis medicine."

Jesse Ray Owens recalled, "We used to sell honey, but I just about
give it away now. We used to sell it in a eight- to ten-pound lard bucket
for a dollar—that was about ten pounds of honey. I've quit selling it
now that the cost of it is so high. I've just about quit the beekeeping
business, but I always enjoyed it."

J. C. Stubblefield added, "We would get anywhere from fifty pounds
to two hundred pounds in one season. We sold the biggest part of it. We
sold it just to individuals around that wanted honey. They'd come and
get it, or if they didn't come, I'd take it to them. We sold to one lady

over on Lake Rabun. We would carry a whole fifty-pound lard can full of honey to her for ten cents a pound. Now, that was way back about fifty years ago. There ain't no bees around much now."

George Prater told us about current prices for honey. "Mainly, right now, I've just been selling my honey up at my office. I used to wholesale some out to stores. But the last few years [1994–1999], I haven't had enough to where I needed to worry about that. You see, some years you don't even get any honey. The weather is a big thing. This year has been the best honey crop we have had in over ten years. I usually get a fair amount of dark honey in June. Last year it rained just about the whole month of June, and I didn't get any. But I got a pretty decent sourwood flow. This year has been an exceptional sourwood flow. Honey brings about forty-five dollars a case now.

"Honey will granulate over time. Honey is a liquid form of sugar, and eventually almost all honey will turn to solid sugar. It is called granulation. Generally, you will see it in the bottom of jars, crystals at the bottom.

"Sourwood honey is supposed to be the slowest honey to granulate of any of them that is made. We have sourwood honey that we have had for several years that has never granulated. A lot of the other honeys—clover, orange blossom, and others—will granulate in a month or two. A lot of beekeepers say on their label, at the bottom: to reliquefy place in a pan of hot water and heat slowly.

"A lot of the big beekeepers, when they extract the honey, they will put it in a big pot and heat it. They will warm it up. It makes it easier to go through all of their equipment. They pump it into big fifty-five-gallon drums. Heating it is supposed to help keep it from granulating as quick. But I think it takes away from the honey to do that."

BEE STORIES

Howard Prater shared the following account with us. "Way back some time ago, I wouldn't call anybody's name, but there was a man in this county that, the way he kept bees, in the spring he'd feed them sugar water, and it makes the prettiest white comb you have ever seen. He would feed them a lot of sugar water and take that comb out and wouldn't extract it or nothing. He would cut it up in combs and put it in his jars. Then he would go down to Cornelia and buy five gallons of strained honey from South Georgia, pour that in it, and then label it 'Sourwood Mountain Honey'! Somebody reported him to the state, or they came up and inspected him, and they couldn't find any reason to prosecute the boy because he kept his bees on Sourwood Mountain! They ruled that it was perfectly legal."

Lessie Conner told us, "Minyard [her husband] used to keep bees, and we had the honey, but he got stung so much, he can't fool with them anymore. [I have helped him collect the honey,] but I turned over a dishpan full of honey one time, and he didn't ask me to help him anymore. I don't know how many stands of bees he did have. He went out there to rob some of 'em, and he said, 'Lessie, go out there and hold that pan for me.'

"I said, 'I ain't gonna do it. They'll sting me.'

"He said, 'I'll guarantee you, they won't sting you.'

"He just kept on begging me and kept on begging me. I said, 'All right, I'll go,' and I said, 'The first sting I get, I'll throw that pan down and I'll leave there.'

"And he said, 'Okay. You can throw her down the first sting you get.'

"So I went on out there, and he had that pan just level with the prettiest white honey you've ever seen. And one dabbed me right there, and about that time another one took me there, and *whup*, it went and down the hill I went!

"He didn't quarrel. I don't think he liked it, but he didn't quarrel for he knowed I'd do it. Minyard had on a net and all."

Minyard continued the story. "The bees was awful calm. It was on the hillside and hard to set a dishpan down with just nobody to help you a'tall, and me a-cuttin' it out of the top of the gum and putting in the pan, you see. I told her not to fight at 'em—if one got around her not to fight at 'em—and they wouldn't bother her."

Lessie concluded the story by saying, "Well, I didn't fight at 'em. I couldn't fight at 'em with my hands full of the dishpan!"

Howard Prater told us about the flight of the bee. "One time I had robbed some bees and taken some honey off, and my boys was just sitting there; we were sitting at the table for supper. They got to asking me questions about bees, and I just give them a little history about it, the makeup of a hive. You got the female bee, she is the working bee, and they can sting. The drones are the male bees, and they don't sting. Then they have got the queen. The queen has to mate with one of the drones before she can lay eggs. And the drones, in the fall of the year, the queen bees take the drones out of their hive and cut their wings off and throw them overboard because they don't feed those drones through the wintertime, and they haven't helped make the honey. So they get rid of them. But the flight of the bee, that new queen comes out, and she is going to mate with the drone. She goes up, she flies up—as far as she can go up—and the drone that is strong enough to stay with her mates, and he dies. I was telling the boys the story, and Lois, my wife, had never heard this story. She said, 'Ah, shut up telling those boys all that stuff.' The next day the magazine section of the Atlanta paper had the same thing in it. So I had proof that I wasn't lying to them!"

George Prater said, "I had a hive one time that had gone queenless, and I had taken a frame of brood from one of my other hives and stuck in there for them to raise another queen. I went in and looked a few weeks later, and I found the queen. So I knew that the queen was there, but there were no fresh eggs. So I went back about a week later and looked in again—still no fresh eggs. I got to thinking, well maybe the queen hasn't mated. So I went over to one of the other hives and grabbed a drone and took it over there and threw it in the front entrance, and he went running right in there. I looked in the next week and there was plenty of eggs in there! I doubt that that made any difference! Drones can go from hive to hive. The bees will let them do that. But in the fall they will run them off and not let them in.

"From what I've been told, there are no wild honeybees anymore. I lost some bees this year when they swarmed. But they tell me that because of the mites, that those bees that swarm won't live over one year in the wild."

TECHNOLOGY AND TOOLS

"He wanted t' be self-sustaining and do his own things as much as he could . . ."

It is almost impossible to comprehend the hardships our parents and grandparents faced in the early part of the 1900s. The tools and technology available for use were limited by what could be made and what had been invented. In order to survive, people had to be skilled woodworkers, toolmakers, farmers, hunters, and doctors. When some task needed to be accomplished, they had to rely on their own ingenuity and make do with what they had. When a tool broke, they couldn't run to the store to buy a new one. Creating a tool was a time-consuming task because they were made by hand, either in a blacksmith shop or at home. They were simple in construction, and the majority were operated by animal or human power.

Numerous tools were used in a farm family's everyday existence. Tools for woodworking included mauls, axes, mallets, shaving horses, broadaxes, foot adzes, chisels, handsaws, squares, rulers, froes, and go-devils. Everyone used plows, hoes, shovels, rakes, spades, and mattocks in preparing and tending the land. Many of the tools that were so important in everyday life have been featured in previous Foxfire books.

By the early 1900s, the available tools and technology had begun to change. Cars and planes were being seen, on a limited basis, in our community. In 1911 the first power plant was being built here. The way of life was changing in Rabun County and all across the country. But even with the newer technology, the people here continued to rely on themselves and, when absolutely necessary, their neighbors. As Buck Carver said about his friend and neighbor Bill Lamb, "He wanted t' be self-sustaining and do his own things as much as he could his own self and not bother the other feller."

Back in those days, that was possible, but now we rely on others, in one way or another, for almost everything. We are a society of consumers; we acquire goods and services rather than producing those goods or services ourselves. If we make something, it is because we choose to, not because we have to.

The tools featured in this chapter reflect the limited technology available to farm families then. The fireless cooker, hydraulic ram, plumping mill, and fertilizer distributor, while primitive compared to our technology today, greatly improved the quality of life back then. They allowed meals to be kept warm without burning, corn to be ground into meal at home, water to be pumped into the house, and the garden to be fertilized easily. All were labor- or time-savers—something the old-timers appreciated. The final section features Connie Carlton, a craftsman who is trying to carry on the tradition of creating handmade tools. He summarizes his philosophy by saying, "I don't think you can beat the beauty in simplicity. That's not with just making things, but that's in living too."

—*Kaye Carver Collins*

THE FIRELESS COOKER

People who don't live on farms anymore enjoy recalling romanticized memories of growing up or visiting relatives on the farm. Those memories are usually charming pictures of an idyllic and pleasant life—a life of few worries, little stress, and simpler times.

But for the people on those farms, life was anything but simple. Everything they did was necessary for their existence. It was hard work from daylight to dark. They had few, if any, conveniences. That is why, when technology made the fireless cooker and hydraulic ram possible, people truly appreciated the time and labor it saved them.

In the old days, fireless cookers were very popular. People used them instead of stoves because they were safer. The fireless cooker was a box with three openings big enough for pots to sit inside them. The box was insulated with wood pulp. It is called a fireless cooker because it cooked food with hot iron wafers instead of fire. The iron wafers were heated

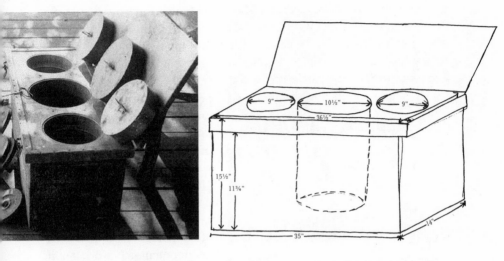

PLATES 106, 107 The fireless cooker

by placing them in the fireplace and then were put in the bottom of each hole of the cooker. There were insulated lids for each opening. Other fireless cookers used soapstone because it held more heat and stayed hot longer than iron did.

The fireless cooker worked like an older version of the Crockpot. Farmers and their families could leave the house for the entire day and come home to a hot meal.

THE HYDRAULIC RAM

George Carpenter recalled, "In 1936 we ordered a ram from Sears-Roebuck and installed it on Backbone Ridge between Cornelia and Demorest. I'd say that a pump at that time would cost probably twenty dollars, and the pipe was probably two or three cents a foot. Many people back then didn't have money to buy the pump or the pipe. They had to carry water. But it was a real convenience in a time when there wasn't many conveniences.

"For many people, it wasn't convenient for them to use rams because the lay of the land and everything was not right for that kind of pump—you had to have gravity. The pump was real reliable. We had a reservoir on top of the ridge where we lived, and we had a continuous flow of water. We never ran out of water with the ram. But many times,

PLATE 108 The hydraulic ram from
Murray Collections

in bad weather, extra water would come into the spring, and there would be a little grit, sand, or maybe little sticks in it. It would have to be cleaned out. I was the only one in the family that knew how to work on it and do maintenance. Sometimes you would have to take it completely apart and reassemble it to clean it. But, basically, I'd say every two months is how often that there would have to be maintenance work on it. Once every couple of years you would have to change the diaphragm in it to keep it in operation.

"There was eight people in my family, and there was enough water for everybody. There was no electricity then, and we had an outside toilet, so the water was just for cooking and taking a bath in the tub. It pumped a stream about half the size of a pencil continually. Day and night, the ram never stopped pumping. If you had a holding tank sufficient to hold the amount of water it would take to supply a family for twenty-four hours, then you would have enough water.

"Ours pumped for about ten years with maintenance work. It never was replaced, just maintenance parts—that's all. Then electricity came through, and we had a well then, and a bathroom in the house!

"There was one other ram in our area at that time. It belonged to C. M. Miller. He pumped water from a lake to a holding tank on top of a ridge in his apple orchard. He used it to spray, but it was a real large one. It was a whole lot bigger than ours. I'd say it probably would have pumped enough water to spray over a hundred acres of apple trees once a week. It pumped continually, but it wasn't pumping all of the water in the stream. Part of it would overflow into the dam.

"There's a limit to how far it can push the water up. The pump was two hundred and fifty yards from the house, and it was pumping two hundred and fifty feet in elevation from the pump to the house. There was a reservoir built there, graded downhill to the pump itself. The ram was really spring-loaded, like a steel spring, and the water pressure would hit it and knock the spring up. Then the spring would recoil and push the water back through a check valve. What went through the check valve was trapped there. It pushed it on up the hill to the house. It would come up again, and the water would spray out each side. Then the spring would overload the water pressure. The spring would kick again and knock more water back through the check valve. This was a continual process.

"Today some seasonal people that come up in the summertime could rely on a ram. Especially in areas where electricity is not easily accessible, it would be real handy. If we ever had a national disaster, a pump like that would be a real convenience. People could have water where otherwise they would have to carry it or make different arrangements to get it to their house."

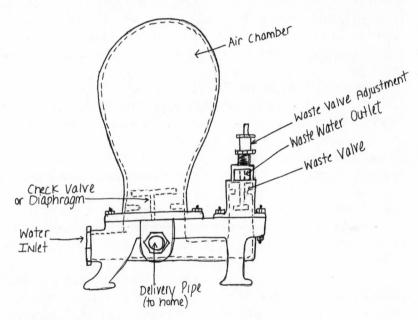

PLATE 109 Hydraulic ram

The water is pumped using two valves and the force of the flowing water to create enough air pressure to push the water up. Out of the column of water that flows into the ram, only a small portion of water is actually pumped. The water that is not pumped is called waste water. The only moving parts are the valves. The first valve to close from the water pressure is the waste valve. When the waste valve closes, water pressure builds inside. This pressure forces water up through the check valve and then into the air chamber, causing the air to compress. When the air has compressed enough to stop the flow of water, the check valve closes and the water is forced out into the delivery pipe. This releases the pressure on the waste valve; then the process starts all over again. This process can happen sixty times a minute. The rate at which the ram "kicks" can be adjusted for variations in the amount of water that comes out. Strangely, the less the ram kicks, the more water it pumps. This is because the less waste water that the ram throws out, the more that goes into the air chamber to be pushed into the delivery pipe.

THE PLUMPING MILL

Mr. and Mrs. Maynard Murray restored the old water mill at Sylvan Lake Falls off of Wolffork Road in Rabun Gap. They also built a pound mill, or plumping mill, as it is sometimes called. Mr. Murray said, "I thought it would be interesting just to have a real old-fashioned plumping mill going. People that had those just ground enough meal for their own use."

Although we could not find an old pound mill in our area to authenticate their use here, we did have several local people who told us that they remembered them when they were growing up, and they were able to draw rough sketches of how they worked.

Mr. Murray told us, "I was reading one of Eric Sloane's books called *Vanishing America,* and in there, he mentioned that in the southern mountains, many of the people used what they called a plumping mill. They called it that because of the noise it made. It was operated by water running into a box mounted on one end of a beam and a stone or hardwood mallet attached to the other end, with a hollowed-out log under the mallet.

"I thought it would be interesting just to have a real, old-fashioned plumping mill going. It's just a thing of interest to show people how they used to do it in the old days. It was never expected to grind any more meal than just what one family could use. Each family probably hand-built their own mill. It's just a simple thing. They weren't all exactly alike. Some of them used a stone, some used a hardwood mallet, and probably some people used much longer shafts than others. It was just a matter of fitting it to the amount of water they had and where it was available.

"I didn't find it too difficult to make. I just went by the pencil sketch and the little picture that were in Sloane's book. I went up on the hills here and found a little locust tree that had a fork in it. Then I cut a groove in a stone and forced that fork around the stone and fastened the fork at the end so it would hold the stone tight, and then I built the box on the end for the water to run into. It took me about a day and a half to make it and get it set up. I put it on some planks so it would be a completely movable unit. I didn't put any stakes in the ground, but put some rocks on the planks to hold it steady, so it wouldn't jar around so much. It should last for a long time. There's not much to wear out on it. There's just one bolt on it that makes the hinge operate when it swings up and down.

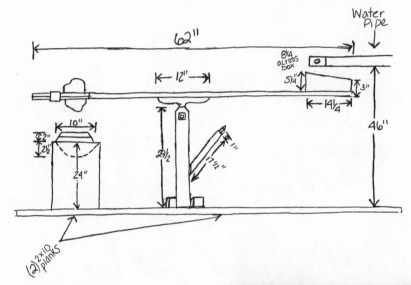

PLATE 110 Diagram of plumping mill built by Maynard Murray

PLATE 111 Plumping mill

"So far, I've ground about three five-pound bags and given them to my friends and said, 'Try it.' They like it very much. It's just a little different in consistency from the meal that's stone-ground. It has more of an appearance of grits than it does cornmeal, because it doesn't go through the [mill]stones. It's just really hammered up fine with a stone pounding on it.

"Most of the time, the plumping mill is run day and night. It doesn't need any oiling or grease or any attention. Just take the meal out and put more corn in it. The water filling that pot [or box or bucket] determines how fast the mill runs. I've got a fair stream of water, which comes from up above the dam just piped here, gravity feed. The pot fills up with water and dumps about once every six seconds. As the water spills out, it drops the mallet into the hollowed-out log filled with corn, hammering it into meal.

PLATE 112 The mallet drops into the hollowed-out log filled with corn, hammering it into meal

"You can [pound the corn] with any hard rock that won't keep peeling off. You wouldn't want to use sandstone because you'd end up with a lot of sand in the meal. I used a piece of rock that looks like granite. It's a fairly hard rock. I took a Carborundum stone and just shaped the end of it so it'd fit down in the bowl pretty good and get a face about two inches in diameter. The corn gets ground fine in the bottom of the bowl. The fine meal keeps working up the sides and the coarse keeps falling down in the center. Every individual grain of corn will be ground if you leave it in there for four or five hours. It seems to rotate the corn itself. There'll be a few coarse pieces of cornmeal in there, but I sift that out and dump the coarse back in with the new corn. I usually put about two or three cups of corn in each morning or afternoon, and I'll get about two cups of cornmeal each time. I haven't tried wheat or any other grain in it. I guess you could put wheat in there if you wanted to."

A FERTILIZER DISTRIBUTOR

Even with newer technology, many of the old-timers continued relying on their own abilities and skills. They enjoyed being as self-sufficient as possible.

Buck Carver tells of his longtime friend Bill Lamb and the hand-operated fertilizer distributor that Bill invented after he sold his horse. Bill passed away in the winter of 1970, and his family gave the machine, which Bill called a knocker, to Buck, as they felt Bill would have wanted him to have it.

Buck explained, "I don't have the least idea how long it took Bill to make it, but I believe Blanche [Bill's daughter] told me 1963 was when he made it. The first thing I knowed about him havin' it was I was down there in the shed one day, and I said, 'Bill, what in the cat hair is this thing you've got here?'

" 'Oh,' he says, 'that's my knocker,' and he told me what he used it for, you know.

"Blanche was talkin' about that right after he died, and decided she'd give the thing to me. I tried t' buy it from her, and

PLATE 113 The fertilizer distributor built by Bill Lamb

she said she didn't know what t' do about that—that he'd left it in his will, or some of his papers where he'd made his requests, that he wanted Floyd [his son] to look after the disposal of all his personal property. She said, 'Whatever Floyd wants t' do about it is all right.'

"I said, 'Well, now, I'd just be tickled t' buy that thing from you, and I'll pay you every dollar I can stand for it.'

"In about six months, I was down there, and she told me they decided they would just give me the thing—that they wanted t' give it to me.

"As t' how long it took him t' make it, I wouldn't have the least idea, but you can look at it and tell it's been a pretty time-consuming job. And Bill was gettin' old. Course his health hadn't gone so bad on him at that time, and he was still turning off work pretty fast.

"He had to scribe out all these circles on there, you know—them wooden circles. I think he used a keyhole saw on them [the cogs on the round wooden disc mounted on the wheel]. They're all the same distance apart, you know, and he had to figger out his circumference around there.

"An' he was particular about everything. It had t' be just so or it was no good. He was a firm believer that everything he done, it had t' be done just right, or he wasn't gonna have it at all. If it wadn't right the first time, he'd tear it up, start all over. He was awful particular. Nearly all the old-timers was. I know from the time I was big enough t' foller my daddy around, he'd tell me, 'Anything that's worth doing at all is worth doing right.'

PLATE 114 Buck Carver explaining the agitator arm's action to Stan Echols

PLATE 115 The arrow at left shows the tip of the agitator arm, the other end of which is attached to the bottom of the box. The arrow at right points to one of the twelve cogs on the wheel's wooden disc.

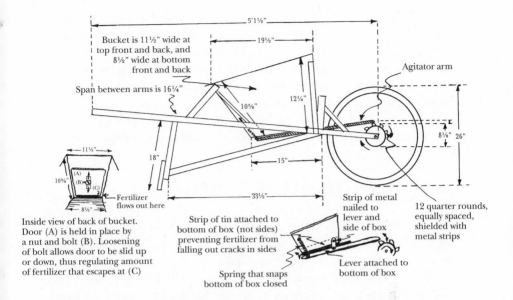

Bucket is 11½" wide at top front and back, and 8½" wide at bottom front and back

Span between arms is 16¼"

5'1½"

19½"

10⅝"

12¼"

Agitator arm

8⅛" 26"

11½"

18"

15"

33½"

10⅝"

8½"

(A)

(B)

(C)

Fertilizer flows out here

Inside view of back of bucket. Door (A) is held in place by a nut and bolt (B). Loosening of bolt allows door to be slid up or down, thus regulating amount of fertilizer that escapes at (C)

Strip of tin attached to bottom of box (not sides) preventing fertilizer from falling out cracks in sides

Spring that snaps bottom of box closed

Strip of metal nailed to lever and side of box

Lever attached to bottom of box

12 quarter rounds, equally spaced, shielded with metal strips

PLATE 116 The fertilizer distributor

"Bill got his materials for this from Roosevelt Burrell's sawmill down there—just scrap lumber. The wheel is an old bicycle wheel. The distributor'll hold about a peck and a half—about a third a bushel, I guess, t' be about as exact as I could. T' put it in pounds, I guess it'll hold around twenty pounds of that ammonia nitrate. It'll hold that level full—but, now, you can't fill the thing level full and still operate it 'cause you'll be shaking too much off a the top. How much fertilizer comes out depends on how you regulate the gate in the rear. The bottom of the box is regulated by a set screw. You can raise or lower it, so it just depends on the opening. It's a pretty constant flow—mostly when it made that bump, it'd throw a pretty good little wad down. Course there'd be a few grains of it trail off, you know. He stepped 'em out. That was another thing. Bill was really good in mathematics t' not have no education. He could figger things out good. He could figger out how far apart them little cogs on the wooden wheel had t' be t' space the fertilizer ten 'r twelve inches apart. He wanted it pretty close t' the stalks of corn and not waste any.

"Bill was good on them things. As far as education's concerned, I doubt whether he finished second grade or not—I doubt like everything. But he had a head full of common sense, and he put 'em t' good use.

"Bill didn't have any plans t' go by. He just thought it up. He'd been a-studyin' about it. He'd been a-borrowin' distributors from other people t' use, and he just had sold his horse, so he just fell on that idea. He didn't just hatch it up in a minute. He'd been studying it up for several days before he started it. He was the kinda man that didn't like t' devil his neighbors no more than he could help. He knowed they had work of their own t' do, and Bill was a fella that liked t' be independent. I didn't mean that he was hateful or anything of that kind, 'cause he certainly wasn't. He wanted t' be self-sustaining and do his own things as much as he could his own self and not bother the other feller.

"So people depended on themselves fer things a that kind."

HANDMADE FARM TOOLS

John Rice Irwin and his Museum of Appalachia in Norris, Tennessee, have, time and time again, given Foxfire unlimited access to a wealth of Appalachian culture and skills.

On one trip, Teresia and Warren Thomason and Dewey Smith were fortunate to meet one of those craftsmen, Mr. Connie Carlton. Connie handmakes a wide variety of farm tools such as rakes, pitchforks, and shovels, using only a shaving horse, a drawknife, and a few other primitive tools. Today we think nothing of running out to the local hardware store to pick up a rake or a shovel; but, in pioneer times, life was not so convenient. Connie, with his knowledge and love for his craft, is working hard to preserve and pass on this fading tradition.

Connie reminisced, "I was born the thirtieth of March 1942 in central Kentucky on a farm near a little town called Lawrenceburg. It was a rural community, and I lived there until I was about eight years old. [Then] my daddy went into the grocery business, and we moved to town. I more or less turned into a city slicker. I was actually raised up

PLATE 117
Connie Carlton working on a pitchfork with his shaving horse and drawknife

in a small town, but all my kinfolks and the customers of the store were rural people.

"I've always liked older people and related to them more. I'd set around and listen to their stories and tales, and they'd show me things. I guess that's the way my interest really started growing. I tell people I was born probably two hundred years too late. It's always been in my ancestral blood to be self-surviving with the bare necessities. I've probably got the reputation of being the youngest old-timer around. I can see and understand so much of your old ways. I think your heritage is as much a part of you as anything else. It's something that should be carried on and preserved in some way for the next generation.

"My wife's name is Judy, and I think she's the best lady in the world. She's stood behind me and given me a lot of encouragement. She's just an old country gal [who] was raised on a farm, and she likes the same things that I like. She's taught school for about twenty years now, and that's what she does. [We] have two boys and a girl. My girl will work with her hands some, but my boys don't have the interest.

"I've had a mixed-up profession. I barbered for thirty years, farmed, and done some carpentry work and crafts.

"I really got started [making tools] around 1982. I was deer hunting [with some friends], and we were killing some time one night. I went by a bookstore and picked up Roy Underhill's book. [Roy Underhill hosts *The Woodwrights Shop* on PBS and has authored numerous books.] It gives a general step-by-step method [for toolmaking]. That's what got me started. After I got interested, [I would read] any books I could find. I've got books piled up, and some of them are just wore to a frazzle. I've had some re-bound. I might want to see how to do just one thing or what they said about it, and I can look at a picture and get a general idea of how it was made and the size of it.

"I got interested in learning these crafts, and I learned the majority of them through research, reading books, and picking up a few pointers here and there from old-timers. I don't know where the spark started. Anything old, pure, and simple will catch my eye. I just see beauty in things like that. I love the simplicity of the finished product. It's got a lot of purpose and usefulness. I get more satisfaction from going out and cutting the tree, taking a few simple hand tools, and constructing something that's practical and beautiful, than from having a shop full of modern tools and making a refined piece of furniture. I don't see as much beauty and craftsmanship in that for the amount of effort [that is expended]. You really have to have a love for it or you wouldn't endure through trial and error. I could make a pitchfork and it break and as long as I can see what caused it to break, I'm learning from that. I've got all the patience in the world there, but when I go to change a spark plug in a lawn mower and get the threads crossed, I'm ready to get the sledgehammer. It's just different interests for different people. I get as much satisfaction and enjoyment out of someone appreciating and admiring my work, probably as much or more so than [their] actually buying it.

"[Carving] kind of grows on you. When you start out, you try to make [your piece] look like [the model you are using]. Then, as you get older and [begin to understand] the reasoning behind everything, you start learning what each wood would do and what you could do with a tool. When I'm shaving a piece of wood on the shaving horse with the drawknife, and I hit the in-grain [where] that wood starts wanting to tear, I just stop automatically. It's just second nature with you. All you've got to do is turn your wood around [in the] opposite direction. I think any craftsman will tell you this, you can learn the basics on anything you want to learn, but it's all the little things that you pick up on your own that you get a feel for. I tell folks sometimes the way that I have a feel for wood is just like crawling right up inside of the log. You've got to have control over everything as it comes together: the wood, the tools, and the shaping. There are things that just come to you. You just don't learn them overnight.

"Anytime that I go to a museum and see a unique piece that was practical and popular in use, I copy it. I make the wooden pitchforks all the way from two tines to five tines. I make various types of wooden rakes, bow rakes, and split-style rakes that have split handles [with tines] that fork out. I make ox yokes, wooden shovels, and meal paddles. I have a little tool that I make; we call them cane strippers back home. They're just a little notched stick that you can walk through a field of sorghum with and knock the leaves off before you cut it. I [also] make dough bowls and spoons. I tried baskets a little bit, but baskets kind of run with the lawn mower. My patience don't hold out.

"The crafts that I make have been a good part of my livelihood for the past eight years. The biggest problem that I have is the love that you have for it. There's so much of it that you want to do, and you can't do it all and be accomplished and end up making it right. You don't know how hard it is to control that. When you get to thinking about the amount of pieces and the amount of money, you may as well just have a nine-to-five job, because that's what it's gonna run into. You've got to keep it balanced where you'll keep that love for it. You've got to put yourself into every piece you make. That's the way I try to do with these pieces. I don't just say, 'Well, I've got to hurry up and get this one done so I can get to this next one.' I can't do that and enjoy it.

PLATE 118 Several of Connie's handmade farm tools

"I start right from the tree with most of the work I do. I pick my cut, cut the tree, split it, and rive [split] it out. I use very little sawed lumber. A lot of times, I'll just buy the beam of an ox yoke or something like that. [All] my farm tools are carved and shaped on a shaving horse, which is nothing more than a vise or bench you set down on to hold your wood.

"[To make a pitchfork,] the first thing I would do is go out in the woods and select a good tree. I would either use ash, white or red oak, or hickory, because these woods all rive and work good with hand tools, and they have a lot of strength about them. You can bend the wood without it breaking. I would select a log [that is] maybe twelve to fifteen inches in diameter. You've got to select a tree that's almost of a veneer quality [no knots or protrusions]. You've got to be able to read that tree [while it's] standing. By reading it, you can look at the bark of the tree, and it'll tell you a whole lot. Where it's growing will [also] tell you a whole lot. [If] you can see a scar on the tree where a limb has been, there's gonna be a knot there. You don't want that. You want that clear wood. [Once] I have selected my tree, I'll cut off a six-foot section and take a wedge and sledgehammer, and half the log. Then I'll fourth it. Then I'll eighth it, load it in my truck, and take it to the house.

"I don't have to worry about hauling it to the sawmill or anything like that. I'll take one of these one-eighth sections, which will look pie-shaped, and I'll knock the very inner heartwood out. I'll put this in a break. [A break] is just a forked limb that's elevated where you can stick the wood through it to hold it. [Then] take your froe and mallet, rive this wood, apply pressure to it, and split it out the way you want it. I'll get a piece of wood down small enough for a pitchfork blank [a piece of wood a pattern is drawn on] and then I'll take my shaving horse and, with the drawknife, smooth up one side of it and draw my pattern of the pitchfork. Then I'll take the hewing hatchet and cut almost down to the line. I can cut that out in the rough with the hatchet to get the bulk of the wood off. Then I'll set down on the shaving horse again, and, with my drawknife, I will cut this out right down to the exact shape, relieve the end where the tines are at, and bend them. After this, I will separate the tines where your prongs come out, and then I steam the wood.

"My steaming box is very crude. It's nothing more than four boards about one by eight, six feet long, nailed together and made [into] a long, rectangle-shaped box. Both ends are open, and I set this box up about two feet off the ground. I have a camp stove, and I heat water underneath [the box with] it. I've got a hole cut in the bottom that I pipe steam up into my box with. I put whatever I'm steaming in the box and stop up both ends. The heat and the moisture is what relaxes the wood enough to make it bend. You can oversteam or not steam enough. It's kind of like cooking. You've got to kind of get a knack for it.

"Then I bend the piece in a jig and that gives it its shape. You let it set in there for two to three weeks. Then you can take it out, go back over it with a spokeshave to smooth it up, and put your spreader rods in. I tell everyone that you can make a pitchfork in two and a half or three hours spread out over a month, on account of the different stages you go through. I enjoy going to craft shows and making pitchforks. I can show them all the different stages where they can actually see where it gets into being a pitchfork. It seems like a lot of people appreciate that.

"With our ancestors, whatever you were making determined the types of wood used, because your woods have [different] characteristics. Some wood is real springy and elastic like hickory, white oak, and ash. Those are the main woods I use. If you're using the same tools that they used back then, and you go about making pieces the way they made them, a lot of times it'll tell you what type of wood to use. It's always got a purpose. Your buckeye and your poplar were your main woods in dough bowls. It was soft and easy working, yet durable. Most of your pitchforks were made of hickory, ash, and oak. Ox yokes [are made from] poplar, sassafras, and ash, because they were strong enough, yet they were light in weight. Your woods always have a purpose or reason behind using them. That's the way I see it, and I think that's the way our ancestors saw it.

"Knowing that the majority of my things are just gonna be hung up on the wall to look at, I [still] try to make everything as original as I can. If you actually wanted to use my forks and rakes, you could. My wife says that's too much trouble. I'm too much of a purist. If something looks good on the outside, but is not functional all the way through, I don't have a good feeling about it.

"If a person took pride in his tools, he'd keep them in first-class shape. I use an oil finish on all of my work. I mix linseed oil and turpentine. Sometimes I put varnish with this. A lot of times, you'll find a pitchfork with black-looking stuff on it. That was pine resin that they would melt over the bends of the pitchfork to waterproof it. If you keep a pitchfork in the dry, it's gonna hold its shape good. If it's set out in the weather, it's gonna gradually straighten back out a whole lot, because wood has a memory.

"Once or twice a year, just rub it down with linseed oil, let it soak in, and wipe the excess off. Actually, using a piece will make it more beautiful than just buying it and hanging it up on the wall, because you put the patina in it. The aging of the wood shows the wear from use. If you could find two original antique pieces that were just alike, [except] one of them was put up and never used and [the other] one was used, the one that was used would be more beautiful, to me, than the other one.

"[My tools consist of] a drawknife, a spokeshave, a froe, a mallet, a maul, wedges, wooden gluts made out of dogwood or locust, axes, and hatchets. I use a hewing hatchet a whole lot. It's made just like your broadax, only it's in a hatchet form. I buy some of my tools, and I make a lot of them. You'll run across them at flea markets and auctions. Tools are getting harder to find, and if you find one, it's in such shape that you can't make it functional. I make bow saws, and I have blacksmith friends who reproduce some old tools that I can't buy nowhere. I tell everyone that everything I make is done by hand and with hand tools, except the chainsaw that I cut the tree down with. That's really about the only way you can make them, and make them as genuine as you can.

"Sometimes I have trouble in bending the wood. One of the biggest things that I had trouble with, in making a pitchfork, was getting a good proportional shape. There's so much that you've got to do in the few minutes that you're bending that fork. I can make ten pitchforks, and you'll see a difference in all ten of them. That goes with any handmade piece. No two pieces ever turn out alike. But in my work I never let it bother me. I broke a pitchfork when it was 90 percent done. When I was driving the spreader rods, the little dowels that separate the tines, it caught in the wood somehow and snapped just like you [had] hit it with a hatchet. But I don't let things like that bother me. It's just like getting knocked down. Just get back up and try again. I've basically learned the trade through trial and error and having enough love to want to seek it further.

"A lot of the enjoyment I get is from going out and finding the tree. I can go out sometimes and look a half a day and never find a tree to suit me. At other [times] I can go out and find one in a half an hour and make twenty-five pitchforks. When I find a tree, it almost makes my mouth water, just waiting to get into it and see how it's gonna work. There's nothing like working a good piece of wood.

"I went out and cut a hickory tree to make my bows for the ox yoke I made. Generally, after I get the bows cut out, I take a metal strip, reinforce it, steam it, and bend it around a jig. I use this metal stripping and the steaming to relax the wood and the metal bands to reinforce and keep it from splintering.

"If you're a traditional craftsman, where you make everything by hand, you're gonna be limited for production and shows. I'm about one hundred and eighty miles from home [Lawrenceburg, Kentucky] right now. I've been to Kingsport, Tennessee, and down around the Land Between the Lakes in Kentucky. That's about as far as I've gone. The Museum [of Appalachia in Norris, Tennessee] is a good show. You meet so many fellow craftsmen that you almost become a family. People down here in Tennessee have welcomed me and my wife. People like Bill Henry and Jesse Butcher have done a lot to promote me, encourage me, and give me a lot of confidence. It's just an enjoyment. It's work to a point, but there's more enjoyment than work.

"The most fun thing of all in my type of work is finding a unique object, like a different-shaped pitchfork or something, and making that for the very first time. It's been a hard road mastering this, but I wouldn't have it no other way—I still think the best things in life are free, and I don't think you can beat the beauty in simplicity. That's not with just making things, but that's in living too. If you could make yourself satisfied with that, I think in the long run, you can get a lot more enjoyment out of life."

FARM ANIMALS

"There's not a mule on the hill now."

People in the early 1900s depended on animals. Animals were used for transportation, food, work, and sometimes a sort of money. Farm animals were part of everyday life. Ernest J. Henning recalled, "I had chores that involved animals. We worked with the animals, fed them, and milked the cows. I had three sisters and a brother. Each of us had our own chores to do. I helped my daddy with the cutting of wood and all the farm chores, like feeding the animals."

Gertrude Keener also remembers having many animals at her home. "The year that I was married, we raised our own meat, had our own cattle, and fattened our own hogs. We had two cows to start and had our own milk and butter. We built us a chicken house down here and raised hatching eggs and pullets and sold eggs. We lived hard back then."

Animals helped generations in the past to be self-sufficient. They carried the owners where they needed to go, plowed the garden that produced the food, and sometimes even became the food. Because of the self-sufficient nature of the people, the only reasons to leave the farm were to attend school and church and to buy the few items that could not be raised or made on the farm. This helped previous generations to become a closer family.

Everyone from small children to adults was involved in some way with the animals. Fathers taught sons and daughters how to work with, feed, and tend the animals. This training prepared the children for the future. June Jones told us, "The old man used to put me in the box on the plow stock when I couldn't even walk and keep up. I followed him night and day. I've tinkered with steers all my life."

While we depend on our cars, trucks, and jobs today, importance was placed on the health and care of the animals in the past. Just as we make sure our cars will run and get us where we need to go now, so the people of the past made sure their animals were in good health. If the animals were to get sick, then that resulted in a loss of food and income for the family. As Ernest J. Henning said, "We took care of the animals like they were a part of the family. We took as much care of the animals as we did each other."

The general care of animals was covered in *Foxfire 3*. This chapter is meant to show how important animals were in all aspects of every-day life.

—*Amy S. York*

HORSES

PLATE 119 Adam Foster's horses

Conway Watkins has been working with horses most of his life, and he shared some of his stories with us. "My mother drove a horse to the store. She couldn't back him up. He wouldn't stop. He was a big red horse Daddy had when I was growing up. He was a good workhorse as long as you didn't back him up. He was a good buggy horse and plow horse. We didn't give him a chance to back into much. We knowed what he would do if we backed him up, so we just turned in a circle all of the time. Clayton had dirt streets and plank sidewalks when we had that horse. We were always afraid that if we backed him up, he would back up over the sidewalk and break all the glass in the store.

"A horse can back two-thirds as much weight as he can pull, but a horse hardly ever wants to back up. I never had many to back up. If they did, I'd just slap 'em with the lines to get their attention and get 'em to go on. I've tried to work a few saddle horses, and they back up.

"It's all right to trot a little stump jumper [a saddle horse] when you

get him out on the highways or trail
riding or someplace like that, but I
won't let a big draft horse trot. He
wasn't made to trot, and he can't
stand it."

Estelle Chastain recalls, "We had
horses, but they was always for the
farm. They wasn't just riding horses
or anything like that. They had to
have them on the farm. They used
them for the crops."

TRAINING HORSES

Most people bought horses that
were already trained or broken.
These horses were then kept and
worked until they were too old to
continue. When age set in, farmers

PLATE 120 Conway Watkins

would take the old horses to a
horse trader and trade the older horses in for younger ones. Some people, however, just enjoyed the challenge of training horses themselves.
Hence, they bought green colts and trained them at home.

"I'll be seventy-six the twenty-first of September [1989], and I've
been fooling with horses ever since I was about twelve or fourteen," said
Conway Watkins. "I've been trading horses ever since I first married in
1934. Farming and logging is just about all I've ever done. To make a
living, I've had to work with horses logging and plowing. I worked them
all the time.

"Back when I was growing up, there wasn't many tractors in this
country. We done it all with horses or mules. We used a straight turning
plow and a team of mules to turn the ground. Then we had the cutaway harrow. We cut the ground and fixed it to plant [laid off the rows]
with the laying-off plow (the single foot). We walked behind the turning plow, but we got to ride on the harrows. When we went to riding a
cutaway harrow in that plowed ground, it took three good mules to pull
it all day. They don't make a cutaway harrow for one horse. They're
heavy enough 'til you have to have two [or three horses or mules].

"[When I first get a horse,] I usually handle him, curry [comb] him,
rub him down good, and get him good and gentle. Then I go to putting
the harness on him a piece at a time. I start with the bridle, then put the

collar on, then put the reins on, and [just continue] to put the pieces on. I just work with him until I get him tame, used to me.

"The best thing you do when fooling with a horse is not to be afraid of it. He can tell the difference just as quick as you can. You don't show it if you're afraid of him. Just walk on in [the stable] to him.

"You don't have to hit a horse if you'll be good to him. I just make sure, to start with, that I'm not gonna let him get away from me. When you tie one, tie him with something [that he can't break] where he can't get loose. If he gets loose one time, you will always have trouble. If you're hooking one [to a wagon or a plow], always keep your lines where you can reach and get 'em. Don't never turn him loose. I've seen people back a horse in[to the wagon traces] and start hooking them up and their lines not even fastened. My lines is the first thing I fix, and then I keep 'em where I can get to 'em.

"I put my lines on him, but I don't put them in no rings. I leave them straight back by the horse. I work him that way. You can learn one to rein easier that way than you can if you put the lines up in the rings. He can turn around with you easier. Don't put the lines in no rings on your reins. Leave them loose. You're holding one end [of the reins], and the bit has the other end.

"I break a horse quiet. [I don't like to handle them rough.] Just let them pull a little load first. I had a lot of old truck chains and automobile chains here, and I just hooked the last horse I broke to them chains. I just let them drag. He didn't pay much attention to them. I made two trips up there [on the trail] with him hooked to them log chains.

"I like to work them to a sled. That's the best thing to hook 'em to. That's better than a wagon or anything else, and I can ride on the sled. I've got me a good seat on it, and I just sit down. That's the reason I use that sled.

"[To break a horse to pull a load,] I start 'em off light and just keep getting [the load] heavier and heavier. I go off with the sled around here, and wherever I can find a rock, I just pick it up and put it on the sled. I just keep on driving until I've got a pretty good load. That's the way I start one off.

"If a horse's mouth is sore, it's because someone was mean with the bit or was too rough with it. The horse will get over [its mouth being sore] if you'll put the right kind of bit on it and handle your lines right. They'll get over that.

"I don't use too rough a bit, just a medium one. I've got a bit out there that don't hurt a horse's mouth. It's got a pretty long shank and three different places that you can fasten up your lines."

WORKING HORSES

As recently as forty years ago, there was no such thing as a pleasure animal. Every animal had a purpose and a job (or jobs) to do. Horses were used season after season, from pulling plows in the spring to sleds in the winter. Aside from the daily farmwork, they were also expected to take the family to town in the wagon and to pull the buggy to church on Sunday.

"I train a horse to start a wagon steady," Conway Watkins told us. "I don't let it jump into the harness [jerk the wagon as it starts pulling]. After you've used them for logging, they don't start a wagon right. They want to jerk it. If they jump into it one time, just stop 'em and try all over.

"If the horses are pulling a wagon up a hill, stop them to rest. Lots of people say that you've got to get over this pull here. If you get stopped, you can't get started. If you've got too much on the wagon to get going again, then you had too much to start with. Pull them short and rest them short. Let them rest for short periods of time at several intervals as they are pulling a load up a hill. It doesn't take but a few minutes for a horse to catch its breath; then you can go on again. I learn them to hold that wagon going downhill and uphill. If I stop them in a steep place going uphill, I make them hold it and not let it roll back. When I go downhill, I spread the horses in the tongue as far as they can be spread. I go downhill that way. The harness will help hold the wagon back off the horses.

"I worked my own horses [whenever I was logging]. I built a horse lot where they could get water and a shed big enough for them to put their feet and head in out of bad weather. [I'd leave them there] and get in the car and go home every night and be back in the next morning.

"The last that I cut and logged was on Warwoman for fifteen dollars an hour. I had my own team of three horses. Two of them were about twelve years old, and the other one was about sixteen. They were just big workhorses. I logged for ol' man John Turner about 103,000 feet [of lumber] that year with horses.

"The first thing I had to do was to trim the skidding trail [a trail for dragging logs out] and clear the J-holes. A J-hole is a clearing on the side of the trail just big enough for the horses to turn into off the skidding trail. Sometimes the J-hole is on the left and sometimes on the right. You run your horses off the road into the J-hole. The horses turn off, and the logs are released to go off down the hill. [Sometimes the horses make their own J-holes] when they want to get out of the way of the logs. The horses hit them J-holes too, boys! You train one, and he knows what he's doing. I've had one or two to pass it up, and they didn't like that too good—them logs chasing 'em on down the hill.

"The horses age fast when you go to logging because it strains them. They have to pull hard all the time."

MULES

Some would say the mule was king of farm life at one time. This importance stemmed from the versatility associated with the animal. It was able to perform most of the same jobs that cattle, oxen, and horses could accomplish.

Several people we interviewed remembered the multiple uses for the mule. Around the smaller farm, mules were good for plowing, laying off rows for planting, dragging harrows, mowing and raking hay, and pulling sleds loaded with cordwood, stovewood, corn, and other sundries. On larger farms, mules were handy for pulling reapers, bailers, combines, potato diggers, and "groundhog" thrashers. They were useful in cattle roundups as well. Settlers, developers, and other commercial businessmen used mules for clearing land, snaking logs for tan bark, pulling crossties and telephone poles, and turning corn crushers and sorghum mills. Mules also pulled hearses, carried the mail, pulled dirt pans in construction work, and turned grinders for clay to be made into pottery. The list of uses is seemingly endless. A local legend tells that some mules were so well trained that they could haul sugar and malt to the mountain stills alone, and then walk out alone, laden with the finished moonshine.

Of the mule's proficiency, Ada Kelly wrote a letter stating, "To begin with, [the mule] helped in the clearing of land of timber so that agricultural products could be planted to produce food for people and animals. It helped to drag logs off the land for building houses and barns, and hauling the logs to building sites. This was in the age of log houses, before sawmills came into use. After they began sawing logs into lumber for buildings, the mule was busy dragging logs out of woods and hauling them to the mills. After they were sawed, they were loaded on wagons (which had been hewn out of wood) and pulled by mules many miles to some place where they could be dried, dressed, and readied for building houses. Then the faithful old mule would haul the lumber back to the building sites.

"In his spare time, he plowed land for crops of many varieties, and then helped to get the planting and cultivating done. Then he was there to help harvest and haul the crops to a place to be stored for winter use.

"Everything that was too heavy to be moved from place to place by man was moved by the mule.

"In the horse and buggy days, it was most often mules instead of horses that was hitched to the buggy, wagon, or whatever the vehicle might be. It was always convenient to hitch up the mule, or put a saddle on him to go to church or anywhere else that it was too far to walk."

Because mules were so adaptable, they often brought a high price. Farms in Kentucky and Tennessee began to specialize in breeding them. Their young mules were taken south and sold in places like Franklin, North Carolina, where, claims R. L. Edwards of Clayton, his uncle once paid $400 for an untrained pair—and that was in a day when a dollar was worth considerably more than it is now. In fact, many claim that a good pair of mules used to cost more than an equally good pair of horses.

The cost led many farmers to begin breeding their own mules and breeding mules for their neighbors. Grover Wilson, a resident of Clayton and onetime sheriff, talked to us about this for several hours. He told us, "Some of them mules raised in this county [Rabun] were huge. Mr. Bill Blalock's grandfather (Uncle Jesse) once had a pair that weighed twenty-seven hundred pounds. Most of the mules in the county were homegrown. There were two or three jacks, and they were owned by Mr. Jim Fisher, Mr. Sam Mitchell, and me. These were carried to farms by request and bred to farmers' mares. After the mare foal produced a mare mule or a horse mule, the breeder would come back around and collect a ten-dollar fee."

Another reason why farmers in Rabun County bred their own mules, aside from convenience and thriftiness, was their belief that mules from Kentucky, Tennessee, and Missouri, though bigger, were not as tough as the smaller "mountain mule." Farmers in the Cotton Belt sometimes preferred the mountain mule too, having great respect for its stamina.

Farmers that did not want to raise their own mule could always buy one from one of the traders that came through the area at regular intervals with a drove of mules.

A favorite time for trading, buying, or just looking was on "Court

Day." The Superior Court convened in Clayton on the fourth Monday in February and the fourth Monday in August. The sessions lasted from four to five days each and drew people from all over the county. Not only were the sixty or seventy jurors present, but also spectators who often came in mobs to watch the excitement—especially if there was a case on the agenda that had captured everyone's interest. Some people came from as far as twenty miles away, and since there were no cars, it was foolish to try to commute back and forth. These people stayed in the local hotels or in the homes of the townsfolk.

Due to the size of the occasion, it was always a good time to buy, sell, or trade for mules and other needed supplies. Mr. Wilson's father often bought mule colts for $75 to $100 apiece when they were old enough to break, and then he carried them to Anderson, South Carolina, to sell again at a small profit.

An extra-good pair of mules often brought $400 to $450, with mare mules bringing $20 more apiece if they were better looking, more "blocky," and less contrary than the males. An average pair of mares commonly went for $200 to $250.

Using mules, as opposed to other livestock, had several drawbacks. Esco Pitts shared his thoughts on several of the disadvantages with us. "The use of mules was slow, grueling labor. Mules had to be fed daily throughout the year, whether they were working or not. Equipment such as traces, harnesses, collars, plow points, and the like had to be kept in perfect working order. And even working from sundown to sunup, the best mules could only cultivate four acres a day. The work could seem endless with two hundred acres to be cultivated."

The expression "stubborn as a mule" was also accurate in many cases. Mr. Pitts remembers many mules who would not go near the end of a field if a ditch was there. The rows would have to be left unfinished, for there was nothing anyone could do that would make the mule continue. And, at other times, they would run away with him and be almost impossible to stop.

Conversations with other farmers in the county turned up other disadvantages. Some reminded us that mules get tired while tractors don't. After two or three good rows, you have to rest a mule and the man left behind him!

Mules are far more expensive than most people will admit. They cost about a dollar a day to feed [a quart of corn or five ears, plus about ten pounds of hay]. In the spring and summer, they can pasture, but simply to have pastureland, one must figure in the cost of fertilizer, weed control, fencing, and other expenses. Wilbur Maney, a former Rabun County extension agent, added, "Figure a mule is costing you about a dollar a day to keep up; that makes about three hundred and sixty-five dollars a year. Add to that the repair for the equipment and shelter for the animal during the winter. Nowadays, for the same price, you could buy a six- or seven-horsepower Sears-Roebuck tractor that would do the same amount of work and do it faster—and after your initial investment, it would only cost you gas and oil. Where a mule can only plow an acre or two a day, a tractor can do the same in about thirty minutes."

PLATE 122 Wilbur Maney

Grover Wilson cited the example of a friend who had once kept many mules. When asked if he still had them, the friend replied, "There's not a mule on the hill now. I just can't pay a man sixty-five cents an hour to plow a flop-eared mule." He went to tractors.

Mr. Wilson explained that "even if a farmer wanted to keep mules, he would not be able to get anyone to help him plow, not even at a dollar an hour. The work is just too tough. No one wants to do it with mules when there are easier ways."

Other farmers added that even on the smallest farms, where crops are grown not for sale but for home consumption during the winter, mules are uneconomical especially considering the price of today's small farm tractors. When asked if these small farms could even afford the Sears-Roebuck tractor, Wilbur Maney replied, "No, but most of them can't afford the mule either. They probably shouldn't even be farming."

Esco Pitts went to work for Rabun Gap–Nacoochee School and was soon named the farm supervisor of the school. As such, he was in the position of ultimate responsibility for the care and upkeep of the animals. His insights into working with mules were vivid. When he arrived at the school, they had two mules named Pete and George and two cows named Blanche and Blackie. Pete was blind in one eye. Before long, the school had more mules [Kit, Mac, Bob, Mandy, Red, and Blackie]. The school was almost run by mule power. The sorghum was ground by using mules. Building foundations and basements were dug out by mules, slip pans, and scoops. Logs were snaked by mules. Everything that had to be hauled—wood, corn, rye being taken to the stacking station for threshing—was hauled by mules.

In farming, Mr. Pitts remembered Mandy, with whom he could lay off a long row "just as straight as a rifle barrel." Two hundred acres were under cultivation, and he could remember seeing eight mules at a time in the fields, each followed by one of the students in the school. Plowing was done in the fall then, to turn the stubble under. If one waited until spring to plow, the ground would be so hard it would be twice as hard to work. Rye and Simpson clover were sowed on September 1. Mr. Pitts recalled the rest of the fall schedule. "Andrew Ritchie, then president of the school, would stand slowly in the dining hall and say, 'This is our program: rye to sow, fodder to take, silos to fill, syrup to make.' "

In the spring, the mules dragged the cutaway harrows out into the fields and readied them for seed. Then the rows were laid off with a mule-drawn "shovel plow" or "laying-off plow," and the planting would commence.

Bill Gravley told us, "I have always heard a mule will live all of its life just to kick you one time. So I was really kinda afraid of mules. I grew up on a little farm—about twelve or fourteen acres—and we always had a horse up until I was about thirteen years old. [Then] Daddy bought a mule, and that mule was about the same age I was—about twelve or thirteen years old. It was a mare mule. A little mule, it weighed about nine hundred pounds. To start with, I was afraid of it. I was afraid it would kick me or bite me or whatever, because I had heard so many stories about mules. But it turned out, she was better than the horses were. She was gentler, easier to work with. I learned how to plow with her, learned how to use a turning plow, and learned how to drive a one-horse wagon. I used her for gathering corn, hauling wood, pulling poles out of the woods for heater wood, and what have you. My grandpa said I could do more with her than anyone else could because I treated her easy and gentle. I didn't holler and beat and knock like a lot of folks did. I reckon she learned to trust me, and she went anywhere I wanted to go and did anything I wanted her to do. I just had a good relationship with a mule.

"We had her for about three or four years. It was always my job to feed and take care of the mule. She got out one night. We hadn't had her long, and we had to get out and try to find her. We did find her and got her back to pasture, no problem. She wasn't hard to catch or anything like that, she had just got out. We found her and brought her back. That night, I was coming back from the barn barefooted, and the old house I was raised in had about seven steps up to the front porch of that house, and coming back from that barn there was a big copper-head right at the bottom of those steps. I stepped on that thing bare-footed, and the next step I took, I was standing in the middle of the front porch! I missed the steps completely. Then they got a light out there and killed that snake.

"A couple of years after that, the mule got sick. We believed that she got some molded hay or something, and it gave her colic, and she died from that. But while she was sick, I remember how we tried to keep her going. The veterinarian came and gave her some medicine. Daddy gave her medicine that he knew how to give. He took a Coke bottle and mixed medicine in it and stuck the neck of the bottle down the throat. We kept her moving because Daddy said if she laid down she would die, or she would roll and get her intestines messed up. So we tried to keep her up and a-going, but she'd try to lay down anyway. The veterinarian came, and he had a bull shocker, and he could get her up with that bull shocker by punching her with it and making her get up. After he left, the only thing we could get her up with was a power saw; he remembered she was scared of a power saw. He run up behind where she was laying with the power saw and cranked it up and revved up the motor on the power saw real loud, and the mule jumped up, but when she did, she hit me. She throwed her front foot out in front of her, and that foot landed right on one of my feet, and when she come up, her weight was on that foot, and her head come right up under my chin. Like to tore me in two and knocked me down on the ground.

"I got over that, but she didn't. She died that night. I guess that was the loss of a first love. She got me kicked before she died, even if it was with her head and her front foot."

"I know about mules. I used to plow them," J. C. Stubblefield stated. "We had a mule one time; it knowed just as well as you did when eleven o'clock come. If you was out there in the field laying off or anything you was doing, that mule would go to the barn with you. I tried not to let him go to the barn down there. I thought I would just stall it down. I had a lay-off plow. I set that in the ground just as deep as it would go, and that mule just went right on with me. It went to the barn. When it come eleven o'clock, you'd better be ready to go. The mule was like that when we got it. Somebody else must have fed it at that time. He was like that all the time we had him. You couldn't stop it, wasn't no way to stop it. But I got to where, just a few minutes before eleven, I'd take the dog-gone mule to the barn and feed him. Of course, I guess somebody else had done that too.

"I had another mule; you had to give that mule a whopping about ever' spring, 'cause it got to where it wouldn't work hardly. It wouldn't go like off the branch bank. We had a good place to walk, you know. It wouldn't go in there, and I was going across the branch to plow some over there. He wouldn't go. I picked up a stick there, and I just mauled that thing over the head. He got to where, when I hit him, he'd go across."

SHEEP

PLATE 123 Terry Dickerson

Terry Dickerson remembered caring for sheep when he was younger. "We had free-range back when I was young. All of these mountains were free-range, and you had to fence your crops in [to keep the cows and other livestock out]. Everybody had sheep, and that called for fetching them from the mountains. Brother Jim and I had to fetch the sheep when we were boys. Then, when I was thirteen years old, my dad died [and we had to take on a lot more chores].

"Brother Jim and I built a sheep pen, and we had a black sheep over there that wore a bell. We would go over there to feed her, and one of us would get on that sheep's back while she was eating her corn, and she'd just twist around and try to shake us off. She'd leave her head in that trough still eating just as intelligent as a pet dog.

"A lot of time in the fall of the year, we would go out and hunt the sheep. [Sometimes, though, they'd come on in by themselves.] The black sheep wore the bell, and I remember I woke up early one morning, and I heard the bell ringing right up there on that ridge. She brought all the sheep in. We had twelve or fifteen of them then, and that old mother sheep—when grass or stuff was bit down in the woods—she'd come home for feed, and the others would follow that bell just like people will go to a bell now. That sheep lived 'til the black wool on her back had turned white, and the wool around her head was white.

"Brother Jim and I would feed the sheep, and we would help shear the sheep. When Mother had to take over [after Dad died], she sheared the sheep and carded the wool, and she rolled it up in rolls about the size around of a broom handle. She'd spin that wool and knit socks and sweaters and winter caps for us children. She'd work 'til ten or eleven o'clock after we went to bed at night spinning that old spinning wheel. It's still upstairs right now. I can hear it hit now. When she'd pull that wool out, she'd get a long [continuous] thread just as true as it is today."

Jesse Ray Owens recalled, "We had hogs, cows, and sheep. We kept enough sheep so we would have wool to make us sweaters and socks. We carded our own wool. My mother spun it. She had two or three [spinning wheels]. The parts of one of them is still around here somewhere [over there in the old house]. She's spun many a night, and she knitted our socks from that wool. I knitted several pairs of socks myself. I had to learn how. I done everything else, but I never could turn the heel."

DUCKS

Addie Bleckley remembered having ducks on her family farm. "Mother raised ducks so she could pick their feathers to make our feather beds and pillows. We didn't have to do anything but catch them and hold them and pick out handfuls of feathers. Every time we'd pull, they'd go 'quack, quack.' I guess it did hurt them.

"When we got through plucking, we'd turn them loose. We'd wash the feathers and put them out in the sun. The ducks would grow more feathers. I guess it was just made for us to pick them that way. They didn't bleed, but they sure could quack when we'd pull out a handful. We had about twelve ducks, I guess, but I don't know how many

PLATE 124 Addie Bleckley

feathers we'd get off them each time. It took a pretty good while for them to grow their feathers back, and then we'd pick them again."

Gertrude Keener recalled, "We had ducks. A lot of fun that I had in the mornings was going duck egg hunting. We had about a dozen ducks, and they would get nests all around our pond and lay their eggs. I enjoyed getting out real early in the morning hunting those eggs."

CATTLE

"People would hit the mountains for making a living," Clarence Lusk remembered. "You see, they could range their cattle, grow hogs and sheep, and fence in their little field. They'd build a fence around their gardens and just turn the cattle and hogs out in the woods and the mountains [to graze]. That's the way they made their living.

"I remember going back in the mountains with my daddy cow hunting. The woods was just full of cows and hogs. We'd mark [our animals] in the ear with so many splits. Some people would brand 'em, but all I ever knowed was cropping them—cutting certain notches out of the ears. I know some people who had as high as three hundred head of

hogs up there and every one of 'em marked. They'd have big gangs of cattle too.

"People used to come down the road here [on the way to market]. There was a man from North Carolina, and he had cow dogs. He [raised] a lot of cattle back in the mountains, and he'd come down through here with a string of cattle. [He and his helpers] rode their horses, and they'd have a big gang of cattle in front of

PLATE 126 Clarence Lusk

'em. Them dogs would stay out on the outside, and if one of the cows [started] to get out of the road, that dog would run down around yonder and put him back in the road. He'd keep that cow in the road. [They were] taking their cattle to slaughter and selling 'em."

Terry Dickerson also remembered working with cows. "We had bells on the cows too. When we'd hunt a milk cow, we'd listen for that bell. You could hear it for half a mile. We knew right where to go. When that bell began to rattle and she'd leave out, the rest of the cows would follow. They had learned. Animal life is sensible. It was interesting to us back then [to watch how the animals took care of themselves].

"[All the cows were out in the mountains together.] They had marks on them, and we used to check the brands and bring ours home. I've walked from Wolffork Valley up behind Taylor's Chapel Church to drive down milk cows. Quite a walk. That would take just about a solid hour."

Minnie Dailey said, "We raised cows and milked 'em. We had steers to work in the fields and haul with. My father used the steers most of the time, because he loved them more than he did the horses. I could catch those steers by the horns, 'cause they was gentle, and we could take a rope and tie it around their necks, and they'd lead like a cow."

Belle Dryman told us, "If you tend t' cattle like I do, I guess they will come when you call 'em. Mine do. I think I'll keep that white one over there, just t' see what kind of cow hit'll make. I don't git much milk. We sell three or four calves a year, and when the cows get older, we sell them too.

"We've had cattle all my life. I turned them into the cornfield and graze them in the morning. I stay out there with them. Sometimes I piece quilts when I'm with them."

PLATE 127 Belle Dryman feeding her pig

DRIVING CATTLE

Because there was no stock law, cattle were allowed to roam freely. To keep them from eating all the crops, getting into fields, and roaming the community, farmers had to drive the herd into the mountains. Here the cattle foraged for survival upon tree leaves, grass, and new sprouts. Each summer, farmers drove the herd to the range. In the fall, they drove them back so as to have the cattle close enough to keep them fed tops of corn through the harsh winters.

"We had a lot of chores when I was growing up. We grew meat and stock," Kermit Thompson remembered. "There wasn't a stock law at that time, and we would drive our cows to the mountains. Most of the time it was to Black Mountain, right over there next to Tate City. We would run them to the mountains through the summer and then bring them back in the fall of the year. Sometimes the cows would get too far out of range, and we would have to go back up there and herd them back where they belonged. We didn't have a car, so we had to walk up there."

Adam Foster told us, "In later days, I got to be the one that had to go to the mountains in the summer season to look about the cattle. Dad sent me one mornin'. He said, 'You get up in the mornin', Adam, and

PLATE 128 Kermit Thompson

go up there and get that big jersey cow.' Said, 'She's supposed to have had a calf a week ago, and we ain't never went and brought her in.' Well, I knew she was gentle, and he did too. I knew right where she run—pretty close. He said, 'You can go up there and be back by eight o'clock. Just get up, saddle your horse, grab you a rope, and go on.' Said, 'You don't need to wait for breakfast. Get your breakfast when you come back. You won't be gone over an hour and a half.' It wasn't but 'bout five miles up there. I went up there, and that cow was gone. I couldn't find her nowhere. She'd had her calf, all right. But she was gone. And I hunted, and I hunted, and I hunted. I knowed all that country. Found all the other cattle but couldn't find her. She had a big bell on. And I never did find her that day.

"I come on back home and told my daddy. I said, 'I put in all day, and I couldn't find her.' 'Well,' he said, 'you go back in the mornin' and get one of them old Smith brothers to go with you up the mountain. He knows the big mountains back there. He'll help you hunt that cow.' I did. I went on back up there. Got one of 'em to go with me. I got up there, and he said, 'Yeah, I'll go with you.' I said, 'Well, we may have to hunt all day, now.' He said, 'That's all right.'

"He went on with me. Hunted, hunted, and hunted and never found the cow. And after a while, I happened to hear a bell 'bout two or three miles away. I knew the bell was on that cow. I could tell the difference of the ring of every cowbell we had. So I said, 'She's in that old field right down over yonder where she used to run.' We went over there, and she was right there pickin' where she used to run all the time. Well, there wasn't no calf there, but we knowed she'd had the calf. She'd have to go to the calf. And she was two miles or better away from that calf, the cow was. She hid it way on back in them mountains two miles. She did it to keep us from finding her.

"After the calf got three or four days old, and we hadn't found it, the cow didn't want us messing with it. She wanted to raise it wild. So I just followed this cow. I'd keep about a half a mile behind her, so she wouldn't think I was a-watchin' her, and she'd go back to the baby. Well, I just kept a-watchin' and listenin' to the bell. So after a while, I seen her turn a trail that went back up in the mountains where it was flat. And she turned up that road.

"I told the man that was with me, I said, 'Now, that calf won't follow the cow. We'll have to do somethin'. I'll just put the calf on the horse, and I'll get on behind it, and the cow will follow me and the calf off the mountain.' And she did. I put that calf up in the saddle, and I got on behind it, and down through there I went with that calf in the saddle. And here the old cow come down behind us, the man drivin' her."

TRAINING STEERS

Many people used oxen or steers to work around the farm. While they were slow, they were also strong, durable animals. They had to be trained to pull plows and other farm equipment and to move appropriately to the common commands of "gee" [go right], "haw" [go left], "whoa," and "get up."

Numerous Marcus explained, "I used to plow oxen all the time before I got my horses. I'd rather plow a horse 'cause he's a little faster, but you can do just as good plowing with oxen as you can a horse. There's a whole lot of difference in working oxen than horses. Oxen are slower and they're contrary. They'd get hot and take a notion to run off to the branch, and if you wasn't big enough to hold them, why then they'd take you too.

"Me and Dad used to have lots of fun breaking a yoke of oxen. I got awful tickled at Dad one time. We had a yoke of oxen broke, and they plowed good double.

"Dad said, 'Well, now, it's getting about time for us to get ready to start laying off and plantin' corn. You've got to learn these oxen to work single sometime.'

"We put one of 'em up there on the hill, and we was dragging wood with him. He started down the hill toward the road, and he was working the finest you ever did see. We had already pulled three loads with him. All of a sudden, he took a notion he wanted to run. Boys! He kicked up his heels and right down that road he went. Dad was going around and around a bush. He was gonna try and run him into the bush so he couldn't go. 'Bout that time, Dad got wrapped around the bush, and that little ol' steer turned right back in below the bush, and Dad run right over top of that steer.

"Dad said, 'Son, look out! You're gonna get run over here directly.' He called that little ol' steer his son. That tickled me. I laughed at him, but Dad held him. He wasn't gonna turn him loose, all right. We thought we had him all right for laying off and planting corn, and then he kicked up his heels and off down the hill he went. We used to have a lot of fun with them things when they'd run away with us.

"Sometimes you'd have to put chains around an ox's nose to keep 'im from running away with you. If the oxen didn't have any horns, then you made a halter and put chains around his nose to stop him. If they had horns, you could tie a head chain on them. Just take a small chain and put around the horns, and if he started to run, give him a jerk and that would slow him down. They wouldn't pull much against the chain. If they got their head down, they could go right on. They didn't pay no attention to much. I used blocks sometimes. They're like reins on a horse. They're just made out of sassafras wood. Or I'd use yokes. I made them myself. It's according to what kind of places you're in and depends on what you're doing."

June Jones has been training steers all his life. He told us, "My dad would use his steers for logging, farming, whatever he needed it for. I was probably four or five years old when the old man give me two calves. They was just mixed-up steers. I have no idea what breed they was. They were just mixed. I didn't have a pair of paired steers until I had a pair of guernseys. They was registered guernseys. I had a pair of holsteins, and I guess they was registered, because they came out of the dairy.

"I have no idea how many pairs I've had. I've had a few that I killed for beef that I couldn't manage. If they don't do to suit me, Blalock's Meat Processing can take care of them.

"Before you can say you got them broke, they have got to be about two or three years old. They got to get about two years old.

"I use cotton lines on the steers, and when I start to drive them, I just put the lines on them and start driving. Mostly, I just play with them— just hook them to the wagon. I hauled all my wood up off the creeks down here with them. That's the biggest thing I do with them. I just play with them.

"I make my yokes, wagon shafts, and everything else. I just make my own. I want everything to be old-time. You can make them out of a lot of different kinds of wood. Hickory and locust is the best thing to make a yoke out of. The only thing that I can get to work to make bows out of is white oak.

"When I put the yokes on steers, I just throw it across their necks and run the bow up by their necks. The last pair of steer that I had, I hauled just like dogs. I could just back up there and lower the tailgate, and they'd crawl in. I don't know if I will ever get the

PLATE 129 June Jones placing a white oak bow into the yoke

PLATE 130 "When I put the yokes on steers, I just throw it across their necks and run the bow up by their necks." —June Jones

ones I'm working with now broke like that or not. Those others I took to work with me every day I went. Those guernseys, I took them with me to work and turned them loose like dogs and put them out. They'd loafer around, and when I got ready to come to the house, all I had to do was holler for them, and they would just load themselves.

"I like to work with steers because I can just do more with them. An old horse, he'll just prance around and jump around. An old mule, he'll work for two or three years just to get to kick you once.

"I could put them to the plow, to the planter. I planted it, plowed it, done it all with those holsteins, just like they do now with tractors. They'd do it slower, but I'm slower too."

BEEF PREPARATION

Slaughterhouses, meat-processing plants, and packing houses were not in existence in the early 1900s; therefore, beef preparation, in its entirety, was done at home.

Terry Dickerson remembered preparing the beef after the animal was killed. "We butchered our beef in the wintertime," he said. "We generally dried our beef. We'd hang up the meat and let it drain, and we'd put it in something like a cheesecloth to protect it from the flies and gnats. We'd hang it over the big wood range in the kitchen to dry. That stove would heat the whole room, and we hung the beef in there. It wasn't too bad to keep. It was all the way we had. There wasn't many people who dried beef. It took quite a bit of work to take care of it, and it was pretty small stuff in those days. They didn't butcher an animal after it got over five hundred pounds. It was too big. Now they butcher some of them weighing nine hundred and even eleven hundred pounds. Animals [like that] were too big for us to butcher. It had to be really small stuff; something we could handle. Something that big, you couldn't dry it all out. There'd be moisture around the bones for months."

Garnet Lovell also told us about preparing meat. The first thing Garnet does is cut up a hindquarter of beef. Garnet said, "You can't dry it with the bone in it. The bone will give it a taste or something. It's not any good. We never did dry the bone, and I have dried lots of beef in my life. And we never would dry any of the forequarter. There is too much bone in the forequarter. We would always can that, or salt it and hang it out and eat off it while it was fresh. In cold weather, it will last for a month or six weeks all right.

"[You dry the meat in big chunks, but] the chunks won't weigh but about three or four pounds when they get dried. [My wife's father] used to cut it up in much bigger pieces. [I want it] to dry fast, so I [don't] cut it as heavy as he did.

"And you'd never cut it into strips. The old people said it didn't have the flavor. If the meat was smoked, hickory was the wood used. I don't recall ever seeing a big beef smoked. I think the only time they smoked it was if it got warm weather. They'd smoke it to keep the flies out of their smokehouse. I don't think they intended to smoke it [to make it have any special sort of flavor or anything]."

After the meat has been cut up, it must be salted down. Garnet sprinkles it with regular meat salt and doesn't use any spices or other seasonings. He does this while the animal heat is still in the meat. Garnet said, "In the past, within four or five hours after the beef was shot, it was salted."

You can tell by looking at it when the meat is ready. There will be no water or blood coming out, and the meat will be dark. The process usually takes about two days, but if the weather is wet, it will take about a week.

PLATE 131 Garnet Lovell cuts up the beef in chunks

After the meat has taken salt, Garnet cuts a hole in the meat and slides it on sweet birch sticks and hangs it about six feet above a fireplace. It usually takes about four weeks to dry. When the meat has dried, he puts it in bags and hangs it up in any dry place. "Now, this, when it's dry, will keep 'til next fall. I've been in homes when they'd have that attic up here hanging full [of] turkey breast and everything," Garnet told us. He said you could also dry deer meat this way.

The only hindquarter meat not dried is that with too much bone, with gristle, or with fat, which keeps the dried meat from being lean enough. Garnet didn't dry the T-bone section, for example, since it has too many bones.

We asked Garnet what he did with the meat that was left on the bone. He replied, "What she'll [his wife, Blanche] do is put it in that big pressure cooker she has got, and cook it off, and then put it in containers and put it in the freezer. We don't need it right now. They ain't no use in throwing it away. No, we don't want to throw anything away. We'll just cook the meat off it."

The fat from the meat may be used in several different ways. Some of it used to be rendered into tallow. Garnet said, "We don't do anything with it [ourselves, but] it makes good shoe grease, [and] old people used to grease the bottoms of kids' feet and chests with it for croup."

BEEF RECIPES

OLD-FASHIONED MEAT LOAF

1½ pounds ground beef
¼ teaspoon black pepper
1 cup tomato juice
2 teaspoons salt
3 cups oatmeal or crushed saltine crackers
2 eggs, well beaten
¼ cup applesauce
¼ cup chopped onion

Combine all ingredients and mix thoroughly. Pack firmly in a loaf pan and bake at 350°F for 1 hour.
—*Margaret Norton*

BEEF SOUP

2 pounds beef, cubed
6 tomatoes
10 carrots
8 Irish potatoes
1 teaspoon salt
Pepper to taste

Cook beef until tender. Add tomatoes, carrots, potatoes, salt, and pepper. Cover with water and cook until vegetables are tender.
   —*Bertha Waldroop*

BRUNSWICK STEW

1 pound chopped or ground beef
1 large onion, chopped
2 cups canned tomatoes
1 cup tomato catsup
$\frac{1}{2}$ cup green pepper, chopped
2 cups fresh, canned, or frozen corn
1 teaspoon sugar
1 teaspoon vinegar
Salt and pepper to taste

Brown beef and onion together. Add tomatoes, catsup, and green pepper. Cover and cook slowly for 30 minutes. Add corn and seasonings and stir well. Cook slowly for another 30 minutes. Stir often, and add water if stew becomes too thick.
   —*Clyde Burrell*

PLATE 132 Clyde Burrell

To expand the above recipe to serve a large crowd or to can a large quantity:
   25 pounds beef
   20 pounds pork
   8 pounds ham
   12 quarts corn
   12 quarts tomatoes
   6 or more onions

Some people put sage in their Brunswick stew.
   —*Lettie Chastain*

Blanche Lovell said, "Slice off a little piece of dried beef the thickness of a fifty-cent piece. Let it soak in water just a little, until it is soft. Then take it out and roll it in flour and fry it, and then you have a piece of regular steak. Or lay it out in the hot grease and cook it until it is tender, and then make milk gravy on top of that. That is the way they used to do it fifty years ago, and still do it that way today. If you are going to stew it, just throw it in water with vegetables in it. But who'd want to stew such good meat as this? It's better fried."

MILKING COWS

Every farm had at least one cow just for the purpose of obtaining milk and milk products. Each morning and evening, farm families across the Southern Appalachians went to the barn to milk the cows. Because the milk cows were milked twice daily, they were never taken to the range with the rest of the herd. Apart from milk, these cows served another important purpose. Each year, they were bred and had one calf. These calves were then raised for milk cows, brood cows, bulls, trained as steers, slaughtered as beef, or sold.

Minyard Conner shared one of his stories with us. "When the children was growing up, we had three or four milking cows—seven head of cattle total, you know—and a mule, horses, and chickens—just name it. Lessie [his wife] always liked cats, and we had three or four cats here. Every time the boys would go to the barn to milk, the cats would follow 'em. The boys would go to milking, and the cats would get down and just open their mouths and let the milk spurt right in. I've also seen the boys just a-spurting milk at one another up there. You know how boys'll do!"

Edith Cannon told us about her early married life. "Robert and I owned a cow. We put it up there in Bill O'Neal's pasture. Robert built a barn to put the cow in. So we had plenty of milk and butter. We milked it every day. We had to milk the cow twice a day. We carried the milk and put it in a box down in the spring to keep it cold. Of course, the spring was nothing compared to the refrigerator that we have these days. We thought the milk was cold. The spring kept it good until supper. What we didn't use for supper would go into our churn to make buttermilk and butter. Robert and I also sold milk to our neighbors who lived down in a little old house right below us. You know, people couldn't go to the store and buy milk like everyone does today. We sold sweet milk for ten cents every half of a gallon. I believe it was a nickel per gallon of buttermilk."

CHURNING BUTTER

Estelle Chastain has been churning butter for many years. "You have to have a churn jar and pour your [sweet] milk [whole milk—not sweetened condensed milk] in the churn jar, and if you want it to clabber [become thick by souring] pretty quick, you put a quart of buttermilk in—that's in with your sweet milk. Whenever it clabbers, it will all be thick, and so you just turn the jar over enough to see if it turns loose of the jar. Then churn it.

"Whenever you take your butter out of it [the churn], whatever is left in the jar is your buttermilk. Then for the taking up of the butter, you have to wash your hands. You have to wash your hands in like laundry soap or that butter will stick all over your hands—we had some laundry soap like we have now when I was growing up. It wasn't quite as strong as what we've got now. You have to wash your hands in that and rinse them in cold water.

"If you had something with holes in it that could dip a pretty good handful of the butter, you could use that and not have to put your hands in it. But I always fixed it like I'm a-telling you.

"You have to have a bowl to put your butter in. Then whenever you get all of the butter off of the milk, you have to put some cold water in with your butter and work it. And your butter will be kinda stiff where it will all be together.

"You'd have to churn it whenever it was cool if you could, because if it gets hot, the butter will get kinda thin. It won't mold as good as it will if it's cold. Some cows, their butter will really be firm, while others feels nearly like a grease is in it.

"[How much milk you use is] according to the churn jar that you got—what size it is. But I don't like to churn any more than two gallons. That pretty well fills up a three- or four-gallon jar; it would be half full or more than that.

"[How much butter you get] is just according to what kind of a butter cow you've got. Sometimes off of two gallon of milk, you'll get maybe four pints of butter. Because that is just half a pound—a pint is.

"[Churning] was always something you had to do at my home. Where I was raised, you had to put up with churning.

"The reason I'm not churning anymore is because people have given 'em [the cows] stuff [medicine] to purify the milk, and whenever they do that, why, then, whenever you churn it, you don't make no butter. You can't get it to churn; it won't even clabber."

CHICKENS

PLATE 133 Mary Cabe feeding her chickens

Claude Darnell said, "We had our own chickens to lay eggs. I tell you, I've carried eggs from right over here in the field there to Dillard for eight cents a dozen. I took ever'one I could carry and brought back as much stuff as you can buy for five dollars now."

Claude's wife, Edith, affirmed, "We bought a lot of stuff with eggs. We used eggs as money sometimes. Lots of time when we went to buy groceries, we would have nine and ten dozen."

Edith Cannon disclosed, "We hardly ever ate the eggs [that the chickens laid]. We [used them] to buy our flour with."

Diane Taylor discussed her childhood memories on her family farm. "I remember my father doing chores on the farm. We had a corncrib, and I would help him

PLATE 134 "We were so busy trying to work and make enough food for our family to eat that we didn't have much pleasure time."—Diane Taylor shell the corn for the chickens and feed the chickens. We were just a farm family. We had all kinds of animals that farms usually have. As a child, I worked on the farm. We were so busy trying to work and make enough food for our family to eat that we didn't have much pleasure time."

Mildred Story told us, "It is funny to me that chicken wings are a delicacy now. Back then, the guests [at my family's hotel; *Foxfire 10*, pages 121–34] ate the thigh, the leg, and the white meat. [Our family] got what was left—now, it doesn't mean we didn't get some of the good pieces too—a lot of backs and wings! You couldn't buy chickens already dressed. My daddy bought chickens by the coop. We killed the chickens, plucked them, and cut them up. Behind the hotel, there was a shack called the washplace where the washing was done with two great big iron pots. We had to kill the chickens by the washplace. I guess we did about twenty-five at a time.

"We couldn't kill those chickens very long ahead, because they wouldn't keep with no electric refrigerators or freezers. [Instead of] electrical refrigerators like we have now, we had a great big icebox."

Minnie Dailey reminisced, "When I was a young'un at home, my mother had a bunch of chickens, and when they'd lay eggs, we'd take the eggs to the store and swap 'em for a nickel or dime's worth of brown sugar, and we'd get a great big pile, more than you'd get now for a dollar, I guess."

Rose Shirley Barnes stated, "When I lived with my mama and daddy, we never went to the store to get a chicken. We raised our own chickens. We went out, and we killed a chicken, and we brought it back in the house and fried it. If we needed money, we would catch some chickens and take them to the market and sell them and their eggs. For a dozen eggs, you could get enough groceries to last a while."

Clive Smith revealed, "We had chickens [to have] our own eggs. We raised chickens for sale and for our own. The chickens ran free, and we'd sell eggs in the summer. When the chicks would set and raise young'uns, we sold fryers."

Mary Pitts, the former postmaster at the Rabun Gap post office, told us how people would order chickens through the mail. "People would order little baby

PLATE 135 Mary Pitts

chicks from different places, and they'd come through the mail by special delivery. The rural carrier would have to take them directly to the owner. If the person who ordered them had a post office box, the postmaster would deliver them. There was a lot of that back then."

Bernice Taylor recalled many stories about chickens on her family farm. "One time when we was real small, we had hens and one of them was a-settin'. Mama tried to break her and couldn't get her broke [from settin']. She called me and J. C. [her brother] in there and said, 'Take them hens in yonder and go out there and dip them in water and see if you can get them to quit settin'.'

"Well, it was cold. We went out to the branch, and we had a big old tub that was sitting under a spout out there—that branch gets cold; in cold weather, it's cold! We dipped them chickens in that water. We'd hold 'em down; we'd pull 'em up; we'd put 'em back down. We just kept doing that, and when we got done, that chicken couldn't even stand up! We come back to the house, and we said, 'Mama, this chicken is gonna die.' She said, 'What'd ya'll do to that?' We said, 'We done what you told us to. We dipped her in the water.' She said, 'You dipped her more in the water than you were supposed to.' She kept watching, and we just knew them chickens were going to die, but after they had time to thaw out, they kindly got over it, and they was all right.

"She deviled us as long as she lived about burying the chickens in water alive and just about letting them die! I imagine we was about maybe eight or ten years old. I can remember her telling everybody about that. She said, 'Them old hens quit settin' too. They didn't set no more!'

"One time after we [she and her brothers and sisters] all got older, they [the family] had a hen that eat so much, and her craw was so full, she was gonna die if they didn't do something. So Mama told them [her brothers and sisters] to catch that hen and bring her there, and one of them come and hold her, and she was gonna operate on her. She was gonna cut that craw open and get that out of there. When she cut it open and got it out down at the bottom—where it wasn't supposed to have been—they was a cocklebur that had crawled in there. It had already sprouted, fixin' to grow. She got that out, sewed the old hen back up with black thread, and turned her loose. She just went along like nothing had happened, said in a few days she was all right, just eating and doing fine.

"I guess we had twenty-five or thirty, maybe forty [chickens] running around on the place—not the same age, [and] different sizes. We used them for eggs, and if we took a notion to have chicken for dinner, we'd kill one and have it.

"They wrung their neck [to kill the chickens]. I never did wring the neck. Howard [another brother] did, though. Mama told him, 'Son, go out yonder and catch that chicken and wring its neck.' Mama already had her water hot. So Howard would just go ahead and do what she wanted him to. [One time] he picked that chicken up and gave it a wring two or three times, put it down, and it just got up and walked off. You had to break the bones and he just twisted it. That was funny!"

CHICKEN PREPARATION

SCALDING AND PREPARING CHICKENS
After plucking the feathers, cutting the head and feet off, and removing the entrails, lightly singe the skin to remove any pinfeathers left. The best way to do this is to make a torch of newspaper and hold the cleaned chicken over the torch with the flames barely touching the chicken.

Next, the chicken is washed with a cloth and soapy water. Then it is rinsed well and cut into serving pieces if it is to be fried or left whole if it is to be baked or stewed.

—*Blanche Harkins*

CUTTING THE CHICKEN INTO SERVING PIECES
(1) With chicken breast-side up, cut skin between thighs and body of chicken. Grasping a leg of the chicken in each hand, lift the chicken off cutting board and bend its legs back as you lift. Continue bending them back until the bones break at the joints.

(2) Cut the legs from the body. Next, bend each leg at the "knee" joint and cut across the skin on the top of the joint. Continue bending at the joint until the bone breaks. Then run the knife's edge under the joint to cut the leg into two pieces, the drumstick and the thigh.

(3) With chicken still breast-side up, remove wings by cutting where they attach to the body. To give them the typical shape, the wing tip is forced under the section that was attached to the body.

(4) To separate the back from the breast, imagine a line drawn from the neck down each side of the chicken to the tail. The line should go through the holes where the wings and legs were removed [as close to the backbone as possible]. Now cut along these lines. The backbone may be used to cook in a stock or for soup.

(5) Since a wishbone, or "pulleybone," is a favorite piece of fried chicken, many cooks around here cut the breast into three pieces, first cutting across the upper part of the breast to remove the pulleybone intact. Then they split the lower part of the body in half, lengthwise, at

the breastbone. It is recommended that this cut be made slightly to one side of the breastbone and cartilage, so that the bone may be lifted out before frying.

—*Bessie Underwood*

CHICKEN RECIPES

CHICKEN AND DUMPLINGS

Boil or stew a chicken until tender, adding salt and pepper to taste. Remove the chicken to a serving bowl and keep warm. Roll out a biscuit dough and cut into strips or biscuits, and drop into the boiling chicken stock. Cover the pot with a lid and cook about 5 to 7 minutes. Test with a fork. They should fall apart when you try to lift them with the fork and will not be doughy. Dip out and serve in a separate bowl. Pour the broth over the chicken and serve.

—*Lucy York*

FRIED CHICKEN

Salt chicken pieces, dip them into a batter made of flour, pepper, an egg, and a little milk or water, and fry them slowly in beef fat.

—*Effie Lord*

Dip the chicken pieces into buttermilk and then roll them in a mixture of flour, salt, and pepper and fry them in hot grease; turn the pieces over as they brown.

—*Lola Cannon*

The chicken parts are rolled in flour and fried in hot grease. After browning on one side, turn the chicken pieces over, let them brown a few minutes, and then cover the pan with a lid and cook over low heat until tender, about 20 to 30 minutes.

If desired, the liver and gizzard may also be fried, or boiled in a small amount of water until tender, and then cut up and used with the stock to make a giblet gravy.

—*Bessie Underwood*

BAKED CHICKEN

First, salt and pepper the pieces and roll them in flour. Place them into an iron frying pan with a small amount of grease in it and place the pan in the oven to cook at a low temperature for an hour or so. You can also use cornmeal in place of the flour sometimes.

—*Addie Norton*

HOGS

Omie Gragg recalled, "We raised our hogs in a pen. [We'd] feed them, just like you feed chickens—every day. We'd feed them, [and] then we got our meat out of them."

Adam Foster remembered, "My great-granddaddy was up at his house, and this old feller, Corn, had some hogs that got in my great-granddaddy's field. Said he had a ten-rail fence, and them hogs was just layin' the fence down. Well, he went over there and told Mr. Corn about his hogs. It was a mile or two over there, and Mr. Corn was just standin' in his field. He said he told him, 'Put them hogs up or I'll take care of 'em.'

"Mr. Corn said, 'Well, I will. I'll put 'em up.' So my great-grand-daddy went on back home.

"And the next day, they was back in again. So he just turned around and walked over the mountain to old man Corn's. And he told him, 'Mr. Corn, I told you to put them hogs up and keep 'em up. If they're in my field when I get back, they'll not get out; I'll tell you that.' He said, 'I'll kill 'em just as fast as I can shoot.'

"So sure enough, just as soon as he went back to the house, he shot what didn't get away before he got through shootin'. They was a big bunch of hogs. He shot part of 'em, [and] just left 'em layin' there. Old man Corn never said a word about his hogs. That was just the way people was then. They meant business when they told you somethin'."

WILD HOGS

Eldon Miller told us about the wild hogs he has on his farm. "[Females grow a tusk] about an inch to an inch and a quarter. That's all. The males average about six inches. We had one here one time [that was] seven and a quarter inches long. Most people, when they catch 'em, break 'em off. I don't never do it. At a year old, they've got a set about an inch and a half long, and they are straight—dangerous. I've caught 'em that had tusks four or five inches long. We caught one three weeks ago, but it just broke itself down. Wouldn't give up. We had it tied down and going to turn it loose wild, but it broke down, and we had to kill it.

"The young Russian breed looks like a chipmunk. They have red and black stripes, like paint. It's that distinctive. The red turns black. Those hogs are coming back now. That's what's wrong with game in these mountains. People kill too much. I just catch 'em. When I was in the army, some of my buddies would drop around and want to see one of them caught, 'cause when I was little, it was fun to catch 'em. But now it's not so much fun. We caught one in Mountain City. I carried my bulldogs all over the pasture. Nelson [his son] has helped me. He got his shirt cut. It came that close. Tore my britches leg.

"You don't make any money foolin' with 'em. It's one of the best sports, though. If people would hunt them right—not see one, shoot it, and leave it laying—why, we could have a good sport. A big hog like that [the one they just caught] will dare the dogs to come in the lot. He seems to enjoy it as much as the dogs do. He'll walk the fence, blow at 'em, paw the ground—just like a bull. [The hog that I have now] has attacked me one time. I didn't have dogs with me at the time. That cur heard me yelling an' come. That's as pure a breed of Russian as you can find in this country. He's two years old. I'm going to keep him for a while, then I'll try to turn him loose in the mountains if I can. If I can't turn him loose, I'll have to kill him, 'cause a lot of time, they get used to corn and come back."

"[I'm not too fond of him to eat him.] I'd enjoy tasting him. He's killed a dog and been pretty rough on the rest, but I'm going to try to turn him loose in the mountains. After he gets wild again, he probably won't come around close. He won't bother you if you don't bother him.

"I have run a hog like that for four hours, so you can judge by that their endurance and how they can run. And I have no idea how many hogs I've caught. I do that for sport. One year, I caught twenty-three. Killed one. The dogs cut it up. Turned the others loose so they could restock."

HOG KILLING

The hog played a vital part in survival for the Southern Appalachian people. Almost every family had at least one hog because they were cheaper than cattle to buy and feed, making them easiest to raise. Even those people who lived in town had them, because hogs could survive in a small pen with table scraps or slop for food. Depending on the size of the family, six to eight hogs could be killed each year to provide meat. Bill Gravley remembered, "My mom and daddy always killed four. There's eight kids, so there's ten of us altogether in the family." Occasionally, a young pig would be killed to roast, but most families waited until they were grown in order to get more meat from them.

Gertrude Keener remembered, "My daddy and the boys usually killed the hog. We didn't have to send out for any help. They'd shoot the hog and 'stick' it so it could bleed well. Then we scalded it in a great big washpot full of water. We'd pull it out and scald the other end. We had a scaffold that we'd lay it out on and scrape it. Then wash it down real good. Then hung the hog up with a gambling stick to take the entrails out." A gambling stick is eighteen inches long and two inches in diameter and is sharpened on both ends with a rope in the middle. The sharpened ends are stuck into the tendons in the hog's feet.

Sallie Beaty told us about killing hogs. "The first thing you had to [do was] to have your water a-boiling. You had to have your water at a certain temperature, or you would set the hair back on 'em, and you couldn't hardly get it off. Sometimes you would take a tow sack and spread it over them and pour the boiling water [on them]. We would take hoes and knives and scrape the hair off of them. Then, when we would get all that done, we would hang 'em up. Then somebody would take their intestines out, cut their heads off, and take the liver and lites [lungs] out. Then we would take 'em to the smokehouse. [Next, we would] cut 'em up like [into] hams, middlin's, shoulders, the pork chops, [and] the backbones and ribs. We would can our backbones and ribs most of the time. [But] we would salt-cure our shoulders, middlin's, and hams."

Buck Henslee shared his experience with killing hogs with us. "I've never killed more than two hogs at a time. Lotta people have more. It takes about two or three fellers all day to clean 'em. You have to have help, because one feller couldn't handle a big hog. You raise the hog as big as you can get 'em.

PLATE 137 Buck Henslee

We've some out there that weigh five hundred pounds. The biggest I've ever had was five or six hundred pounds. You start 'bout November when it gets cold. You have to start when it gets cold so your meat'll turn out. You have to heat your water first. Build you a fire under the scaldin' barrel—the scaldin' barrel is just a great big ol' tub, not really a barrel. Heat your water to scald 'em; then go out there an' shoot 'em. You have to shoot them in their forehead an' then cut their throats so you can bleed 'em. If you don't bleed 'em, the meat will be 'bloodshot.' Then bring 'em to the scaldin' barrel an' scald 'em by pourin' boilin' water over the hogs. Then take sharp knives an' scrape the hair off of 'em. Hang the hog up by its feet an' pour hot water down it to clean it off. Cut the head off an' wash it off. Then start at the top of the hog an' split it down its stomach; an' when you're done, pull the sides back. Then gut 'em. Then the tenderloin is stripped out an' then laid on a table to be cut up. Then take the hog down. Lay the hog on the table with its legs up, an' take an ax an' split it down the backbone. Cut the ribs out an' cut 'em up with an ax. Take the fat off. It's for cracklin's, an' the rest of the meat is cut into sections of streaked meat, fatback, shoulders, and hams. Then put 'em in the smokehouse an' salt 'em. It won't ruin if you put salt on it. You can wait as long as a year to eat it if you want, but you won't have enough to last you a year! Ha-ha! You can eat it right then if you can get someone to cook it."

PREPARING THE MEAT

PLATE 138 "Then take sharp knives an' scrape the hair off of 'em. Hang the hog up by its feet an' pour hot water down to clean it off."—Buck Henslee

Amanda Turpin told us how she cures hog's meat. She explained, "We killed our own hogs and cured our meat with salt. We'd have hams and shoulders and sides [of pork]. We didn't smoke it, though. We just cured it with salt, and it would be good too. We don't have any good meat now like we did back then. My daddy was a great hand to salt meat, and he salted it just right, and it was good! Sometimes he would kill a beef, hang it up, and salt it. Nowadays everything spoils. You can't keep things. I don't know why, but it just don't keep. The weather's different.

"We'd just butcher whatever [hogs] we had—one, two, or three. We'd build up a fire out in the yard and heat the water in big pots. I helped, but I didn't like to. We made sausage out of beef or mixed the beef and pork together for sausage."

Belle Henslee informed us about the many uses for hogs. "You can use the cracklin's from the hog to make short'nin' bread. You cut it up pretty fine, an' then you put it in a pot and wait 'til the cracklin's get good 'n' brown an' kindly comes to the top, and then you strain the cracklin's out of it an' then pour that lard in the buckets.

PLATE 139 "You can use jus' 'bout all the hog for somethin'."—Belle Henslee

"You can use jus' 'bout all the hog for somethin'. You can take the head an' make sousemeat out of it. Sousemeat tastes kinda like sausage. To make it, you cook it off the bone good an' mash it up an' put in pepper, sage, an' a little salt. Put the feet, tail, an' head all together to make sousemeat out of it, all of it. It makes a good sandwich. You put it in the bowl and press it down. Then, when it gets hard, you put it in the 'frigerator or set it out where it's cold an' let it get hard. Then you slice it off, an' it really makes it a good sandwich. You eat it cold. You don't cook it! I bet this is the craziest thang that ever went on!"

Sallie Beaty gave us her instructions for curing meat. "[To salt-cure the shoulders, middlin's, and hams of two hogs, we] would use one twenty-five-pound bag of plain salt with one box of red pepper and one box of black pepper in it. [We] rubbed it on our meat on both sides and then either hung it up or put it on a shelf. [We would] put our middlin's on the shelf in the smokehouse. Between each layer, we would put corncobs. Sometimes it would [be] three layers high. Then [we] would go back in a week or two weeks and turn it over so all the water that had drained in there and was settling would run out. [This curing would] take six to eight weeks. We would wrap the shoulders and hams—right when they put the salt on it—up in brown paper and hang it up in sacks. [They] always hung the leg down so it would drain out through it. [Once wrapped, they would] tie up [the bottom]. While the meat was being salt-cured, we would be smoking it too.

"The jaws [would be] fried like streaked meat. A lot of people would cook their liver into liver mush. Some people would put part of the heads in their liver mush. We also used the intestines and paunch for chitlin's. You'd wash them real good and soak them in salt water for two or three days. Then you would take 'em out and roll 'em in flour and cornmeal and fry 'em 'til they were brown."

Gertrude Keener recalled curing meat. "We raised all of our pork. We didn't know what it was to go to the store and buy bacon or sausage or anything like that. We made our own sausage and dried our own bacon meat. We made sousemeat. That was one of our favorite dishes. Cook the hog's head and grind it up after you get it cooked. Then season it with sage and red peppers and press it down to get all the grease out of it. Of course, it's already been cooked, but by putting the weight on it, it gets all the rest of the grease out. It keeps for the longest time."

Lettie Chastain told us, "Hogs are killed when it's cold weather. We'd have a wooden meat box and put a layer of meat, layer of salt, layer of meat, and a layer of salt. We'd get it covered good and let it stay about six weeks. Then we'd take up the meat and wash it good. My mother always made a plaster of brown sugar, flour, and syrup to cover hers over. After she washed and dried the meat, she'd cover it with the brown sugar mixture and wrap it in a brown paper. Then she'd put it in a cloth flour sack and hang it up in the smokehouse to cure. Everybody cured their meats and kept them in the smokehouse. When I was a kid, I loved to get in the old smokehouse. They kept the meat, canned stuff, pumpkins, just anything that would last through the winter."

PORK RECIPES

LIVER MUSH
1 hog's liver
2 cups cornmeal
2 tablespoons seasoning salt

Boil liver until done and then run through a food chopper. After you have done this, add meal and seasoning salt. Preheat oven to 350°F. Put mush in a pan and cook for about 30 minutes.

—*Margaret Norton*

Hog's liver
Cornmeal

·Boil liver until tender. This must be made shortly after the hogs are butchered. Mash up the cooked liver with a potato masher, leaving it in the stock. Add enough cornmeal to the hot stock and liver to get it to the consistency of mush. While it's still hot, pour into a pan or bowl to mold it. Let it cool. It can then be sliced and heated [and] browned in a pan when you are ready to serve it. Liver mush serves as bread and meat for a meal.
    —*Lucy York*

CHITLIN'S—KONK'S
    Clean all the fat off pig's intestines, run warm water through them, and then split them open and wash thoroughly. Link into chains. Boil in salt water until tender and then cut into one-inch pieces. Sprinkle with cornmeal and brown in hot fat.
    —*Lettie Chastain*

HUNTING STORIES

"Most anywhere in these mountains is a good place to hunt."

People depended on animals to survive. Whether it was animals raised on a farm or wild animals in the woods, it was still food. All that they had to help them hunt were intuitions, knowledge passed down from previous generations, weapons, and an occasional lantern. There were no camouflage clothes, paint, masks, flashlights, or any of our modern equipment. Now hunting is mainly for sport rather than survival.

If a person wanted a deer, a coon, or a turkey, he would go out and hunt one no matter the time of year. Many times hunters would stay for days or weeks in the woods to catch food for their families. As Talmadge York said, "I've spent just about as much time in the woods as I have at home, I guess." Nowadays only a few months of the year are set aside to hunt for certain animals.

In the past, hunting was a way for families to be self-sufficient. If they could not raise enough meat on their farm, they would hunt for it. Gertrude Keener recalls how her family would hunt for many different animals. "My daddy and brothers would go squirrel hunting and coon hunting and sell the skins. Sometimes they'd catch muskrats. They were pretty bad on the creek banks, so we always tried to trap them and keep them thinned out. My brothers would go hunting in the snow. That was a good kind of boy that would go rabbit hunting in the snow. They ate the rabbits; they never did throw them away.

"In the wintertime, my daddy would take us bird thrashing. That's what he called it—going hunting birds at night. We'd take a pine torch or a lantern or something for light." Hunting allowed families to survive the winters. No part of the animal was wasted. If it was not used for food, it was used in another way. The hide of larger animals was often traded for food or another needed item.

Many hunters chose to get a little help from dogs. The dogs could find the animals when their owners couldn't.

Hunting was also a form of pest control. Many rabbits and other small animals would destroy a garden, and if a farmer killed the animal, he protected his garden and provided another source of food.

After the animal was caught, it would be prepared at home and put in the smokehouse (see the "Farm Animals" and "The Old Homeplace" chapters).

As fathers take their sons hunting now, they also took them years ago. The children who learned to survive by hunting have taught their children to hunt, not for survival, but for sport. However, some of the techniques and strategies for hunting are the same as they were in the past.

The how-tos of hunting are featured in *The Foxfire Book*, but since hunting was such an important part of our ancestors' lives, we decided to share with you the experiences and memories of several hunters.

—*Amy S. York*

BEARS

Adam Foster remembered this story about his grandfather catching a bear. "My grandpa caught a bear one time and raised it. He caught the bear out in the mountains somewhere. It was small when he got it.

Well, he kept it around there and made him a scaffold up in a big pine tree in the front yard. He made that scaffold for that bear to climb up and lay on. That suited the bear. He put a chain on him and let him go up there and sleep. So he raised that bear up around there, and he got to where he'd turn it loose. It'd go anywhere around there. So finally it went back out in the field, and some of the neighbors shot it; they didn't know it was his. Somebody come through and shot it."

PLATE 140 Adam Foster with his great-niece

Frank Rickman remembers encounters with bears for a very different reason. "I like to hunt bears. I don't like to kill them, but we've worked at it pretty hard. The only ones that I've helped catch is the bears tearing up people's beehives. A bear likes honey better than anything. He'll go for miles and tear up bee gums and get the honey. A lot of people make a living off that honey, and they ask us to come fool with them. I've been trying to keep dogs that we could catch them with. I've really gotten a kick out of that bear hunting because I've always liked to take these young'uns and all these men [to hunt with me]. I always [like] to see how much grit they got, 'cause when that bear stops on them, [those people] will go over the top of something or up something or do something [to get away]. I always liked to do that."

COONS

PLATE 141 Shorty Hooper and his coon dogs

Shorty Hooper told us about coon hunting. "Most anywhere in these mountains is a good place to hunt. A lot of people don't like to tell where they catch their coons at or how they catch 'em, but it doesn't matter to me. I don't mind telling a man where I coon hunt or where I catch 'em.

"One time we were coon hunting, and we got after an old coon that had gotten away from us before. That old coon would get away every time we got after him. The dogs would run him good and hard for a while, and then they would lose him. They would circle around and never could get it straightened out [as to where he went]. That old coon did us that way for about five or six years. So I got without a coon dog, and I bought an old lemon-spotted dog. I told some of my hunting buddies that this old dog would put John in the sack. [We got after the coon and let him get away so many times that I named him John.] I said, 'Well, this dog will put the ol' John in the sack.'

"So one night it was sprinkling rain, a pretty good heavy little drizzle.

I started out, and I was by myself with the old dog that I had bought; his name was Junior. Old Junior struck that coon, and he lost it. He come back, circled back, and he struck that old coon again. There was a dead chestnut tree part of the way down, and it had fallen into the top of a big crooked white oak tree, and that old coon had a den in that oak tree. What he would do whenever the dogs got after him was to go up the dead chestnut tree and jump off the side onto that oak tree. All of the dogs that we had had to run old John would run to that blown-down tree and tree on him there, but the old coon wouldn't be there.

"Junior went up in that blown-down tree as far as he could to where that old coon had jumped off; he walked up as far as he could, and he would turn and come back standing on his hind feet. He marched around up in there where the old coon had jumped off, and he struck him again somehow. [The coon come out,] and the old dog run that old coon up the creek there for about a mile I guess, and directly he gave a big 'boo-oo' there—a tree bark, I call it. He circled an' treed right under a big set of rock ledges. 'Well,' I said to myself, 'there ain't a tree up in there big enough for a coon to climb—back in under those cliffs.' Old Junior is looking at that coon, but I walked on up around the edge of the ledge of the cliffs, and there were two big persimmon trees. I guess I hunted ever since I was young up in there, and I had never seen those two big persimmon trees. I bet you that they were fifty or sixty feet tall, and that old coon was curled around the trunk of a little limb where it forked. He was just wrapped around there, and that was the biggest coon I ever caught. And that was the end of old John. I'd run him for about five years, and I finally put him in the sack. He weighed twenty-two and a half pounds. He was a big one!"

HUNTING COON WITH DOGS

Shorty Hooper told us, "What matters to me is whether or not another man has got as good a dog as I've got. That is the sport in it with me. I've had some awful good dogs. I've had dogs that would just

PLATE 142 Shorty Hooper's coon dog Katy

get out there and coon for me all night long, and I've had some that I would give away because they never would make it. They might tree a coon, but I wouldn't call 'em a coon dog. I've had some that really made it, and them I always hold on to unless something bad happens that I have to get rid of 'em.

"Yes, sir, a good dog is the answer to good coon hunting. You can get out here with just any kind of a dog, and you'll be running these wild-cats and deer and everything else besides a coon. But when you one time get you one trained up for a good coon dog, why, every time you hear that ol' dog bark, you can bet he's after that ol' ringtail. And we get after some tough ones that's hard to do anything with.

"I loaf through this mountain area here. That way you can get after more old smart coons, these here old longtime trailers that would be hard for a dog to tree. And that's what I love to hear—a old dog when he gets after a coon. He'll 'boo-oo' here and he will 'boo-oo' yonder, and he'll go a little farther and mess around, and maybe you'll plumb quit hearing him for a long time. Directly, you'll hear 'boo-oo' on that ol' coon's track again. Just makes you think he has just plumb quit. Then all at once that ol' dog will set down and give a big howl up the tree there, and he'll circle around—and that's the good part about it that I like. Then when you go to your dog, you can look up there and see that old coon sitting up there with them eyes shining like a star look-ing down at you there.

"You can tell a pup's makeup by his head and his ears, and a lot of times [you can tell] if he's going to make a good coon dog. What really counts, though, is putting them in the brush and wearing out that shoe leather out there training on that coon.

"The way I'd start out with this young pup is I'd hunt him with my old dog, and I'd try to get him in there with my old dog on every trail or track that he got on—encourage him to go with my old dog and to be with him when the coon was treed.

"A lot of people will hold their old dogs 'til the young dog catches the coon, but that's the wrongest thing a man ever did. The thing to do is when the young dog trees and gets to staying in there a little better, leave that old dog loose there and cripple that coon and make it walk out of that tree, and that old dog, he knows exactly what to do—he ain't gonna back up. He's going in there and get ahold of that coon. When he does, that's gonna encourage this young dog, and he's going to fall in there. Nine times out of ten he's gonna get bit and eat up a little bit. But still as long as Grandpa stays in on that there coon, why, this young dog ain't gonna back up much. It's too exciting for him to stay out of it, and he can't help hisself. He'll just go right on in there.

"Be good to your dog. Treat him right, and every time he trees one, why, just pet him. Love him up. Hug his neck if you have to. Show that dog he's done the right thing. Then the dog gets to know you, and he gets to know what you're hunting for, and then he will get out there and coon for you all night long. And he won't fool with nothing else if he's trained right.

"The best coon dog I ever had was one I called Little Red. He was half redbone, a quarter cur, and a quarter walker. He was just a straight-out coon dog. That's just all you could make out of him. Take him hunting anywhere, and he'd find you a coon. He didn't come back 'til he had a coon. A lotta times I could turn him up a branch [creek] and wouldn't even have to go with him. If he didn't come, I'd start up the branch 'til I heard him tree or found him somewhere treeing, and many a time with a gang [of coons] up a tree or one big ol' barren sow [that's a coon that never raises up no kittens]. I guess, to my notion, Little Red is the best dog I've ever had in my life.

"A man likes his dogs, and he don't want to part with them. That's the reason they cost so much. Everybody likes a good-trained dog. A good-blooded pup at three months old would cost you anywhere from seventy-five to one hundred dollars. A good trained dog now would cost you—well, from the prices things is today, and by coon hunting being such a good sport that people really loves and enjoys [that brings the price of a dog up]—from five to seven hundred dollars to a thousand, twelve, fourteen hundred. And there have been a few coon dogs sold for more money than that. If you take and train him up, why, you have worn enough shoe leather off to get whatever you can out of him, and it wouldn't be too much. So that's one reason why coon dogs are so high. It's just a good sport that people likes, and always has been—from our old grandparents' days back to now—and always will be, I guess.

"Now, I have had my dog to run a coon a couple or three hours before he ever treed. And I have had it to just cold-trail one from say about nine or ten that night when I first hit the woods until about four that morning before he ever dragged him down. It would take all night to track him down and tree him. A lot of times, maybe nine times out of ten, one like that will be up an oak tree, and you can get him.

"I'd say just on a straight run and race on a coon, he wouldn't last but fifteen or twenty minutes 'til a dog would tree him. But the old coon tricks the old dog. What takes a long time is getting a beatened-up track where he's been or a track that's been rained on, and where he's been feeding around.

"If a dog strikes a good track and gets the coon to going, I'd say fifteen to thirty minutes, why, your dog will have him treed. It's just according to how young or old the coon is and how much he's been dogged and the kind of rough country you're hunting in and how quick the old coon will tree. And an old sow, she'll take care of her kittens. She'll stick her neck out taking care of them. She'll put her kittens up a tree and maybe try to fool a dog and go on a pretty good piece.

"You take a fellow that loves his coon dogs, and he loves to coon hunt for a sport, why, he ain't going to shoot ever' coon he sees noway. He's gonna want to go back and get some more fun out of 'em later.

DEER

Adam Foster's memories of stories about his grandfather seem larger than life, like Paul Bunyan. "Grandpa was a big, stout, long-armed man. He didn't care. He'd catch a bear as quick as he'd catch a ground-hog. There used to be a big mill dam right over the hill there, and his dogs got after a deer. They run it into this mill dam. It was a big old buck deer, and it was a-fightin' his dogs, 'bout to drown 'em. And, of course, Grandpa was stout, and he just pulled off his coat, and into that dam he went to where the deer was. And them dogs was tryin' to catch it in the water there, but it was about to drown them. [So] he just reached in and got them big horns and put it under the water and held it 'til it drowned. He was a big stout man—bigger than I am and longer-armed."

BOBCATS

Talmadge York remembers going hunting for small game, but coming home with much more than he bargained for. "I went squirrel huntin' one time up on Glassy Mountain. I'd

PLATE 144 Talmadge York with the bobcat he killed and mounted

killed six squirrels, and they's some boys scared up some turkeys. So I decided I'd hang my squirrels up and call these turkeys up. So I got down behind a tree; I called a few times, and I looked down below me, and there was the biggest something a-comin' toward me I ever seen. Scared me nearly to death, but I seen it was a bobcat. I had a shotgun, so I shot him off. He wheeled down this way and come right back up on this log. I shot him out again and knocked him off, and the next time he got up he started right toward me. I shot him in the mouth, and that killed him. I was so excited I tied him up and put him around me and started off the mountain with him. [I] got about a half a mile, and I forgot I'd left my squirrels I'd hung up. Instead of laying my cat down— he weighed about twenty-five pounds—and goin' back and gettin' my squirrels, I toted the cat and all back. I had him mounted and kept him for a long time."

FOXES

Edd Hodgins shared his unusual method of catching foxes bare-handed. "I've shot a lot of foxes, but when I could get one treed, I'd try to get him alive lots of times. If you can get him treed in a hole or some-thing, he'll come out with smoke. You get a little smoke, and they'll run out. [When they] start out, grab them by the back of the neck, and they sull up just like a possum! Then I had him!

"One time one jumped out too quick for me. I didn't think I had fire enough. He was in a big hole—hollow log—and boy, I was gonna give him a good one. So I turned my back around to get something more to put on the fire—just had got it started—and out come that thing. Boy, he was out of there! He was one of them big yellow ones. I was glad I had my back to that one! One of my dogs grabbed him, but he was as big as my dog, and it was a big dog! That fox jerked loose, and he got in another hole. I could hear him, but I never could smoke him out. But I would have grabbed him before I seen what I was a-grabbing, and that thing was as big as any dog I had. If I'd grabbed him, I'da had a fight sure enough, so I was glad I had my back to that one!

"My wife's daddy come up here one day, and he wanted to go a-hunting. He was getting old and couldn't hear too good, and them old foxhunters always hunted of a night. I'd go in the morning. My dogs was just as good in the day as their dogs were at night. Them other fox-hunters had high-thoroughbred dogs, and they thought they had the best; and I had old stock dogs—just black and tans and blueticks—but my dogs would catch 'em, and theirs couldn't. I knew that. Anyway, he come up to stay all night with me and go foxhunting in the morning. He'd say, 'You think you can get 'em up of a day?'

"I'd say, 'I can get up one or two.'

"So we went up this ridge here the next morning and jumped one, and one of my boys brought him on up to us dead, and about that time the dogs jumped another one off in there. I said, 'There's another one, Grandpa.'

"He says, 'I'm going after it.' He said, 'You take this one on to the house.' And about that time, he heard them tree down there on the other side of the mountain. I said, 'You take this one to the house. I'll go get that one.'

"He said, 'I ain't going to the house. I'm a-goin' with you.' So we went on to where that one was treed in an old mica hole, and I crawled in. It scares me yet to think about it. The hole was a little sloping; it had been a tunnel, but it was about filled up. You could go fifteen or twenty feet back, but the dogs were still on back beyond that. I figured I could crawl in there as far as I could, and start a little smoke, and give him plenty of room to get the dogs out of there and out of the way, and get back and catch him. But I crawled down in there and started me a little smoke, and the smoke backfired on me worse than it was going the other way [the way he planned for it to go], and me fanning it with my hat. But I couldn't get it back, you know. I got back out of there—I had to back out—but I seen that fox a-comin' directly, and I just lied still. He come out and had a great big hole—four foot square I reckon—to get around me. Had a lot of room to dodge me, but I guess the smoke had his eyes about shut, and I got him. Old Grandpa was sitting over there on the bank, and he went to laughing. He said, 'I've foxhunted all my life, and I've caught more today than I've ever caught!'

"We had a lot of fun. My boys are about as bad to hunt as I was, but they don't take the hard hunts that I had to take. Now you can ride. They've got Jeeps, and you can go down to mule trader's country [flatlands], and you don't hardly have to leave your car to catch something. But here you got to hit these mountains and pull 'em. Boy, I've tramped all over. I don't believe they's many trees in these mountains within four miles of here that I ain't looked at, or seen, or been in."

HUNTING FOXES WITH DOGS

Bell Jones told us how he became interested in raising foxhunting dogs. "I'd go with [my daddy] to look after the cattle, and I got to liking the woods; and later, my brother and I would go out together and rabbit hunt around the farm. Finally, we got to going back in the woods with the dogs at night possum hunting, coon hunting. Finally, we got to running foxes a little bit. [I] had some old dogs—called them pot-licker dogs—you don't never hear tell of them no more. [They were something] like what the black and tan is now. That was a nickname for them. I think it's from licking pots. They used to claim that if you had pot-licker dogs, you had to take a pot with you when you went hunting, and if he wouldn't leave you, you rolled the pot off down the hill and sent him after it to get him away from you—get him out from under your feet. So we kept on at that until later on [when] we began to get us in some more fox dogs that would run better. [That] kinda done away with them old pot-licker hounds. The boys around Clayton began to get in some Walker dogs, and we got ahold of a few of them and got to mixing them. We run them dogs for several years and raised a few of them. They was a mixture—half 'n' half—and they run a fox so much better. They was so much better than the pure old pot-licker dogs and run so much longer.

"So then we [Bell and his brother] decided, after we both got grown, that we'd get us some thoroughbreds—them mixed-up ones was better than the ones we'd had, and thoroughbreds oughta be even better—so we went over in Kentucky and got four (three of them was littermates and one of them was unrelated). And we bought a fifty-acre tract up here on Black's Creek after we had both moved to Mountain City. We both lived here. We lived about a mile apart, so we kept our hounds together. We bought these together—bought that land—and put in a kennel up there. Then we started raising thoroughbred dogs and training some of them. Then we went to advertising them in *Chase Magazine* and *Hunters Home* and we got a lot of calls for dogs. Finally, they got to wanting to send their females to breed to our stud dogs, so we went over to Wheeling, West Virginia, and bought a stud dog. [We] give three hundred dollars for it. That was high for a dog then. His name was Wheeling Steel—named him after Wheeling, West Virginia. We advertised him as stud in magazines. They'd send us females here from a lot of different places, some from Oklahoma, Texas, and Ohio. They'd send them here, and we'd charge a twenty-dollar stud fee.

"Now, in training them, if it was possible, we took the mother of them, and we didn't take any other fast dogs. Usually, she would be broke down [and] old. Naturally, these puppies would follow their mother. Usually, after two or three times carrying them out, they would begin to run pretty good, and then we'd take them with our own pack. But we had to see that they didn't have to run the first race or two with too fast a dog if we could possibly do it, 'cause if you break them down to start with, they're never no more good.

"Ten months old was the best time to start training, we thought. Start them off right, and they would usually make good dogs—good tough dogs. But you could break one down by running them too hard too young, just like anything else. Like riding a colt too young—you'd ruin it. A lot of hunters has ruined good dogs by running them too young. We ruined one of the fastest ones I know of. He was might' near nine months old, and he could run with any of them; he did one night, and that was it—never would run another lick. But he led that pack part of the time, that first night. He was after a red fox, and after he come in, he was so weak that he couldn't get up, and he never did run no fox after that. One of the main things was to get them dogs to where they would come back to you. You had to train them to that, and that was a hard, hard thing.

"But we had a lot of fun at [foxhunting], and it was good sport. I thought about it lots. It was the only one good sport that I know of that I never knew of nobody gambling on. And I guess they were twenty-five, thirty, or more hunters in this county that foxhunted, and I foxhunted with all of them nearly. They'd come and go with me and my brother, or we'd go with them. But you never did want to get too many together. If you got too many strange dogs together, they didn't run. They'd stay split up. If you had a pack and I had a pack, and we carried them together (a pack was about four or five; if you had four or five good dogs, why, you had a pack), you had just about what you needed. But if you go and put three or four more packs in there, why, it wasn't never no good. You done better when you jest went out with two packs."

WILD HOGS

The following is an interview with Eldon Miller on hunting wild hogs as told by the interviewers, Barbara Taylor and Sheila Vinson.

One of the most exciting events that has happened to us was the day we were invited over to Eldon Miller's to see what a wild Russian boar chase was like. Eldon had one he had caught some time ago fenced in his pasture, and periodically he likes to "catch" it again, both for the sport of it and to keep the dogs trained and fit. He claimed that both the dogs and the hog seem to enjoy all the excitement. In fact, even though the hog would scream as though it were the end of the world each time it was caught, within a few short days he'd be back at the fence pawing the ground and snorting and teasing the dogs on the other side into a frenzy.

PLATE 145 Eldon Miller training his dogs with a wild hog

Before we went down to the pasture in search of the hog, Eldon explained each dog's job. The hold dog, for example, was a seventy-pound bulldog named Caesar. "I could put him on one of you, and he'd catch and hold you, but where he catches, it'll hurt." The hold dog locks his jaws so he can hold for hours—if necessary, for days. Eldon said that a hound, on the other hand, won't hold long. "He'll turn loose and fight that hog." The hold dog is the main key. He tries to bring the hog to the ground, and then the hounds move in for the kill. The latter are also called bay dogs. If Eldon had not been there to pull the dogs away, they would have killed the hog while the bulldog held tightly to one ear.

Another key dog is the leopard cur. He protects the hunters from the sharp tusks of the wild boar by staying between them and the hog. He also stays on the job night and day to keep captured boars from jumping the fence, escaping, and roaming free in the community. Eldon said, "The fence don't mean nothin' to th' wild boars. They could jump it."

The average size of the wild boar is anywhere from two hundred twenty-five to two hundred fifty pounds, and that's a big hog. They are very dangerous. They could seriously harm a human with one slash of their tusks.

Frank Rickman shared his feelings about why he hunted hogs in the mountains. "After World War II, the mountain people used to live out of the woods. One of their main cash crops was wild hogs. While I was in the army, the government passed a law that you couldn't free-range animals in the mountains. The old mountain people had hogs and stuff in there and had nobody to catch 'em because all the young people was gone. The hogs multiplied and sorta got out of control. When I come back, there was a lot of them, [and] I got hung up on catching them. I never have wanted to really kill nothing; I just always wanted to man-handle it and show it that it could be manhandled. That's the reason I've wanted to catch them hogs. I caught eighty-something big boars one time in a little over a year right out of this country.

"I helped destroy them, and it hurt my feelings because I'd seen the mistake I'd made. When I caught all them old boars, I didn't want to catch the sows and the pigs; I wanted to catch them old hogs that had them big teeth and stuff. When I done that, all the hunters come in and they killed all the pigs, sows, and mama hogs. Then I seen I'd made a mistake."

FISHING

"I'd like to see just one more speckled trout."

I am not a native of Rabun County, but my mother's family is. My family moved here when I was eight years old. One of the first things I came to realize about this county is the natural beauty that it holds. There are mountains and fields that have never been touched by human hands, and the numerous streams and lakes add to that beauty.

When I go fishing, I get a feeling I can't describe. There is nothing like grabbing your fishing gear and going to spend a day trying to catch one of nature's most beautiful inhabitants. It doesn't matter if I catch a fish or not; I just love trying. That is the fun for me.

The individuals interviewed for this chapter enjoy fishing too. They do it now because they want to, but during the Depression many had to fish in order to have food on the table. Years ago, they had to fish with equipment like cane poles, string, pressed-out lead for sinkers, and, in some cases, pins for hooks.

People have told us about the time when there weren't any limits on the number of fish you could catch in one day and of the times when you didn't have to have a license to fish. That was before there was a danger of some of the native fish becoming extinct. Now the Department of Natural Resources (DNR) puts limits on the number and kind of fish you can catch. The designated limits vary from state to state and can change from year to year. The DNR also stocks the streams here; the fish are raised in a hatchery and released into streams and lakes, adding to the population of that body of water. People say they can taste and see the difference between native and stocked fish. Doug Adams, former president of the Rabun County Chapter of Trout Unlimited, told me, "Stocked trout can develop the same coloring and markings as a native trout within approximately seven months of release into a stream." The one difference is the color of the meat. Native trout have a pink color to their meat almost like that of a salmon, whereas stocked trout do not have the coloring. Their meat is whitish.

Fishing has changed a great deal since the early to mid-1900s. But many secrets and techniques of previous generations are still applicable today and have been passed down to younger generations.

My granddad Buford Garner was an avid fisherman. He took my brother fishing many times and passed on his knowledge to him. My brother, in turn, passed that on to me. I never had the chance to go fishing with my granddad, but I feel that in a way I learned from him. And I'm proud to carry on his fishing knowledge.

—Robbie Bailey

TYPES OF FISH

There are numerous species of fish in the streams and lakes of North Georgia and western North Carolina. This chart lists the most common by type, family, and common name.

BASS

Black Bass
Largemouth—Bigmouth,
   Bucketmouth, Black,
   Green, Green Trout
Smallmouth—Bronze-
   back
Redeye—River Trout,
   Shoal Bass, River
   Bass

White Bass
Striped Bass—Rockfish
White Bass—Striped
   and Silver Bass

Sunfish
Bluegill—Bream
Redbreast Sunfish—
   Yellowbreast Sunfish,
   Shellcracker
Warmouth—Rock Bass,
   Redeye,
   Goggle-eye

CRAWFISH
Crayfish, Crawdad

EEL

CARP

SUCKER
White Sucker, Redhorse, Hog Sucker

PERCH

Yellow Perch   *Walleye*
Ringed Perch, Yellow Bass   Walleyed Pike, Walleyed Bass

TROUT

Brook Trout   *Brown Trout*   *Rainbow Trout*   *Golden Trout*
Brookie,   German Brown,   Bow
  Mountain   Speckled Trout
Trout, Native
Trout, Speckled
Trout, Speck

PIKE

Northern Pike   *Chain Pickerel*
Pike   Pickerel, Pike, Jack

CATFISH

Channel Catfish   *Brown Bullheads*   *Blue Catfish*
                         Bullhead, Mudcat   Channel Catfish

SCULPIN
Molly Craw Bottom, Craw Bottom

MINNOW
Shiner, Dace, Darter, Chub, True Minnow

CRAPPIE
Black and White—Calico Bass, Bridge Perch

HORNYHEAD
Knottyhead

NATIVE VS. STOCKED FISH

Stock, stocked, stocker, stockard, or *hatchery fish* are fish that were spawned and raised in a hatchery on processed feed, then stocked in a stream or lake. *Wild, native,* or *original fish* are fish spawned in the stream or lake and raised in the wild on natural foods.

There are no written records of when fish were first stocked in Rabun County. Doug Adams told us that brown trout were first brought to North America in the 1880s and released in Michigan. In the 1890s they were brought to the New England area, and the South received them in the early 1900s. The Chattooga River was the first body of water in Rabun County to receive brown trout, and rainbow trout were stocked shortly after the brown trout. According to Perry Thompson of the Lake Burton Fish Hatchery, there is no documenta-tion of when trout were first stocked in Rabun County, but the DNR started intensively stocking trout in the late 1940s to early 1950s.

L. E. Craig explained the differences in appearance of native versus stocked fish. "You can tell the difference between the native rainbow trout and the stocked rainbow by the color. The native will be kind of a brownish color with a pretty rainbow down his side. The stocked ones will be just as black as tar when they put them in the creek. They'll have a white streak instead of rainbow colors. The stocked brown trout will be kind of black-looking. Their spots won't show up."

Buck Carver emphatically stated that stocked fish were not fun to catch. "When they went to stocking with them blamed pond-raised fish, that took out all the fun of fishing for me! That took all the sport out of it! They bring them out of the fish hatchery and throw them in the river, and you stand there with your pole and catch 'em out just as

fast as they throw 'em in it. Any-body can catch a fish when you step up to the bank and put the hook in the water. They know something's coming for them to eat. They seen it around them 'raring pools' so many times, they don't think about getting hooked. They're not wild, and they're not skittish."

Andy Cope told us it would take an expert fisherman to

PLATE 146 Andy Cope

catch a native fish. "There are not many native fish anymore. They're very few and far between. There are a few speckled trout deep in the heads of the streams, but so far back it's hard to get to them. To go out camping a night or two in the woods and to catch some of those speckled trout, now, you can't beat that, but as far as having a mess of fish to take home, that's a rare thing. That probably won't happen unless you're a very special trout fisherman. Just anybody can't catch them like that.

"I don't think that the native fish taste any better than a fish grown in a pond. The Game and Fish Department used to feed the hatchery fish liver, and that's what made the stocked fish in the lake mushylike. They don't feed them that anymore. They feed them pellet feed now, made from grains and fish meal."

Lawton Brooks stated, "A wild game fish is harder to catch and will put up a big fight when you get ahold of a good one. He's wild, and you'll have something on your hands. He does everything he can to break loose.

"There's a few wild trout but not too many because they have so many roads to nearly all the streams. They've got to putting them old stock trout in streams, and the wild trout are just about gone. You've got to get a way back to get you a mess of wild trout.

"I don't like to catch them stock fish too good. It's kinda interesting but not like it is to get one of those wild fish. A stock fish is one that game wardens dump in the water. Stock will bite anything you throw in to 'em."

Florence Brooks won't eat a stocked fish. "Native fish got a pretty color, and their meat is firm. Sometimes you'll catch these stock fish, and they'll turn white-spotted before you get 'em home. Their meat's real soft. They keep 'em in these big vats, and they feed 'em chicken feed before they turn them loose in the lakes. The native fish don't do that. They just eat what they can catch, and they are stronger, firmer, meat and all. The minute those stock fish that I've caught turn white-spotted, I throw 'em away. I don't like them white spots."

According to Parker Robinson, "Fishing is my favorite sport. I really love to trout fish, but it's hard work. I'd rather catch them than the others, but it's rough. This day and time you have to get off the road a little and out away where people don't fish so much. I go down the creek kind of in the roughs, and I catch some pretty nice trout. Natives [trout] are smart fish, 'specially if they've been fished after. Rainbow is the best eating trout, I guess."

Talmadge York explained to us, "German brown trout were brought here and stocked. Same way with rainbow, brook, bream, and bass.

They were brought in and stocked in the lakes. They used to stock some brown trout here, raise 'em over at the hatchery and stock 'em, but they didn't do well in these small streams.

"Brown trout are sharp fish. They can see you a long way off. They'll put up a fight, and they'll get off your hook after you've caught 'em. Brown trout have big red spots on them, from their tails to their heads, about the size of dimes when they get to be about twenty-three inches long. Just as red and pretty as you've ever seen."

L. E. Craig said, "And a lot of people call a brown trout a speckled trout. Brown trout are, but they're not the original speckled trout. I can tell one just as quick as I see it. The brown will be kind of black-looking. Their spots won't show up. A brown trout is pretty, and if you ever see a big brown, it'll have red spots on it."

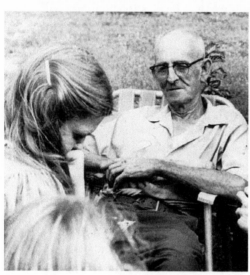

PLATE 147 Willie Underwood

Willie Underwood reminisced, "The first rainbow trout in this section here was shipped here in a barrel when I was six or seven years old. Now there are rainbow in nearly all the streams."

KINDS OF TROUT

"Mountain trout spawn in February and rainbow generally in the spring [February to April]. You ain't supposed to be fishing then," Parker Robinson said. "You take these mountain trout here. Now they'll have a winter coat on them. They don't have scales on them. It's right along now, the beginning of February, when they begin to lay eggs, and they're getting a thick coat on them. If you catch two when they're like that, and let them be against one another and they dry a bit, it's just like glue. You can hardly pull 'em apart, and you can hardly get that coat off of there when you're trying to clean them. I never would eat 'em when they had that coat on them, that spawning coat that mountain trout have."

Talmadge York told us, "We used to fish in these little ol' trout streams for specks. Original specks [native speckled trout] won't get but about six inches long. That's all. They don't have no scales on them at all. They're just as slick as a catfish."

Willie Underwood shared with us his feelings about why there aren't many speckled trout left in Rabun County. "The speckled trout is a small species. They don't have scales but do have little specks on them. There are only a few in the streams because they have to have more oxygen than anything else. It's got to be pure, clear water. The speckled trout are a thing of the past. There has been so much pollution in this clear water, and the lakes have been fished so heavy, the speckled trout are just nonexistent now. Speckled trout cannot compete with the fish that eat one another."

L. E. Craig agreed with Willie Underwood. "I don't know where a creek in this country is that's got any speckled trout. They can't stand for one bit of mud, silt, or anything [to be in the water]. I'd like to see just one more speckled trout. They are the best eating fish. A lot of people call brown trout a speckled trout, but they're not."

Andy Cope, who owned a trout fishing resort, told us, "Brown trout is a stream trout. It's not a good trout to grow in lakes and ponds. They bite slower than the other trout, and that's why there are some large brown trout caught in our streams. The main Betty's Creek stream is stocked with brown trout by the Game and Fish Department."

Jake Waldroop explained, "The brown trout doesn't have any scales, and he's brown all over. I've fished for the brown trout. They grow big. I caught one out there in the creek by my house that weighs three and a half pounds. Got him in the freezer right now."

FISHING EQUIPMENT

The fishing equipment of today is fancy but fairly easy to use. Yet it wasn't always easy to get fishing equipment. Some people made their own fishing poles out of cane or bamboo, their lines out of horsehair or string, and their sinkers from a piece of lead beaten out thin and folded around their line. People back then had it hard just to go fishing.

Willie Underwood explained the basic equipment. "Our fishing poles would be made out of creek canes, alder bushes, sourwood, or whatever we had.

"Fly rods have been around for years, but they wasn't used in this area until after the Depression. Fly rods was for people that had money. People didn't have them much around here because they couldn't afford them. I was forty years old when I got my first fly rod, and I bought it myself."

Melvin Taylor told us, "My daddy used a cane pole, and that's what I started fishing with. The people that had a lot of money had a reel

PLATE 148 "My daddy used a cane pole, and that's what I started fishing with."—Melvin Taylor

and rod. The rest had cane poles, which you can find on creek banks.

"Daddy caught bass that weighed eight and a half pounds with a cane pole. That's the biggest fish I could remember. It came out of Burton Lake. Boy! They put it in a tub at that store on display. That one was a whopper on a cane pole! That's the biggest I've ever heard of."

Andy Cope said, "We would make our fishing poles out of birch saplings. We'd cut a birch sapling and peel the bark off it, then hang it up by the fire and let it dry. When it was dry, we would use it for a fishing pole. Sometimes folks who lived in an area where there was a river would get river cane poles. Where I grew up, there wasn't any river cane."

"Years ago, I used to fish with a cane pole—only thing we had to fish with," L. E. Craig remembered. "There wasn't much bamboo in this country, but you could buy 'em at almost any store for a dime—big, long-tipped ones. Boy! You could catch bass on that thing that weighed two or three pounds. You talk about sport! It was! Have your line just about as long as your pole.

"I used to go down to Seed Lake in a boat and catch eighteen or twenty bass in a couple of hours. Bream could make your line whistle if they got on your pole. A few people had level winding reels to cast for bass."

Jake Waldroop said, "We would make our own fishing poles. Mostly, we would get out there and hunt us a little straight hickory. Hemlock, black gum, and hickory was hard to get. I would always prefer a cane if I could get it. Cane is almost like bamboo.

"I have made lots of cane poles. We would go to the Little Tennessee River and cut sometimes ten or fifteen of them, take them home, and hang them up by a string in the barn. We would cut them off the length we wanted them and tie a great big rock, three or four pounds, to them and let them hang there. Keep 'em from crooking up. Keeps 'em straight as a gun barrel and makes good fishing poles. If you didn't hang 'em up and put a weight on them, they would be warped. The pole should be a little bit bigger than my thumb by the time it's through hanging up. The tip will be as little as a knitting needle, but it will be strong. We could always get them from eight to ten feet long. A cane pole is hard to beat!"

Talmadge York reminisces, "Back when I was a boy, we made our line. We'd take a spool of thread and double it and beeswax 'em. And then we used to use what they called a silk line. You could buy lines made of silk before plastic came out."

Willie Underwood told us, "We used to use sewing thread off a spool for fishing string. It would break easy, so you would have to double and twist it. Sometimes we'd twist it four times because the lines weren't that long. We just had poles. We didn't have any reels to put it on. We'd buy standard fishing hooks at the store, but we didn't have fishing floats like we do now."

Minyard Conner said, "I can remember when I used to fish with horsehair for a line. All you would have to do to it was twist some horsehairs together. You had to have a good smooth place to make 'em. Put them horsehairs on your leg and rub them. That'll twist 'em together, and then when you want to set another one in there, just stick it in and keep a-rolling. They just roll on out there—make it as long as you want—and not have a knot in it. It'll hold too, about three or four horsehairs twisted together. Some of them would put four or five horsehairs together to catch a big fish. A three-horsehair line will catch a twelve-inch rainbow. I'd say it's six-pound test leader.

PLATE 149 Minyard Conner

"Put a sinker on your horsehair line to fish underwater. A horsehair won't tangle up like your other lines. If you throw it over a limb, it might wrap around it three or four times, but you give it a little pull, and it'll unravel by itself, and it's straight. You take a cotton string and throw it around a limb, and it ties right there."

Jake Waldroop recalled, "Sometimes we would buy hooks and tie them to the line, and sometimes we'd get them already made with the leader tied to them. Sometimes it's faster getting the hook out of the fish's mouth, if you can fish with bait with a sinker. 'Cause if they're bitin' good, when he grabs the bait, he'll just swallow hook and bait plumb down, and I have had to tear a fish's whole mouth open to get the hook out."

Leonard Jones told us about an alternative to using store-bought hooks. "I know one feller that said he wasn't never able to buy him no hooks. He'd fish with a straight pin. He'd bend it, you know. It didn't have that barb, and when he hooked one, he had to throw it out on the bank. If he didn't, it'd come off, and he'd lose it."

Leonard also explained how to make homemade sinkers. "Before they got to making sinkers, you'd just get you a piece of lead, cut it in strips, beat it out right thin, and then roll it around the line. You can buy any size sinkers now, great big ones or small ones. You want a sinker on it if you're fishing with bait, but if you're fishing with a fly, you don't."

Andy Cope recalls, "We used store-bought hooks, but we made our own sinkers out of shot from a shotgun shell. It was folded and put in a big spoon and melted on a fire. That run the lead together. Then we'd hammer the lead out flat and cut it into little pieces and roll it around fishing line for sinkers."

Talmadge York told us how to fix up a trotline. "To make a trotline, first tie the hooks to two-foot lengths of string. Then tie these to a long piece of binder twice about six or eight feet apart to keep the hooks from getting tangled up. Then go to a good root or something on the edge of the lake and tie one end of the line to that. Take your boat across the lake, maybe a hundred yards, somewhere where the lake's not too wide, and have the other end of your line tied to a big rock. If you don't tie the string to a big rock, it'll stay right on top. Put it down to where it'll be four or five foot under the water.

"I have set 'em and gone back the next morning, and every bait was still on. You work two or three hours to fix one up and set it and then go back and don't get nothing—that's hard work. I just quit fooling with it."

Leonard Jones explained what to do with the fish you catch. "I use a stringer instead of a chain to put the fish I catch on. All you do is run the line up through the gills and out their mouths. The first one that you put on, you've got to run it back through, make a ring. The rest is just strung through the gills and out the mouth without having to make the ring. You carry your stringer along with you, but most of the time you're setting down somewhere. So just throw your fish out in the water and take the end that has the sharp metal cover and stick it down in the ground. That'll hold 'em."

BAIT

"Trout will eat crawfish," L. E. Craig told us. "If you ever clean a trout of any size, and you don't find one in him, there's something wrong. Nearly any kind of fish will bite a crawfish. If he sees one, he wants to get him. Boy! It hurts to get bit by a crawfish."

Minyard Conner informed us that "minnows are good bait, but they don't live long." Talmadge York added, "I used to fish in the lake with minnows, and I fished for crappie with them. I reckon minnows are the only thing crappies will bite."

Lots of fishermen think red worms are the best bait. Jake Waldroop told us, "Red worms are good bait. Sometimes I have caught six fish with one red worm. I've tried them all, and red worms are the best." Buck Carver believes that "trout will all bite red worms in the wintertime and the early spring, but not all year round. They'll go for flies a lot of the year." Melvin Taylor told us, "Bass bites red worms and night crawlers real well in the spring. They're better than a lizard anytime." And Lawton Brooks said, "Red worms are pretty good for wild trout. Just regular earthworms. Them little ol' speckled trout—you can catch them with those worms. Just pitch a little ol' worm over there where the water ain't real deep. He'll come up and bite that worm, and you don't know where he come from."

Willie Underwood recalled, "We'd catch those ol' black crickets that you see in the fields, but that was hard to do. They're good for trout."

Carl Dills told us about flies used by fishermen. "These old mountain people calls 'em stick bait, but the regular name for them is caddis fly. They live among sticks and rocks in the edge of the creek, and you just pull them out."

Lots of fishermen preferred night crawlers. Blanche Harkins told us how her

PLATE 150 Carl Dills

sons caught them. "My sons uses night crawlers and red worms. Night crawlers come out at night, and fishermen catch 'em. They're just like red worms but a whole lot larger. The later at night they wait to catch them, the more they come out. If you wait till real late, they'll be out on top of the ground, and you can just pick them up. You use a flashlight, and if you don't dim your light, they jump back in their holes."

Parker Robinson explained how to create a "bed" for night crawlers. "You can make a place in your yard to raise night crawlers by putting your food peels in a pile. That dirt's gonna be rich where you have all that stuff, and your worms will come to that."

Willie Underwood told us to "burn a hornets' nest or yellow jackets' nest and get the young larvae. They make awful good bait, but they're tender enough that if you don't catch your fish when he first hits that bait, you'll have to bait your hook again."

Talmadge York told us about some of the different baits he uses. "I have got these little fellers [hellgrammites] out from under rocks and fished for trout with 'em. They'll sting you if you don't catch 'em just right. They look like a great big worm. We used them for when we trawled for bass. You can find what they call stretcher worms in the edge of the water."

Jack Waldroop recalled using mayflies as bait. "That's a fly that's down in the water. When he begins to come on top of the water and starts trying to fly, them fish come up to eat him. I've seen seventy-five to one hundred fish coming up at one time for those flies when they started hatching out. If you put a different kind of bait in there when the mayflies are in season, the fish won't strike as much. Just about all fish like mayflies."

Buck Carver reminisced about using wood sawyers. "The best luck I've had on a sinker or an eagle claw snail was these big ol' white sawyers that you get out of trestle timber. Used to, they would repair these railroad tracks and would throw out the old timber, and them ol' big sawyers would get in there. A sawyer is a termite-type worm. They'll be anywhere from a quarter of an inch to three or four inches long. Sometimes you can find them in rotten pine logs."

Another kind of worm used was the catawba worm. Minyard Conner told us, "The old catawba worms that are on the catawba trees—they're good bait. You'll never find the catawba worms on any other tree, just that certain kind."

Talmadge York agreed that those worms were good bait, especially for bream. "Old pea trees is what we call the trees they grow off of. There's another name for them but we always called 'em a pea tree. They have big ol' long peas on 'em. Bream bite catawba worms pretty good. Take a little stick or match and turn him wrong side outward. Take his head and push him plumb through. When he turns out, he's white. They'll bite him better white than green. If you fish with them, you usually catch big bream. Little ones won't fool with 'em."

Many fishermen used lizards for bait. Talmadge York recalled, "I have fished with what they call a red dog. It's a type of lizard except he's redder, like blood. They are good to fish with for bass. We used to go spring lizard hunting and stay out 'til twelve or one o'clock if we were going fishing the next day. You'd tear your fingers all to pieces scratching under rocks and catching them with a flashlight. Them spring lizards are awful good bait for bass if you fish slow with 'em. You get more big ones that way because the little ones don't pay much attention to the lizards."

L. E. Craig told us he used spring lizards to catch the biggest fish he ever caught. "I like to use spring lizards for bait. I don't like artificial bait. The largest fish I ever caught weighed seven and a half pounds, and I was using spring lizards. I've caught lots of trout with little-bitty lizards about two inches long. Bream and trout bite them small lizards you get out of a spring. Them ol' lizards live for half a day almost."

Jake Waldroop described using chicken parts for bait. "A good thing to bait your hook with for trout is chicken innards. Just throw a great big wad of them out in the water. Directly a fish will come and get 'em and start dragging them off. All you got to do is drag your fish out."

Corn is commonly used here to attract stocked fish. Jake Waldroop recalled, "Corn is good bait. Put a little red worm on a hook and then put a piece of corn on after it. Throw your line out there, and the stocked fish will come right for it. You can catch them better than natives with corn. The natives don't care too much about that corn."

Talmadge York told us, "Here, lately, the stocked fish bite corn better than anything, whole-kernel corn. The reason they bite this whole-kernel corn is because they've been fed on pellets, and they're used to that."

Many fishermen debate the use of artificial or real bait. Talmadge York told us, "I'd rather use artificial bait because it's less trouble. Fish bite 'em just as good. At times, I believe they hit 'em better. I've been fishing with boys that's been fishing with 'em while I was using live bait, and they'd catch 'em out of a hole where I wouldn't."

Carl Dills disagreed. "Fish go after live bait better than they do artificial bait. It's like if you went down here to the café, and you ordered a steak and they brought you a hot dog, you'd tell them you wouldn't take it. A fish is smart. They don't grow up to be twenty, twenty-five inches biting every hook that comes along either. They get smart as they

grow. A big trout hardly ever feeds himself of a night. Once in a while, he'll bite, usually if you use a big enough tackle to hole 'im."

Other fishermen change bait as needed, depending on what the fish are biting. Buck Carver said, "When you find a good fishing hole, and one day you come down there and throw your hook in, and they don't bite, you know that they've got tired of the same ol' thing. Fish are just like women—they change their minds all the time."

PLATE 151 "When you find a good fishing hole, and one day you come down there and throw your hook in, and they don't bite, you know that they've got tired of the same ol' thing."—Buck Carver

FISHING BY THE SIGNS

Many of the old-timers believe the signs of the zodiac play a part in whether or not the fish will bite. Buck Carver recalled, "Different times of the moon makes a lot of difference when you're fishing. When the sign is in the heart, they will bite better than usual.

"I tell you what you can do at home. Find a bottle like a small Coca-Cola bottle that's round and fill it to the top with water. Place the bottle upside down into a glass. When the water in the bottle rises in the glass up to the neck of the bottle, get your hooks and go!"

Leonard Jones doesn't follow the signs when fishing. "Lots of people go by the signs of the moon, but I never did pay it much attention, just to be honest with you. I go anytime. There's days you can go out there, and I don't care what kind of bait you've got. They won't bite. There's times you can go, and they'll bite like anything. Now, I don't know what causes it, whether it's the signs or what. Lots of people notices the signs to a great extent. I never did pay much attention to them."

Talmadge York agreed. "I don't go by the signs. But now I believe that on a dark night is the best time to fish. I don't mean to fish on the dark night, but just that time of the month when the moon is not shining bright. It seems like when there is a light night, the fish feed all night, and they're not hungry the next day. They take it by spells. When they're feeding, you couldn't catch a one. It'd be just like there's not a fish in the water."

FISHING TECHNIQUES

All the people we talked to had different ideas about the way they caught fish and what worked best for them. We asked each fisherman to tell how he caught the kinds of fish he does and any methods he recommends.

Lawton Brooks told us, "Crappie will bite in one place for a while, and then they'll quit. They move a lot. They move in schools like white bass. If you get in a bunch of crappie, and they start biting good, the first one you catch in the lip where it won't hurt him, ease him up and cut the line, leaving your hook in him. Cut you off a little bit of leader and tie it to a lightbulb and just drop it back in the water, and he'll stay with the gang. Watch where the lightbulb goes, and just take your boat and follow him. Just keep a-catching them because he will follow the gang of crappies, and you will know where the fish are.

"I'll tell you about a catfish. He's so slow about biting. Maybe you'll set there for hours before one ever bites. Maybe you'll catch one, and sometimes you'll be there the rest of the day and night and not catch nothing. I haven't caught but two catfish in my life in the daytime. Caught one of them out of Hiawassee Lake and caught the other one down here above Tallulah Falls. I went down to Tugalo one time with another feller and caught a bunch of little catfish about four inches long. It wasn't interesting. They was too small to eat."

"Anytime my wife will let me go fishing is the best time to go," Carl Dills declared. "When I get all my work done and she'll let me—that's the best time. You take one of the dark nights. The fish will bite better in the daytime than they will of a light night. I reckon they feed more when the moon is shining all night long than they do of a dark night.

"When it's raining, it washes out the food into the water, and they'll go to feeding. There's a certain time a fish will go to feeding, and other times you swear there wasn't a fish in the creek. Then in maybe ten minutes, there's fish everywhere you look.

"You take a catfish. It feeds by smell, and they'll bite when the water's muddy quicker than when it's clear. A bass or a trout feeds by sight, not by smell alone, and they bite better when the water's clear. Dark water that's dingy, though, and using night crawlers, trout will bite 'cause they're looking for worms that's washed in the water from a heavy rain. They're out there looking for 'em."

Parker Robinson revealed some of the secrets to his successful fishing. "I like to use two fishing poles because I'll be trying to catch one on one pole and maybe another one would bite the other. I like to fish from land because I can catch more fish, but they're about the same size

PLATE 152 "I like to use two fishing poles, because I'll be trying to catch one on one pole and maybe another one would bite the other."—Parker Robinson

you'd catch from a boat. I don't like to fish in the wintertime because you can't catch much. You can catch more fish when it's not raining, but it don't matter if it's cloudy."

Buck Carver informed us, "When you get to the headwaters of these little trout streams, and the water is extremely clear, I like to wade downstream because that stirs up the mud, and fish in their holes can't see you. You can catch more going downstream than you will going up.

"When you're fishing for native trout, fish uphill. There'll be one laying out on guard duty at the bottom of the hole. If you can, slip up behind him and throw out the hook above him and let it drift down to him. If you can get that one on guard duty, you'll be able to catch two or three more out of that same hole. But if he sees you and sails into that hole, you're lucky if you get any of 'em 'cause he comes in there so fast, the rest of 'em knows that he's done set the alarm. They ain't fools. If one comes in there like a scalded dog, the others in that hole knows there's a dead cat on the line somewhere."

Leonard Jones stated, "A good time to go fishing is when it's raining, if you [don't mind] getting wet. They'll bite as good or better than they will any other time. I think maybe the rain causes the water to rise, and they learn that when the water rises, it washes in stuff for them to eat. When it commences to raining, they get to stirring around, and the more they stir, the apter you are of catching them.

"You take the bream. They go in droves around. Maybe you'll catch several right now, and then they'll be gone for a while, then come back around, and you'll catch another bunch. They don't stay long at the same place. Now, a big ol' trout, if he's got a certain hole in the river, he'll stay there most of the time in that same place.

"You should go fishing early of a morning or late of a evening. You can catch trout or catfish at night. From daylight 'til nine in the morning, you'll catch more fish than you will the rest of the day 'til about five or six that evening. Any kind of fish will bite a heap better early of a morning or late of a evening. They don't bite too awful good at noon. They'll bite some along and along all day. When it gets on up about the Fourth of July when it gets real hot, they don't bite good at all. They'll bite in the winter if you can stand to stay out there and fish, but you freeze to death. I caught bream one time up yonder on Bear Creek Lake 'til I got so cold baiting my hook that I got to where I didn't have no feeling nearly in my hands. Every time I'd throw my hook in, one would bite it. I just kept fishing 'til I froze myself good before I quit.

"In the wintertime, fish eat anything they can get. If a lake has been down and rises, why, that washes in a lot of food."

Melvin Taylor believes the best time to fish is when it's calm. "I don't remember me doing much good when it was cloudy with the wind blowing and white clouds in the sky, but that's the time my daddy said was best. I say the best time is when it's clear and calm. The spring of the year or fall is better than any other time for bream fishing.

"A good place to fish is where the stream runs into another one. In the spring of the year, they're looking for a place to bed. That's when you'll catch most of the trout. They bed on a full moon, when it's warm. They'll be out in the shallow water, so you just travel out 'til you find their beds. Then stop and fish until they stop biting. They'll just bite for so long. Then you just crank up and find another bed. You can see the beds in early morning, but still you can see them plain as day in shallow water in the evening.

"Bream fish, that's my favorite kind of fishing. One thing about it, you can always catch one of them. They bed on every new moon. In the spring of the year, you get some red worms and go on a new moon and ride around in your boat until you find a bed. If you find them in a bed, you can catch them.

"When you're out there, you don't necessarily have to be quiet, but the aluminum boats have to be pretty still because of the vibrations from them. The bass, they won't hear you coming up. You can just about run across them. I've ran right over a bed and not even seen them.

"A good time to go catfishin' is when it's dark. They go to feeding then."

Jake Waldroop shared his fishing techniques. "It's better to catch fish early in the morning or late in the evening. Now, rainbow bite better of a night than of a day. I remember the time when they would just eat you up at night.

"I would rather fish upstream when fly-fishing. When you're fishing upstream, just let your line float back downriver.

"It don't take a person long to learn how to catch a fish. By the time you go fishing four or five times, you get along pretty good. You can just sit on the side of the bank and fish out in the water and catch them. Let your hook come around the edge of the bank. He'll be laying back under there. He'll run out and grab it. You take that net, and when you hook one out in the water somewhere, you can pull him up to you on the pole and reach out with the net and get it under him. Lots of times, if you don't have that net, he will float off the hook.

"You have to throw them back in now if they're under seven inches long. It doesn't hurt a fish much usually, but if you hook him pretty deep, you just might as well throw him on the bank. If you just catch him in the lips, you can throw him back in.

"I've had a lot of fish to get away. If you can miss him, that's about it. If you hook him a little, you can tell it, you can feel it. If he struck at your hook, if you didn't snag him, he may not come back again. About nine times out of ten, you will miss one.

"When I was a boy, and we went fishing, we had to walk about four miles, but when we got over there, we fished for about two hours and then went back home. Sometimes we would go and stay all night. When we did that, we would just fix us a mess for supper and breakfast. Then after breakfast, we would go back and catch us some fish to bring home with us. Sometimes we went on Monday morning and didn't come back 'til Saturday. We would stay a whole week at a time.

"You don't have to be too quick when the water is right clear. It's best for you to keep the bushes between you and the hole you fish in. Back then, there was so many they couldn't help from biting. They didn't pay much attention to you. It still don't take too long to catch a fish. I just walk up to a hole, have my hook baited, and throw it in. Jerk it right back out of that. Those trout, when they bite, they really come after it. You don't have to wait on them too long."

FAVORITE FISHING HOLES

"My favorite place to fish is down on the Chattooga River," said Talmadge York. "Anywhere you can get to in the Chattooga is a good place. Sara's Creek is a good place in the summertime. There's so many people fishing there now that there ain't many fish left. For the last few years, me and my wife have camped up there at Sara's Creek—stay a week at a time. When they stock 'em up there, you can catch 'em right when they first put 'em in. We always catch our limit. Have enough to do us. It ain't so much fun catching them stocked ones as it is catching the wild ones, though."

Melvin Taylor prefers lake fishing. "The best fishing place is Lake Rabun. If you want to catch fish—fish Lake Rabun. They've got 'em all. It's the best fishing place you'll find. If you want to catch bream, you go to Lake Rabun anytime in warm weather up into October and November. In fact, I caught a mess down there during deer season."

Florence Brooks prefers fishing in streams. "I'd rather fish in a stream because you can just catch them better, and then I just like stream fishing. We used to walk from Rabun Gap to the head of Betty's Creek and then fish back down. We'd catch a pile of fish! Walk along, and if you feel something, jerk it. But in a lake, you just stand still, wait for them to get on, then jerk it. I fish right around here, all over Rabun County, just anywhere I can get a hook in the water."

Lawton Brooks agrees with his wife. "I like to fish anywhere there's a good stream. I like to fish streams better than I do lakes because there is more sport in it. Just get in there with them. Trout have more action. Give you more sport."

PLATE 153 Florence and Lawton Brooks holding their fishing trophies

Jake Waldroop said, "I never did have a favorite fishing hole. Everybody could locate them just as well as I could. There is lots of rivers that runs right under these mountains here. There's Long Branch, Park Creek, Kimsey Creek [North Carolina]. I would rather fish in them than any other. I have caught lots of fish from them."

Minyard Conner told us, "I like to fish almost anywhere. I don't like fishing in trout farms much. I'd rather fish after a trout where it's raised out in the wild where you just have to outwit him to get him. If he sees the shadow of your pole, he'll run. He knows something dangerous is on hand."

CLEANING FISH

Leonard Jones explained, "It depends on what kind of fish you have as to how you clean it. If they're small, take a trout for instance, I just scrape them good, take their innards out, and cut their heads and fins off.

"You have to skin a catfish. It ain't got no scales on it. Cut it around the neck, split it down the back and stomach, and take a pair of pliers and pull that skin off. You can skin 'em just about as quick as you scrape 'em. If I catch a great big fish of any kind, I skin it. Small ones, I don't."

Minyard Conner told us, "To clean a speckled trout, just take a knife and split him open and take his guts out. Then he's ready to cook."

Buck Carver said, "The rainbow and the brown trout have scales, and you have to scrape them. Though the speckled trout has scales, they're so fine you needn't try to scale him. All you do is rub that slime off with some sand."

COOKING OR PRESERVING FISH

Minyard Conner stated, "There are a lot of ways you can cook trout—bake 'em, fry 'em, or stew 'em. First, you cut their heads off and clean 'em. Now, these stockards [stocked fish], I'd stew 'em and take the bones out and make fish patties out of them because their meat's too tender to hold together to fry.

"To bake a fish, you coat them with a little grease and lemon juice. Heat your oven to about 350 degrees and cook 'em about thirty minutes."

Florence Brooks told us, "Mama used to fry fish for us for breakfast. Nowadays I usually give away what I catch, because we don't eat fish. When I do cook them, I just roll the fish in cornmeal and a little salt and fry them in grease on the stove. Some people can't eat fried fish, but my kids just like them fried brown. They eat them that way with hush puppies."

Minyard Conner revealed, "I've eat fish eggs! I've caught a lot of big fish with big rolls of eggs under them. Boy, I like them! That's caviar! That's good!"

Blanche Harkins stated, "Trout are easy to cook. I scrub them with a scrub pad or dishrag gourd to get the slime off. Then I cut their heads off and cut their stomachs open to take their innards out. Then I wash 'em again and roll them in cornmeal. I have a big black frying pan that I put Crisco in and get it hot enough to smoke. I turn the heat down some and brown them about ten minutes on either side, and they're ready to eat."

Jake Waldroop told us, "Before we had a freezer, we had some cool springs, and we would put any fish we weren't going to cook right then in a bucket or half-gallon jars and stand them under those springs where the cold water would run over them. We could keep them for four or five days or more."

Minyard Conner recalled, "Well, I was raised with the Indians. They wouldn't do like the white man. You know, catch too many of anything and have to throw 'em away. They'd just catch what they could eat, and that's all they took. If they could eat ten, then that's all they took. They didn't usually try to preserve them. They didn't do a thing with 'em."

PLATE 154 Blanche Harkins

"THE BIGGEST FISH I EVER CAUGHT"

Florence Brooks related, "The biggest fish I ever caught lacked one inch from being two feet long. It's been ten or fifteen years ago, I guess, when we lived at Dillard. I caught a brown trout right about Betty's Creek Bridge. It was as long as my arm and weighed four pounds and a half. I was using an ol' cane pole, and my line had been on there no telling how long.

"They all took a fit when I caught that fish—thought somebody was a-drowning! I had it caught deep in its throat, and it couldn't cut up a bit. I just drug it to the bank. Lawton [her husband] and Kent Shope got down in the water and lifted it up on the bank with their hands."

Minyard Conner stated, "The biggest fish I ever caught was a twenty-four-inch rainbow over in Smokemont, in the Smokies [North Carolina]. I have fished all year long and maybe not caught one fish over a foot long. I seen one over there in the Smokies that was thirty-six and a half inches long that they'd caught in the Pigeon River."

Talmadge York recollected, "I never had a really big fish that got away. One maybe twelve or fifteen inches long got off before I could get him out of the water. About the biggest fish I ever caught was a twenty-three-inch brown trout. I caught a blue cat one time that weighed nine pounds. I guess the biggest bass we ever caught was about a six-pounder."

"I'VE HEARD, WHAT GROWS THE FASTEST OF ANYTHING IN THE WORLD IS A FISH AFTER IT'S CAUGHT 'TIL YOU TELL ABOUT IT."

The first thing we thought about when we decided on an entire chapter dedicated to fishing were the stories fishermen are reputed to tell. The main focus of all our interviews was probably "Do you know any good fishing stories?"

Some of these are events that happened to people as they fished, or stories that had been told to them about people fishing, or stories they know about other fishermen. Some of the stories are exciting; some are funny; some are kind of hard to believe but are said to be true; and some are just informative.

Lawton Brooks told us, "I found this fish, oh, I guess four or five months ahead of the time I caught him. But I couldn't get him to hit nothing. I tried everything. My wife'd catch lizards, and we'd try those. I didn't tell nobody where I fished at. It was right down the railroad going by our house. The creek went right in beside the mountain there, hit a big rock, and turned back right under the rock there. It was right deep, and it was swift through there. It might be that when you put your bait in there, it went by too fast for him to catch it. He didn't want to fool with it or something.

"I'd slip down there sometimes and see him out. I'd look over in there, and sometimes he'd be in a deep hole. I'd go to the house and tell Florence, my wife, 'I'm gonna catch him.'

"So they started a revival meeting down there at the church below the house. One evening—it was the prettiest evening to fish—I went out there, and I fished and I fished, and fooled around and caught me a little ol' crawdad. I cut his head off, hooked him on that hook, and had me a line—I mean a stout'un. I had me a big ol' cane pole, long as from here to the door yonder, and I put that thing on that pole. I put me on a great big ol' beaten-out piece of lead, and I rolled it around there.

"I throwed that line right on over in there with that crawdad, and I went on off to church. I put the pole up under a rock and stuck it in the bank. We come on back, and he'd bit my line. He was on there!

"I tell you what I done. I'd pull him out from under that rock, and he'd go back. And I'd get him back out, and he'd go back under. He'd swallowed the plug I had on the line way down. There wasn't no way he could have got loose without he broke the line all the way because he'd done got it down past that tough place in his throat here. If it ever got below there, it'd pull his head off, and he'd still come out of there, or he'd come out dead. He ain't gonna get that hook out. As long as you've just got him up here in the mouth, he can throw 'em out. But I know he swallowed that thing, for I had it hooked right through both his lips, and I knowed he'd have to swallow the whole hook, and sure 'nough, he had.

"I fooled with that ol' rascal a long time, pulling him in and out. Thedro Wood come up. He had his arm broke, had it in a sling. He said, 'What's the matter here?'

"I said, 'I'm trying to get this big fish outta here. I've got a big'un under here. You watch 'im in a minute.'

"Boy! I brought him out of there, and back he'd go. Thedro said, 'Yea, God! What a fish!' He said, 'Next time bring him plumb on out in those bushes. Bring him out on this sandbar, and I'll catch 'im.'

"I brought him out there, and he went back in. The next time I started with him, I just took right on out through yonder just a-runnin' with my pole, draggin' him. Sure enough, he come out on the sandbar, and Thedro fell down on top of him. He said, 'Come in here. I've got it. He's under me here.' Says, 'Just reach under there and get it. He's under there. I'm on top of it.'

"So I reached around under there, and I finally got to his head and got right up in his gills, and I said, 'We got 'im now.' I forgot how long he was, but boys, he was a whopping fish! And no telling how long he'd been in that creek. And everybody had fished by him. I'd been a-fishing by him for over a year before I ever knowed he was in there. Of course, I bet he'd laid right there in that same place.

"I had my pole back in under a bank, just as far back as I could drive it in the bank. I fixed it a purpose, so if he did get on there, I meant to have him. I got a line that I bet would have held fifty pounds and tied on that cane pole! And I wrapped the line way down the pole, so if he broke the end of the pole, I'd still have him down near to the bottom of it."

Florence Brooks recalled, "I was fishing over there above Lake Burton, right down in the mouth of Timpson Creek. I put my plug out there, and I whipped one. I was bringing it in, and all at once, it got a whole lot heavier. I said, 'My word, he must be an awful big one!' He come out, and I saw that a bigger fish had the one I caught in his mouth. I had two hooks on my line, and the other fish was caught by that one. I come out with two of 'em.

"One time when I was fishing up yonder on Burton Lake on a bridge, I saw a pretty hole way up across there, and I just drew back and threw my hook under there. I hooked something, and it broke loose. Since Lawton was fishing above there, I just thought, 'Doggone it, he's caught my fish!' And I swear, I liked to have caught a deer in the nose!

"It was in that water covered up, all but its nose sticking out. I thought it was a rock. When I got it in the nose, it jerked loose and got out of the water and left there. It's the truth! It tickled Lawton to death. This was last summer. I knew it was a big one, but I wasn't sure if it was a fish. I told Lawton that if I'd have got him good, he would have jerked me in! I don't want to catch me another deer!"

Buck Carver explained, "If you ever slip up to a hole and hook a rainbow or a brown, either one, and hook him pretty hard, you might as well forget about that rascal if you lose him, because he ain't gonna bite again that day.

"One time in my life I caught one over here in Kelly's Creek. One of the biggest ones I've ever caught. It was about sixteen and a half inches long. It was awful broad.

"Anyhow, I was up on the side of the bank, and I dropped my hook in. It had a red worm on it. That fish hit the hook, and I got him about five foot out of the water, and he splashed off and went back in. The hook tore out. I went on up the creek. I was gone about two hours or two hours and a half. I didn't think he'd bite again that quick, but he took it so fast when I dropped it in there the first time, I figured he must be pretty hungry. I come back down on the other side of the creek where I could get down in the water with that fish. That thing hooked up again. I scrambled around and let him wrestle around over that hole and finally got 'im out. He was about a pound, pound and a half, and there in the roof of his mouth was a big 'ol tore place where I'd hooked him the first time. That was the quickest I've ever got one of them durn things to bite again, and know it."

Minyard Conner informed us, "I'll tell you a fishing story that happened while I was fishing last summer. We was up yonder at the creek, and there was just so many people, I couldn't get in. I had on a pair of wading boots, and they had just thrown a stockard in there about twenty inches long—one of them stripers. He was as long as your arm. He'd swim in there, back and forth, and everyone would throw their hook at him. Well, there wasn't no place for me to stand, so I decided I would wade the river. There was laurel on the other side, and I went over there. That fish had come down and around over there, and everybody was throwing their hooks at him.

"I said to myself, 'Directly, he'll come up here, and I'll snag him.' He swam up that channel, and I saw him coming. I placed my hook in the water in that channel and gave it a yank and caught him on the right side of the head. He like to have jerked the pole out of my hand. He went round and round, and everyone pulled their hooks out of the water so I didn't tangle him up with none of them. He just run everywhere, and I guess there must have been over a hundred people standing there fishing. After a while I slung him out and stuck my finger in his mouth and said, 'Whoopee!' And it was all over."

Leonard Jones related, "I used to go fishing, and if I had any luck and come home, my wife, Ethel, would say, 'Well, did you buy them?' Well, one time I went and caught one or two cats, real good ones. They's some fellow there that had four more real good ones. He said he'd take a dollar for 'em. I just give him a dollar and strung them up with mine. Ethel said, 'Well, where'd you buy 'em at?'

"I said, 'Every time I catch any you always accuse me of buyin' them.' I guess it was two or three years before I told her that I bought them. I wouldn't tell her. That's the only ones, though, that I have bought, but she always accused me, if I had good luck, of buying 'em."

Melvin Taylor reminisced, "We were out in a boat. We were up early in the morning. We saw [a] fish, but there was something wrong with it. I thought at first he had a shad hung in his mouth, but I think his floater was busted. You know, when he runs, he bails that water and takes off. We'd come up on him, and when he saw the boat motor, he would go out of sight and come up way over on the other side of the lake. First thing we'd see was a break of water, so we'd crank up the boat and run on over there. We'd see him dig off again, so we had run him around the lake about thirty minutes or longer, and I told Wesley [my son] if we ever run him into shallow water, we might get him. So we went way on the other side of the lake, and we saw him jump. When we got back over there, he took off again.

"Wesley said, 'Daddy, I'm glad it's early in the morning. Ain't nobody around. They'd think we were drunk or crazy one.'

"We went on over there and sure enough, he went in, broke water, and went out to shallow water. I told Wesley, 'If we slip up behind him so he can't see us, we might get him.' So that time I saw him, his head was at the other direction. I told Wesley to get a net and both hands. 'Boy! It's a big one.' I couldn't see the fish. I was paddling and Wesley, he was a-looking. He was bent down, had the net in the water. About that time Wesley came falling over backwards in the boat with that fish in the net. Wesley told me, 'He ran that way, and when he seen the shallow water, he whirled around and run right slap into the net, headfirst!'

"That's how we caught that one. Wesley said, 'How are we going to tell how we caught it, Daddy?'

" 'Well,' I said, 'we'll just have to tell the truth, son.'

"He said, 'Ain't nobody going to believe you.'

"And I said, 'I know they're not. We'll have a lot of fun out of this.'

"So we fished around a while longer, but wasn't doing no good. We went over to Jack Hunnicutt's bait place about daylight or a little after, and there were four or five men buying bait. We came in, and they asked us what we caught him on. We told them we caught it on one of Jack Hunnicutt's smiling night crawlers. They said, 'Sure 'nough, how did you catch him? What kind of outfit did you have?'

" 'To tell the truth, we didn't have him on no line. We just run him down and caught him in the landing net.' Boy, they just punched one another and was laughing and going on, you know, and we come on and showed him around. We had more fun out of that, and they rode me and Wesley about that for two or three months. That's the way we caught that fish.

"Everybody said, 'Well, that's not no fun to catch one like that.'

"And I told them, 'I tell you what. You try running one down with a motorboat and catching him in a landing net. You'll find out it's a pretty good sport.'

"That was really an experience. That one weighed eight pounds and ten ounces—that's a nice one. You don't get many that size in this country."

Jake Waldroop recalled, "Yeah, a fish has taken my hook off before. You just have to go out on the bank and tie you on another one and go right back after 'im.

"I was a-fishing up there on Kimsey

PLATE 155 Jake Waldroop

Creek one time, and I had caught me a big brown trout. He was about sixteen inches long. I got him pulled out and put him on my string, then went on and throwed my bait in. I seen another coming at it, and he struck at the hook. I pulled, and I had him, and I said, 'That's the biggest fish I've ever caught in my life.' He just took off right down the river with me, and I just had to let go. He got down in some muddy water, and there was a sandbar there. I finally got him out. I had caught him by his tail. He wasn't as big as nothing, but he had more power to pull because of where he was caught. The hook had missed his mouth and caught in his tail. That hook is just as sharp as anything that can be made.

"We had a big fish on Kimsey Creek, a big old rainbow. We fished for that fish for three years and never could catch it. One time it rained all night, and the next morning, while we were getting breakfast, a big old crawfish came crawling out the camp door. Al jumped up and got him and put him in a box that we had. He said he was going up the creek and catch that big trout that morning. I had to round up the sows and feed them. While I was down there, I heard Al yell. You never heard such in your life! So I went back to the camp and he said, 'He got away.'

"I said, 'No, he didn't. What's that you've got covered up over there?' He had him covered up in some leaves. He uncovered him and took him out, and he was twenty-one inches long.

"He said, 'I put that crawfish on and started up at the head and come down, and I felt him [on my line]. I let him chew on it a little bit until I got him.'

"He had already swallowed that crawfish plus two more and two big chubs about five inches long. He had all that in him when Al caught him. He was a greedy one.

"We played a trick on a man one time. His name was David Rouse. Frank Long and I were up there at our camp, and David came along. He was camping down at another camp, and we told him to go get his stuff and come on up there with us. He said, 'Do you want to go fishing?'

"We told him we were planning on going. So he said he would be back directly. He came on back in, got supper, and got ready to go. There was an old log laying out in the water. It would go down, then back up, down, then back up. I got my hook caught in it. It looked just like a fish when it went down and up, so we thought we would have some fun out of him. We told him there was a big fish down there at the river that he ought to get out of there. He went and put a number six hook on and went on down to the river. He pulled and pulled trying to get that big fish out. He said, 'Oh, I got him.' He pulled 'til the end of his pole broke off. That old man died believing he had a fish at the end of his pole. We never did tell him no better."

PLATE 156 Talmadge York

Talmadge York told us, "A bunch of us, we'd take ol' man Will Zoellner, and we'd camp. We'd set up at night 'til twelve or one o'clock listening to him tell these big ol' fish tales. He said he caught 'em so old the fish had moss on their backs back in them streams. Course we believed all that back then.

"It tickled me to watch him eat 'em. He could eat fish! Especially trout. After that, we got to going to these stocked streams. Went to the top of Wildcat one time and caught a bunch of them. He wouldn't let you cut their heads off. He eats heads and all. He can take a trout eight to ten inches long and start at the head and never spit a bone out. Eats every bone in there. I told him one time, 'If I eat them bones, it'd choke me to death.'

"He said, 'When they get about right there [bottom of the trachea], they're gone.' And I seen him eat six or eight trout, bones and all.

"Another time, me and Bobby Alexander was fishing. We was wading one side, both of us fishing from one side of the river, and there was fish right next to the bank under the bushes. It was deep out there, and we didn't want to get in over our heads and get our stuff wet. Bobby reached up to hold on to a bush, and he pulled a hornets' nest down. He didn't even see it. That bush with that nest hit right on me. They liked to have stung me to death. I'll bet there was twenty-five stings right around the back of my neck.

"I went in under the water trying to get 'em off and finally did. We went on up the river, and there was a man and a woman camped up there. She had some alcohol and got me down on the table and fixed my neck up with that alcohol. They liked to have made me sick, so many of them.

"Fish won't never give up. I got one twenty-three inches long down in Dick's Creek up in Kay Swafford's field. I had a fly rod, and I had a lot of line out. I was fishing with worms that day, and I was pulling my line down through there, and he hit it. It was just a small creek, and he went thirty or forty feet. That's how much line I had out. I just run down the creek with him trying to take up line and finally got him up to the end of my pole. I thought I just run him plumb out on the bank. I started running up that bank, and the end of my fly rod hit the bank and broke it slap in two. I just kept a-running, and I got my fish. He was a nice fish.

"I don't know of no big fishing tales. One time a bunch of us went over to a little stream in the Glades. The season wasn't open yet. Me and my wife and Noah Hamby decided to go too. They was going to catch enough out of there for us to cook and eat. We got down in there. Cecil was watching for Bobby to fish, and he had hip boots. The little ol' stream wasn't three foot wide, but it was early spring. He had his spinning rod, and he was fishing in there.

"My Jeep was just like the one the game warden had then, and Cecil thought it was the game warden coming in there. He hollered to Bobby that the game warden was a-coming, and he took out right across the hill. His spinner caught in a bush, and he just kept a-going. He run all his line off and broke it, and just kept right on a-going. We drove on down there and kept hollering for him to come back. I guess it was thirty minutes before he come back, scared to death. He had on them hip boots and had a hard time running.

"One time a bunch of us went down to this old mill. Me and Harry walked across the mountain. We went different ways for different parts of the river. We fished down[stream] and didn't get a strike below Bull Shoulder—way down—and it was just as cloudy as it could be and thundering. It come up a rain, and we waited just a few minutes.

"Then we started fishing back up the river where we had already fished, and everywhere we'd throw that plug, we'd catch a fish. I reckon that rain started 'em a-biting.

"Some of the boys would take us down to the river. Then they'd take the car around, and we'd fish up to them. A lot of times we'd camp, and cook and eat those fish right on the bank. We caught several good trout, brown trout.

"One time down on Licklog, we fished for them little catfish that wouldn't be but about six inches long. Every once in a while, we'd catch one of them big white suckers. You can't eat them. You have to throw them back, but you have a lot of fun getting them out. They cut up awful. We caught some of them that weighed two pounds.

"The last few times I went in there and fished that river, it was pretty rough and deep in places. I got to where I couldn't get over the rocks, couldn't get my feet up over them. But we had a lot of fun back in those times."

APPENDIX

Compiled by Doug Adams and Kyle Burrell

THE BASS FAMILIES

Bass are in either the black bass "family" or the white bass family.

BLACK BASS

Black bass is a collective term used to indicate any one of ten large members of the sunfish family. They live in warmer lakes and ponds, as well as warm to cool rivers. All black bass build nests in which the male guards the eggs.

Largemouth Bass (a.k.a. Bigmouth Bass, Black Bass, Bucketmouth Bass, Green Bass, Green Trout). The largemouth bass is one of the most important freshwater game fish in North America. It has dark stripes on its sides, but they disappear as it matures. Young fish have dark lateral bands. Their mouth is large and extends back beyond the eye. Largemouth bass usually weigh less than ten pounds. It spawns in spring from March through May in waters that are sixty to seventy degrees. Large females can lay up to forty thousand eggs. They eat small fish, worms, insects, crawfish, small turtles, and frogs. They strike artificial lures or live bait.

Redeye Bass (a.k.a. River Trout, River Bass, Shoal Bass). The redeye greatly resembles the smallmouth. It is a small bass found in rivers. Redeye bass are up to fourteen inches long and are very common in the Chattooga River. They eat small fish and crawfish. They can be caught on spinners and lures. Many anglers prize them because they are scrappy, colorful, and highly palatable.

Smallmouth Bass (a.k.a. Bronzeback Bass). The smallmouth bass is considered by many to be our greatest freshwater game fish. The color of smallmouth bass is golden bronze-green or brownish green with distinct faint vertical bars on the side of the body. The mouth extends to the pupil of the eye, but not beyond. There are scales on the base of the fins. Smallmouth bass usually weigh less than six pounds. They prefer deeper, cooler waters and are found in clear streams and lakes. They spawn in the spring in waters that are sixty-five to seventy degrees. They feed on minnows, worms, insects, frogs, crawfish, and hellgrammites. Smallmouth bass will strike artificial lures and live bait.

WHITE BASS

The white bass are the true bass family. White bass are found in rivers, but seem to prefer large lakes with relatively clear water. In the spring, they run up rivers and spawn in running water without building nests where the eggs free-float or settle to a gravel bottom.

Striped Bass (a.k.a. Rockfish). The striped bass is colored greenish or brownish on the upper part of the sides, silvery or brassy below, and white on the belly. Seven or eight dark, well-defined stripes run from the back of the gill cover to the base of the tail. Size ranges of ten to twenty-five pounds are common. Good fishing occurs during the spawning run. The bait commonly used is shad.

White Bass (a.k.a. Striped Bass, Silver Bass). This white bass looks like a striped bass but is much smaller. Sizes range up to four pounds. They swim in schools and are often seen chasing shad on the surface of the lake. They will strike minnow lures and spinners.

THE CARP FAMILY

Carp are large minnows. They are golden in color. The goldfish raised in aquariums and ponds are part of this family. The carp family includes over three hundred American species. They can grow to three feet long and over twenty pounds in weight. They are found in lakes and slow streams. Carp are bottom feeders.

THE CATFISH FAMILY

The catfish family contains over one thousand species. They have smooth, scaleless bodies with long barbels around the mouth. Depending on species, catfish can mature at less than a pound but can grow up to 150 pounds. Most catfish live in quiet waters, but some live in moderately fast-running streams. Catfish are scavengers and will eat other fish, frogs, crawfish, insect larvae, crustaceans, clams.

Blue Catfish (a.k.a. Channel Catfish). The blue catfish color is a rather dark bluish gray on the back, which fades into a lighter slate gray on the sides. It has no dark spots. The average size is two to five pounds. Blue catfish weighing twenty pounds are common, and they can grow to over one hundred pounds.

Brown Bullheads (a.k.a. Bullhead, Mudcat). Brown bullheads are light

brownish yellow to black-brown in color and are found in slow or stagnant water. The average size is less than a pound, with large brown bullheads reaching four pounds.

Channel Catfish. Channel catfish are considered the sportiest member of
the catfish family. They are colored silvery olive or slate blue with
round, black spots. Channel catfish have a deeply forked tail and fairly
slender body. They can weigh up to three or four pounds and prefer
clear moving water. Most of their feeding is at night. They spawn in the
spring with an upstream migration.

THE CRAPPIE FAMILY

Black and White Crappie (a.k.a. Bridge Perch, Calico Bass). The crappie is
closely related to sunfish and black bass. The two species, black and
white, are very similar. They can grow up to sixteen inches long and can
weigh over two pounds. Crappies eat small fish, insects, crustaceans,
and worms. Jigs may be used in casting for them. They are easily
caught in the spring and make excellent pan fish.

THE PERCH FAMILY

Yellow Perch (a.k.a. Ringed Perch, Yellow Bass). Yellow perch are the
best-known perch. They are yellowish, and their sides are distinctly
barred. Their fins are tinged with red. The average size is less than a
pound. They are found in lakes and are a school fish. Spawning occurs
in the spring, and the eggs are laid over sand. They eat insects and small
fish. They will strike live minnows and artificial lures.

Walleye (a.k.a. Walleyed Bass, Walleyed Pike). Walleye is a large dark
perch. They are becoming less common in local lakes. Walleye weigh
up to ten pounds and are also very good to eat.

THE PIKE FAMILY

Northern Pike (a.k.a. Pike). The scaling, which covers the entire cheek but
only the upper half of the gill, identifies northern pike. They weigh up
to thirty-five pounds and can grow to over four feet long. Northern pike
are slender with narrow pointed heads and duckbill-shaped mouths.

Chain Pickerel (a.k.a. Jack, Pickerel, Pike). Chain pickerel are much
smaller than northern pike, but look almost identical. They grow to a

maximum of three feet in length and also have a duckbill-shaped mouth.

THE SUNFISH FAMILY

Sunfish are smaller than bass, generally about eight inches long. They spawn in the spring. Shallow, saucerlike nests are fanned in the sand and gravel. The male guards the nest. There are hundreds of species.

Bluegill (a.k.a. Bream). Bluegills are small fish about as big as your hand. They can be caught in large numbers in our lakes using crickets, worms, and artificial flies.

Redbreast Sunfish (a.k.a. Bream, Shellcracker, Yellowbreast Sunfish). They are the same size as bluegills and are often found in cool rivers.

Warmouth (a.k.a. Goggle-eye, Redeye, Rock Bass). The warmouth looks similar to a bream but has a larger mouth. They live in lakes and streams and are usually found near shorelines. Maximum length is about eleven inches. They will strike almost any bait and are not good fighters.

THE SUCKER FAMILY (a.k.a. Hog Sucker, Redhorse Sucker, White Sucker)

The sucker is a carplike fish. It is a freshwater fish found in streams, rivers, ponds, and lakes. Suckers spawn in the spring with a definite upstream migration. Their mouth is directed downward rather than forward. They feed on aquatic plants, insects, worms, and mollusks.

THE TROUT FAMILY

Trout are related to salmon but are smaller. Trout are usually found in fresh water. They require clean, cold water to successfully spawn. Wild trout are spawned in the streams. Trout are also raised in hatcheries and are released in suitable fishing waters. The state of Georgia classifies all of the streams in Rabun County as trout streams.

Brook Trout (a.k.a. Brookie, Mountain Trout, Native Trout, Speckled Trout, Speck). Brook trout have light olive-green worm-tracked markings on the upper parts of their body and white on the leading edges of their belly fins. Wild Southern Appalachian brook trout rarely exceed twelve inches in length. Hatchery brook trout can be raised to over sixteen inches in length. Brook trout thrive in water below sixty-five degrees. They spawn in the fall. The female fans a nest with her tail, and when the nest is completed, she spawns with the male. Afterward, she covers the nest with fine gravel. Brook trout eat insects and small fish. The brook trout is actually a member of the char family and is the only trout native to the Southern Appalachians. When they are hatchery-raised, they are called brook trout, and when they are wild, they are called speckled trout.

Brown Trout (a.k.a. German Brown, Speckled Trout). Brown trout are marked with large, lightly bordered red spots. They are brownish in color with a golden yellow belly. Wild brown trout can grow to a length of thirty inches in the Southern Appalachians. They require cold, clean water, especially for spawning. They spawn during the fall in the same way as the brook trout. They eat insects, crawfish, and small fish. The brown trout are native to Europe and were introduced to the Southern Appalachians about a hundred years ago.

Golden Trout. The golden trout, found in some commercial trout ponds in this region, are albino trout. They are the products of a hatchery, and they are not the same as the wild golden trout found in remote areas of the western United States. They are popular in some commercial catch-out ponds because of their unique coloration.

Rainbow Trout (a.k.a. Bow). Rainbow trout have a dark olive back with black spots all over their bodies. They have a broad, red, lateral band extending down the side from the cheek to the tail. Wild rainbow trout in the Southern Appalachian region rarely exceed sixteen inches in length. They spawn from February to April, depending on the water temperature, in the same manner as brook and brown trout. They eat insects and small fish. The rainbow trout is native to the West Coast of North America and was introduced to the Southern Appalachians within the last hundred years.

OTHER FISH

Crawfish (a.k.a. Crawdad, Crayfish). Crawfish are not really a fish, but a crustacean that looks like a miniature lobster. Crawfish make excellent bait for trout, bass, and most game fish.

Eel. An eel is a long slender fish that looks like a snake with a fin on top and bottom. Eels spawn in the ocean and swim up rivers and streams to live. They have sharp teeth, are olive brown in color, and have no scales.

Hornyhead (a.k.a. Knottyhead). This small fish grows up to ten inches long and has little hornlike spikes on its head. This fish is not particularly good to eat and is usually caught by accident when trout fishing. It is the adult member of the chub and minnow families.

Minnows (a.k.a. Dace, Darter, Chub, Shiner, and True Minnow). These are the small fish that live in lakes and streams. They are often used as bait for bass and crappie. They are usually small—less than three inches in length—and are silver in color.

Sculpin (a.k.a. Craw Bottom, Molly Craw Bottom). Sculpin live on the bottom of the creek between rocks and are brown in color. They have a big head and a narrow tail. They are small, with the largest reaching about four inches in length. They make good bait for brown trout.

PERSONALITY PORTRAITS

"It was a happy time to live . . ."

Imagine rising well before daylight to do the chores around home so that when daybreak came you could begin working in the fields or garden. As Annie Chastain said, "We'd walk in there in the morning and hoe corn 'til the sun'd be just about gone down." Then you would walk back home, do the evening chores, eat supper, and go to bed shortly after dark. They rarely complained, and, looking back, the majority of them remember it as a happy time in their lives—a time when people were closer to one another, more neighborly. As Lillie Nix says in one of the following sections, "If people loved one another, they wouldn't want to harm each other, but would want to help each other, like they did back in my childhood days." The people featured in this personality section grew up in a time when folks were resilient, hardworking, generous, and self-sufficient. They relied on God, the land, and their own industriousness for survival.

They worked from daylight to dark with extremely limited technology, in isolation from the world outside these mountains, and with none of the modern conveniences. As Billy Long said, "I don't know but what people could get along just as well back then as they do now. Of course, they didn't have all the utilities and conveniences they have today."

On the following pages, Annie Chastain, Billy Long, and Lillie Nix describe how hard work, family, and faith in God have allowed them to have happy lives. They all describe the differences between then and now and share their wisdom for making the world better by incorporating some of the old ways into our modern-day lives.

—*Kaye Carver Collins*

ANNIE CHASTAIN

"I Really Love to Work in the Dirt."

*B*ecause this is my last article as a high school senior, I wanted it to be a very memorable experience. *With that in mind, I set off one day in 1997 with Jennifer Ramey, another Foxfire student, for Annie Chastain's house to interview her about the tornado of 1932. She and her husband, Irvin, live in a modest white frame home surrounded by huge hydrangeas, delicate rosebushes, and eye-filling flowers. The minute she opened her front door, two things were very clear: her incredible warmth and goodness. She met us, both of us being complete strangers to her, at the door with warm hugs and friendly welcomes. As we entered her house, she immediately started a conversation with us that eventually led to this article. It was one of the easiest interviews I have ever conducted. Finally, Jenny and I had to leave to get back to class, but both of us hated to go. Once again, as we were leaving, we were both given warm hugs and invited to come back anytime.*

A few weeks later, having encountered difficulties with my original topic idea and wanting to go visit Mrs. Chastain, I decided to change the topic and do an article just on her. She is eighty-three years old. Her white hair and a weathered face are a testament to years of hard work, working outside her home in housekeeping, farming, and cooking, while raising her family. Her kindness, love, and spirituality had helped her during adversities. I couldn't think of anything more memorable than doing an article on such an incredibly sweet woman, a woman whose faith and religion show not only in her words but also in the way she treats others, whether they are strangers or friends. So, a few days after that, I went to her house again for the second interview.

This article is a combination of those two interviews. In it, Mrs. Chastain talks about the years she has spent farming, a tornado she experienced as a teenager, and a little about her Christian faith. I wanted my last article to be a memorable experience, and I can truly say that this one was.

—Lacy Hunter

I'll just tell you about my farming. I went to the field with my older sister and my daddy when I's seven years old. And we's tending a new ground over yonder on Wolffork over there at Jess Tanner's, a big old field up through there. My sister and daddy, they took me with them to tote water for them. Well, they sat down to rest and eat their dinner, and

PLATE 157 "We made good stuff
back then in them new grounds."
—Annie Chastain

when they did, I picked up a hoe
and started hoeing corn. That
just ruirnt [ruined] everything.
The next morning, I had to
take me a hoe and go to the
field and go to hoeing. I hoed
from then on. Well, I even hoed
some last year—I planted me
some beans and hoed them. But
back then we'd clear new
grounds in the wintertime when
it would be sometimes a-sleetin'
and a-snowin' a little. We'd cut
them bushes down and have us a
big fire burning in that place. We
made some awful good stuff.
There wasn't nothin' back then to
destroy it much like there is now.
There wasn't no bean beetles and
things like that. We made good
stuff back then in them new
grounds. My daddy loved to work
new grounds.

We didn't have no team to
plow our crop with, and this here
little lady who lived over here in Mountain City, I forgot what her name
was, but, anyhow, she had this big old steer, you know, and she told my
daddy if he wanted to take the steer and feed it for its work, well, he could
take the steer and use it to plow with. So he got it. It was so gentle 'til I'd
get out and hook that steer up and just plow like everything. They said I
kept the garden plowed up into dust nearly, because I liked to plow that
thing. It went just like a mule, though; it'd step right on out with you.

We tended a field down on Wolffork. We'd walk down, well, they call
it the Billy Branch Road now, but we called it Billy Mountain when we
lived there because it was a mountain you had to go up. We would plant
corn down in the valley on Wolffork, and we lived up in little Germany
at the head of the mountain. We'd walk in there in the morning and hoe
corn 'til the sun'd be just about gone down. Then we'd go back and climb
that mountain back home. Since we didn't have no team, sometimes we'd
hoe corn for other people, me and my older brother Eddie and
Frances, my sister. We hoed corn for other people to get their team to
plow sometimes, you know, when we's farming. We always made a

good garden, and we always had plenty of corn and stuff to do us during the wintertime to make our bread. Always raised us some hogs and had some cattle and had chickens and just a big ol' farm.

We lived over on Germany then, and that day [when the tornado came on March 24, 1932], it had been the queerest-lookin', foggiest-lookin' day, you know, just yallerish-lookin'. One of our neighbors' boys was a-plowin' the field for us, and it hadn't rained or thundered or lightnin'ed or nothin'. That night, my daddy come in from work, and we eat supper and cleaned our table up and sat around a little while. Then they went to bed, my mama and daddy and my younger brothers did, and me and my younger sister that was at home, we was a-sittin' up a-sangin'. We set up and sung 'til I don't remember what time o' the night it was, but it was over 'bout ten or eleven o'clock, I guess, and then we went to bed. Just about the time we went to bed, it started thunderin'; ooh, just sounded like it was rollin' under the floor, and just a-lightnin' like that. Oh, it was just a-lightnin' so fast—just kept the place lit up. And my brother, I had a brother that was real nervous, and he said, "Mama, I can't go to sleep with this lightnin' a-comin' through this winder." So my mama, she got up and hung a quilt over the winder where he was sleepin', and she started back to bed, and I remember her saying to my dad, "This here's the worst storm we've ever had." And it hadn't got there then, you know, I mean, the bad part of it.

They say it started on Burton Lake, and, buddy, it was comin'—just like freight trains across that mountain. It come right through Germany over there and blowed Mrs. Jim Parker's kitchen off. They had a kitchen on the porch, and it blowed it away and broke the top of the house. Never blowed it off, but it broke it and blowed his barn away—ever' bit of his barn. It blowed Eula Parker's and Gordon Dickerson's houses off of the pillars.

When we heared it a-comin' so bad, my dad rolled out of the bed on his knees and started prayin'. Course the rest of us was prayin' too, the ones of us that prayed, and askin' the Lord to take care of us. We just lived in an old common house. You know, that storm, it was a-comin' right towards us; but, instead, it just took the whole mountain above us down, just blowed ever' bit of it down, all the timber and a big ol' tree right above the house, so big around I couldn't reach around it. It blowed it down just right above our house. Then it went on across the mountain, but it come down there at our house, went on across the mountain, and come down at Sylvan Lake. They'd built a big ol' dance hall down there, right pretty close to the lake, and a whole lot of cabins. Well, it blowed all them cabins and that dance hall—piano and all—into the lake.

I guess I was about sixteen or seventeen years old when this happened. It was the worst storm I've ever been in. And after that, then we had a little place Papa dug out in the bank and fixed us a cellar to put our canned stuff in so it wouldn't freeze, and when it'd come pretty bad wind and start stormin' like windy, my daddy'd say, "Let's go get in that cellar." So we'd go get in that cellar and stay 'til it got gone. That storm didn't even touch our house. I don't know, the Lord just blessed us, I reckon. It just passed, just barely heard a little wind hit it one time, and it just went on by. Everything was just fine; our barn, you know, it was just an old shack of a barn, but it was still a-standin' the next morning, and our cattle and everythin' was all right, and everythin' we had was all right. There wasn't nothin' blowed away nowhere, but it sure destroyed the stuff on down the hill.

We didn't stay there very long 'til we moved down on Wolffork. Then we moved from Wolffork up in here to Mountain City, and we've been up in here ever since. We ain't had but about one since then I reckon, a pretty bad one that blowed the apple house away over yonder on the Cathey farm, but we've got a dugout down there in the bank. When it gets to blowin' pretty hard, we usually take off down there and get in it.

PLATE 158

[Later,] when we moved down from up in little Germany, we moved down to Wolffork at the Rickman place over there, and we lived there, I don't remember just how long, but we lived there a pretty good little while. We tended all them big old bottoms. Course, my daddy wasn't hardly able to work; he had a nervous breakdown. Me and my older brother, we worked a lot, you know. We worked in the field, and then we worked out for people too, to buy his medicine. Then, after he got better, they moved back out here to what they call Turkey Cove. I still stayed over on Wolffork. I stayed with my sister that lived over there awhile, and then, after I got married, why, we lived up there a little while up at the upper end of Black's Creek.

Then we moved off—well, we moved several times. We moved to the same house where my younger sister was born, where we lived on Wolffork. We put in a big crop over there, and we had to get my daddy's horse and buggy to do our plowing. So we got that horse and buggy, and we got through plowing. We had a little A-model car, and so my husband said, "Y'uns can drive the buggy," 'cause I couldn't drive the car—never did learn to drive. He said, "And y'uns can drive the horse an' buggy back up here, and I'll take the car for us to come back home in."

Well, he told us, said, "Now, I'll beat y'uns up there." I had my two daughters, Mary Ethel and Laurie Anne, with me. Mary Ethel was about five years old 'cause Laurie Anne was just a small child, about a year, I guess. Anyhow, we got in the buggy, and we took off, and, buddy, we was there a long time before he got there 'cause he had a flat tire and had to fix it. He said, "Well, I won't never tell y'uns no more that I'll beat y'uns there, 'cause I had bad luck."

Then we moved from there. My daddy had a big farm over there on Wolffork, below the Baptist Church on Wolffork. He tended all that land in here and we lived in that little house there awhile, in front o' the church. We had a garden there too—we had big, big ol' fields of beans, corn, and all kind of stuff like that. Of course, my children, we'd send them out to work in the garden, and they'd leave the weeds and cut the stuff down, you know. We had a whole lot of field peas planted in the corn, and they left the ragweed—thought they was the peas—and cut the peas down. I told 'em I believed they done that just to keep from hoeing in the garden. They laughed at me, but I think they finally found out, you know, what to do.

I've just worked and worked and worked and worked, farming and building houses. Well, I've helped build two houses. We built one up yonder [above her present house] first, and I helped build it. Then I helped build this'un. And my brother-in-law that's dead, Mark Chastain, he built a house up in North Carolina, so we went up there and helped him work on it some. I told 'em I reckon I'd done everything but work in a sawmill. I ain't never worked at no sawmill, but I've sawed wood and cleared pine mountains and everything like that, and built pasture fences and milked cows and fed hogs and chickens and just a little of everything.

Of course, my children, after they got up a bit older, they knowed how to work in the gardens and everything, but Mary Ethel ain't never had a garden. Laurie had one. She likes to garden. Mary Ethel set her out a 'mater plant or two, but she'd rather work out on a public job as to farm.

I really love to work in the dirt. Last year, I just prayed and asked the Lord to give me strength to be able to plant some beans and be able to work. Then I went down there and planted me five rows of beans in the garden, and planted them and covered them and everything. And then, when they come up, I asked Him for strength to be able to hoe them, and I worked them beans, and I made quite a few beans last year. I didn't even have to buy none. I usually have to buy beans every year, but last year I didn't even have to buy none, and I had beans to can, and some I give my neighbors and all.

I've done got two little pea patches planted this year. I got my English peas up about two inches high, one patch of them; the other ones was up about that high, the tender ones that you eat hull and all. They're growing faster than the tough ones. They're really a-comin' on. By the last of May, anyhow, they'll be having peas on them. Irvin, my husband, planted a few potatoes down there, and he said they's comin' up.

Somebody called me the other day and asked me if I was happy. I said yeah. They asked me if I'd been happy all my life, or if I'd been sad, and I told them, I said, "Well, I've been happy. When I was seventeen years old, I give my heart to the Lord, and I've been trying to live fer Him ever since, and He's blessed me and give me strength fer almost eighty-three years." If I live to the twenty-first of July, I'll be eighty-three. And that's how old my brother-in-law was that was buried yesterday. He was from the twenty-fifth of March 'til the twenty-first of July older than me, [that] was all the difference in our ages. They said, "You mean you've been happy?" and I said yeah. I said, "The Lord's been with me," and I said, "He keeps me happy."

Then they asked about my family, if I had any family, and I said, "Yes, I've got some. I've got a husband and two daughters, and I got a brother, and I got three sisters." Said, "You ain't got a mama and a daddy?" and I said, "No, they're both dead." I said, "I've got three brothers dead and a sister dead." And they said, "Well, and you mean you've still been happy?" and I said, "Well, it was sad when I lost 'em, but I can't bring 'em back, but I can go to them 'cause they all said they's ready to go when they left here, and that's a good feeling fer 'em to tell you that they're ready to go, because He promised us a mansion. When He went to prepare us a mansion, He said He'd come back and receive us unto Hisself. Where He was, we'd be also, and so I'm a-looking fer it." The Bible said to lay up our treasures in heaven where moths and rust won't corrupt and thieves won't break through to steal, so I just talk to the Lord. Irvin goes to work at the Forest Service, but seems like I'm not alone. I can talk to the Lord and seems like I've got company all the time. I just feel happy about it.

BILLY LONG

"A garden is about half a living."

*B*illy and Annie Long live in the extreme northern part of Rabun County near the Georgia–North Carolina line. Their home, at the head of Betty's Creek Road, is a modest, one-story house with a covered porch across the front. They have lived in this house since it was built in 1954. At that time, the old Long family homeplace, where Billy had grown up and Annie and Billy had lived since their marriage in 1938, burned to the ground. A longtime acquaintance of the Longs, Lena Shope, told us that when the Longs' home burned, all of the families on Betty's Creek pitched in and rebuilt it. This was once a common tradition in many of the communities around here. Besides, Billy and Annie Long had done so much for the people of their community that it was only natural for their neighbors to return the favor.

Billy and Annie Long are both small people physically. Billy is about five and a half feet tall and probably weighs little more than a hundred pounds. Annie is tiny and delicate. They appear to be very quiet, retiring people when one first meets them, but then the smiles come out and Billy's blue eyes sparkle. Our interview centered primarily around Billy's farming methods and his plowing with a horse as a principal means of cultivation. However, the conversation sometimes got off onto canning and preserving techniques, and he often turned to Annie to verify some comment he had just made. She'd just quietly agree or explain something in more detail.

When we were there, the house was tranquil, and there were no other visitors, no grandchildren running in and out, but there were photographs and reminders of a big family, three sons and three daughters, throughout the kitchen and living room. All during the visits, there would be comments about their children, so I know they visit often and stay in close touch.

The hillside and fields directly across the road from the house are where much of Billy's farming life has taken place. These are the same fields that Billy's father farmed when Billy was a young boy. The garden is now covered with old, dry cornstalks, but in early spring, Billy will plow it, preparing it for new crops. He will probably use a tractor to get the job done, but that wasn't always the case. He once used a horse or mule and plowed for up to fourteen hours a day. On one visit to his house last spring, he gave us a demonstration of how this was done. We photographed this technique after he had trained his horse. He wryly stated that he didn't want pictures published of him "being dragged all over the field."

Billy has been a farmer since he was a boy and did chores in the field for his father. When I first saw him, I couldn't imagine this small-framed man doing such hard work for such long hours. He said it was just a way of life and necessary, and that the crops raised were not usually sold, but provided food to feed his family and livestock.

Realizing that people in our area used to grow and preserve most of their own food from family gardens, we called on Billy to tell us his experiences in working with the land. From his recollections, gardening was once an even more backbreaking job than it is today. With country stores stocking only scant and basic supplies, gardening was certainly considered a necessity to survive. However, it did not stop with the garden. After the food was harvested, Annie had her own job of preparing it for preservation to feed their family of six children. Billy put both jobs in a nutshell for us: "A garden is about half a living."

—*Kelli Marcus*

PLATE 159

My daddy had four girls by his first wife. I don't know how long it was after she died before he remarried, but he married again and had me and Edith and another sister, who died when she was young. And then my mother died when I was small, and my half sister raised us. She was the oldest girl. I think she was in her twenties, maybe thirty.

Here lately, I've often thought about all she did. I didn't think about it much then. My daddy always called me about five o'clock to get up and build a fire in the fireplace in the stove and to get my lantern and go feed the animals. As soon as I got the fire started, I'd call her. She'd get up, and when I got back, she had breakfast cooked—meat, eggs, syrup, and jelly, dried fruit, and whatever I wanted. Then she done the milking and took care of the milk and the cow. She'd come back and go about washing dishes and just everything.

I bet there's not three women that done the work that she done. She'd go all day long. I'd ask her that night if she was tired, and she'd say, "Nay, I ain't tired." Why, I knowed she was give out. She didn't make us help her like she ought to either. She'd do it herself. We'd eat supper and go in there and sit down by the fire in the wintertime, and she'd wash the dishes. She'd never ask us to, and of course, we wasn't going to volunteer. She made Edith help her after she got big enough to wash dishes, but after Edith left to go to school, she never asked us young'uns to do nothing. [Edith went to Mars Hill College to study to be a teacher.]

She'd can apples and dry fruit. Daddy always kept plenty of racks made up out of little old thin boards. He'd make them about three or four foot square and put her some poles outside for those to set on. Some of them were bigger than a table. She had different sizes. She'd peel her fruit, slice it pretty thin, and take it out there and spread it out all over those racks. She'd just cover them up with her apples and lay them out there in the sun 'til they'd dry and shrivel up. She would transfer them off of one and onto another, and when she got some empty, she just peeled her some more apples and put them on there. Most of the time, if it didn't look too rainy, she'd just cover them up at night. The racks was fixed so you could just set them on top of each other without hurting the apples. She had six, eight, or ten at a time, and after you got them stacked up so high, you just cover up the top one. That was it. If it rained then, it wouldn't hurt none of them.

My half sister was the main one who took care of the garden too, and the rest of us worked in the field most of the time. Of course, we helped. That's the way it was done back then. Men would help in the garden if they was needed, and if the men needed the women in the field, they'd go help in the field.

When we wanted to clear up a field, we'd cut the trees off, burn the brush, snake the logs off or burn them, or whatever we wanted. We couldn't plow it much the first time, so we'd take a plow and just kind of scratch it up. Then we'd lay it off the best we could, and lots of times we just planted us a bean patch. We didn't use fertilizer and didn't have to spray then. We just grew them. Usually, we'd get out in kind of a hollow where your soil is pretty rich to do things like that.

I think one reason there's so many insects today is people quit burning the woods. You know, they used to burn the woods up 'bout every year. Certain times of the year you could burn it, and if you burned it right, there wasn't enough stuff in there to kill the timber much. We didn't have any problems out of ants, and we didn't used to know what a beetle was. We had little old flea bugs and things to get on the sweet potatoes and Irish potatoes. The children would clean ashes out of the fireplace every few days, and we'd just broadcast them on the tater ground, and them flea bugs would leave. We didn't have no more trouble out of them. We had a lot of cutworms. They'd get on our tobacco and cabbage and cut them down, but we never did spray for them back then. We'd just go through and hunt for them and kill them when we would find them. We didn't have too much trouble with the birds, and we never did bother them. I imagine they ate a lot of the insects. We would put out a scarecrow for rabbits and groundhogs, and my daddy used to trap a right smart for muskrats. We had more trouble with muskrats than anything about cutting the corn down. They'd set in on a field, and they would just clean it up for an acre or more.

Anyway, after we got the field broke up pretty good, we'd usually sow it in grass and make a pasture out of it. If there was rocks, we just hauled them off, but we never did get all of them big rocks in some pastures. We'd just keep piling them up. I know one field over there that my daddy pretty well cleaned up before I came along. It seemed like every time we plowed it, the plow would just gather that many more rocks. We kept on 'til we got most of them off. And there's one four- or five-acre piece up there that had a lot of stumps in it, and we'd generally just plow around them until they began to rot. Then when they got loose enough, we'd run a plow over them, or take horses, and just pull them out and snake them out of the field.

PLATE 160 "When we were breaking up the new ground, we never did use but one horse, so we just used a single-foot plow."—Billy Long

We didn't have a 'dozer or nothing like that. We had a bottomland plow, and we'd use two horses to pull it. And we had what I call a hillside plow. That's the one you can just flip over and plow backwards and forward in the furrow. With a bottomland plow, you go around just one way where it's level. We'd take so much of the field and cut it up into what we called lands. When we were breaking up the new ground, we never did use but one horse, so we just used a single-foot plow. You couldn't use a turn plow for new ground 'cause it was too heavy to lift around. If we got a big rock or stump that left a hole, we'd fill it back up with dirt. Then maybe we'd run the harrows over it and smooth it up.

After we plowed in the spring, we'd always take a drag harrow and run over a field and smooth it up. Then we'd take the disc harrow and disc it, and cut it good, and take the drag harrow and drag it again. Then we'd lay it off and plant it. When the corn began to come up, we were about ready to go to work on it with a cultivator. We had three different cultivators: a five-foot, a four-foot, and a double-foot. We'd use that double-foot in the new ground and the four- or five-foot in our land that was already broke up good.

We never did have any terraces in the field as I knowed of. My daddy never did tend that steep ground many times. He'd sow it in grass.

Now and then we made compost. We'd build us a ten-by-twelve-foot pen or take a shed or clean out a stall in the stable. We'd take a wagon to the woods and bring in a wagonload of rich dirt and leaves and sprinkle a layer of that in our pen. We bought fertilizer—called it acid back then—in the hundred-pound bags at the store and sprinkled that over the leaves. Then we'd throw on a layer of manure and sprinkle more acid. Next time, we'd put more dirt and leaves on it and just keep building it up. We've had twenty-five and thirty wagonloads of compost. Then when we went to plant our corn, we'd just take us a tow sack, split it open, cut holes in it to run our arms through, and make a apron, a throw sack. That's the way we used manure most of the time, put a handful of manure or compost to each hill of corn. We'd broadcast it over the ground by hand, because you couldn't have even got machinery in there on them hills.

Planting crops in the same field every year is not too hard on the ground if you keep fertilizing it. My daddy would rotate his crops. He would sow the field he had in corn this year in rye, or maybe clover, the next year, and then turn it under.

I've made lots of hoes out of a saw blade. Just take an old crosscut saw that's wore out, cut it or break it up in pieces, five to eight inches wide or whatever width you want it, and punch you some holes in it.

Then just take nails or something to make brads out of, and brad that blade onto that neck that you trimmed off from a hoe that was wore out. Put three brads in the neck; I always have a brad on each side of the neck and then one down at the lower end. That makes the best hoe of any I've ever used. It's a lot thinner than a regular hoe; it's easy to sharpen, and it stays sharp. A saw blade really makes good hoes.

When we was all growing up together, we'd always work in the field at hoeing time. We'd all get us a hoe, and sometimes we'd divide the row up: each one would take so far and just go until we met each other. We'd do what we called keeping up with the plow. When Daddy covered up corn, we'd straighten it up, chop down what weeds was there, and maybe put a little more dirt on it. My daddy said that the best time of the year was when you got your ground ready, and it was warm enough to plant.

We raised lettuce, turnips, beets, tomatoes, onions, cabbage, and beans. We didn't have these half-runners like we do now, just old-timey beans. We usually saved them from year to year. We let them stay on the vines until they got dry; then we'd pull them off and shell them out and bag them up and keep them for the next year. We'd always have some corn in the garden with patches of roasting ears, and we'd have a sweet potato patch somewhere.

We always planted what we called a little clay pea with the corn. We gathered eight and ten bushels of peas at a time, after they was shelled out. And we'd always have plenty of cornfield beans. We'd hang them up and let them dry and make soup beans out of them. They call them leather britches too, you know.

We had about an acre or two in apple orchards. Then Daddy'd have just three or four peach trees in a place here and yonder. We had a plum tree and pear trees. And we could get a lot of berries—buckberries and huckleberries. Those buckberries make the best pies of anything I've ever eaten.

There wasn't much of anyplace up here to get wheat ground, so rye and corn and a few oats were about all my daddy raised in the grain line. We'd grind the rye up and make bread out of it a lot. We used corn for feed, and to eat, to make cornbread or a big pot of hominy for the family, for roasting ears [corn on the cob], or we'd put it with beans and have pickled corn and beans. Besides that, we'd feed corn to the horses, cows, hogs, and chickens.

Back in my daddy's lifetime, about all we used for hay was fodder. We'd cut the tops off of the corn, shuck them, and tie them up. We'd strip the fodder off of the stalk as far down as it was green—plumb down to the ground nearly—and tie it in little "hands" and hang it on the stalk. When it was cured out, we'd take about four of those hands—all the blades you could hold in your hands at one time made up one hand—tie them together, and make what we called the bundle. Then we went to stack it. According to how big a stack we was stacking, we'd put maybe seventy-five or one hundred bundles to a stack. We always put the tops down first. We'd stand up about forty or fifty around the bottom of the bed, just stand them on their ends with the tops sticking up. Then we'd start right up the pole. Somebody would get up on the pole, and we'd lay a bundle down and step up on it. Then somebody'd start throwing it to you, and you'd just go round and round that pole, laying it on it. We'd start the fodder down pretty close to the lower edge of the tops, but we'd keep pulling it in and tapering off pretty sharp as we got up the pole. Always heard talk about things "tapered like a fodder stack"—well, that's the way we'd do it. Then we'd take two or three bundles, tie them together by the loose end, and make a big bundle out of it. We'd slip that right down over the stack pole, and we called that the cap bundle. That's what we put over it to keep it dry, and it would shed water. That's about all we used for hay and roughage.

My half sister would get the inside of the corn shuck and wrap it around the spindle on a spinning wheel, and then she'd weave her off a little thread and wrap it around the corn shuck 'til she got it tied. Then she'd tie the next piece onto that, and she'd just spin it and roll it up on that corn shuck. When she got her spool of thread as big as she wanted it, she'd just slip it off the spindle. That's what she called a spool.

Back when I was a kid, we'd pick up enough chestnuts in the fall of the year to buy our shoes. You could always sell those chestnuts.

We had plenty of rhubarb, and we always kept peppermint or catnip in the garden. It would come up every year; you didn't have to plant it. We'd gather it, put it up 'til it'd get dry, and use it all winter to make tea. We'd get out on the branch banks around and gather horsesnips and other herbs. Very little we wasted.

Well, we raised about everything except salt, soda, coffee, a little kerosene oil, and some sugar. We used syrup more for sweetening than we do now. Daddy always raised a big cane patch. We'd fix the ground, put fertilizer and stable manure in it and work it about three or four times, plant it in hills, and keep the weeds out of it. When the cane got ripe, we'd strip the fodder off of it, cut the heads off, and cut it down. We'd pile it up in the patch and then haul it to the syrup mill, where we'd grind it, boil it, and make syrup. Everybody in the settlement, even as far down as Dillard, would bring cane for Daddy to grind. He'd make it on the halves with them. He'd get part of the syrup as payment for making it.

So we had plenty of syrup, milk and butter, meat and bread. Some people say, "I can remember we like to have starved to death." But I'm telling you the truth, as far as eating goes, we never knew there was a Depression. Back then people didn't depend on money to buy nothing. They made what they needed!

Mostly, I think we've come a long way since the 1920s and 1930s. In some ways, the living has improved a lot from what it was back then. And in a way, I don't know but what people could get along just as well back then as they do now. Of course, they didn't have all the utilities and conveniences they have today. We used a spring box to keep our milk and butter in. We didn't know what a refrigerator or a freezer was, and we kept our meat in a smokehouse. But people's not as close as they used to be. Back when I was growing up, if your cow was dry, you still got milk. If your neighbor had milk, you had milk. We'd divide the milk as long as we had it and lived close enough together. Of course, people are still neighborly. You take the people up here on Betty's Creek. They always come to the rescue if you need help. But I'll sure say this is unusually good up here. I don't know whether it's as good everywhere else.

LILLIE NIX

"We made do when we didn't have, just the same as when we had."

*M*y grandmother Lillie Nix is one of the most loved people in my life. She married Earnest Nix in October 1923, and they had four children, one son and three daughters. Earnest died in November 1934 from complications of sugar diabetes. In 1936 Lillie married his brother George Nix, my grandfather, and they had two sons and two daughters.

My grandmother worked in the fields, as well as raising her children and coping with housekeeping without the modern conveniences of washing machines, dishwashers, and vacuum cleaners. My grandfather George worked in the asbestos mines early in their marriage and later on started farming in Scaly, North Carolina, where they still live.

I interviewed Grandmother one afternoon back before she and Granddad left for their winter stay in Demorest. For several years, I had wanted her to tell me about her early life, her childhood. Some of the things she told me were things I had heard her talk about before. Others were new to me. She told me about some old people she had visited when she was a child, and she related it in such clear detail, I could almost envision the place.

The house where I've always lived is very close to my grandparents' home, though not next door as city houses are because we live on a large farm. My parents operate the farm now, but it still belongs to my grandparents. They now spend their winters in Demorest, near one of my aunts, and their house in Scaly stands empty through the cold weather. I miss their not being there as I come home from school. When spring comes, they'll be back and the yard will bloom with dahlias that Grandmother has planted over the years. She'll plant a vegetable garden as she does every year, and their place will come to life once more.

—Pam Nix

I was raised in Northeast Georgia, just a little ways from the North Carolina line, on a farm, pioneer style. There was a big family of us, eight children. We all had to work, and we worked hard. Our father taught us to work with our hands. That taught me when I grew up how to make a living with my own hands.

PLATE 161 Lillie Nix (center foreground) and her family

We raised all of our food we ate. We raised our own meat, our own vegetables, and everything that we needed. We had cows. Nearly every family in that community had a cow. My father also raised hogs. It was open range where we lived. That meant there wasn't any fence law. You had to fence your crops in to protect them from the animals. Our farm animals roamed at large, wherever they wanted to go. They roamed loose in the woods. My father had lots and lots of hogs in the woods, and come fall of the year, those hogs would get fat off of the mast that fell from the trees.

In spring of the year, about March, the men of the community would go out and burn the woods. It didn't kill the timber because the sap wasn't up, but it caused the grass to come up tender, and the cattle would feed on that.

My father had two good hog dogs. One big bulldog was the catch dog, and a big cur dog was the bay dog. The bay dog was the one that would run and stop the hog. The hog would wheel around and face the dog, and the dog would bark with a vicious bark 'til my father would get there with the catch dog. He would tell that bulldog to catch. The bulldog would catch that big hog by the ear and lay close by the hog's side, holding it there until my father could cut its throat and let it bleed to death.

We also had sheep. In the spring of the year, we would gather up those sheep and bring them in, and put them in the stables and shear them. We had a table, and we would tie the sheep's feet together and lay him up there. We'd shear one side and then flop him over and shear the other side.

My grandmother lived with us. My grandfather was dead. She and my mother would wash that wool nice and white with homemade soap. They'd dry that wool on a scaffold and sack it up. In fall of the year, my mother would spin that wool into thread on her spinning wheel. Mother and Grandmother knitted all the socks and stockings that the family needed. Sometimes Mother would spin thread and send it over to a neighbor and have the neighbor to weave some cloth. Mama had a sewing machine, and she would sew shirts for my daddy. We had some cotton clothes that we used for Sunday, and we had gingham dresses too.

We planted big crops. We planted lots of cornfield beans with our corn. They would grow to the tops of the corn. We would pick those beans and bring them up on the front porch and ask our neighbors in to a bean stringing. They would come over and help us string those beans out. Mama and Grandmother would lay those beans out on scaffolds to dry and then put them in white sacks to have to eat in the winter.

My mother didn't can too much. She dried most of her vegetables. For our kraut, we had a sixty-gallon barrel up in the little springhouse. We would chop that full of cabbage and make a barrel of kraut. Then Mama would put up a sixty-gallon barrel of pickled beans.

We had lots of apple trees. There was old fields around where we lived. My daddy would take the wagon and us kids, and we would go to those fields. He would climb up in the trees and shake the apples off. Us kids would pick 'em up, put them in the wagon, and we'd bring them in. Mama and Grandmother would cut those apples, put them on scaffolds, and dry them in the fall of the year. They dried most of them with the peeling on them. Therefore, we got more vitamins from what we ate by having the peeling on them.

The store was five miles from our home. We didn't need to go to the store much. We had all we needed at home. It just had little items that was necessary for the pioneer people back then. They would keep horseshoe nails and things like that. And they would keep a little coffee, but they didn't keep ground coffee like we have today. It was in the grain, and it was green. You had to bring that coffee home, put it in an iron skillet, and put it on the stove to parch; or you could parch it before the open fireplace in a Dutch oven. You could put a few coals under the Dutch oven, heat the coffee slowly, and keep stirring it 'til you toasted it a dark brown. Then we poured it up in a can so it wouldn't lose its flavor. We had a little coffee mill fastened to the side of the wall, and we would pour our coffee beans in that little coffee mill, put a cup under the little spout, and it had a little crank to it. We would grind enough to make a pot a coffee. You could smell that coffee all over the house. We only used coffee in the morning.

Sometimes we would run out of kerosene, so our mother would send us kids up on the hillside with a tow bag. We would fill that tow bag full of rich pine knots and bring them to the house. She would throw them, one or two at a time, in the fireplace, and it would light up the whole room where we sat. She has knit socks many hours by that crackling pine knot fire. We made do when we didn't have, just the same as when we had.

To make lye soap, we needed ashes and lard. The longer you burn ashes in your fireplace, the stronger the lye you get from them. When the ashes get cool, you take them out and put them in your ash hopper. In the bottom of the ash hopper, you put something like straw to make a filter for the lye to come through, so the ashes won't go through with it. You put a vessel under that little spout that's under the ash hopper, and you pour water on the ashes a little at a time and very slowly until the ashes get wet enough for the lye to start being leached out and dripping through. You then keep pouring a little water along until the ashes have been thoroughly saturated. You put your lye water in a black iron pot and put grease in there in order to make the soap. It won't make without some kind of grease—old butter, tallow, fat from hogs that you kill, or anything that's grease.

It might take a day or two to make a big pot of soap. You boil it until it's as thick as you want it. It never did get plumb hard, that kind of soap, but it would be like a thick liquid soap. We'd usually pour it up in some kind of a container, usually a trough that had been hewed out, because that soap was strong. It would eat through most metals! It was stored in old jars or a wood trough. That's what people washed their clothes with.

They would take a bucket of that soap and go down to the spring or to a branch to wash their clothes. There wasn't any washboards back in that day, like people used on up later. People had what they called a battling block. The menfolks would saw off a great huge block of wood about waist-high for the battling block. And they'd make a big paddle with a handle to it for a battling stick. The women would soak those garments good, take them out of the water, soap them and put them on that block, take that paddle, and just paddle them. Knock every bit of the dirt loose in them and put them into the washtub. If they wasn't cleaned up by then, they would soap them again and onto the block and battle them again. That's the way they cleaned their clothes.

Our house was a two-story home. It had some bedrooms upstairs and two bedrooms at the back of our living room. The kitchen and dining room were together in an L-shape that run off the back of the house. We had two fireplaces in that house. We had one in the living room, and the other one in the kitchen, and my mother did a lot of her cooking in the fireplace. She would bake bread in the Dutch oven. We cooked lots of bread before the open fireplace. She would cook pots of meat and those dried applies or dried pumpkin, and keep a pot of something cooking nearly every day for us from the open fireplace.

My daddy had about thirty stands of bees. Whenever he would rob those bees, we would have so much honey that we wouldn't have vessels to put it in. I remember one time that my mother had to use her big black washpot to help hold honey. And we always had a barrel of syrup too. Back then people didn't eat white sugar like they do today. We didn't use much sugar, because we didn't need it. We had plenty of syrup and plenty of honey for sweetening.

For our brooms, we would go out to an old field and cut broom straw. Each one of us would cut big bundles of it. We'd take a string with us and a short knife and cut the straw off at the ground. We'd get all that we could carry. We'd bring it to the house and put it in the dry to make brooms that winter. To make a broom, we'd take as much straw as we could grasp in one hand, wrap a cord around that bundle, and fasten it to where it wouldn't come undone. Using the ax, we'd cut the end of the broom to make it square. That's the kind of brooms we had, and

PLATE 162 A picture displaying Lillie's in-laws and their family. Back row: Ralph, Henry, and Earnest. Front row: Garnet, John (their father), George, Sally (their mother), and Marvin.

the longer we used them, the better it was. I was half grown before I saw a store-bought broom!

I enjoyed my childhood days. I was happy. Our parents were real good to us, but we had to mind them. Our father didn't have to speak to us the second time because we knew to mind him the first time he spoke. That discipline meant a lot to me through all of the years. It helped me in raising my children. Of course, my children didn't mind as good as we minded our father. I'm very grateful to my parents for the way they raised me. I can't remember that my daddy ever whipped me. He didn't have to. We was afraid not to mind him, but we loved him and respected him for that. That's why I thank my parents now for the way they raised me. They raised us to respect them and to respect other people and especially our schoolteachers when we went to school.

We never had any trouble with our schoolteacher nor any of our neighbors. Everything was peace and love. We went and visited each other and talked with each other because we loved one another. Sometimes we would get out of meal or coffee, and we would go and borrow from the other. Then when we would get some, we would go and pay it back to them.

We had a little accident at our home one day. My two younger sisters was out at the woodpile, and one of them had the ax in her hand up over her back. They was barefooted, and my other little sister put her foot up on the chop block. My sister said, "If you don't take that foot off," she says, "I'll cut your toe off." And she told her she'd not take it off. So my sister with the ax came down with the ax and cut her big toe off and left it a-laying at the woodpile. Well, my grandmother was there, and she was the doctor in our house. She knew just what to do. She and my mother got my sister, took her in the house, bandaged it up, and got the bleeding stopped. Grandmother sent somebody out into the woods to skin a red oak tree to get the bark off of it. She boiled that solution and put alum in it. She would wash that foot several times a day. She had some kind of salve that she had made from herbs that she used on it. In a few weeks, it was well.

My grandmother says, "Now, that toe out there at the woodpile, if the ants gets on it and crawls over it, she'll have the same feeling on her foot—just like ants are crawling on her foot." So Grandmother goes, gets that toe at the woodpile, puts it in a bottle of alcohol, fastens it up, and buries it. There never was a doctor in our house as long as we lived at that place. There was a doctor in the community, and he went to other houses, but he didn't come to our home 'til I was almost grown.

Sunday was our biggest day—going to church. Everybody looked forward to whatever was going on at church, and everybody went. They would come from miles around, and everybody walked, sometimes four or five miles, but they didn't mind that. We all enjoyed it. The road would be full of people walking to the church. Sometimes we would go to Hale Ridge. They would have big days out there, church services twice a month. And sometimes we'd come to church up here at the Flats.

There was very little money back then. The only money we got would be in the fall of the year whenever my daddy would go peddling. He always made a late garden and set out lots of cabbage in order to have them to peddle. He'd take apples, beans, cabbage, and chinquapins. There was lots of chinquapin trees around our place. We'd go out and pick up gallons and gallons of chinquapins and he would take them to market, and they would really sell. He got about five cents a cup for them and that was good pay back then. Lots of the people in our community would take a barrel of kraut in the back of their wagon. They would dip out half a gallon or a gallon to each house. He peddled on Cotton Mill Hill where the people worked in the mill. They didn't make gardens or didn't have any vegetables or anything like that, so they were glad to buy from the peddlers.

Now, there is another place I would like to talk to you about. It was in the same community where I lived. It was a real pioneer home. There was an old couple that lived in this log cabin, a one-room log cabin. This old couple was a brother and sister. I just loved to go there and visit them when I was a child. I don't know why, because they weren't talkative people. They would just answer when you talked to them, but I loved to go there.

In front of the cabin was an old-fashioned zigzagged rail fence, and in the zigzagged places was beds of the most beautiful flowers you've ever seen such as bachelor buttons, fall pinks, Jerusalem cherries, Mexican honeysuckle—all kinds of old-time flowers that you don't even see now. It was a beautiful sight to look at.

Beyond the end of the house where the chimney was, there was a trough that had been hewed out with a foot adze from a pine log. It had the ends in it, but the middle was hewed out down deep. That's where this lady kept her homemade soap. She kept it covered up good so nothing wouldn't get in it. At the back of that cabin was an old-fashioned ash hopper, made in a "V" shape, where she put her ashes from the fireplace and dripped the lye to make her soap. She made it in a black washpot. She'd cook it maybe two days before she'd get it as thick as she wanted it. Then she'd pour it in that log trough and keep it covered up. That's what she washed her clothes with.

Now, let's go on to the inside of that cabin. About three feet from the wall in the back of that cabin was the old lady's bed. She slept on a feather bed. In making up that bed, she would fluff those feathers up 'til that cover would just stand up as soft as it could be. The covers of that bed was as white as snow and looked like a snowbank. Everything in that cabin was just as clean as it could be.

Over on the other side on the wall was the brother's bed. It was a homemade bed he made himself. He nailed the back of it to the log wall and he cut him some little poles and made legs for the front of it. That's what he made his bed on, and there's where he slept.

There was a little water shelf next to the front door on the outside; and there's where they set the water. The lady'd carry her water from the spring in a wooden water bucket, and for her dipper, she used a long-handled gourd that they'd cut open and cleaned out.

There was a big rock hearth in front of the fireplace, and that's where she did her cooking. She didn't have a stove of any kind nor never had [one] in her life. She always cooked on the open fireplace. She had her Dutch oven and lid setting on the side of that rock hearth, and her pot hooks was hanging right above the oven and lid. That oven was what she baked her bread in, and sometimes she would bake potatoes in one side, bread in the other, all at the same time. She cooked her other food in black pots in front of the fire. If she fried meat, she would take out coals from the fireplace and set her frying pan on those and fry her meat. And her coffeepot was a black iron kettle with a long spout to it, and she kept that little spout corked up so nothing couldn't crawl in her coffeepot.

Her chair set by the side of the fireplace, and she had a pocket from an old pair of pants tacked to the wall by the side of her chair. In that pocket, she kept leaves of dried tobacco. She smoked a clay pipe with a long cane stem in it. She'd reach into that pocket, get her some dry crumbs of tobacco, put 'em in her pipe, and pack her pipe full. Then she'd take her little fire shovel and reach into the fire and get her a little live coal. She'd put that coal on top of that tobacco in her pipe, take a few puffs, get the tobacco lit good, and she'd put the coal back in the fireplace. She'd sit there and smoke that pipe and talk to you if you wanted to talk. That was a real pioneer home.

Times were different then. There wasn't any war when I was a child. I was born in 1905, and the first war that I ever heard tell of started out in 1914 and went on a year or two before the United States had to go over there. Things didn't go too high during World War I. Because we made what we needed on the farm, we didn't know what it was to go buy. Things might have been scarce somewhere, but not where we lived.

It was a happy time to live, far different from today. We didn't have any crime, no hoodlums. You could travel miles and miles by your lone self, and you would never meet a human being. There was nobody to hurt you, and you could go where you pleased. It was a peaceful time.

If I could change anything in the world, I'd make the world different by people loving one another. People don't love each other anymore. They hate each other. Before they'll work to make any money, they'll kill, rob, and steal. The main thing is if they would get right with the Lord, then they could see the right thing. They wouldn't want to take this dope, and they wouldn't want to drink and carry on like they do today. Love is the thing that's missing in their lives. The reason a lot of them are in that condition is that they were children that were unloved and unwanted. Love is the thing that is missing today. That's the main thing. If people loved one another, they wouldn't want to harm each other, but would want to help each other, like they did back in my childhood days.

PLATE 163 "If people loved one another, they wouldn't want to harm each other, but would want to help each other, like they did back in my childhood days."—Lillie Nix

CONTRIBUTORS

CONTACTS

Doug Adams
Alvin Alexander
Furman Arvey
Rose Shirley Barnes
Dean Beasley
Sallie Beaty
Gail Beck
Addie Bleckley
Lassie Bradshaw
Florence Brooks
Lawton Brooks
Mrs. Varn Brooks
Harry Brown
Ross Brown
Millard Buchanan
Clyde Burrell
Kyle Burrell
Mary Cabe
Ruth Cabe
Edith Cannon
Lola Cannon
Connie Carlton
Aunt Arie Carpenter
George Carpenter
Buck Carver
Leona Carver
Annie Chastain
Estelle Chastain
Jo Ann Chastain
Lettie Chastain
Lessie Conner
Minyard Conner
Andy Cope
Ethel Corn

Pat Cotter
L. E. Craig
Ada Crone
Minnie Dailey
Claude Darnell
Edith Darnell
Arizona Dickerson
Terry Dickerson
Carl Dills
Belle Dryman
R. L. Edwards
Ruby Eller
Adam Foster
Dr. John Fowler
Nora Garland
Lelia Gibson
Harley Gragg
Omie Gragg
Bill Gravley
Kimsey Hampton
Blanche Harkins
Mary C. Heffington
Ernest J. Henning
Belle Henslee
Buck Henslee
Roberta Hicks
Edd Hodgins
Hugh Holcomb
Ruth Holcomb
Shorty Hooper
Mrs. Selvin Hopper
Bell Jones
June Jones
Leonard Jones

Coyle Justice
Daisy Justice
Oakley Justice
Gertrude Keener
Mrs. Hershel Keener
Ada Kelly
Dorothy Kilby
Jimmie Kilby
Juanita Kilby
Oza Kilby
Hazel Killebrew
Bill Lamb
Billy Long
Effie Lord
Blanche Lovell
Garnet Lovell
Winnie Lovell
Clarence Lusk
Wilbur Maney
Numerous Marcus
Bob Massee
Carrie McCurry
Mrs. Myrtle
    McMahan
Marie Mellinger
Oliver Meyers
Eldon Miller
Roy Mize
Lizzie Moore
Gertrude Mull
Maynard Murray
Gladys Nichols
Lillie Nix
Addie Norton

312   FOXFIRE 11

Algie Norton   Varina Ritchie   Jim Turpin
Margaret Norton   Parker Robinson   Bessie Underwood
Richard Norton   Doug Sheppard   Willie Underwood
Jesse Ray Owens   Clive Smith   Eva Vinson
Edith Parker   Susie Smith   Frank Vinson
Bill Patton   Billy Joe Stiles   Bertha Waldroop
Laura Patton   Mildred Story   Jake Waldroop
Beulah Perry   J. C. Stubblefield   Conway Watkins
Esco Pitts   Bernice Taylor   Marvin Watts
Mary Pitts   Diane Taylor   Mrs. Marvin Watts
Andrea Potts   Glen J. Taylor   Grover Wilson
George Prater   Melvin Taylor   Lucy York
Howard Prater   Kermit Thompson   M. S. York
Bessie Ramey   Perry Thompson   Talmadge York
Clara Mae Ramey   Charles Thurmond
Frank Rickman   Amanda Turpin

STUDENTS

Allison Adams   Brenda Carpenter   Brandy Day
Matt Alexander   Lee Carpenter   Melanie Deitz
Ruth Arbitter   Maybelle Carpenter   Scott Dick
Glenda Arrowood   Patricia Carpenter   Julie Dickens
Pat Arrowood   Faye (Bit) Carver   Anthony Dills
Robbie Bailey   Kaye Carver   Melissa Easter
Rabun Baldwin   Dickie Chastain   Arjuna Echols
Mitchell Barron   Patti Chastain   Stan Echols
Russell Bauman   Rosanne Chastain   Baxter Edwards
Amy Beck   Tessa Chieves   Richard Edwards
Shayne Beck   Chris Clay   Shannon Edwards
John Bowen   Chuck Clay   Angie English
Donna Bradshaw   Jenny Coleman   Rance Fleming
Julie Bradshaw   Eddie Conner   Kim Foster
Alicia Brown   Mike Cook   Ricky Foster
Kathy Brown   Karen Cox   Shay Foster
William Brown   Renai Crane   Rodger Freeman
Laurie Brunson   Pingree Crawford   Mike Galloway
George Burch   Leah Crumley   Darryl Garland
Libbi Burney   Barbara Crunkleton   Jeff Giles
Melanie Burrell   Doug Cunningham   Carrie Gillespie
Kurt Cannon   Emili Davis   Paul Gillespie
Scott Cannon   Jenna Davis   Gary Gottchalk

Sharon Gravley
Teresia Gravley
Brian Green
John Grewer
Wendy Guyaux
Gail Hamby
Kim Hamilton
Suzanne Hassell
Keith Head
Kim Hendricks
Dana Holcomb
Shane Holcomb
John Thomas Horton
Carla Houck
Kari Hughes
Lacy Hunter
Suzanne James
Anita Jenkins
Richard Jones
Terri Jones
Beverly Justus
Eddie Kelly
Tonia Kelly
Kara Kennedy
Ken Kistner
Tommy Lamb
Georganne Lanich
Gwen Leavens
Julia Ledford
Tammy Ledford
Lori Lee
Rusty Legett
Jenny Lincoln
Hope Loudermilk
Kaleb Love
Mechelle Lovell
Billy Maney
Kelli Marcus

Mary Ann Martin
Wayne Mason
Jason Maxwell
Preston McCracken
Bridget McCurry
Randy McFalls
Robert Mitcham
Amy Nichols
Susie Nichols
Chris Nix
Lois Nix
Pam Nix
Kirk Patterson
Sherita Penland
Myra Queen
Mary Sue Raaf
Crystal Ramey
Jennifer Ramey
Sheryl Ramey
Tommy Ramey
Annette Reems
Jeff Reeves
Aline Richards
Cristie Rickman
Renee Roane
Vaughn Rogers, Jr.
Heather Scull
Jolynne Sheffield
April Shirley
Beth Shirley
OhSoon Shropshire
Dewey Smith
Leigh Ann Smith
Steve Smith
Shannon Snyder
Gabe Southards
Judy Speed
Anthony Stalcup

Greg Strickland
Brant Sturgill
Annette Sutherland
Greg Talley
Marty Talley
Barbara Taylor
Becky Taylor
Mary Thomas
Don Thompson
Sandra Thurmond
Sheri Thurmond
Teresa Thurmond
Dawn Timko
Donna Turpin
Linda Underwood
Sheila Vinson
Cheryl Wall
Vance Wall
Daniel Wallace
Sarah Wallace
Dawn Watson
Greg Watts
Curtis Weaver
Rudi Webb
Deedee Welborn
Chet Welch
Kim Welch
Kenny Whitmire
Frenda Wilborn
Craig Williams
Lynette Williams
David Wilson
Amy York
Greg York
Suzanne York
Carlton Young
Matt Young
Wendy Youngblood

PLATE 164 Foxfire editors (left to right), back row: Kaye Collins, Lacy Hunter, Amy York, and Teresia Thomason. Front row: Robbie Bailey

Kaye Carver Collins is the Community and Teacher Liaison at Foxfire. Lacy Hunter is a sophomore at Brenau College in Gainesville, Georgia. They, as well as the other editors, are former *Foxfire Magazine* students. Current and former students involved in Rabun County High School and Rabun Gap-Nacoochee School's *Foxfire Magazine* class conducted the interviews featured in this book.

The
Naturopathic Way

The
Naturopathic
Way

How to Detox, Find Quality Nutrition, and Restore Your Acid-Alkaline Balance

Christopher Vasey, N.D.

Translated by Jon E. Graham

Healing Arts Press
Rochester, Vermont

Healing Arts Press
One Park Street
Rochester, Vermont 05767
www.HealingArtsPress.com

Healing Arts Press is a division of Inner Traditions International

Originally published in French under the title *Petit traité de naturopathie à l'usage des malades qui veulent retrouver la santé et des bien-portants qui veulent le rester: suivi du Dictionnaire thématique des concepts de la naturopathie* by Éditions Jouvence, S.A., Chemin du Guillon 20, Case 143, CH-1233 Genève-Bernex, Switzerland, www.editions-jouvence.com, info@editions-jouvence.com

Note to the reader: This book is intended as an informational guide. The remedies, approaches, and techniques described herein are meant to supplement, and not to be a substitute for, professional medical care or treatment. They should not be used to treat a serious ailment without prior consultation with a qualified health care professional.

Library of Congress Cataloging-in-Publication Data
Vasey, Christopher.
    [Petit traité de naturopathie. English.]
    The naturopathic way : how to detox, find quality nutrition, and restore your acid-alkaline balance / Christopher Vasey ; translated by Jon E. Graham.
       p. cm.
    Originally published in French under the title: Petit traité de naturopathie: à l'usage des malades qui veulent retrouver la santé et des bien-portants qui veulent le rester: suivi du Dictionnaire thématique des concepts de la naturopathie. Genève : Éditions Jouvence, c2007.
    Includes bibliographical references and index.
    Summary: "How naturopathy works to establish good health and protect against the toxic causes of illness."—Provided by publisher.
    ISBN 978-1-59477-260-3 (pbk.)
    1. Naturopathy. I. Title.
    RZ440.V3713 2007
    615.5'35—dc22
                                                                2008041957

Printed and bound in the United States by Lake Book Manufacturing

10   9   8   7   6   5   4   3   2   1

Text design and layout by Virginia Scott Bowman
This book was typeset in Sabon with New Baskerville and Avenir as display typefaces

Contents

༄

Foreword

⁓

Our medical system is ill, and Western society, like the rest of our planet, is not faring well. Iatrogenic illnesses (illnesses actually caused by allopathic treatments) and nosocomial illnesses (those that develop in hospitals) are increasing at an alarming rate. We promise the children being born today that they will live to see one hundred, but we are confusing medicated old age with an enjoyable quality of life.

At the same time, it's been demonstrated that 90 percent of all cancers are linked to nutritional and environmental factors. Doctors are developing more and more cases of depression in the two years following establishment of their professional practices.

Should our response to these paradoxes of the modern world be to maintain our comfort level with an ostrichlike denial of the evidence, or to hold an alarmist and paranoid discourse? Naturopathy believes that this picture, dramatic as it may be, can be studied calmly and solved positively if we can manage to awaken the awareness of both consumers and decision makers, most of whose views have been framed by a single philosophy.

In fact, whether it involves ecoplanetary or health

imbalances, everything rests on the philosophy, points of reference, and points of view that determine human behavior. Most of the problems we currently face have their origin in materialistic thinking and the egotistical belief that humanity can operate independently of the laws of nature or biology.

Naturopathy's chosen objective is health and well-being, but in the framework of a profound and authentic reconciliation with these laws, which are often simple and full of common sense: How do we best nourish ourselves, breathe freely, and take care of our bodies and their natural elimination processes? How do we optimize our sleep, our vitality, and our libido? How do we recharge ourselves through the natural elements—earth, water, air, and light, for example? Why should we carefully alternate times of activity and times of rest? How can we purify and regenerate the internal cellular environment of our bodies? How can we be consumers without endangering our planetary resources?

Good sense such as this is to be found, in fact, where it has always been: in the heart of the great health-sustaining recommendations and medical traditions that date back to the fabled teachings of the Sumerians and the Essenes. This includes Ayurvedic, Native American, Chinese, and Tibetan practices, and more specifically for us in the Western world, Hippocrates' noble philosophy. The most surprising thing, perhaps, is that beyond the contextual differences in their details, all of these traditions are based on the same foundations, and only allopathic medicine (the institutional Western form that prevails in most of the world today) has been established in total opposition to these universal concepts.

What, then, are the common elements in these traditions? Prevention is preferable to healing, teaching is preferable to treating, and giving the individual responsibility for his or her health is preferable to taking charge. Other common features include considering the whole person rather than the symptom, remaining humbly and respectfully attuned to the laws of a healthy life, and working with the energetic processes of regeneration and spontaneous self-healing rather than putting your faith in the effectiveness of a remedy. In short, an entire program.

After more than a century in the United States and seventy years in Europe, naturopathy has become the discipline that offers another kind of medicine, one in which the practitioner is first and foremost an educator of health, perfectly effective in the treatment of all the chronic diseases—the so-called functional diseases—as well as in primary prevention and quality of life. This does not make the naturopath just one more practitioner in the vast field of natural medicine that includes, for example, phytotherapy and homeopathy. He remains, rather, the general practitioner of health, as the allopathic physician is the general practitioner of illness. Is it now possible to envision the ideal public health system—perhaps modeled after the integrated medicine practiced in some parts of the United States—in which the allopathic doctor, the natural medicine practitioner, and the naturopath can congenially complement one another's services in an atmosphere of perfect mutual respect, all for the benefit of the patient?

The French Federation of Naturopathy (FENAHMAN) states that naturopathy is founded on the principle of the vital energy of the body, and that it combines the practices that have emerged from Western tradition based on the ten natural aspects of health: diet, hydration, psychology, physical exercise, respiration, plants, reflexology, light therapy, and manual and energetic techniques. It aims at preserving and optimizing the overall health and quality of life of an individual by allowing the body to regenerate itself through natural means. Faithful to these concepts, my colleague Christopher Vasey has realized a work of remarkable synthesis here, because it is no easy task to summarize the essence of our art, as well as its useful application, in so few pages. He's earned my great respect for his precision, and my sincerest congratulations for his teaching ability.

In this work, we have the pleasure of rediscovering the essential keys of the five columns treasured by Hippocrates and all of our European teachers (Sebastian Kneipp, Paul Carton, Henri Durville, Pierre Valentin Marchesseau, André Roux), and North American teachers (Benedict Lust, John H. Tilden, Henry Lindlahr, Bernarr Macfadden, Bernard Jensen), namely: serology, the science of bodily fluids and their disorders (excesses, deficiencies, obstructions); vitalism, the study of our intrinsic vital energy and its invaluable capabilities (homeostasis, regeneration, self-healing); prevention, maintaining our connection with the natural world and a wholesome lifestyle; causalism, the methodical quest for the primary origin of symptoms, which always comes back to not only the condition of the bodily fluids, but also the energetic state, meaning psychology, spirituality, or ecology; and holism, the global approach to the human being and the way he interacts with his environment.

Thank you, Christopher, for this new reference work, and pleasant reading to all.

DANIEL KIEFFER

Daniel Kieffer is the president of FENAHMAN, which is the French Federation of Naturopathy, and president of the UEN, the European Union of Naturopathy. He is also the director of CENATHO, the European College of Traditional Holistic Naturopathy, and a member of OMNES, which is the Organization of Natural Medicine and Health Education.

Introduction

꩜

For many people, naturopathy distinguishes itself from allopathic medicine only by the remedies it employs. These remedies are natural (found in nature—medicinal plants, hydrotherapy, and so forth) rather than "chemical" (created in a laboratory). In reality there is another stark difference: the naturopath has a completely different concept of disease from that of the allopathic physician.

Naturopathy, therefore, does not do the same thing by different means, but actually does something quite different, using extremely dissimilar means. Its therapeutic objectives are, in fact, governed by a completely different logic.

What is this logic?

The purpose of this book is to present the different aspects of naturopathy by revealing the foundations on which it is based (theoretical framework), and by describing the means it uses to bring relief to the sufferers of illness (practical application).

1

The Naturopathic Concept of Illness

ॐ

WHAT IS AN ILLNESS?

*The Importance of the Body's Internal
Cellular Environment*

It is rare for any person whose health has been compromised to ask himself, "Why am I sick? What is really happening in my body?" To the contrary, all of his attention—and that of those around him—is focused on his blatant, disagreeable, or painful symptoms, which are actually just surface manifestations of his deep-rooted illness.

It seems self-evident that the normal reaction would be to make a vigorous counterattack to the assault represented by the illness. As a general rule we behave as if disease were an outside entity independent of the patient, which, by entering the body, suddenly makes the patient sick. From this perspective, we consider the individual stricken by illness to be an innocent victim requiring our assistance because, through bad luck, he or she suffered an unhealthy assault.

The expressions used to speak of illness clearly support this premise. We say that we "fall" ill, that we have been "stricken," or that we have "caught" a disease.

According to this hypothesis, taught by allopathic medicine, each "assailant" determines different characteristic disorders. There are, therefore, as many diseases as there are assailants; this is what is known as multiple causes, or the plurality of disease. Since there are no common elements among diseases in this framework, each must be treated with its own specific remedy.

What Is Allopathic Medicine?

Allopathic medicine is a therapeutic method that deals with disease by using methods that, generally speaking, oppose the curative effects of the body's vital forces. By suppressing toxins into the depths of the body, anti-symptom remedies do banish the symptoms from the surface, but this is to the detriment of the biological terrain.

In naturopathy, however, all diseases are considered as different manifestations of a single, common disorder. This common denominator, this profound illness from which all others result, resides on the level of the biological terrain, or internal cellular environment. This terrain consists of all the fluids in the body, including those contained within cells and those in which the cells are bathed, as well as the blood, lymph, and cerebrospinal fluid.

How Is Naturopathy
Different from Allopathy?

Naturopathy treats disease using natural methods, and takes action to improve the biological terrain rather than to diminish the symptoms. In supporting the body's own healing power, it addresses the deep roots of illness, rather than the effects.

The intra- and extracellular fluids, along with the blood, represent 70 percent of the body's weight. These fluids are crucial, inasmuch as they constitute the environment of our cells. Intracellular fluid fills the cells, gives the body its shape and tone, and allows the exchanges that need to take place between the organs. Extracellular fluid carries oxygen and nutrients to the cells, and carries waste from the cells to the excretory organs.

Our cells depend entirely on these fluids. They deliver nutritive supplies (food, vitamins, water, oxygen, and so

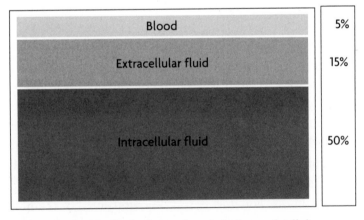

*The bodily fluids that make up the internal cellular
environment and their weight percentages in the body*

on), eliminate toxins created by the metabolic process, and transmit messages from one cell to another, ensuring their coordinated and harmonious interaction.

Just as our environment provides conditions that are favorable for health or that make us sick, depending on whether or not it is polluted, the environment of the cells plays an influential role in the state of their health. If they are bathing in a milieu that is deficient in oxygen and over-loaded with wastes, they will be incapable of performing their tasks properly.

Health: A Definition

Health is not the absence of detectable disease symptoms, but corresponds to a state of the biological terrain in which the composition of the bodily fluids ensures and provides the conditions favorable to the cells' unhampered normal activity. Health is determined by the state of the body's internal cellular environment. If this biological terrain is healthy, then the body is healthy; if it is unhealthy, the body is ill, even if there are no apparent symptoms.

Our body is made up of cells. If these cells are not functioning normally, the entire body will function poorly and enter the state that we call illness.

There is a precise and ideal composition of the internal environment that permits proper functioning of the body. Any major quantitative or qualitative change in these fluids leads to illness. For this reason, the vital force of the body is constantly struggling to maintain the internal cellular environment in perfect balance.

The body does this primarily by neutralizing and expelling all wastes and toxins that are a consequence of metabolism. This purification is carried out by the emunctory, or excretory organs—liver, intestines, kidneys, skin, lungs—which filter and eliminate waste.

Health, therefore, is founded on a very precarious state of balance that must be constantly restored. For example, if the body's biological terrain becomes overloaded on an irregular basis with small amounts of toxins—caused by overeating, or ingesting a stimulant like alcohol, or certain medications—the consequences won't be dramatic because the body is perfectly capable of purifying itself and restoring the ideal composition of bodily fluids. On the other hand, if these unhealthy incidents start becoming regular or daily habits, the body's capacity for restoring its own balance will be quickly exceeded.

These wastes accumulate in the bloodstream, which eventually deposits them along the walls of the blood vessels. As the diameter of the blood vessels shrinks and the blood itself becomes thicker, blood circulation becomes less and less effective. The exchanges made between the blood and the cellular fluids slow down. The wastes that cells are constantly discharging collect in the tissue instead of being flushed rapidly out of the body. The organs of the body, increasingly saturated with wastes, are unable to perform their work properly, and the congested excretory organs are no longer able to guarantee sufficient purification of the bodily fluids. All of the body's activities are then thrown out of kilter, whether these activities involve the cells, the enzymes, white blood cells, or biochemical reactions.

This constricted state of the body's internal cellular environment is what natural medicine considers to be the intrinsic illness.

This state can be found in all diseases. It forms both their unique characteristics and their common base. So it is not because an illness "enters" the body that its overall state deteriorates; it is because the state of the biological terrain has been degraded that illness manifests.

Since bodily fluids never stop circulating and there are constant exchanges taking place among them, toxins will necessarily spread throughout the body, and not a single part of the body will be spared. Hence this fundamental aphorism of natural medicine: "Illness has one cause—it is the congested state of the biological terrain." This concept of one unique malady, the unity of disease—that all health disorders are the expression of a single illness, which is the degradation of the biological terrain—is the opposite of the premise of multiple causes for diseases that is found in standard (allopathic) medicine.

At first glance there would seem to be a contradiction between this concept of the unique illness and clearly differentiated forms of disease with which we are familiar. Naturopathy, however, considers every local disorder not as an illness in its own right, but as merely the surface manifestation of a deeper problem, a result of preexisting obstruction. This illness could not make its presence known unless the internal cellular environment had already been overloaded with wastes. The specific local disorder it causes is comparable to the tip of the iceberg. The biggest part of the iceberg remains invisible: it is the overloaded biological terrain.

Local disorders are, therefore, not intrinsic illnesses but simply the secondary consequences of the root malady: the biological terrain overloaded with wastes. Hence another aphorism of natural medicine, "There are no local diseases; there are only general diseases."

This is clearly the case because local disorders evolve as a result of the state of the biological terrain: the more it deteriorates, the more the disorder escalates. Whether the local disorder is a case of the flu or a cancerous tumor, the process is the same. The increase in the rate of the body's overload—toxins that dangerously burden the biological terrain when they collect in overly large quantities—aggravates the illness and encourages the development of the disorder. Conversely, the local symptoms will diminish proportionately with a reduction in the rate of toxic overload. They will vanish entirely when the terrain has recovered its stasis, in situations when this return to a balanced state is still possible.

The localization of "surface" disorders depends on the particular weaknesses of an individual's body. All the body's organs are immersed in fluids that are overloaded with wastes. They are all irritated and attacked similarly by toxic sludge. The first organs to give way, the first to find this environment intolerable, are obviously those that are genetically weakest or have the greatest demands placed on them. For example, for people whose profession requires them to talk a lot, it would be the throat; for those most often affected by stress, the nerves will give way; miners, painters, and others who breathe in dust or noxious gases at their place of employment are likely to have problems with the respiratory tract. The illness is one and the same in all cases, but manifests differently in every individual.

We owe this concept of a single cause for every disease to Hippocrates, known as the father of medicine. In the time around 500 BCE he wrote: "The nature of all illness is the same. It differs only in its seat. I think it only reveals itself in such diversity because of the multiplicity of places where the illness is established. In fact, its essence is one, and the cause producing it is also one."

Twenty-five centuries later, Alexis Carrel, the 1912 Nobel Prize winner for medicine, stated: "The body is ill in its entirety. No illness remains strictly confined to a single organ."

> ❧
>
> When the state of the biological terrain deteriorates, illness appears. Every local disorder is only the surface manifestation of a deeper disorder: the congestion of the body's internal cellular environment.

WHY DO WE FALL ILL?

The Role Played by Toxins and Deficiencies

When we understand how the state of the terrain becomes degraded, we also realize that it depends entirely on outside sustenance to build and renew itself. The nutritive substances contained in the foods we eat are used to manufacture cells and bodily fluids. Our bodies function thanks to them.

If the intake supplied by one's diet is greater than the body's needs, the body accumulates substances it is unable to use. As the body is forced to store them, they collect in the tissues. This can include chemical or synthetic ingredients in food, such as coloring, preservatives, and so on. Since nature has never provided any instructions to the body for their use, these more or less toxic substances will collect in the tissues and alter the biological terrain in accordance with their specific characteristics.

Even when the diet—the body's primary source for retaining or restoring health—is adequate, it is still possible for wastes to accumulate in the body. This occurs every time that worry, stress, fear, and so forth disturb the multitude of biochemical transformations that take place in the body—the body's metabolism. Digestion functions poorly, so the foods ingested engender a plethora of wastes, generally designated as toxins. This includes crystals, which, produced by the metabolism of proteins, are acidic in nature and can be hard and painful to excrete; and colloidal wastes, such as phlegm, which are produced by the metabolism of starches and fats and do not generally cause pain.

THE TWO KINDS OF TOXINS

	Crystals	Colloidal Wastes
Sources	proteins, white sugar, acidifying foods	starches, fats
Excretory organs responsible for elimination	kidneys, sweat glands	liver, gallbladder, intestines, sebaceous glands, lungs

All of these substances, whether toxic or not, when present in excess amounts prevent the body from functioning properly and are considered to be the primary cause of the deterioration of the biological terrain, and therefore the source of disease.

The body may also become overloaded with wastes due to the poor breakdown and utilization of food substances caused by a lack of physical activity and the insufficient oxygenation that results from a sedentary lifestyle. Additionally, when the excretory organs designed for the elimination of toxins are not working efficiently, the body is compelled to store the retained wastes in its tissues.

Normal cellular activity also produces wastes, but only a fairly minimal amount. There is a much greater danger when the cells are diseased. They then can release far greater amounts of wastes that gradually will poison the entire body.

The factors that come into play with regard to the deterioration and congestion of the biological terrain are, therefore, multiple, but in all cases involve wastes formed by poorly metabolized ingested substances. This is why life hygiene, meaning personal health care, and vigilance about nutritious foods are so vitally important.

The food, beverages, medication, and stimulants that we consume can either keep our biological terrain healthy and disease resistant, or cause it to deteriorate.

~:~

There is another major cause for degradation of the biological terrain, one brought about not by an excess of one or more substances in the body, but by a deficiency in a substance it requires to function properly.

A deficiency is a lack of essential nutrients that are indispensable for the body's ability to rebuild itself and function. Such nutrients include proteins, carbohydrates, fats, minerals, vitamins, and trace elements. The composition of the body's internal environment can be maintained only when there is sufficient intake of all the elements it requires. If one of these elements is not supplied in sufficient quantity, there is an immediate slowdown in physical function. When this element is entirely lacking from the diet, the body functions that are dependent on it can no longer be assured. If this state of complete deficiency extends for a prolonged amount of time, death is a real possibility.

In our society of abundance, it might seem difficult to imagine falling ill due to dietary deficiencies, but the truth is it is very possible and even quite easy. The foods available today supply less and less of our body's needs because they themselves are suffering deficiencies, due to modern farming and husbandry practices. The countless refining processes our food undergoes before reaching the grocery shelves exacerbates the problem.

Another cause of deficiency resides not in the inadequate intake of nutrients, but in their destruction by chemical ingredients in foods and medications, substances that act as anti-vitamins or inhibit the activity of trace elements. Specialized diets, those which systematically exclude certain kinds of food (for example, carbohydrates), also contribute to the production of deficiencies because of the lack of variety in the foods they provide the body.

When deficiencies are present for an extended time—which is the case when poor eating habits are maintained—they create substantial changes in the composition of bodily fluids and cause an insidious, gradual weakening of the body's resistance.

Furthermore, because most nutritive elements work interdependently to ensure their most effective use by the body, a deficiency in any one of them will create a series of other deficiencies, in a chain reaction.

A body suffering from nutrient deficiencies functions less well and eliminates waste poorly. Consequently, the ratio of excess waste and toxin in the body will only increase.

THE TWO CAUSES OF DETERIORATION OF THE BIOLOGICAL TERRAIN

Overloads	Deficiencies
Toxins (urea, uric acid); toxin-creating substances (tobacco, alcohol, coffee); food additives (food coloring, preservatives); poisons from pollution (lead, cadmium)	Water, oxygen, proteins, carbohydrates, fats, vitamins, minerals, trace elements

Illness arises, therefore, when the biological terrain is overloaded with wastes and is suffering from deficiencies. The functioning of the body is disrupted and can no longer defend itself properly. This phenomenon is not as unknown as it may appear, as it is used strategically in standard medical research. In fact, for studying bacterial activity or testing new remedies, animals are inoculated with germs. If these animals are enjoying good health, and their internal cellular environments are experiencing neither overloads nor deficiencies, infections either do not appear, or do so with much less frequency.

The way modern medical science attempts to overcome this obstacle to experimentation speaks volumes: healthy animals are made susceptible to bacterial attack through a "scientific" devastation of their biological terrain. They are fed deficient food that is not adapted to their digestive capabilities, too much food, cooked food, and chemical cocktails. A stress condition is created in the animals by placing them in darkness, putting their feet in cold water, and so forth.

༄

Disease arises when the body is overloaded with waste and is suffering deficiencies.

HOW DO WE HEAL?
The Wisdom of the Body

Everyone has, at least once, recovered from a disease without taking any medicine, or products containing active ingredients for treating illness. And yet, when someone is sick, the main concern is always to procure medication. This need for a remedy at any cost has been engraved deeply into our brains, as it is commonly accepted that without medicine there is no recovery.

Medications are supposed to contain all the curative powers necessary to restore a sick body to health. And yet, how many patients have recovered their health without taking any medication, either because it was unavailable or because they simply did not want to take medication? Also, how do animals cure themselves, since they do not have any medicines naturally available to them? Is there another option?

Natural medicine talks about a "medicalizing" nature or "vital force of the body." This force cannot be identified with any one organ of the body; its existence is revealed only in the effects of its action. Hippocrates said, "The vital force of the body is the most powerful force of cohesion and action in existence. However, it is invisible to the eye; only reasoning can conceive of it."

Vital Force

The vital force organizes living matter and orchestrates, synchronizes, and harmonizes all its organic functions. It is intangible and therefore cannot be identified with any single organ of the body. Its existence is revealed only by its effects. All its efforts are aimed at maintaining the body in an optimum state of health. It is this force that enlivens the organs and governs the processes of respiration, circulation, digestion, exchanges, and elimination. It also triggers reactions by the body's defense system; it scars wounds, neutralizes poisons, and prompts healing crises.

In the healthy state, the vital force orchestrates and harmonizes all physical functions of the body. It works constantly to maintain the body in the healthiest state possible.

In the event of injury, it is the vital force that directs the repair of tissue by scarring over wounds. When the body is attacked by products that threaten its integrity, whether they originate on the outside (venom, poison, microbes, and so on) or inside (toxins and metabolic waste), it puts the entire body on alert and implements its defense system.

When confronted by a rising tide of overloads and congestion of the tissues, the vital force does not remain on the sidelines as a passive spectator. It reacts vigorously to restore order to the physical organism so that it can continue—or resume—its normal functioning. All its efforts aim at reestablishing the purity of the biological terrain by neutralizing the toxins found in this internal cellular environment, and expelling waste from the body by means of the various excretory organs. This eviction of toxins from the body often can take a spectacular form. Such events are called detoxification crises, also known as cleansing crises, or healing crises, due to the abrupt intensity of their inception.

Elimination during these kinds of crises will be made through the same excretory organs as in conditions of normal health, but with greater forcefulness. Colloidal waste will be expectorated through the respiratory tract, and urine will be laden with waste. The skin may eliminate waste through heavy perspiration, pimples, or various forms of eczema. The digestive tract also plays a role by releasing diarrhea, or abundant secretions of bile.

Which excretory organs are pressed into service depends on the nature of the waste and the strength of a patient's different organs, so there are significant variations from one individual to the next, and multiple possibilities for the localization of disorders. These local disorders are the visible manifestation of the vital force's defensive reaction as it seeks to correct a much more profound ill: the congestion of the biological terrain.

In standard medicine, every local defensive reaction is catalogued according to its characteristics, is given a specific name, and is then considered an illness in its own right. The eliminatory nature of illness is something Hippocrates proclaimed centuries ago: "All diseases are resolved either by the mouth, the bowels, the bladder, or some other such organ. Sweat is a common form of resolution in all these cases." The seventeenth-century English physician Thomas Sydenham wrote: "A disease, however much its cause may be adverse to the human body, is nothing more than an effort of nature, who strives with might and main to restore the health of the patient by the elimination of the morbific [disease-causing] humor." Closer to our time, in 1924, Dr. Paul Carton—the Hippocrates of the twentieth century—stated: "Disease in reality is only the translation of an inner effort to neutralize and clean out toxins, which the body performs for preservation and regeneration and is not an effort to destroy health . . . "

The body is, therefore, quite capable of working all alone toward its own healing. Thanks to the vital force, it contains the capacity for self-healing through its immune response. Hippocrates called this ability of the vital force its "medicalizing" nature.

The immune response is the body's capacity to resist and defend itself when confronted with disease-causing processes. It is present in the body from birth, and remains present in both sickness and in health. But the body's immune system is only powerful and effective as long as the biological terrain remains pure and balanced. Looking at it from the reverse perspective, the more the biological terrain is saturated with waste and deficient in other substances it requires for health, the greater the reduction in the body's ability to defend itself.

The different elements of the immune system (bone marrow, lymph nodes, white blood cells, and so forth) are also bathing in the bodily fluids, and their effectiveness is dependent on the quality of these fluids. The degradation of the biological terrain can become so pronounced—either because the toxic overload is so great, the deficit of nutrients so profound, or both, as is most often the case—that the immune system loses, for all practical purposes, its ability to take action. The body is then left almost defenseless against assaults.

Although natural medicine considers the internal cellular environment of the body to be the deciding factor in health, the harmful influence of germs is not minimized. Germs, viruses, and parasites are a reality and represent a certain potential danger to the human body. It would be inaccurate, however, to consider them to be the primary cause of disease. A good many illnesses are not due to a bacterial attack. For example, heart failure, diabetes, asthma, digestive disorders, and nervous disorders are not caused by germs. Furthermore, the immune system, if it is functioning properly, is capable of defending the body against all microbial attacks. If this were not the case, the human race would have vanished from the face of the earth long ago.

There is a subtle balance between the body's defensive force and its vulnerability to attacks from germs. The stronger the immune system is, the sooner germs are rendered powerless or destroyed. They can enter the body but not cause any damage. On the other hand, the weaker the body's defense system, the more germs can develop, proliferate, and invade the entire body with their devastating activity. The now-famous phrase attributed to Pasteur on his deathbed sums it up admirably: "The germ is nothing; the internal environment is everything."

Healing is accomplished not by attacking the secondary cause, but by eliminating the primary cause of disease. In other words, healing requires cleansing the body's internal cellular environment and restoring its health.

> Illness is the expression of an effort by the body to purify and preserve itself. It is not a task aimed at destroying health.

REMEDIES AND THERAPIES

Helping the Body to Heal Itself

If all the health problems occurring in specific regions of the body (local disorders) are a result of the defective state of the body's biological terrain, and if the ability of germs to launch a successful attack is also dependent on those weaknesses, then it is simply good sense for the therapist to focus first and foremost on this internal cellular environment. The unity of disease concept has its correspondence in therapeutic uniqueness: the correction of the biological terrain through purifying it and amending its deficiencies.

The first objective, therefore, is to free the body of toxins and waste. To achieve this goal, it is necessary to completely clear all the body's exits, or organs of filtering and elimination: liver, intestines, kidneys, skin, and respiratory tract. These organs are always working at a slower pace in sick individuals. The wastes that accumulate there, which the organs are unable to expel from the body, are then forced deep into the tissues. The various drainage methods, intended to stimulate the excretory organs, will first seek to rid these organs of their wastes, which then allows them to gradually flush out the rest of the wastes stored in the body.

A person needs to have personally experienced or witnessed a drainage cure to truly appreciate just how much

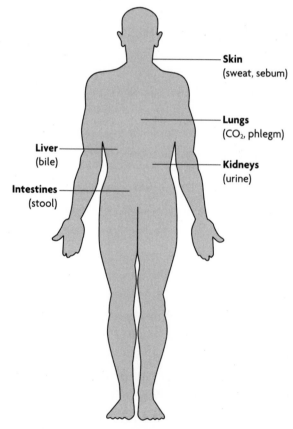

The five excretory organs and their waste products

waste and poison can insidiously collect within the body. Individuals suffering from lethargic intestinal transit are always quite astounded at the quantity of matter that their intestines expel, even after several days of fasting from food, while taking in only water. The strong and nauseating odor of the perspiration of seriously ill individuals is also a well-known phenomenon. By the same token, the deeper color and concentration of urine during a detoxification crisis is always cause for surprise to the novice, as are the many other forms that waste assumes when it is expelled through the skin (pimples, infections, oozing). Despite the often unpleasant nature of these eliminations, they should not be viewed as either discouraging or frightening; it is far preferable to have these wastes outside the body, rather than inside.

Naturopathy calls upon a variety of cleansing methods to stimulate the elimination of toxins. Invariably the techniques are chosen for the particular patient. Depending on the case, the therapist will choose a therapy from medicinal plants, sweat-inducing procedures, enemas, poultices, reflexology, and so forth.

In conjunction with the clearing of the body's avenues of elimination, it is also essential to encourage the emergence of toxins that are embedded in the body. Over time, concentrated wastes not only permeate the bodily fluids, but also become buried in the cellular tissue. These wastes are, of course, much more difficult to eliminate, because they first need to be dislodged before they can be ejected from the depths of the tissues and carried to the excretory organs by bodily fluids. The techniques used for this purpose either encourage a significant increase in the flow of cellular fluids, accelerate circulation, or break down wastes embedded in the tissues into smaller particles that are easier for the body to transport and eliminate. These techniques include fasts, mono diets (limited to a single food), balneotherapy, lymphatic drainage, specific physical exercises, and so forth.

By stimulating the intestines with laxative (elimination-inducing) plants or enemas, encouraging the elimination of urine with diuretic plants, encouraging expectoration with essential oils, and perspiration with hydrotherapy or balneotherapy, the naturopath is doing nothing other than imitating the healing procedures implemented by the body itself. The vital force triggers abundant elimination of waste through the digestive tract (diarrhea, vomiting), kidneys (thick, acidic urine), respiratory tract (mucus), and skin (sweat) to purify the body and restore it to good health. In mimicking this process, natural medicine respects the great truth proclaimed by Hippocrates: "Medicine is the art of imitating the healing procedures of nature."

The second objective of naturopathy is to correct the biological terrain by supplying what it needs to recover its equilibrium, and satisfying its deficiencies. If deficiencies in essential amino acids, minerals, vitamins, and trace elements have a dramatic effect on bodily function, it is simply because our bodies are unable to manufacture them and must get them from the outside.

A body that is given substances it was previously deprived of for a significant length of time will feel reborn and, amazingly, recover all its strength. All the physical and mental functions that had been dulled or lethargic will resume activity, all work left in suspended animation will be put back in motion, and the body will revive. The biological terrain will then be purified much more quickly, and the immune forces will recover their normal strength.

One can satisfy body deficiencies by regular consumption of foods containing the missing substances, or with the help of restoratives like bee or flower pollen, royal jelly, brewer's yeast, sprouts, seaweed, or certain shellfish. The abundance and concentration of vitamins, essential amino acids, trace elements, and minerals in these food supplements support the body's natural vital forces and fill its deficiencies more rapidly.*

༴

In allopathic medicine the diagnosis of the patient is considered to be the most important point to be resolved, because medical prescriptions will be determined by clues that indicate a specific disease. These clues are revealed by examination of the patient. This kind of therapy looks like a kind of equation: this disease = this medication. Until there is a diagnosis, treatment cannot begin. The patient is therefore placed under observation, which in reality means that the biological terrain will be left to continue to deteriorate until a diagnosable local disorder appears.

It is only then that a course of treatment can be initiated and the correct therapeutic agent chosen to combat the illness.

There is another major inconvenience with this concept of medicine. When a new and unknown disease appears, such as AIDS, the patient is forced to invest all his hope in the day when the disease will be fully identified and a cure manufactured.

Naturopathy does not allow itself to be halted by a "new" and "unknown" disease. All that is new about any illness is the way it manifests a disorder buried in a constricted biological terrain. Even in the absence of a diagnosis in the standard allopathic sense, treatment can begin.

---

*See also the glossary entry for Naturopathy for an outline of techniques used by naturopaths to restore and maintain health.

There is no need for the patient to be placed under observation, to wait while his problems grow worse and hope for the discovery of a cure. The correction (draining wastes and filling deficiencies) can be started at once.

In allopathic medicine the diagnosis is based on the illness; in naturopathy it is based on the patient. It is not so much a diagnosis as it is a health assessment indicating what imbalances need correction. The therapist takes an interest in the patient's lifestyle, organ strength, immune system, deficiencies, and the nature and causes of body fluid congestion.

The therapist is concerned with the total human being—physical, mental, and spiritual—rather than isolated fragments of his or her total being, because the corollary to a fragmentary diagnosis is a fragmentary treatment. Naturopathy strives to realize an in-depth treatment that addresses the profound nature of the illness rather than its superficial manifestations.

ॐ

It is worth taking a moment here to ask ourselves what makes a remedy effective. How does it work? Customarily, one has the impression that the remedy encompasses all the healing powers necessary to effect a cure, and that it is the unique active agent. If we define the effectiveness of a remedy by its ability to cause the symptoms of a disease to vanish, this is the way it can seem. But if we consider disease to be a defective state of the body's internal cellular environment, we need to question how a remedy, versatile as it may be, can stimulate the excretory organs, purify the tissues, strengthen the immune system, fill the body's deficiencies, and dissipate local symptoms all by itself.

The remedy does not heal the disease; it helps the patient self-heal. The powers of healing reside within the body. They are the body's vital forces, what the ancients called its medicalizing nature, and what moderns call the immune response. Therefore the conversation is about self-healing, not just healing. No remedy is capable of healing the diseases of a dead person. A corpse lacks the vital, organic force that will be able to stimulate, direct, and support it.

However, it is important to note that naturopathy is not opposed to the use of remedies. It makes use of them, but uniquely, as a supplement to its treatment of the body's deep-rooted issues. Rather than pinning all possibility of a cure on a sole specific remedy, as allopathy does, naturopathy acts on the biological terrain that is responsible for the specific local disorder. Furthermore, because the specific remedies it employs for local disorders are physiological and not chemical, they are accepted into the body's metabolic circuitry, and can be easily used and eliminated by the body. When this is not the case, remedies will only increase the degradation of the biological terrain, creating an effect that is more harmful than beneficial.

It is certainly sometimes necessary to use remedies whose "cure is worse than the illness" when their temporary use makes it possible to get through difficult junctures: an explosion of bacterial activity, intense pain, abrupt weakening of an organ, and so forth. But whereas the use of these remedies should be the exception, it has become the rule. This is why we're witnessing an explosion of iatrogenic diseases, illnesses that are caused by the medications themselves. The rationale that the iatrogenic illness is less serious than the initial disease is not a valid argument for the use of these medications. Local symptoms and disorders may appear less grave, but the degradation of the biological terrain is aggravated even further by the medication-induced toxic overload, prefiguring new diseases.

It is always disconcerting for those who prescribe chemical medication, as well as for those who use it, to see the procedures employed in natural medicine. How can herb teas and tinctures compete with products that have an incomparably higher concentration of active ingredients? How can applications of water, diet, or massage claim to bring about healing where the most powerful medications remain impotent? Here we should recall that the value of a remedy does not reside in itself but in its capacities to aid, support, and stimulate the body's own healing powers.

٭

The forces of healing are located inside the body.

The value of a remedy does not reside in itself but in its ability to stimulate these vital forces.

FICTITIOUS HEALING VS. TRUE HEALING

Addressing Causes, Not Just Symptoms

Since illness is rooted in the body's internal cellular environment, healing must transpire on this same level of the biological terrain, and not at the level of the local disorder. Health is not the absence of surface symptoms, but corresponds to a particular state of the body's biological terrain in which the composition of the bodily fluids permits and encourages normal cellular activity. True healing is the kind of healing that restores the biological terrain to its optimum state.

The clearing up of local disorders cannot be considered

to be a healing of the illness if the biological terrain upon which these disorders appeared has not also been changed. Of course the cessation of painful or debilitating local disorders can be hailed as a good thing, but this gain will not last for very long if the root of the illness has not been addressed.

Unless there is change in the status of the bodily fluids, we will experience or witness many relapses, often incorrectly identified by standard medicine as new attacks that will then require new treatments to repress the symptoms. This is a real battle against the seven-headed hydra. Hardly has one local disorder been put down than the vital force will trigger another healing crisis at the same excretory location (known as a relapse) or at another location in the body (a transfer of disease, which is simply a redirection of wastes to another excretory organ).

Multiple attempts by the vital force to purify the body can take place simultaneously at several locations. The unknowing and poorly advised patient will then race from one specialist to the next for treatment of the different local disorders, whereas a single treatment—the correction of the biological terrain—would cause all of them to vanish. Let me repeat, the illness is always one and the same, it only manifests differently depending on where in the body it is located.

Superficial healings obtained locally by treatments targeting the symptoms ultimately fail, because toxins remain buried in the depths of the tissues. The body is thus forced to tolerate an increasingly elevated rate of overloads. The patient seems cured, but his or her biological terrain continues to degrade. In reality, the patient is becoming sicker and sicker.

A real healing can be obtained only by restoring the

norms of the biological terrain, which can be achieved only by purifying it completely. These measures addressing the depths of the body will automatically bring about the disappearance of local disorders—and in a definitive manner—if the errors that created the degradation of the biological terrain are not repeated.

The defined and labeled local disease is only the ultimate culmination of a long process of degradation of the body's internal cellular environment that may have stretched over months or even years, so there should be no illusion of a fast and easy cure by a miraculous remedy. A cure can be obtained only through the implementation of a process that is the reverse of the one that caused the degradation of the biological terrain. All toxins that have entered the body must be eliminated, all deficiencies need to be replenished, and all damaged tissue must repair itself.

In all diseases, but especially in serious diseases, one must fortify oneself with patience and look at the long term. There are no possible shortcuts. The disappearance of a local disorder does not mean that the internal cellular environment has been cleansed from top to bottom. To the contrary, the symptoms can disappear fairly quickly, precisely because they are only the terminal culmination of a deep-rooted disorder. They are like the last drop of water that causes the glass to overflow, or the straw that breaks the camel's back. The most important thing to emphasize here is that it would be a mistake to stop treatment at the point when the local disorder disappears.

Halting one's intake of pharmaceutical medicine as soon as the symptoms have vanished fits into the logic of the medical approach that considers these local symptoms to be the integral disease. This way of doing things cannot be transposed into treatment that will correct the body's biological terrain. Naturopathic treatment should be continued for some time after the symptoms disappear.

The treatment of the biological terrain does not, however, offer protection against new assaults by toxins, or deficiencies in other essential substances. Any change in the patient's lifestyle that was adopted to obtain a cure must be maintained afterward, with some adjustments, lest the same causes recur and prompt the symptoms to reappear. This lifestyle change is the price of true and lasting healing.

The disappearance of local disorders cannot be considered a healing of the disease unless the biological terrain hosting the disorder has also been changed.

THE DIFFERENT STAGES OF DISEASE

From "Not Feeling Well" to Serious Illness

The difference between a benign illness and a serious disease is not a difference of type, but of degree. Fundamentally, all diseases possess an identical nature. But in serious illness, the degree of deterioration of the biological terrain and the scope of the damage it causes are much greater than in more common illnesses. The deficiencies are more pronounced, the overloads more abundant, and the disruption of cellular life more significant. The state of decay in the biological terrain is such that the physical and mental functions of the body are not only restricted or perturbed, they have deviated significantly or stopped completely. How is it possible for living matter to reach such a state of chaos?

As we have seen, diseases do not make a sudden

appearance but are the culmination of a long process. Serious diseases such as cancer, AIDS, or multiple sclerosis do not suddenly strike someone enjoying good health. They constitute the terminal manifestation of a state of defective health that may have been building over many years.

The fact that children, as well as adults, may be stricken by serious illness shows how immensely important it is to avoid fictitious healings that create only the appearance of health, and to concentrate our search on cures that guarantee true health. These alone will permit the transmission of strong, healthy cellular terrain to our descendants.

Disease progresses through three different stages before it becomes a serious and degenerative illness.

First Stage

The first stage is the stage of warning signals, when a person who has been enjoying sound health observes the appearance of minor health problems. These warnings that the person is leaving the ideal state of health may be, for example, a loss of enthusiasm and a lack of pep, temporary indisposition, difficulty recovering after exertion, or even pimples or digestive disorders. The skin may lose its sheen and the hair turn dull and lackluster. All of these are signs that the biological terrain is becoming degraded. The rate of overload is still low during this stage, and these kinds of disorders will disappear quickly if the individual considers them as warning bells and takes appropriate action. In other words, she should scrutinize her lifestyle over the days or weeks preceding the appearance of any health problems to identify what has produced these alterations in her biological terrain.

Has she put a strain on her health from overeating,

consuming toxins, overworked nerves, lack of sleep, or being too sedentary? The biological terrain deteriorates every time the lifestyle exceeds the body's working capacity, or every time the body's physical and mental capacities are diminished for one reason or another and can no longer perform the tasks required of them.

If the patient refuses to listen to the warnings being issued by her body and continues living extravagantly without making any course corrections, the biological terrain will continue to deteriorate. The collection of waste and toxins in this internal cellular environment will go on until it reaches the threshold of tolerance, when a vigorous reaction by the body's vital forces will trigger a health-restoring cleansing crisis.

Second Stage

The second stage, that of acute illness, is reached at this point. Any further possibility of tolerating the rising level of toxins has been exceeded, and all of the body's vital forces are mobilized to expel the excess waste from the body. Depending on the location or form taken by these cleansing crises, allopathic medicine might diagnose the flu, measles, bronchitis, and so on, labeling each of these defensive reactions of the body as diseases in their own right.

In general, acute illnesses are violent and spectacular. The fever accompanying them reveals the intense activity the body deploys to renew itself. This activity is extended all over the body, moreover, and calls on the services of all the excretory organs. The flu, for example, is characterized by abundant secretions from the respiratory tract, intestinal upset, profuse sweating, and waste-laden urine. Acute illnesses are of short duration because the intensity of the effort of organic purification is sufficient to restore order rapidly.

Fever: Why We Heat Up

Fever is a reflection of the body's attempt to defend itself from a biological terrain overloaded with toxins. The acceleration of immune defenses, blood circulation, respiration, and cellular exchanges produces heat and thereby increases body temperature. Fever is, therefore, a manifestation of the body defending itself, which is why it is a common symptom of so many different maladies. It is the body's brilliant way of incinerating and eliminating a large amount of toxins in a short space of time.

Unless the patient's temperature climbs so high that it poses its own risks to the body, breaking a fever will only obstruct the body's defense system.

The confusion at this stage is to mistake the effect for the cause. If these defensive reactions are erroneously perceived as the cause of the disease and not as an effect of the deterioration of the body's internal cellular environment, the therapy will not be directed toward helping the body in its efforts to purify itself, but toward repressing unwelcome and troublesome symptoms. The treatment for the symptoms will halt all efforts of the vital force—in other words, the immune system—and push the toxins deep into the depths of the body. The result will be an increase in the level of toxicity and a decrease in the body's defensive capability.

If the patient, content with the disappearance of his symptoms, resumes his earlier lifestyle, the accumulation of

waste will resume. Every new palliative treatment undertaken to repress the efforts of body detoxification (symptoms) will bring about an increase in wastes and reduce the
vital force's ability to respond. Subsequently, at the stage
of serious illness, it will be a cause for surprise that the
immune system is, for all practical purposes, nonexistent.
Yet throughout the patient's entire life, every effort has
been made to destroy it.

Third Stage

In the third stage, diseases stop being acute and progress
to becoming chronic, or recurring. The overload rate is
far too high and the vital force too compromised for any
one round of physical cleansing to be sufficient, as is the
case with an acute illness. We then see cases of bronchitis, eczema, or liver trauma repeating every few months
or weeks. Detoxification efforts need to be renewed constantly, as they never completely succeed in purifying the
internal environment. At this stage, the body absolutely
requires outside assistance because its own forces are no
longer fully capable of dealing with the congestion of
the biological terrain. This support can be provided with
cleansing cures, combined with filling the body's deficiencies, as well as the use of specific physiological remedies.
In this way, the biological terrain will recover an almost
normal composition and health can be reestablished.

⌁

Alas, far too often the patient continues to believe a remedy is required for each illness, and that each more serious illness demands a stronger remedy. She continues to
eliminate the effects without ever removing the causes. The
resistance of the biological terrain and the vital force progressively deteriorate.

In the first three stages of the illness, the vital force was still strong enough, to a greater or lesser degree, to expel wastes from the body. But once the fourth stage has been reached, the stage of serious and degenerative disease, this possibility is gone. Wastes and toxins no longer can be expelled properly, and the body's attempt to accommodate itself to their massive presence disrupts its proper functioning. It must fight to survive the highly toxic condition of the biological terrain.

These days, more and more people are coming into the world with such compromised immune systems that, in the evolution of their health problems, they do not even go through the first three typical stages of illness. From birth their bodies have been so overloaded with wastes that no cleansing and regenerative crisis can interrupt the continued degradation of their internal cellular environments.

THE STAGES OF DISEASE

First stage	Warning signals
Second stage	Acute disease
Third stage	Chronic disease
Fourth stage	Degenerative disease

Fourth Stage

During the fourth stage of an illness, what's left of the vital force is still trying to save the life of the patient, but any attempted solutions must take place in the restricted framework of the internal environment, making them increasingly difficult to achieve. Where can the vital force direct the new waves of wastes and toxins relentlessly invading the tissues? How can it continue to protect the cells?

The cells, which should be bathed in nourishing and vivifying pure fluids, are suffocating in fluids saturated with wastes and toxic substances. They are forced to live in a kind of poisoned swamp. In addition they are suffering from a shortage of essential nutrients.

Every kind of physical dysfunction is then possible. Cells become progressively less normal and living matter becomes increasingly disorganized, which is revealed by the destruction of certain kinds of tissue or organs (sclerosis—hardening of a body part, irreversible lesions, deformities); aberrational behavior on the part of the cells, which are no longer subject to the intelligent guidance of the body's vital force (cancer); or by the body's inability to defend itself as an organized unit against microbial and viral assaults (AIDS, various immune deficiency disorders).

At this stage there is much less hope than in previous stages for a remedy or other arbitrary form of intervention that will restore order to the physical chaos reigning in the body. The logical solution is to alter the biological terrain as much as possible in the direction of health, and while waiting for this to be accomplished, support the patient with specific remedies.

The difficulty researchers encounter when attempting to perfect effective remedies against fourth stage diseases stems from the fact that diseases of this nature cannot be cured via shortcuts. It is instead imperative to retrace one's steps while there is still time, and make a focused attempt to cease and amend whatever mistakes have been made against the body's internal cellular environment.

That this is the sole sure means of obtaining remission or a true cure has been abundantly proven by all who have taken this course of action.

~~~

Illness goes through three different stages before becoming so serious that it is the terminal manifestation of a state of failing health, one that has been defective for many years.

2

The Causes of Illness
and the Reasons
for Health

ॐ

Because the state of our health is dependent on the state of our biological terrain, anything capable of causing this internal cellular environment to deteriorate will inevitably threaten our overall health.

The more crucial and numerous the factors causing degradation of the biological terrain, the more it deteriorates and the greater risk we run of falling seriously ill. It is, therefore, in our best interest to understand these causes so that we can avoid them. We should not expect to find these causes in exceptional situations (poisoning or accidental intoxication, for example), but in the habits of our daily lives.

Our biological terrain is composed of what we ingest as solid, liquid, or gaseous nourishment (the air we breathe), as well as everything else that enters the body (food additives, medication, tobacco, and so forth). Every influence to which our body is subjected becomes encapsulated in our biological terrain. Simple logic, then, invites us to examine our lifestyles.

The influence of lifestyle on our health does not always appear obvious because the errors that we make do not always affect us in a way clearly related to what we are doing. These bad habits first bring about changes that eventually grow larger in size—a process that can take months or even years—and become visible on the surface in the form of localized disorders.

Let's take a look at how these mistakes and bad habits break down our biological terrain and make us ill.

> All the influences to which our bodies are subjected become encapsulated in our biological terrain, hence the importance of examining our lifestyles.

OVEREATING IN GENERAL

In general, the first and foremost ill effect attributed to eating too much is that it leads to obesity. But eating more than is necessary has a number of other negative repercussions.

Organ Exhaustion

Digestion represents a major task performed by the body. It needs to carry out a series of transformations on the foods ingested, so that they can be absorbed and the valuable nutrients they offer can be made usable by the body.

The force expended for digestion increases with the amount of food consumed. Overeating inevitably leads to general body fatigue. The negative effects of overworking first strike the digestive glands, followed by the heart and the circulatory system that has to transport the excess food products, and finally the excretory organs that are responsible for expelling this vast quantity of waste from the body.

Intestinal Fermentation and Putrefaction

The body's digestive capacity is not limitless. When the amount of food eaten is too large, or when too many different kinds of food are eaten at the same time, the different stages of digestion perform poorly. Food that has not been digested sufficiently will ferment and putrefy in the intestines.

Intestinal fermentation and putrefaction produce a plethora of toxic substances: pyruvic acid, scatol, indole, ptomaine, and so forth. If these substances can be speedily flushed out of the organism, they will cause hardly any damage. But because of the fatigue of the digestive and excretory organs, this is exactly what doesn't happen. This is the way the body poisons itself with toxic substances.

Self-poisoning

Depending on the degree of the intestinal breakdown, the speed of the intestinal transit can be slowed so considerably that fecal material remains inside the intestines for days, or even weeks, causing self-poisoning. The intestinal mucous membranes are attacked and irritated by these unexcreted poisons with which they are now in prolonged contact. Eventually they develop lesions and become porous. From this point, instead of allowing only nutritive substances to flow into the bloodstream, the destroyed mesh of their walls also allows the passage of larger toxic molecules.

By creating a situation that leads to lesions in the intestinal mucous membrane, overeating throws open the doors to intestinal poisons and wastes. As long as the liver can manage to neutralize these wastes, they will not cause the body any undue suffering. But once the anti-toxin function of the liver has been exceeded by the mass of wastes it is receiving on a daily basis, the liver can no longer protect the body and little by little will become completely overrun by these toxins. The patient actually poisons himself with his own wastes.

The Accumulation of Overloads

Even if digestion is functioning perfectly well, overeating will still cause the biological terrain to break down. Indeed, when overeating takes place, the body is receiving more food than it needs. What should it do with the excess nutritive substances?

It can place part of them in reserve, storing them in anticipation of future needs, as it does with fat or glucose. But the body's storage capacities are not unlimited either. When there is an overabundance of any stored substance in the body, even a useful one will become harmful. Just think, for example, of diabetics who suffer from a variety of ailments, all of which can be traced to the poisoning of their body by sugar. Likewise, the excessive fat collected in the tissues of obese individuals will eventually cause them major problems such as slowed circulation and cellular exchange, useless fatigue of the heart and organs, and clogging of the organs.

Instead of storing excess substances, the body also can try to eliminate them. It first needs to break them down into a form the excretory organs will find easy to expel. However, the breaking down of these substances, which would free the body from undesirable overloads, does not take place properly because of the overall slowed pace of bodily functions. Breaking down glucose, for example, does not end with the normal production of easily eliminated

water and carbon dioxide, but comes to a halt at an intermediary stage that produces numerous toxic acids (pyruvic
acid, succinic acid, fumaric acid, and so on).

Even if the breakdown of excess substances takes place
normally, it is still producing toxins. For example, the degradation of proteins inevitably leads to the production of
urea and uric acid.

Overeating does not necessarily lead to gaining weight.
It can also, without any increase in pounds, congest the
body enough to cause significant changes in the composition of bodily fluids.

Excretory Insufficiency

The body's use of food substances always produces waste
and toxins. This involves a normal and entirely anticipated
process, since the role of the excretory organs (liver, intestines, kidneys, skin, and lungs) is specifically to eliminate
these wastes. Of course, the greater the quantity of food
consumed, the greater the quantity of wastes that will be
produced.

When they exceed the eliminatory capacity of the excretory organs, toxins clog the "filters" and cause congestion
in the organs. As elimination becomes unable to take place
properly, waste starts collecting in the tissues.

How Does One Overeat?

Practically speaking, there are two different ways in which
it is possible to overeat, although they can be combined:
eating too often or eating too much at one time.

In addition to their three regular meals, many people take breaks around 10:00 a.m. and 4:00 p.m. to eat
snacks. These foods are intended to "just tide me over,"
but teatime and coffee break snacks are often just as rich

as the three main meals of the day. These people are actually eating not just three meals a day but rather five or more! The cakes, cookies, chips, sandwiches, coffee drinks, and candies that are the usual "snack" culprits represent a substantial portion of the daily dietary intake.

In the second kind of overeating it is not necessarily the amount of food that is most important, but its questionable nutritional value. These foods are too rich, with too many calories and too few nutrients.

At mealtime, instead of consuming the recommended 70 percent "light" foods (salads, raw and cooked vegetables, fruits) and 30 percent concentrated foods (meat, cheese, eggs, grains, fatty foods), the proportions are reversed. The core of the meal is formed by meat, often served with fattening, flour-thickened sauces, whereas the portions of fruit and vegetables are extremely limited. Sometimes it seems as if these latter foods are only for decoration.

Overeating is rampant in every strata of the population. Although the real needs of an adult are placed around 2400 calories a day, actual intakes are much higher. The average daily caloric intake in Switzerland is around 3,380 calories, 3,633 calories in France, 3,651 in Belgium, and 3,654 in the United States.

❧

Overeating wears out the body and overloads it with waste.

OVEREATING SPECIFIC SUBSTANCES

In overeating in general, the subject eats everything in too large a quantity. When there is overconsumption of specific foods, these are cases in which a single kind of food is consumed in quantities higher than the body can properly digest and utilize.

All the problems encountered with general overeating are also problematic in specific foods, but with the addition of the distinct problems specific to the foods being consumed in excess. There are primarily four foods incriminated in this group: sugar, meat, fat, and salt.

Diets Too Heavy in Sugar

The digestion of foods rich in carbohydrates—fruit, grains, bread, potatoes, refined sugar products—provides glucose for fuel, which the body requires in order to function.

In order to be transformed into energy, glucose goes through two metabolic phases: an anaerobic phase (in the absence of oxygen), and an aerobic phase (in the presence of oxygen). During the anaerobic phase, through the action of different enzymes, glucose is transformed successively into citric acid, alpha-ketoglutaric acid, pyruvic acid, succinic acid, fumaric acid, malic acid, oxaloacetic acid, and finally lactic acid. These different acids are called the toxic intermediate metabolites (TIM).

In the subsequent aerobic phase, the TIM are oxidized, thereby releasing the energy the body needs. The residue left by this last transformation is composed of water and carbon dioxide, both of which are eliminated easily by the body.

But when there is excess consumption of carbohydrates, the body receives more glucose than it can possibly transform. Instead of culminating with the production of energy, the breakdown of the glucose is interrupted during one of the stages of the anaerobic phase. Whether it is at the pyruvic acid stage or malic acid stage, the intermediary metabolites are toxic residue that will poison the body.

The presence of TIM deteriorates the biological terrain in numerous ways. Blood and lymph have less liquidity, thereby slowing the rate of circulation and exchange and causing congestion in the organs. The mucous membranes of the organs and the walls of the cells are attacked and injured, which increases their vulnerability. A certain number of biochemical reactions no longer can occur because of the change in the pH, or acid-alkaline balance, of the internal environment. The biological terrain becomes increasingly acidic and the body depletes itself by surrendering its alkaline substances to neutralize the excess acidity.* The more carbohydrates consumed, the greater the deficiency in the vitamins and trace elements required to activate the enzymes involved in the breaking down of glucose, and the more the conversion of glucose runs the risk of being halted during its anaerobic phase, which produces TIM.

Consequently, the glucose from foods that are rich in vitamins and trace elements, such as fruit and whole grains, is metabolized much more effectively than the glucose from foods that have scant amounts of these substances, refined foods for instance. Refined sugars (both white and brown) and grains (white rice, white flour, pasta made from refined flour) are large producers of TIM. And yet, the consumption of foods made from white flour and refined sugar is increasing at an alarming rate. The use of white bread is widespread, and the annual consumption of sugar per capita in the United States has gone from 64 pounds in 1900 to more than 139 pounds. The latter figure includes both refined

---

*For more on this, see the section at the end of the chapter, "The Rupture of the Acid-Alkaline Balance," and my book *The Acid–Alkaline Diet for Optimum Health,* Rochester, Vt.: Healing Arts Press, 2003, Revised second edition 2006.

white sugar (62 pounds) and the high fructose corn syrup (77 pounds) found in almost all processed foods. Sugar consumption in the United States is double the European average.

A heavy carbohydrate diet is especially harmful when it includes too many foods containing refined sugar: candy, chocolate, baked items, preserves, commercial soft drinks (averaging 100 grams, or nearly half a cup, of sugar per liter), and sweetened yogurt (16 grams, or more than 3 teaspoons, of sugar per 100 grams) . . . and let's not forget the sugar we add to coffee and tea.

Diets Too Heavy in Protein

Foods rich in protein, such as meat, fish, cheese, eggs, grains, and beans provide the body with the essential amino acids it needs to grow new replacement cells for those that are worn out. The minimum daily protein requirement for the average individual has been strictly established, and it is not large. For healthy adults it is 0.8 gram per kilogram of body weight, which converts to only about 36 grams of protein for every 100 pounds of body weight. All the excess protein that is ingested still needs to be broken down and eliminated, because the body's capacity for storing amino acids in reserve is practically nil. The breaking down of proteins engenders three kinds of extremely toxic waste: uric acid, ammoniac acid, and ketonic acid. While the body is capable of breaking down ammoniac and ketonic acids into less toxic substances such as urea, which is eliminated through the kidneys and the sweat glands, it has no such ability to neutralize uric acid.

When high protein foods are eaten in too high quantities, the body's capacity to neutralize and eliminate the wastes generated by metabolizing them is quickly exceeded.

The result is ammoniac poisoning and accumulation of uric acid in the tissues.

The overeating of high protein foods is the most serious kind of food overconsumption, because the waste created in metabolizing them is the most toxic type of waste that can be created by food in the body.

Additionally, when these proteins are ingested in the form of animal products, the waste does not come merely from the metabolizing of these proteins. Animal tissue also contains all the metabolic waste generated by an animal when it was still alive; in other words, the animal's uric and ammoniac acids, and so on.

At the beginning of the twentieth century in what is commonly known as the developed world (primarily Western Europe and the United States), the annual consumption of meat per capita was around 90 pounds. A century later this figure has more than doubled to 201 pounds, which is a daily meat consumption of more than half a pound. This figure does not include all the protein consumed in foods such as dairy products, eggs, beans, and grains.

These days, a meal without meat is not considered to be a real meal. Furthermore, many people do not take into account that the meat products eaten as a snack, like salami or hot dogs or beef jerky, also represent an intake of meat. Excessive consumption of protein also can come from overeating cheese, eggs, or beans.

Diets Too Heavy in Fats

Fat plays both a building role and an energetic role in our bodies. Fats can be found in oleaginous foods like nuts and seeds (fat content 35–60%), eggs (11.5%), meat (up to 30% fat), sausages (up to 50%), cream (30%), and butter (81%).

Modern studies have proven the existence of two kinds of fat: saturated and unsaturated fatty acids. Unsaturated fatty acids are of vital importance to the body, and are easily metabolized. Saturated fatty acids are another story, however, as the body finds them difficult to use.

It is the latter that are the first to collect in the body's fat reserves (cellulite, obesity) and which adhere to the walls of the blood vessels (cardiovascular disease). Once established in the tissues, they are extremely difficult to dislodge, break down, and eliminate. It should also be noted that excess carbohydrates are stored in the body in the form of saturated fatty acids.

All foods containing fatty substances are composed of both saturated and unsaturated fatty acids, but their proportion varies from one food to the next. The foods that hold the highest concentrations of saturated fatty acids are of animal origin, but this list also includes palm and coconut oils, which are used to make margarine. However, these kinds of margarine are distinctly different from vegetable margarines that are rich in non-hydrogenated and unsaturated fatty acids and are manufactured from cold-pressed virgin oils.

In their natural form, unsaturated fatty acids, generally of plant origin, produce a beneficial effect on the human body by providing it with vitamin F, also known as the Omega 3 and 6 fatty acids. When they are subjected to overly high temperatures, they are adulterated. For this reason, when cooking, it is better to use a good-quality refined oil (sparingly) than the virgin cold-pressed oils.

Excess consumption of fats often goes hand-in-hand with the overeating of meat. This is not only because meats themselves are rich in fats (beef 20%, veal 11%, ham 30%, salami 35 to 49.5%), but also because they are often cooked in grease and fat, and served with equally fat-laden sauces.

Excess ingestion of fatty substances can also be the result of the excess consumption of dairy products, especially butter, whether on bread or vegetables, in sauces and dips, or used in cooking.

The harmful effects of fats are increased even further when they are overheated. In fact, the carbonization of oils or grease during cooking—primarily in frying, deep-frying, and barbecuing—gives birth to substances that are especially toxic and carcinogenic.

Diets Too Heavy in Salt

The foods we are offered by nature contain very little salt. Plant-based foods contain less than 100 milligrams of salt per 100 grams and animal products contain less than 250 milligrams per 100 grams. The salt that we consume is primarily added to foods as part of their preparation (in bread and cheese, for example), as they are cooked, or when they are eaten at the table.

Salt helps maintain the proper rate of water in the body, which means it contributes to ensuring that there is enough fluid within the cells, blood, lymph, and so forth in order for the body to function properly. One of the properties of salt, in fact, is its ability to retain large amounts of liquid (11 grams of water per 1 gram of salt). Salt also helps maintain good muscle tone and blood pressure.

Too much salt in the tissue leads to retention of more fluid than the body needs. This accumulation of water causes weight gain (in the form of water), creates edemas, and tires the heart because it is forced to circulate a fluid mass much larger than what is necessary. Blood pressure will also increase and continue to increase in proportion to the amount of excess salt in the body. This can bring about a variety of health problems associated with high blood pressure as well as cerebral congestion and heart fatigue. Furthermore, the kidneys, responsible for the elimination of salt, will either be assaulted (resulting in inflammation) or clogged (causing kidney stones) by the amount of salt they need to expel. Also, as salt retains water in the tissues it also retains the toxins being held that may otherwise have been eliminated.

Overconsumption of salt is extremely common today. This can be attributed both to a tendency to add much too much salt to our foods before we eat them and to the overconsumption of highly salted foods such as cheese, cold cuts, chips, salted nuts, canned soups, and ketchup. Salt can even be found in sweet foods such as cakes and cookies.

❧

The body cannot digest and properly use excess substances.

STIMULANTS

In addition to the actual food we eat, we regularly consume products we mistakenly consider to be food. These are stimulants like coffee, tea, cocoa, soft drinks, and alcohol. Tobacco is another commonly used stimulant, but no one considers it to be a food.

Stimulants contribute practically no nutritive substances to the body. However, one reason they are so widely consumed is that they give the impression of providing energy.

Because of our unnatural—even anti-natural—habits of life (stress, lack of sleep, and so on), we are always tired and consequently we perpetually attempt to energize ourselves with the aid of stimulants. In reality, the energy that is felt on taking a stimulant is not provided by the stimulant itself but is extracted *from our body's reserves.* The truth is that all stimulants contain numerous toxic substances. In order to protect the organism, the vital force triggers a defensive reaction by accelerating the body's metabolism to neutralize, break down, and eliminate these poisons.

This acceleration of the metabolism is experienced as a jolt of energy from outside, whereas in reality the body is only wearing itself out by being forced to react against repeated poisoning. A truly vicious cycle is established: the more the body is revived by stimulants, the more it exhausts itself; the more exhausted it is, the greater its need for stimulation.

During any exertion, there is wear and tear on the tissues and waste production from the breaking down of fuel used by the cells. When it collects in the tissues, the toxins of fatigue can dangerously overload the body's internal cellular environment, especially if the effort is sustained for a prolonged stretch of time. Fatigue is the signal we are given to interrupt our efforts so as to allow the elimination of wastes these efforts have already generated.

If this purification period represented by rest is not respected, and if, by virtue of stimulants, new forces are extracted from the body's reserves to make the continuation of the effort possible, then new toxins are produced. These will combine with those that have already accumulated, and which were the reason for taking the stimulant. When the body is not granted the rest it needs, it becomes more and more poisoned by its own waste.

This endogenous intoxication within the deep tissue is produced by the toxins of fatigue, and only exacerbated by the intoxication resulting from toxins in the stimulants.

Coffee, Tea, Cocoa, Cola

Beverages made from coffee, tea, cocoa, or cola contain varying proportions of one or more of the three following alkaloids: caffeine, theosphylline, and theobromine. These three elements are soluble in both water and in oil. Consequently, they are able to penetrate any kind of tissue; the protective membrane of the cell, which is fatty, cannot function as a filter against them. The toxic state caused by these alkaloids is, therefore, capable of afflicting even the best-protected tissues, such as those of the nerves and the brain.

The ravages caused by these beverages do not stop there. They also make a significant contribution of tars and oxalic acid. Furthermore, the amount of purine—a substance that gets broken down by the metabolism to become uric acid—contained in these beverages is quite high. Approximately 1 to 2 teaspoons of dried tea (the recommended quantity for one cup) provides as much uric acid to the body as one would get from drinking more than six quarts of milk (approximately 24 glasses).

Alcoholic Beverages

Everyone is familiar with the ravages caused by alcohol, but because we are so used to hearing about them we no longer pay enough attention. People have a tendency to say, "A little alcohol cannot do a body harm," which is essentially true. However the daily consumption of 10 ounces (3 deciliters) a day of wine with 12 percent alcohol by volume will add up to an intake of 4 gallons (15 liters) of pure alcohol in a year's time. The consumption of a liter (most wine bottles are 0.75 liter) of wine with 10 percent alcohol content corresponds to the ingestion of one hundred grams of pure alcohol (nearly one-half cup). Alcohol is not a food but a poison that wears out the liver and irritates and ossifies the tissues.

Tobacco

Although it is constantly repeated that the nicotine, carbon monoxide, cadmium, arsenic, ammonia, and up to 599 legal additives inhaled with every cigarette by smokers—and those around them—are violent toxins, the warnings concerning tobacco poisoning are not taken seriously enough. In fact, there seem to be a large number of people surviving this poisoning, despite daily doses of tobacco higher than what is otherwise believed to be fatal.

It is therefore necessary to specify that the doses commonly cited as fatal are the levels that would be deadly if found *in the blood*. But thanks to the ceaseless efforts of the vital force, the poisons contained in tobacco—just like those of all toxic products of any kind—are rapidly removed from the bloodstream to be eliminated by the excretory organs, if these organs are functioning properly, or buried in the depths of the tissues if they are not. Confronted by such poisoning on a daily basis, the excretory organs are quickly overwhelmed, of course, and the poisons are then deposited out of the bloodstream in the tissues, thereby saving the smoker from poisoning by keeping the blood within norms compatible with life.

But while a quick death is averted, the smoker is still subjected to a slow, widespread poisoning. Throughout the rest of his or her life, the smoker will be beset by numerous disorders that will eventually lead to a slow death through profound degradation of the biological terrain.

⸙

When a stimulant is taken, what is felt as a rush of new energy imported from the outside is actually a defense mechanism of the body.

CHEMICAL POISONS

For what is now decades, human beings have been consuming and being poisoned by enormous quantities of chemical ingredients added to their food. This is a critical cause of body fluid congestion.

The different sources of these chemical substances are the following:

Products Used in Farming
Plant fertilizers, as well as the products used to protect crops (insecticides, fungicides, pesticides, herbicides—often twenty to thirty treatments between planting and harvest) partially permeate the tissues of vegetables, fruits, and grains and enter our bodies when we eat the treated foods.

Products Used in Raising Animals
All the medications (antibiotics, vaccines, and so on) and fattening agents (hormones, special diets) given to animals permeate their flesh or their by-products (eggs, milk, dairy products) and ultimately are swallowed by consumers and embedded in their tissues. Only recently, a new threat has emerged—the danger from GMOs, or genetically modified organisms, contained in livestock feed.

Food Additives

These substances are manufactured for the purpose of preserving food products, as well as for making them appear attractive to consumers. They include preservatives, stabilizers, food coloring, flavor enhancers, and so forth. Some of them are perfectly harmless, such as the beet juice that adds red color to fruit yogurt, but others are now recognized as violent poisons. There are several thousand substances used as additives. Although there are only minuscule amounts of each in different foods, there is an estimated annual consumption of several pounds of additives per person each year!

Medications

The majority of medications produced by the pharmaceutical industry are either synthetic products or dangerous chemical substances. Convincing arguments for this are provided on the medications themselves. Simply read the warning labels for the many contraindications and possible side effects. Their risk becomes only more apparent when we see them abruptly pulled from the market for unexpected, disastrous side effects. We also should keep in mind the many iatrogenic diseases discussed earlier.

Household Products

Some of the ingredients in cleaning and beauty products commonly found around the home—detergents, cleansers, shampoos, hair dyes, and so forth—are toxic. Although their toxicity is not extremely high, their regular use is dangerous.

The Products of Pollution

Pollutants contaminate the air, water, and soil. They come from factory smokestacks, automobile exhaust, emissions generated by heating and cooling, and the wastewater created by both homes and industries.

The levels of all of these chemical substances are overseen by official agencies that determine the admissible amount of toxic content in various products and in our environment. Against all normal expectations, toxic or carcinogenic products are not banned outright, but quantities of substances known to be dangerous are regulated so that only very small doses of each can be used. These doses are far below what are deemed to be fatal amounts, and even if they accumulate over time, must not exceed the quantities compatible with life.

You might try to reassure yourself that the experts surely know whether or not the body can tolerate these substances and in what amounts. But a plethora of events and experiments show that they do not really know, and that the human body does not handle being poisoned at all well—even when this chemical poisoning has been approved by the appropriate regulating authorities.

The large-scale usage of additives and chemical medications, which has been accelerating only over the last few decades, is still too recent a phenomenon in terms of human history to allow us to truly measure the long-term effects. The repercussions of toxic poisoning are not always visible immediately. Sometimes lung cancer doesn't declare its presence until thirty or forty years after the smoker takes his first puff.

Furthermore, different experiments seem to show that the appearance of cancerous cells is more rapid when there's a larger daily dose of a carcinogen—in keeping with what one might expect—but surprisingly, that the dose necessary to produce a tumor is practically constant. In other words, it doesn't matter whether the incidents of carcinogen ingestion are close together or spaced further apart, because it is not the quantity contained by the body for a given moment that counts; it is total quantity that has traveled through the body. The effects of each ingested dose, therefore, continue to add up, without any subtraction, over an entire lifetime. Whether the critical level is met by small doses over long periods or just one large dose, it is equally disastrous.

There is yet another concern that needs to be addressed here. While we know very little about the effect of each additive when taken individually, we are even more ignorant about what happens when they combine in our tissues to give birth to completely unknown compounds that might be extremely toxic.

The current multiplication of new forms of serious disease is directly connected to this discreet and insidious chemical poisoning of the body, for which man alone is responsible.

The repercussions of a poisonous or toxic state are not always immediately visible.

POOR ELIMINATION

Our bodies are endowed with five organs charged with filtering all the metabolic waste and residue out of the bloodstream in order to expel it from the body. These five excretory organs are the liver, kidneys, intestines, skin, and lungs.

When functioning properly, they are capable of eliminating all the waste produced by ordinary daily life. Even when mistakes have been made, the purity of the biological terrain can still be safeguarded for a certain period of time because the vital force of the body will intensify the filtering and eliminatory work performed by the excretory organs. However, this increased work level cannot be sustained indefinitely.

Sooner or later, the excretory organs will become exhausted and their activity will diminish. If the conditions forcing them to work overtime continue, eventually they will suffer injury and become incapable of functioning normally. It is therefore imperative to rapidly correct all the errors that created this unhealthy condition.

Several figures will allow us to realize the speed with which an organism can become saturated with wastes. The kidneys normally eliminate 25 to 30 grams of urea every twenty-four hours. If they eliminate only 20 grams, that represents a retention of urea of 5 grams a day, adding up to 150 grams (more than five ounces) a month! If, instead of eliminating the 15 grams of salt (NaCl) that are typically absorbed from food every twenty-four hours they expel only 12 grams, this adds up to a retention rate of 90 grams (more than three ounces) of salt in one month.

Of course these figures are not an exact depiction of reality, because the waste that one excretory organ is incapable of eliminating can be eliminated by another, provided the latter's capacities have not been exceeded by overwork as well. But these figures can give us a greater understanding of the quantity of waste that can collect and begin to degrade the state of our internal cellular environment if we do not pay attention to elimination.

So what are the criteria for the proper, healthy functioning of our five excretory organs?

The Liver

The liver filters wastes out of the blood and expels them from the body with the bile. It has an excretory function in addition to its digestive role, inasmuch as it permits the emulsification of fats, an important stage in the digestive process.

Bile insufficiency reveals its presence by overall digestive troubles, abdominal pain, nausea, fermentation, bloating, coating on the tongue, bad breath, and headaches after meals. Another common reaction is feelings of disgust at the mere thought of eating fatty foods such as eggs, fried foods, fat-laden sauces and gravies, and rich pastries; individuals will be incapable of consuming these foods.

The consistency and color of the stool can also reveal this insufficiency. In the absence of bile, the individual is generally constipated and has hard, dry stools that resemble goat dung more than human excrement. The brownish-yellow color of stool is due to the presence of bile pigments. The skin and eyes become yellow when bile is not eliminated properly, because the pigments remain stagnant in the region of the liver, from whence they can easily travel into the bloodstream. A few other revealing symptoms include greasy skin, the propensity to have pimples, and the tendency to suffer inflammation in the respiratory tract.

But even if we are not suffering from any of the problems mentioned above, there is still always the possibility that our liver may be in the midst of becoming deficient because the entire anti-natural lifestyle that is prevalent today contributes to this condition (overeating, chemical poisoning, stress, vaccinations, and so on).

The Intestines

When the intestines are functioning properly, they empty themselves once or twice a day (not necessarily at a set time), and the stools are firm, eliminated easily without straining, and do not have a very strong odor. After one has passed a stool, there should be a feeling of having thoroughly emptied oneself.

But how many people produce only one stool every two or three days, if not less frequently, or have stools that are either dry and hard, or completely loose and repulsive? These individuals often have great trouble evacuating and never have the feeling following a bowel movement that they've emptied themselves completely. This impression is quite accurate—matter is continuing to collect in the intestines, distending and deforming them. Moreover, by fermenting and putrefying while still inside their bodies, this non-eliminated fecal matter starts attacking the mucous membranes of the intestines, which become porous as a result. Instead of being evacuated, some of the wastes are reabsorbed by the damaged mucous membranes and spread throughout the body via the bloodstream.

The Kidneys

The kidneys excrete the wastes they filter out of the blood by diluting them with water. The quantity and characteristics of our urine reveal much about the state of the renal excretory organ. Normally an average 1.5 liters (about 6.5 cups) of urine should be eliminated daily, which means around five to six urinations a day. Because it is carrying waste, urine is colored (golden yellow) and has a distinctive odor.

An individual is suffering from renal insufficiency when the quantity of urine falls below the norm, if she urinates only two to three times a day, or if the urine is too clear and resembles water. In this case the kidneys are certainly eliminating fluid from the body, but not enough waste to give the urine its characteristic yellow color. This observation about color is obviously not valid for people who drink a lot of water—three liters (more than three quarts) a day, for example, as this dilutes the urine and causes it to lose its color.

The Skin

With its sebaceous glands that secrete sebum and its sudoriferous (sweat) glands that secrete perspiration, the skin has a dual elimination system at its disposal. These various glands are quite tiny but numerous. Consequently, they are able to eliminate substantial quantities of waste. During a fever, for example, the skin can perspire quarts of sweat loaded with urea, uric acid, and salt.

Skin that is functioning properly will perspire during times of exertion and when temperatures are high. A person who never perspires or who perspires only from specific locales of the body has an excretory organ that has been practically sealed shut. Because it is incapable of performing the eliminatory duties expected of it, the other excretory organs are forced to work harder. Another sign of poor function is overly dry skin, or, conversely, skin that is too oily or has acne.

The appearance of a pimple or a case of eczema is certainly a defensive reaction of the excretory system, but it is also a sign that eliminations must not be functioning well, because wastes are stagnating in the region of this excretory organ.

The Lungs

Wastes that are eliminated by way of the respiratory tract should first and foremost be of a gaseous nature—carbon dioxide and water vapor. Solid wastes should be extremely rare and primarily consist of dust that has been inhaled and trapped in the filters of the upper respiratory tract. It is not normal to have a constantly runny nose or to be coughing and expectorating. People prone to inflammation in the mucous membranes of the respiratory tract (colds, sinusitis, bronchitis) are showing evidence of congestion of

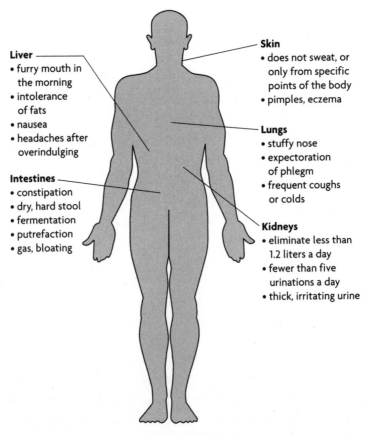

Liver
• furry mouth in the morning
• intolerance of fats
• nausea
• headaches after overindulging

Intestines
• constipation
• dry, hard stool
• fermentation
• putrefaction
• gas, bloating

Skin
• does not sweat, or only from specific points of the body
• pimples, eczema

Lungs
• stuffy nose
• expectoration of phlegm
• frequent coughs or colds

Kidneys
• eliminate less than 1.2 liters a day
• fewer than five urinations a day
• thick, irritating urine

Signs of excretory organ weakness

the biological terrain and overworked excretory organs.

The inhalation and exhalation of air should be regular, deep, and easily adapted to a change in rhythm during intense periods of exertion. Someone who runs out of breath too easily, even during slight exertion, or who is often gasping for air or frequently needs to spit out colloidal waste, has an overloaded pulmonary excretory organ wherein gaseous exchanges are not taking place properly.

⋰⋱

Expulsion of waste from the body is not the sole task performed by the excretory organs. They must first filter and extract these wastes from the bloodstream, then prepare them in a way that allows them to leave the body without injuring the tissues.

Each excretory organ filters and eliminates specific wastes. When one of these organs can no longer manage to eliminate all the wastes presented by the body, another excretory organ steps in and eases its workload. For example, colloidal wastes that the liver is incapable of filtering can be expelled through the sebaceous glands or respiratory tract.

A system of mutual aid, therefore, exists between the excretory organs and allows them to protect the purity of the biological terrain by ensuring that the essential task of eliminating waste continues to take place. Of course this system can only function as long as the assisting excretory organs are not themselves overworked. If this is the case, deep and rapid congestion of the body will occur.

It is easy to see that the deficiency of one excretory organ does not lead directly to serious illness. But the chronic insufficiency of one or several of these organs will certainly lead to a state of poor health eventually, because of the progressive saturation of the biological terrain with wastes. Those suffering from serious, or big illnesses are all "small eliminators."

> ❧
>
> Big illness patients are all "small eliminators."

A SEDENTARY LIFESTYLE

In addition to weakened muscles and organs, a sedentary lifestyle causes decreased oxygenation, slowed metabolism of food intake, and poor elimination of toxins.

Our ancestors were much more physically active than we are today, simply out of necessity. Elevators, automobiles, supermarkets and the like have created an "easy life" that's not so easy on our bodies. Our motor capacities are underutilized, either because of jobs that require us to remain seated, our use of motor vehicles to travel rather than walk even short distances, the absence of physical activity during leisure time, or all of the above.

The lack of time that often serves as a pretext for not walking, taking the stairs, or preparing foods manually is just that—a pretext because time that is saved in this way is used by most people in sedentary pursuits, like sitting for hours in front of the television or computer, or traveling long distances to get to . . . the gym.

DEFICIENCIES

The body does not hold within its tissues all the nutritive substances it will need over the course of a lifetime. It is, therefore, necessarily dependent on what is provided by sources outside the body. Our food should regularly bring us sufficient quantities of all the nutrients (amino acids, carbohydrates, fats, minerals, vitamins, and so forth) that are essential for the formation and maintenance of our organs as well as their functioning.

Once the body is deprived of one of these nutrients, its functioning is disrupted; the first sign is the slowing of one or more body functions. Subsequently, if the deficiency lasts too long, certain physical and mental functions can grind to a halt. If it remains uncorrected, death will eventually ensue. For example, depending on what substances the body lacks, tissues will no longer be repaired, the resistance of the mucous membranes diminishes, there is a loss of muscle tone, enzyme activity is reduced, secretions stop, the blood becomes thinner, and white blood cells lose their defensive ability.

In illnesses caused by deficiencies, nothing can halt the evolution of the disorder and the degradation of the biological terrain other than restoring an adequate supply of the missing substance. As long as this substance remains absent, the body will continue to go downhill. Because the body is totally dependent on the missing nutrient, no medicine is capable of taking its place. Just as the solution to this problem is simple—the ingestion of several milligrams of vitamins, for example—a disorder can remain serious so long as the deficiency remains unaddressed.

Even a deficiency of a single nutrient can have catastrophic consequences. In fact, nutrients work interdependently with one another. The absence of just one can, therefore, render the utilization of the others completely ineffective, and like a chain reaction, create a state of multiple deficiencies.

Although we live in an era of abundance, it is much easier to experience deficiencies of this nature than one might think. It might be a deficiency of supply (the foods ingested by the body do not contain all the necessary nutrients), or it could be a deficiency of utilization (the nutrients are supplied to the body but the body is unable to make use of them).

Deficiencies of Supply

In the simplest case, foods containing the missing substance are not being eaten by the individual. In the past, this was a common occurrence for inhabitants of extremely isolated regions that had a limited number of foods at their disposal. Today, deficiencies of supply are more likely to be due to a deliberate—but erroneous—eating choice. Many people, perhaps because they have been misinformed or have not grasped the entire picture, totally banish one food or entire food category from their diets and practice skewed diets that lead directly to the various diseases caused by deficiencies. Some people indiscriminatingly eliminate all fat from their diets after having read somewhere that fats were implicated in cardiovascular disease. Others avoid eating a certain fruit for fear of being poisoned by pesticides, and so on.

Diets that are practiced for philosophical or aesthetic reasons can also create serious deficiencies, if these individuals do not take into consideration the physiological imperatives of the body.

Another very common cause for deficiencies of supply today arises from the fact that our food no longer contains all the nutrients it should. These elements have been removed by various procedures that alter the food's outer appearance or increase its shelf life. Perhaps grains have been refined, a process that makes it possible to obtain extremely white flour, but which deprives the consumer of precious nutrients that are located in the part of the grain that gets discarded in the refining process. Vegetable and plant oils are also subjected to a series of mechanical, caloric, and chemical transformations that cause them to lose their vitamins and trace elements. The same holds true for refined sugar, which, stripped of all living elements, can be preserved almost indefinitely. Additionally, the depletion of soil and inadequate farming or livestock-raising methods is likely to result in a sharp drop in the nutrient content of foods, as is the drying of fruits at high temperatures, eating only cooked foods, and throwing away the cooking water.

A special word needs to be said concerning water. Of all the substances our bodies need, water is a top priority inasmuch as our bodies primarily consist of fluids. Daily intake of sufficient water is, therefore, essential. The reality is that many people are not drinking enough water; their daily consumption is clearly below the 2 liters, or slightly more than half a gallon, that their bodies require every day. This shortage of water creates a state of chronic tissue dehydration that hampers the body's normal functioning.*

Deficiencies of Utilization

This kind of deficiency is caused when the body finds it impossible to utilize some of the nutrients with which it has been provided.

This could be either because the nutrients were destroyed in the intestines before they could be absorbed into the bloodstream by toxic substances resulting from intestinal fermentation and putrefaction, or because the biological terrain is so saturated with wastes that exchanges

---

*For more on this see my book *The Water Prescription,* Rochester, Vt.: Healing Arts Press, 2006.

are occurring poorly. In either case the result is the same: the nutrients don't reach the area of the body where they can be used.

Numerous chemical substances from additives, pollution, and pharmaceutical medication have an inhibiting effect on vitamins and trace elements. When this occurs, they can be described as anti-vitamins, or chelators of trace elements. The nutrients are present in the body but have been rendered inactive, or even destroyed, by chemical pollution. The individual suffering from deficiencies can supply her body with all the proper nutrition it needs, but in vain; the consumption of these inhibitors creates a state of deficiency in the body, in addition to other toxic effects.

The simple consumption of stimulants causes deficiencies because their use demands more nutrients that will allow the body to neutralize the poisons of the stimulants. The consumption of tobacco increases the body's need for vitamin C, alcohol for vitamin B, and so forth. It is important to note that deficiencies in vitamin C reduce the body's capacity to defend itself, and deficiencies in vitamin B disrupt the nervous system and encourage clogging of body fluids because of the poor utilization of food that results.

Another reason why the body finds itself incapable of benefiting from the nutrients it is supplied stems from the fact that they are removed before it can put them to use. In fact, numerous deficient foods, such as refined sugar, white flour, and refined oils, as well as all the food products prepared with them, are known as "vitamin thieves." Because these foods are incomplete they no longer carry the enzymes, vitamins, and catalytic metals required to digest them. In order to make the digestive breakdown of these deficient foods possible, these vital substances will be pilfered from the body. Refined and processed foods, even before they give the body whatever nutritive substances they might still carry, are desecrating what is already there.

When incomplete and deficient foods like these are consumed on a regular basis, the body's reserves end up being pillaged, and serious deficiencies can be established.

> ❧
>
> Once the body has been deprived of any one essential nutrient, its functioning will be disturbed.

THE RUPTURE OF THE ACID-ALKALINE BALANCE

Our bodies function best when the acidic and alkaline substances that enter into the composition of tissues and bodily fluids are present in equal quantities—what we call the acid-alkaline balance.

A Precarious Balance

The body contains both acid and alkaline substances, and the balance between them is critical to our good health. This balance—the degree of acidity or alkalinity in the body—is measured as pH. The normal pH of blood, and of the biological terrain in general, is 7.39. When there is movement away from this ideal pH, frequently caused by our acid-producing diet and lifestyle, the bodily terrain becomes highly susceptible to disease.

Any disruption of this balance will lead to illness. The most common rupture, extremely widespread at present, is the one characterized by a disproportionate amount of acid in the internal cellular environment, or acidosis. The health problems that this can cause are quite varied: chronic fatigue, stress, excessive nervousness, depression, rheumatic disorders, tendinitis, eczema, tooth decay, and so forth.

How are these disorders formed? Acids have virulent properties that irritate the tissues and can go on to cause inflammations, for example of the joints and tendons. In order to defend itself, the body seeks to neutralize the excess acid with the help of its buffer system. To do this, it steals the alkaline minerals found in the blood and tissues. In times of heavy demand or regular withdrawals, the organs and tissues lose their mineral content and become weaker and more fragile (dental cavities, eczema, nervous fragility . . .). Furthermore, an acidic biological terrain is an environment that provides unfavorable working conditions for enzymes, those "little workers" responsible for all the biochemical transformations that take place in the body. Energy production, tissue regeneration, and cellular exchanges all diminish and are replaced by chronic fatigue, depression, reduced defenses, and a marked loss of enthusiasm.

The principle cause for the rupture of the acid-alkaline balance toward acidity is dietary. The proportion of acidifying food (meat, flour, fat, refined sugar) we consume is generally much higher than that of alkaline food (salad greens, raw and cooked vegetables, potatoes, almonds, bananas). Because it is receiving a much greater quantity of acids on a daily basis than it is alkaline substances, it is a big challenge for the body to neutralize the excess acid. It is therefore obliged to pillage its alkaline reserves from the tissues, with all the unhealthy consequences this theft entails. Usually the body is unsuccessful at reestablishing a perfectly normal pH and must live with this excess acid, which creates a chronic state of recurring disease due to acidosis.

The other causes of acidity are the consumption of stimulants, poor elimination of acids by the skin and kidneys, vitamin deficiencies, and lack of oxygenation. In addition, a negative mental attitude (anxiety, aggressiveness, bitterness, and so forth) will disrupt the metabolism and engender more production of acid by the body. Insufficient sleep and overwork will produce acids as well.

Summary: The Causes of Acidification of the Biological Terrain

- Excess of acidifying and acidic foods and beverages
- Insufficient alkalizing foods
- Under-oxygenation
- Vitamin deficiencies
- Poor elimination by skin and kidneys
- Stress
- Negative mental attitude

As we have ascertained, the major causes for degradation of the biological terrain and those for the formation of an acidic biological terrain are the same. There are, however, several different kinds of biological terrain degradation, of which acidification is just one. It is extremely widespread, because many people have trouble from the outset metabolizing acid, and the excessive quantity of acids consumed in the typical diet rapidly exceeds the body's ability to deal with them.

One means of determining if your biological terrain is acidic is to measure your urinary pH with the help of litmus paper. The normal acid content of the urine is the same as that of the entire body, which we have seen is a pH of around 7. When a person's lifestyle and diet is acidifying,

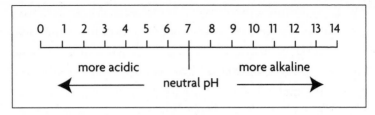

The pH scale

more acids will be eliminated through urination, which will lower its pH to around 6 or 5.

NEGATIVE MENTAL ATTITUDE

Everyone has personally experienced the influence of mental attitude on the body's functioning. The simple nervous anticipation experienced before exams is enough to cause all sorts of disruptions—loss of the desire to eat, sweating, accelerated heartbeat, trembling hands, upset stomach and other intestinal problems, and the persistent desire to urinate. A quarrel that breaks out during the middle of a meal can also be the cause of indigestion. Moreover, grievances can cause loss of appetite, worries can prevent sleep, and so on.

Also, who doesn't know people with liver complaints (hepatics) who experience a liver crisis (nausea, indigestion, vomiting) over the smallest worry and asthmatics who have an attack whenever something upsets them? There are also those who regularly get sick on Monday mornings—both adults in the workforce and schoolchildren—from dread about the week looming ahead.

If the episodes of our mental life, limited in time like the examples just mentioned, can momentarily overwhelm various bodily functions, how much worse are the disorders engendered in someone who agonizes perpetually about everything, dwells on dark thoughts, is easily depressed, fears falling seriously ill, is impatient with those around him, attacks his neighbors, and explodes in rage over the merest trifle?

It would be wrong to think that we are unable to do anything about our individual fortunes and are simply the victims of events. In fact, what is most important is not the situation we are experiencing, but *our attitude* toward it. Some people get irritated at the slightest thing, whereas others are capable of keeping their calm even in the most stressful circumstances.

Two people experiencing the same situation in which both are involved equally—following the death of someone close to both of them, for example—can react in totally different ways. One may be completely stricken by it and fall into a slow decline, whereas the other, although profoundly shaken, will get a grip on his or her feelings and, full of enthusiasm, find new meaning in life.

The power of our attitude and thoughts over events is also revealed by the fact that just to *imagine* an unpleasant situation is enough to cause a change in bodily functioning. The simple mention of forthcoming exams, even weeks in advance, can create anxiety and tie one's stomach into knots. Thoughts of violence and hatred are capable of creating tension even if the person against whom these violent thoughts are directed is absent. Likewise, the joy inspired by an anticipated visit can work positive changes on the overall state of a patient's health.

The influence of thoughts is such that, up to a certain point, even life and death are dependent on them. The will to live of certain seriously ill individuals or accident victims can help them to rise above absolutely desperate situations.

On the other hand, sick or injured people who "give up" or "just let everything drop" sometimes die from disorders that are quite within the scope of therapeutic healing methods.

Because the attitude of the patient has such profound influence on his or her illness, it is clear that the therapist guiding the treatment of these individuals, even when their problems are quite serious, should never diminish the mental aspect of the question as a minor matter while concentrating solely on the material and physical aspects of the patient's case. The psyche exerts its influence on the physical at all times. Just as a negative attitude can increase the serious nature of health problems or hamper their treatment, a positive attitude can lay the groundwork for improvement.

But how, in concrete terms, does a negative attitude cause the state of the biological terrain to deteriorate? Our thoughts and the feelings they engender alter the normal functioning of our organs by means of the sympathetic nervous system and the endocrine glands.

The sympathetic nervous system, which is a part of the autonomic nervous system, regulates unconscious body functions such as salivation, perspiration, air flow to the lungs, and so on. It acts on our body's organs by slowing or accelerating their function, adapting their activity at every moment to the constantly changing needs of daily life. For example, when we need to confront a danger, the digestive functions are inhibited because they are useless as a means of defending ourselves.

Once the danger has passed, the autonomic nervous system slows the circulatory and respiratory functions and stimulates the digestive function so that any interrupted digestion can continue.

But when a person has an erroneous attitude toward life that puts her in a state of constant tension, her digestive functions, to borrow the preceding example, are in a state of chronic indigestion, which is a huge producer of wastes and toxins that contribute to the deterioration of the biological terrain.

Depending on the responses of the sympathetic nervous system to the requests made of it, other changes can occur: elimination will be poor if the excretory organs are permanently inhibited, or there could be a problem with oxidation if it is the respiratory system whose activity is constrained, and so forth.

The endocrine glands, including the thyroid, adrenal glands, and so on, will become disrupted in the same way as the sympathetic nervous system. For example, fear stimulates the release of adrenaline by the adrenal glands, constant irritation and agitation accelerate thyroid function, and so forth. Hormonal secretions also affect the functioning of the organs, and can cause poor digestion or elimination, or a slowing of circulation that will bring about the deterioration of the internal cellular environment.

The influence of mental life over physical health can be subtle, but the fact remains that it is of fundamental importance. More than any other unbalancing factor that asks us to initiate change in our lifestyle, this one demands—if one really wants to be truly cured—profound self-transformation.

꙳

The influence of our thoughts is such that, up to a certain point, life and death depend on them.

3

Naturopathy in Practice

*Correcting and Balancing
the Internal Cellular
Environment*

_෨

The first question to leap into the mind of every person in good health who has grasped the importance of the state of the internal cellular environment will be, "What can I do to maintain this state?"

For those suffering from poor health, whose bodies are already overloaded with toxins and deficiencies of essential nutrients, the question obviously will have to be rephrased to, "What can I do to correct my biological terrain?"

In both cases the guiding principles for maintaining or repairing the biological terrain remain identical. The manner of applying them, however, varies enormously from one patient to the next, and from one stage of illness to the next. The advice provided here will necessarily confine itself to introducing and explaining the guiding principles. They can be adopted to great benefit whether someone is sick or enjoying good health. However, they do not suffice in any case for constituting the treatment, properly speaking, of people stricken by serious disease. It is imperative that individuals in this situation seek the help of a qualified medical practitioner. In fact, precisely adjusting the advocated methods to the health needs of every individual, and changing them in accordance with each person's overall state, is an art. Furthermore, the correction of the biological terrain of individuals suffering from serious disease involves a much stricter and more intensive application of the principles presented here.

The guideline for repairing the body's internal cellular environment was given to us by Hippocrates: "Treatment should aim at opposing the cause of the disease and not allowing it to persist." Since illness results from the degradation of the biological terrain by the collection of waste and deficiency of nutrients, the logical treatment would consist of:

- causing those wastes present in the body to be removed,
- preventing new wastes from entering,
- and filling deficiencies.

This approach, like the methods for draining overloads or filling deficiencies, is astonishingly simple. The knee-jerk reaction of the twenty-first-century human being, accustomed to much more sophisticated procedures, will be to doubt the effectiveness of these methods. But they truly are effective because they are based entirely on conformity to natural laws and physiological imperatives. This approach follows the direction of these laws and supports them.

ॐ

"Treatment should aim at opposing the cause of the disease." —Hippocrates

SHUTTING OFF THE SOURCE OF OVERLOADS

Draining wastes out of the body will not lead to any positive result if, at the same time, other toxins are still being allowed to enter. Over the course of a normal day, new wastes are able to enter our bodies because of our detrimental life habits. If we can correct these bad habits, only one front remains to be conquered. All the body will have to do is eliminate the old, accumulated wastes. It is, therefore, fundamentally important to shut off the perpetual source of new overloads and monitor what we consume.

The regulation of which foods are supplied to the body will of course be more meticulous and precise for someone seriously ill than for someone suffering a minor disorder. When the diet is constantly being adjusted to be in tune with the digestive and excretory capacities of the body, a kind of status quo will be reached. The rate of excess substances does not rise and the organs are never overworked. The strength that is saved in this way is then available for the healing process.

Regulating Quantities

In our era of abundance and chronic overeating, regulating the quantity of food ingested generally means reducing it. But eating less is in no way synonymous with always being hungry and following draconian diets. In accordance with the famous maxim, "You should eat to live, not live to eat," quantitatively regulating your diet merely means that you eat only what your body needs.

If the overeating is due to eating meals that are too big, steps should be taken to make them more modest, either by pure strength of will, preparing smaller quantities, or replacing concentrated foods (meats, fried foods, flour-based foods) with foods of little concentration (vegetables, salads, raw food, fruit).

The overeating we see today is partially due to the poor nutritive quality of our foods. We are instinctively driven to eat more in an attempt to obtain the minerals and vitamins our bodies need but cannot find in the refined foods we offer it. By eating whole foods, and therefore increasing the value of what we ingest, we inevitably will reduce the quantity of food we eat.

Chewing food more thoroughly and for a longer time also helps to reduce the quantity of food ingested. The impression of being full is partially established when the taste buds are saturated with impressions.

Overeating may also be due to an excess amount of snacking between meals. In this case, it's important to be on the lookout primarily for sugar intake. The hunger felt between meals is most often caused by a lack of glucose in the blood. This can be remedied by eating sweet foods (fresh or dried fruit, honey) at the same time as proteins, for example cottage cheese or yogurt. The carbohydrate-protein combination interrupts and stabilizes the use of sugars by the body and makes it possible to maintain normal glycemia, or sugar levels, between meals. Refined sugars in their various forms (chocolates, candies, desserts) are to be avoided at all costs because they encourage the hypoglycemic crises that arouse hunger pangs.

Regulating Quality

Out of ignorance, incomplete information, or thoughtless habit, many people follow irrational and unhealthy diets. Often we consume far too much of one kind of food or totally neglect another. For example, meat is present at every meal but no fruit is eaten at all throughout the day.

The foods eaten excessively in error are primarily meat, refined sugar, fat, and salt:

- With respect to meat, a person will feel much better by consuming this food only once a day, or even better, every two days. If one is sick, it's best to abstain from meat completely for a certain period. Fish is generally less loaded with toxins than meat. It is, therefore, a viable and valuable substitute.

  Total elimination of meat from the diet is only warranted for those suffering from serious disease. Their risk of deficiency is practically nonexistent since meat is extremely low in vitamins and minerals, and the sole valuable nutrient they supply—protein—can be found in many other foods.

- The need for sugar or sweet foods is a legitimate one inasmuch as carbohydrates are an essential fuel supplying energy to the body. But why choose refined sugar, a fuel that makes us sick through demineralization and acidification, when there are others such as fruits and honey that contribute to our good health?

  Individuals suffering from serious diseases should abstain completely from sweets and other food containing refined sugar. This alone will bring about huge health improvements, and would also be beneficial for those with no symptoms.

- Determining the best fats to consume depends on the way they will be prepared and eaten. When cooking, it is best to use a good-quality refined oil (but sparingly!) because they don't adulterate at high temperatures as cold-pressed, virgin oils do. To eat on bread, real butter in small quantities is fine as are vegetable margarines rich in unsaturated fatty acids. For salad dressings, use cold-pressed virgin oils and not refined oils.

- The daily salt requirement is somewhere between 3 and 5 grams. In actual practice, we easily consume much more than that—with some people ingesting as much as 12 to 15 grams a day, three to four times more than the body needs.

  To avoid too much salt in one's diet, first eliminate the "fake" foods that are so high in salt such as chips and salted peanuts. These are not real foods; they are food products that have been manufactured solely to appeal to people's taste buds. Then work toward reducing the salt added during cooking and refrain from adding any extra salt to foods once they reach the dining room table. This will allow for discovery of the true taste of these foods, which is all too often replaced by the taste of salt.

An unbalanced diet can also be caused by the absence of certain foods. Often the deficiency of one food will bring about the excessive consumption of another. The absence of vegetables at a meal will compel the diner to eat more pasta or rice. The food most often absent from the table is fruit, closely followed by vegetables.

For the qualitative regulation of food, we again turn to Hippocrates: "We should reduce what is in excess and add what is lacking."

Eliminating Stimulants

Shutting off the source of overloads also means eliminating all the stimulants in widespread use by people who give little thought to the poisons they contain, and against which the body must fight to render them harmless. In addition, stimulants interfere with the ability to get the hours or quality of sleep required to maintain a healthy body.

When this problem is pointed out to them, consumers of stimulants immediately ask, "Do I really need to do without my morning coffee?" or "Is *one* glass of wine bad for my health?" No, a cup of coffee or a glass of wine is not bad for someone in good health. On the other hand, both are definitively not good for someone who is ill. Furthermore, it is generally not a question of one cup or one glass, but several.

In addition to the well-known ill effects of stimulants like tobacco, alcohol, coffee, and tea, the sleep disruption they can cause is acidifying to the body. Their elimination from the diet will benefit anyone, and is an absolute necessity in cases of serious illness.

However, the weaning period must be handled delicately to prevent any disruption of the already enfeebled bodily functions by abruptly putting the patient in a state of sharp withdrawal. Achieving a dependency-free state should be done as quickly as possible, but gently and gradually so that the body can become accustomed to it without incurring too much disturbance in those functions that have been dependent on habitual stimulation.

Eliminating Chemical Pollution in Food and Medication

Ill individuals are poisoned by waste; their bodies are extremely sensitive to any new form of poisoning, and they will have great difficulty fighting it. Since the body is already working overtime to process accumulated toxins, it is essential to eliminate all possible causes for additional struggle by avoiding any food that contains chemical poison. As much as possible, the ill should eat only food that doesn't contain any dangerous additives: organically grown grains, fruits, and vegetables; and animal products from healthy animals raised in a wholesome environment.

Chemical "medication" is another cause of poison in the body. Sometimes medication is essential, but more often than not it is taken in excess or ill-advisedly. Why not use natural remedies (plants, homeopathic preparations, and so forth) that the body can tolerate easily and which are incontestably effective? All the daily aches, pains, and minor sicknesses can be treated with these remedies. Chemical tranquilizers, pain relievers, and sleep aids often can be replaced by plant-based remedies. More importantly, the practitioner can combine a natural anti-symptom treatment with a treatment targeting the causes of the symptoms.

꿍

When food intake has been adjusted to match the body's digestive and excretory capacities, the organs are no longer overworked. The body forces that are preserved in this way are then available for use by the body's healing process.

ELIMINATING TOXINS

When the biological terrain is overloaded with toxins, when the organs are congested and the blood is polluted, when tissues are poisoned and the cells are asphyxiated by wastes, there is only one way to begin to restore the body to health: cleanse it.

An individual truly needs to personally experience a body-cleansing cure to fully appreciate the considerable size that a mass of toxins collecting in one body can assume, and also to appreciate how getting rid of them produces such remarkable health improvement.

The "exit doors" that need to be cleared to allow the toxins to leave are the excretory organs: liver, intestines, kidneys, skin, and lungs. They provide the necessary passageways leading out of the body, and are also responsible for filtering wastes out of the bloodstream.

By stimulating the excretory organs, one is also stimulating the elimination of the wastes that have collected in these organs, thereby encouraging the purification of the blood. But this is not enough to really cleanse the body thoroughly. The great mass of wastes is not found in the bloodstream but has become embedded in the depths of the tissues. These wastes will need to be dislodged from the tissues so that they can make their way into the bloodstream, which in turn will carry them to the excretory organs. To dislodge these toxins permeating the tissues, it is necessary to turn to various methods that differ from those used to stimulate the excretory organs. These methods are used to ensure the removal of the encrusted toxins.

In the application of cleansing cures, these two points have to follow one another in order: The exit doors from the body have to be opened before efforts to dislodge the layers of deeply buried toxins can begin. If one proceeds in the opposite order, or takes both steps simultaneously, the dislodged toxins will arrive in a mass too huge to be processed by the insufficiently opened excretory organs. It is preferable to eliminate all surface toxins before initiating any efforts to excavate toxins buried in the tissues.

Opening the Excretory Organs

There are numerous methods for opening the excretory organs and increasing the elimination rhythm. Those listed here are the most effective and easiest for general application.

The stimulation of the excretory organs can be expedited beautifully by medicinal herbs, if the correct dosage is used. Too weak a dose will not provide sufficient stimulation to the excretory organs, and doses that are too strong will trigger violent reactions that irritate and exhaust these organs. The best way to find the optimal dose without too much difficulty is by starting with weak doses, then gradually increasing the dose every day. One should stop at the dose just below the level that begins to unleash violent reactions.

The several plants or preparations discussed in the following pages, along with instructions for using them, will allow you to put them to work immediately, but this is by no means an exhaustive list. It goes without saying that other plants or preparations can be used with equal success.

When taking drainers—products that encourage the drainage of toxins from the body by stimulating the function of the excretory organs—the patient should be able to objectively observe an increase in elimination of toxins; for example, urine is darker because it is more charged with wastes, and the intestines are emptying properly.

Since the clogging of the body takes place over a span of years, it is important not to nurture false hopes that a draining lasting several days will be enough to unclog and purify the internal cellular environment. Drainage cures, well-adapted to the patient's capacity, should be pursued for several months. When confronted with the length of time these cures require, some patients will worry about becoming dependent on the medicinal herbs they are using, and be hesitant about taking them over a sustained period of time. On the contrary, in their efforts to avoid a potential dependency on these plants, which is an illusory fear, they are only making themselves more dependent on their toxins!

At the start of a cleanse, the various excretory organs will be opened successively to avoid overworking the body. In the next phase they will be stimulated simultaneously, if the patient's health permits. If not, they should be stimulated in alternation, with treatments lasting three to four weeks. Some drainers work on only one excretory organ. For example, hepatics and renal drainers target the liver and kidneys, respectively. When a drainer works on several excretory organs, it is called a depurative.

Drainage of the Liver

If we had to select only one organ to stimulate, it certainly would be the liver. The sound functioning of the entire body is dependent on this organ's healthy functioning. It plays a key role in all vital functions. Not only does it filter and eliminate wastes, but it also neutralizes and destroys poisons and toxins, carcinogenic substances, and germs.

To function properly, the liver requires heat. The liver's optimum working temperature is 102–104°F (39–40°C), thus it operates at a temperature that is higher than that of the rest of the body. Simply sending heat to the liver encourages its proper functioning. One easy solution is to place a hot water bottle on the body near the liver for around ten to thirty minutes, three times a day, generally after a meal. One should not be misled by the simplicity of this procedure. Its amazing effectiveness results from the fact that it works in conjunction with the principles of nature.

There are three plants that stimulate the liver quite well: dandelion, black radish, and rosemary.

- Dandelion (*Taraxum officinalis*) as a mother tincture (maceration of a medicinal herb in ten times its weight in alcohol): 10–50 drops, three times a day with water before meals.
- Black Radish (*Raphanus niger*) in tablets: 1–3 tablets depending on the manufacturer, three times a day with water before meals.
- Rosemary (*Rosmarinus officinalis*): 1 teaspoon of leaves per cup, steeped for 10 minutes, three cups a day before meals.

There are also numerous commercial herb teas indicated as "for the liver and gallbladder," "hepatic depurative herb tea," or some such variation.

Drainage of the Intestines

Together, the small and large intestines form a tube that is approximately 23 feet long and 1 to 3 inches in diameter (7 meters in length, 3–8 centimeters diameter). The intestines can contain an enormous mass of stagnating fecal matter. Draining them means getting rid of this mass that, as a rule, is fermenting and putrefying, thus serving as the starting point for countless infections brought about by the degeneration and mutation of the intestinal flora. This also encourages intestinal disassimilation, the process by which toxins pass through the 1968 square feet or 600 square meters of surface area within the intestinal mucous membranes. The intestines, like all the excretory organs, filter the blood that passes through their tissues to remove the wastes. These wastes are then eliminated with the fecal matter.

A sufficient quantity of roughage (vegetable fiber) is essential for filling the intestine and stimulating its peristalsis. Increased and regular consumption of raw and cooked vegetables, fruits, and whole grains (brown rice, whole grain pasta, whole wheat and other whole grain breads) is most often sufficient to reestablish proper intestinal functioning.

Drinking enough water over the course of the day also encourages the intestinal transit, because the stools require a certain amount of moistness to be easily eliminated. The stools of people suffering from constipation are always dry and hard.

If necessary, one can increase the volume of roughage by adding wheat bran to the diet (1 to 3 tablespoons a day) or flaxseeds (1 to 2 tablespoons a day). These can be added to foods like yogurt and soup, for example. Both of these products have the property of swelling on contact with water, and thereby filling up the intestine.

The laxative effect of plants varies, and can thereby be easily adapted to different intestinal capacities. Chemical laxatives, however, tend to be harsh and difficult to regulate, and are to be avoided.

Gentle Laxatives

- Steep three to six prunes, or two or three dried figs in a glass of water for an entire day. That evening, eat the fruits and drink the juice.

Average Strength Laxatives

- Buckthorn in a mother tincture: take 20–70 drops with water before going to bed. You will feel the effect in the morning, upon awakening.

- Common mallow (*Malva sylvestris*) in mother tincture: take 20–50 drops with water three times a day before meals.

Strong Laxatives or Purgatives

- Castor Oil: take 1–3 capsules depending on the brand, with water in the evening.

Intestinal enemas are also extremely effective. A wide variety of these treatments exist from the rectal douche to complete cleansing of the colon via colonic irrigation. With the exception of the latter, all are easily performed in the comfort of one's home with the help of minimal equipment. Here is one example:

The Two-Quart Enema

An enema consists of the introduction of water into the colon so that the fecal matter will dissolve in the support liquid and be eliminated easily when the liquid is expelled. To introduce the water, you will need an enema bag, which can be easily purchased in most drugstores or stores specializing in health products. The enema bag also includes:

- a 2-quart container for the liquid
- a long rubber tube
- a cannula (tube suitable for insertion into the anus) with a faucet

Bring 2 quarts of water to a boil, and steep five chamomile sachets or twelve chamomile flowers for 10 minutes. Allow this to cool until it has reached a temperature of 95–98.6°F (35–37°C). Pour the "tea" through a strainer and fill the 2-quart container, placing it at a convenient height so that the water pressure will facilitate its entry into the intestines.

The part of the cannula that can be introduced into the anus should be pushed in entirely, making sure that its faucet is closed. Get down on all fours leaning your head and torso forward. Open the faucet of the cannula and allow the water to enter the intestines. It is easy to facilitate the irrigation of the intestines either by changing how deeply you are breathing, subtly shifting your position, or even by massaging your abdomen in the area directly over the colon.

If the water pressure is too strong or causes pain, close the faucet for a minute or two. Once the water has been introduced into the colon, the cannula is removed. The liquid can be held inside for several minutes to ensure that the stools are thoroughly liquefied. Then seat yourself on the toilet so that the intestinal contents can be evacuated, a process that usually takes several waves to complete.

Two-quart enemas can be performed on a daily basis for one week, or twice a week for two months. They also can be performed every now and then, as necessary.

Drainage through the Kidneys

The kidneys eliminate the wastes they filter out of the bloodstream into a back-up liquid: urine. Insufficient consumption of fluids will lead to the stagnation of toxins at the level of the filter, because they lack the support they need to take them out of the body. It is therefore important to drink enough fluids, at least half a gallon (2 liters) daily, and to eat juicy fruits and vegetables.

Medicinal plants that stimulate the kidneys to work are called diuretics. When proper doses are utilized, the volume of urine will be clearly higher than normal, or even doubled. The urine will also contain a greater amount of wastes, and consequently will assume a deeper color and thicker consistency.

The kidneys can be gently stimulated with:

- Artichoke (*Cynara cardunculus*): 1–3 tablets or capsules three times a day with water before meals.
- Pilosella (*Pilosella officinarum*) in mother tincture: three times a day, 30–50 drops with water before meals.
- Juniper Berries (*Juniperus communis*): 1 teaspoon of berries per cup, steep for 10 minutes, three cups a day.

There are also quite a few herb teas that advertise their use for "kidneys and bladder," or their "diuretic" or "renal" properties.

Drainage through the Skin

The skin expels many wastes from the body through perspiration, evidence for which is the strong body odor of people suffering ill health. Repeated periods of heavy sweating are necessary to cleanse the biological terrain thoroughly.

For those who are capable, sustained physical exercise represents the best option for perspiration, because sweat is much more concentrated when created by exertion. To encourage the process, the individual must engage in the exercise of choice (jogging, bike riding, and so on) while wearing enough clothes to accumulate the heat necessary to trigger sweating. To further assist breaking a sweat, the effort should be rather long in duration and induce sufficient exertion. At least one session a week is necessary to guarantee sufficient elimination.

The practice of taking a sauna has a long history. The only necessary precaution is that the number of sessions and the temperature of the cool bath that follows should be adapted to the vitality of the individual. Like physical exercise that induces sweating, the sauna remains a fairly athletic practice.

The High-Temperature Bath

In contrast to saunas, high-temperature baths are one of the simplest and most effective means of inducing heavy sweating. They also offer the advantage of being easy to practice at home. The patient enters a pleasant temperature bath, then gradually adds hot water until it becomes quite hot. The addition of hot water should stop just before it becomes too hot for comfort. This sensation of "too hot" varies widely from one person to the next. However, the important thing is not the objective temperature but the subjective sensation, because this is what will trigger perspiration. The individual should be able to stay in the hot bath for ten to twenty minutes.

Drinking an infusion of elder or linden flowers before the bath will facilitate perspiration (1 tablespoon per cup, let steep 10 minutes).

In addition to the heavy sweating this process triggers, another advantage of this kind of bath is the bracing effect it has on the bloodstream. In increasing circulation, it dislodges a large amount of waste from the deep tissues. To avoid an abrupt and massive exodus of these toxins toward the excretory organs, it's best to start with one weekly bath, and gradually work up to a rate of three baths a week. Several baths are sometimes necessary before the skin "opens" and sweating takes place properly.

The bath is followed by resting horizontally for at least half an hour with the body wrapped in towels or sheets. Sweating can continue during this resting period.

Drainage through the Lungs

The lungs are equipped to expel primarily gaseous wastes. However, when the biological terrain is greatly overloaded with wastes and the excretory organs are exhausted, the respiratory tract serves as a kind of emergency exit. The patient begins expectorating, spitting, and coughing up solid waste in the form of phlegm, or colloidal waste. This defensive reaction can be intentionally triggered for therapeutic purposes. In fact, all physical activity causes some degree of shortness of breath, and a more intense rate of oxygen exchange in the lungs facilitates the elimination of colloidal waste burdening the bronchia. To create this eliminatory shortness of breath, simply take a walk, jog, go for a bike ride, or walk up the stairs.

Certain medicinal plants activate this kind of elimination and make it easier by liquefying the wastes.

- Eucalyptus (*Eucalyptus globulus*): 1–3 tablets, three times a day with water before meals.
- Thyme (*Thymus vulgaris*) in a mother tincture: three times a day, 20–40 drops with water before meals.
- Coltsfoot (*Tussilago farfara*): 1 teaspoon of flowers per cup, steep 10 minutes, three to four cups a day between meals.

Dislodging the Wastes

The opening of the excretory organs allows a large number of wastes to leave the body. However, some of these wastes have been in the tissues for so long that they are

now encrusted within them. They therefore need to be
dislodged and sent back to a blood vessel so they can find
their way out through the most appropriate excretory organ.
To accomplish this, the overall circulation of fluids in the
body should be activated to increase exchanges between the
blood and the cellular fluids. It is also possible to "burn
off" and break down wastes where they are lodged in the
tissues by increasing bodily combustions through a process
called autolysis.

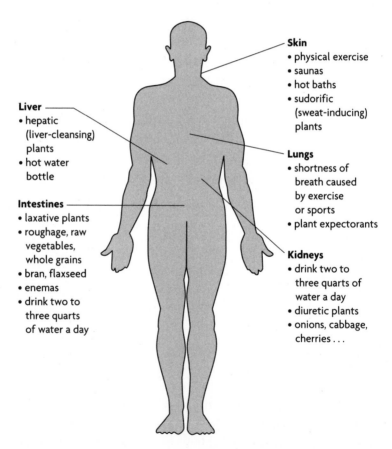

Liver
• hepatic
  (liver-cleansing)
  plants
• hot water
  bottle

Intestines
• laxative plants
• roughage, raw
  vegetables,
  whole grains
• bran, flaxseed
• enemas
• drink two to
  three quarts
  of water a day

Skin
• physical exercise
• saunas
• hot baths
• sudorific
  (sweat-inducing)
  plants

Lungs
• shortness of
  breath caused
  by exercise
  or sports
• plant expectorants

Kidneys
• drink two to
  three quarts of
  water a day
• diuretic plants
• onions, cabbage,
  cherries . . .

The excretory organs and their drainers

Accelerating Exchanges

The practice of a sport like bike riding, long-distance running, hiking in the mountains, and so forth vigorously stirs the bodily fluids in the depths of the tissues because of the physical exertion these exercises require. Repeated muscular contractions crush the tissues as if they were sponges, thereby setting the waste-saturated fluids of the body in motion.

Sick individuals who are no longer capable of making a sustained effort can benefit from this kind of churning of deep bodily fluids by either extremely hot baths or massage. With massage, the crushing of the tissues does not result from muscular contractions but from pressure exerted by the massage therapist. By adapting the type and strength of the massage to the individual patient, a highly beneficial acceleration of exchanges on the cellular level can be obtained.

Special mention should be made of a particular massage technique known as lymphatic drainage, which is intended to drain the lymphatic system. During this process, lymph, which normally travels quite slowly through the body, is pushed forward through the lymphatic vessels. The nodes are also encouraged to disgorge stagnating lymph in this way. The drainage of toxins and the resulting cleansing of the biological terrain through this process can often be quite remarkable.

Increasing Combustion

By increasing combustion within the body, wastes can be "burned away" on site, which offers certain advantages. All the body then has to do is eliminate the "ashes," wastes that are much tinier and easier to transport. In fact, without such a process, wastes are often too large in size to be extracted from the tissues and guided out of the body through the excretory system.

This process, in which wastes are broken down into smaller particles and digested by the body, is known as autolysis. It is caused by the activity of enzymes produced by the cells themselves, in response to special diets and fasts.

Autolysis is only triggered during particular situations when the body is not receiving sufficient nourishment. This means the body will digest its own tissues to make available to the vital organs the essential nutrients they require to function. The body withdraws nutrients from its less vital regions—for example, fat cells or muscles—to transfer them to more vital areas such as the heart, brain, or liver.

By virtue of the wisdom that governs the phenomenon of autolysis, the tissues are attacked in the reverse order of their importance, starting with those that are least important to the body's ability to function. Wastes and toxins will therefore be broken down before the more important tissues.

It is possible to trigger this autolysis of wastes and sick tissues (tumors) intentionally by following a restrictive diet. The greater the restriction of this diet, the more intense the autolysis will be.

There are a great many restrictive diets. The main thing is to reduce the quantity of different foods ingested, while keeping in mind that this is meant to be a therapeutic procedure and, as such, should be followed for only a limited time and adapted to the capacity of the patient (from several days to a week as a single cure, or repeated several times over a longer period). For cures of extended duration, it is crucial to seek the guidance of a competent health care practitioner.

When this restriction eliminates all food except water, it is a fast. If all foods but one are eliminated, it is a mono diet (grape diet, carrot diet, or similar).* Diets in which two or more foods are retained are included under the term *restrictive*. Examples include the low-calorie diet, or diets that set a limit to the number of carbohydrates or fat grams consumed during the course of a day. The restriction can be centered on one food (meat, salt) or a group of foods (red meat, fats, refined sugar). Fasts, mono diets, or restrictive diets that are adapted to the specific health needs of the individual patient figure among the most effective and useful natural means for treating disease.

A restrictive diet that is followed for a fairly extended period of time, or repeated, quite often leads to the breaking down and elimination of substantial quantities of waste. The internal biological terrain of the body, the cradle for all disease, will thereby find itself purified with a resulting improvement in overall health.

Summary: Different Kinds of Diets

- Restrictive diet: partial or complete elimination of one or several foods, as opposed to the standard diet
- Mono diet: one food plus water
- Fast: water only

᠁

Increasing combustion and accelerating the metabolism through physical exercise or high heat baths, or by triggering the process of autolysis, replicates the purifying and healing process that nature itself triggers with fever. Fever is one of the most potent healing methods employed by the

---

*For more detailed information on diets, see my book *The Detox Mono Diet: The Miracle Grape Cure and Other Cleansing Diets,* Rochester, Vt.: Healing Arts Press, 2006.

vital force of the body, and for this reason it is present in many illnesses. Fever certainly signals that the body is in danger, but it also indicates that it is still capable of fighting back. Thanks to fever, the body can compensate to a certain extent for its past shortfalls and sluggish activity by functioning more vigorously and burning away toxins that have collected in the tissues.

Some individuals suffering from ill health no longer have the physical strength necessary to "create" a fever. The methods for raising body heat described in this section on dislodging wastes are copied from nature and enable us to re-create nature's beneficial defense system.

> ❧
>
> When organs are congested, blood is dirty, the tissues poisoned, and the cells asphyxiated, there is only one logical action to be taken to restore the body to health: clean it.

BENEFITS OF EXERCISE

The benefits of physical activity are so numerous that by themselves they can compensate for, and partially eliminate, the harmful effects caused by the congestion of the biological terrain with toxins.

Increasing physical activity makes it possible to burn off the excesses created by overeating. Physical exertion activates physical functions and thereby encourages the abundant elimination of toxins. Through the acceleration of cellular exchanges and blood flow, the wastes embedded in the depths of the tissues can be dislodged and carried away to the excretory organs to be expelled from the body. The deeper breathing caused by physical exertion causes a considerable increase in the body's supply of oxygen, which encourages the breaking down of toxins and, thereby, the purification of the biological terrain.

Nothing is more capable of bringing about deep changes in the body's internal cellular environment than physical exercise. Just as a fresh breeze rekindles the almost-extinguished sparks beneath a bed of ash, exercise will reignite and cleanse the body.

But doing "physical exercise" does not refer only to those privileged and limited moments during which we visit the gym, bike, or play tennis. We also can be very physically active in our regular everyday lives if, instead of hopping into the car to drive to the office, we get there at least partially on foot; skip the elevator and take the stairs; carry our own bags; and instead of using an electric mixer or blender, beat or pulverize our foods by hand. As an added bonus, physical exercise releases endorphins, which are known to improve mental attitude.

స్రి

By adding only physical exercise, we can create profound changes in our biological terrain.

FILLING THE DEFICIENCIES

A sick body, if it is overloaded with wastes, is also generally suffering from deficiencies in a number of nutritive substances: vitamins, minerals, trace elements, and so on. Supplying it with these missing substances will allow it to repair its injured and depleted tissues, strengthen its organs, and resume normal functioning.

The sicker the body, the more ravenous it is for the nutrients it is lacking. Supplies of these missing nutrients need to be provided regularly and over an extended period of time. In this way, the deficiencies will be gradually satisfied and the patient's body will recover its former strength and vitality.

A healthy, natural, and varied diet would be the best way to fill the deficiencies and supply missing nutrients, if the foods available were not so often lacking in these same nutrients. For this reason, it is essential to also include nutrient-rich dietary supplements in the patient's daily intake, in order to compensate for these deficiencies as rapidly as possible.

> ✷
>
> The sicker the body, the hungrier it is for the nutrients it lacks.

A Non-Deficient Diet

The ideal non-deficient diet is the one offered by food farmed organically or biodynamically, as both of these methods respect the natural development of plants and provide the most favorable growing conditions. These farming methods produce grains, fruits, and vegetables capable of maintaining the health of those who consume them.

In order to enjoy the benefits offered by non-deficient foods, it is obviously necessary to avoid creating shortages in the food by overcooking it, for example. Additionally, all refined foods should be avoided, as some of their essential nutrients have been removed. Instead of white bread and pasta, people should eat whole grain or brown bread and whole grain pasta. Refined oils should be replaced by cold-pressed, virgin vegetable oils (except in cooking). Refined sugars should be replaced by unrefined cane sugar

or other natural sweeteners like honey, maple syrup, pear
concentrate, or agave. Candies and other sweets should be
replaced by fresh or dried fruits.

SUGGESTED REPLACEMENTS FOR
COMMONLY EATEN FOODS

Commonly Eaten Food	Suggested Replacement
Fruits and vegetables grown by industrial farming	Fruits and vegetables grown using organic or biodynamic farming methods
White flour	Whole grain flour
White bread	Dark bread, whole grain and semi–whole grain bread
White flour pasta	Pasta made from whole grain flour
White rice	Brown rice
Refined white or brown sugar	Unrefined cane sugar, honey, maple syrup, date extract, pear concentrate, agave
Jam	Honey, whole fruit concentrate, maple cream, hazelnut or almond butter
Candy, chocolate	fresh and dried fruit, fruit butter, yogurt or kefir with fruit, fruit leather, whole grain cereal and fruit bars
White flour crackers	Whole grain crackers
Iodized kitchen salt	Sea salt, aromatic herb blends, soy sauce, gomasio (ground sesame seeds and sea salt)
Refined oil (in salad dressing)	Virgin, cold-pressed oil (sunflower, corn, olive, rapeseed, thistle, safflower)

SUGGESTED REPLACEMENTS FOR
COMMONLY EATEN FOODS (CONTINUED)

Commonly Eaten Food	Suggested Replacement
Coffee	Roasted grain beverage coffee substitute
Black tea	Herb tea
Commercial carbonated beverages	Mineral water, herb tea, fruit or vegetable juice, juice mixed with seltzer water

By eating a variety of foods, one will avoid a unilateral diet, which is one of the main causes of nutritive deficiencies. In short, to avoid scarcities in your diet and the deficiencies that then appear in your body, eat a varied diet composed of whole grain and organically grown foods.

Food Supplements
The healing process can be accelerated, thanks to the use of pollen (bee and flower), brewer's yeast, various seaweed products, cod liver oil, spirulina, blackstrap molasses, wheat germ, royal jelly, and so on. The strong concentrations of vitamins and minerals contained in these foods, and their easy assimilation by the body, helps fill deficiencies much more rapidly because of the quantity, quality, and variety of nutrients they supply. In fact, each nutrient depends to some extent on the presence of other nutrients in order to be assimilated properly.

Since certain food supplements are more effective for some patients than others, it's important to look for advice, or experiment to find the most suitable options. Healing by means of these supplements can take several weeks, or even months.

It is possible to take several different products at the same time without any adverse effects.

SOME OF THE CRUCIAL FOOD SUPPLEMENTS

Vitamin supplements	Bee pollen, brewer's yeast (in powder or liquid), sprouted grains, wheat germ and flaxseed oil, concentrates of acerola or sea buckthorn, spirulina
Minerals and trace elements	Tablets made from powdered bone, seaweed, or shell; sea water (Quinton products); magnesium; blackstrap molasses; spring water; horsetail
General revitalizers	Royal jelly, ginseng, fish roe, a cocktail made from liquid yeast and fruit and vegetable juice

℞

By repairing deficiencies, the sick individual is better able to eliminate toxins; likewise, when the body rids itself of toxins, it's easier to supplement deficiencies. The two processes are inseparably bound together.

RESTORING THE ACID-ALKALINE BALANCE

An overacidic biological terrain is corrected primarily by means of food. Rather than consuming more acidifying foods than alkaline foods, as is generally the case, the individual must keep track of what is eaten to see that the proportion is equal, or even reduce the proportion of acidic foods to fall below that of alkaline foods. The proportion of alkalizing foods consumed should be 50 percent in an individual with a normal pH balance, but 60 to 80 percent in someone with overacidity. Simply put, this means eating more vegetables—green salads, raw and cooked vegetables, potatoes—than meat and flour products. An additional measure aims at eliminating all foods containing refined white sugar, which is, in fact, a powerful acidifying agent.

Alkaline foods that must be increased to make up for the acidifying foods are all the green and colorful vegetables, which come in great variety. Potatoes, which are extremely alkalizing, should replace grains as often as possible, although grains should not be totally excluded from the diet. Chestnuts, almonds, avocadoes, dates, and bananas are other foods that are highly alkalizing. Dairy products such as cottage cheese along with eggs are balanced proteins to substitute for meat and fish. Whole sugar from the cane or agave nectar should be used in the place of white sugar, and maple syrup, fruit concentrate, and honey can take the place of preserves and jellies.

Acidifying Foods

These foods may seem to be alkaline in nature, but make the body's pH more acidic:

- Red meat, fowl, processed meat products, meat extracts, fish, shellfish (mussels, shrimp, and so on)
- Eggs
- Cheese (strong cheese is more acidic than mild cheese)
- Animal fat (lard, suet)

- Vegetable oil, especially peanut and refined oil, and oil spreads (margarine)
- Whole and refined grains: wheat, oats, and especially millet
- Bread, pasta, cereal flakes, and all foods made from refined grains
- Legumes: peanuts and beans (soy, white, broad, navy, and so on)
- White sugar
- Sweets: syrup, pastry, chocolate, candy, preserves, jellied fruits
- Oleaginous fruits: walnuts, hazelnuts, pumpkin seeds, and so on (except chestnuts and almonds)
- Commercially made sodas, sodas with cola base and others
- Coffee, tea, cocoa, wine
- Condiments such as mayonnaise, mustard, and ketchup

Alkalizing Foods

These foods help to combat overacidity and restore acid-alkaline balance:

- Potatoes
- Green vegetables of all types (raw or cooked), salad greens
- Colorful vegetables: carrots, beets, red and yellow peppers, and so on (except tomatoes)
- Corn (kernels or cooked as polenta)
- Milk (liquid or powder), cream, butter, well-drained cottage cheese
- Bananas
- Almonds, Brazil nuts

- Chestnuts
- Dried fruits, especially dates and raisins (except those that are tart to the taste: apricots, apples, and so on)
- Alkaline mineral water
- Almond milk
- Black olives preserved in oil
- Avocadoes
- Cold-pressed oil
- Natural sugar

Weak Acid Foods

The acidifying effects of these foods vary according to the individual's ability to metabolize acids:

- Whey, yogurt, curdled milk, kefir, cottage cheese that has not been drained well
- Fresh fruits (the less ripe the fruit, the greater the acidity)
- Fruit juice
- Sauerkraut, lacto-fermented vegetables
- Honey
- Vinegar

Setting aside the dietary factor, there are other measures that should be taken. Better oxidation of acids occurs when there is physical activity—such as walking, sports, gardening—and elimination of acids already present in the tissues can be increased by the consumption of diuretic medicinal plants (for the kidneys) and sudorifics, or sweat-inducing plants, for the skin.

Another extremely important measure, one proven essential for most cases, is the taking of alkaline mineral supplements to help the body not only eliminate acids ingested daily, but also, and primarily, to facilitate the evacuation of acids lodged in the depths of the tissues. This measure is of major importance because the body resists allowing acids embedded in the tissues to be pulled back into the bloodstream—en route to the excretory organs—because their return to the bloodstream represents a dangerous alteration of its pH. These acids, therefore, have an unfortunate tendency to be kept in the depths of the tissues to protect the blood. However, a substantial delivery of alkaline reserves to the body makes it possible to eliminate these embedded acids. Buffered by the alkaline supplements, the acids can drift back to the surface in the form of neutral salts, a form that will not harm the blood pH.

Alkaline supplements are blends of calcium, magnesium, potassium, and so forth in a form easily assimilated by the body. Available in tablet form or powder, these preparations are to be taken three times a day with a little water, before meals. To assure appropriate dosage, it should be calibrated in accordance with the urinary pH of the individual concerned. The general rule is to take as much supplement as necessary to obtain a urinary pH between 7 and 7.5, based on the second and subsequent urinations of the day (not the first one). Therefore, if a dose of 2 tablets, three times a day pushes the pH from 5.5 to 6.5, the dosage will have to be increased so that it can get to a normal pH of 7 to 7.5. This important rule ensures that correction of the acidity in the biological terrain is done properly.

The various measures undertaken to deacidify the biological terrain will gradually cause all the acids embedded in the depth of the tissues to come to the surface and be expelled from the body. Over time, this deacidification of the depths of the biological terrain will not only heal the patient from current ills, but also prevent any relapses.

SPECIFIC REMEDIES

In addition to the general therapeutic maneuvers described in this chapter, it is sometimes necessary to give additional support to the weak points of the body. Treatment ceases to be general, focused on the entire biological terrain, but addresses a specific organ, strengthens a deficient function, soothes irritable tissues, disinfects, and so on. Every patient has vulnerable points that need to be taken into consideration during treatment, along with the major steps being taken to correct the biological terrain.

Among specific remedies that can be utilized are such dissimilar but effective therapies as medicinal plants, aromatherapy, magnetics, homeopathy, facial and foot reflexology, acupuncture, hydrotherapy, and many more. But, let me repeat, these specific treatments should all be employed as complements to the overall treatment of the biological terrain.

POSITIVE MENTAL ATTITUDE

The tool we know as the human body functions in accordance with its own inner logic, but it is also highly influenced by our mental life. A balanced nature, confronting life with confidence, trust, and optimism provides the most favorable conditions for the body's harmonious functioning. Conversely, negativity, fear, and aggressive attitudes disrupt this functioning and slow it down, and can throw the body completely off kilter. The physical state espouses the fluctuations of thoughts and emotions. Physical functioning so clearly mirrors state of mind that it is often enough for a patient to believe his illness is growing worse for it actually to become worse.

Depending on the patient's mental attitude, the healing process can be hampered and blocked, or, to the contrary, supported and even stimulated. It is therefore of enormous consequence that the patient adopt an appropriate attitude in confronting his illness. How can the body keep fighting if the patient has abandoned the struggle, or even worse, is fighting the healing process? The will to get better, along with active participation in the remedial treatment by freeing the body from the pressure of negative thoughts, mobilizes the defense system and supports regeneration.

Conclusion

꒰꒱

A clear and realistic vision regards the human body as a tool that has been placed at our disposal. This tool functions in accordance with precise instructions that must be followed to maintain its proper working order. In other words, there are a certain number of physiological imperatives—laws of health—that set out conditions for the proper functioning of the body. The body must be used and maintained in conformance with these instructions, and not as momentary moods, whims, and desires dictate. A person loses healthy equilibrium and falls ill when the laws of health, as described in this book, are not respected. As long as they are adhered to, the body will remain in excellent health.

Every disease has a cause. Its very existence necessarily implies mistakes have been made in the physical and mental circumstances of the person afflicted. So long as these errors are not detected and eliminated, health problems will persist and be provoked. It is therefore absolutely necessary to alter one's personal health regimen. *Changes* must take place. The patient can and should take control by beginning to eat differently, eliminating the sources of toxic buildup, leading a more physically active life, or adopting a new mental attitude.

Therapeutic methods are available to help the patient, but these changes are something that only the patient, not the naturopath, can make happen. If the naturopath leans toward optimism, it is not for the purpose of planting suggestions that will encourage healing in the patient's mind. The confidence and hope the naturopath can give is based on a concrete reality, one confirmed by countless cases of remission and healing.

Now, in closing, I leave you with a summary of six basic rules for recovering and maintaining health:

1. Eat a varied diet of whole, preferably organic foods, consisting predominantly of plants.

2. Eat too little rather than too much.

3. Drink more than 2 quarts of water a day.

4. Engage in physical activity every day.

5. Get enough sleep every night.

6. Approach all of life's challenges with a positive and constructive attitude.

Glossary of the Concepts of Naturopathy

༈

The numbers following each definition refer the reader to pages in the book where the concept is discussed.

acid-alkaline balance: This is the balance between acid and alkaline substances in the body that permits it to remain in good health. The unit used to measure the degree of acidity or alkalinity is pH (*see also* pH). The normal pH of blood, and of the biological terrain in general, is 7.39. When there is movement away from this ideal pH, disease appears. Acidosis, or excess acid, is the most common example of an acid-alkaline imbalance, and is a common result of our acidifying lifestyle and diet. Acidosis can be corrected by following an alkalizing diet, oxygenation, and by taking alkaline supplements. (67, 101)

acidosis: The state of the body when the acid-alkaline ratio is out of balance and the biological terrain is acidic. (68)

acute and chronic illness: Diseases are crises of detoxification or cleansing triggered by the vital force as it seeks to eliminate the surplus of toxins encumbering the biological terrain. An illness is acute when the vital force is strong. Elimination is violent, spectacular, and short in duration . . . and it achieves

110

its goal: the renewal of the biological terrain. Chronic diseases are the same efforts made by a weakened vital force, and are, therefore, of lesser intensity. Incapable of repairing the biological terrain in one attempt, these crises will recur regularly, hence their chronic nature. (30)

allopathic medicine: A therapeutic method that deals with disease by using methods that, generally speaking, oppose the curative effects of the body's vital force. By repressing toxins into the depths of the body, anti-symptom remedies are successful in banishing symptoms from the surface, but this is to the detriment of the biological terrain. The opposite method of health care is naturopathy. (3)

autolysis: Autolysis is a physiological process triggered by special diets and fasts during which the body digests or breaks down (*lyse*) its own tissues (*auto*). When it stops receiving any or enough nutrients from outside, the body is forced to draw on its own reserves for nutritive substances, which it does by first self-digesting diseased tissue and toxins. Autolysis, therefore, has a curative effect because it rids the biological terrain of the wastes with which it is encumbered. (94)

biological terrain: Just as a plant will either prosper or wither depending on the quality of the terrain in which it grows, our cells and the organs they form will function properly or not depending on the "biological terrain" in which they find themselves. This biological terrain is composed of the bodily fluids in which the cells are immersed, in other words the fluids around them (extracellular fluid, lymph, and blood) and those inside them (intracellular fluid).

The liquid environment of the cell ensures it receives the supplies of oxygen and nutrients it needs, and thereby, this environment is the ultimate guarantor of health. Because of its crucial function, any overly large quantitative or qualitative alteration suffered by these fluids leads to disease. Two primary imbalances are possible: either the presence of an excessive amount of certain substances (toxins, poisons), which leads to diseases caused by overloads; or the absence of certain substances (nutrients, minerals), which will engender deficiency-caused diseases. (3)

chronic illness: *See* Acute and chronic illness.

colloidal waste: Colloidal waste is one of the primary varieties of toxins (*see also* Crystals). These toxins are non-soluble in liquids. For example, phlegm, the viscous substance that is eliminated by blowing one's nose, is a colloidal waste. When mixed with water these substances do not dissolve, but retain their appearance. Sputum, pus, and so on are all colloidal wastes.

Colloidal wastes are eliminated by the liver, the intestines, the sebaceous glands, and also sometimes by the lungs. The illnesses caused by colloidal wastes are not painful as those caused by crystals are, and they are fluid in nature: inflammations of the respiratory tract, acne, oozing eczema, and so forth.

The sources of colloidal waste are starches and fats. (10)

crises—cleansing, healing, detoxification: The vital force governing the body does not remain a passive bystander when confronted by the collection of toxins in the biological terrain. When the tolerance threshold has been crossed, it abruptly intensifies the functioning of one or more excretory organs to rid itself of the wastes with which it is encumbered, giving rise to the description of a cleansing, or detoxification crisis. These crises are also curative, because by eliminating the primary cause of illness—the accumulation of toxins in the biological terrain—they banish the health problem. (15)

crystals: Crystals are one of the two major kinds of waste (*see also* Colloidal waste). They are hard and can wound like real crystals, but like sugar or salt, they dissolve in water. Crystals are eliminated by the excretory organs that evacuate liquids—the kidneys and the sweat glands.

Crystals are generally acidic, like uric acid or oxalic acid, but also can be discarded mineral salts. The sand we have in our eyes when waking, and the substance that makes our joints creak are composed of crystals. Crystalloid diseases such as rheumatism, kidney stones, sciatica, tendinitis, dry eczema, and neuritis can be painful and are not "runny."

The sources of crystals are proteins, white sugar, and acidifying foods. (10)

deficiencies: A deficiency is the absence or insufficient amount of an element that is essential for the body's nutrition. The shortage may be of protein, calcium, vitamins, or any other nutritive substance. Deficiencies can involve one or more nutrients, and be temporary or long-lasting. They also can be major or minor depending on the importance of the missing substance. In deficiencies of supply, the missing nutrient does not reach the body because the food containing it is not eaten or has been extracted from the food before consumption; the refining process, for example, strips grains of their vitamin B content. In deficiencies of utilization, nutrients enter the body via their host foods, but are destroyed by harmful substances (anti-vitamins or chelators—drugs or other substances that inhibit the metabolic action of a vitamin or trace element) before the body can use them. Deficiency-based diseases are treated by providing the missing substance in order to satisfy the deficiency. (11)

depurative: A drainer that works on several excretory organs. (84)

diagnosis: In allopathic medicine, a diagnosis is made to determine what illness is afflicting the patient. The goal of a diagnosis is to identify a malady before prescribing a specific remedy. In naturopathy, there is a diagnosis but it evaluates the overall health of the individual (*see also* Health assessment). (22)

diet: Diet is one of the primary factors for remaining in, or restoring, good health. The body is entirely dependent on food for building and repairing itself, and for carrying out its functions. A poor diet causes the deficiencies and toxins that are at the root of any degradation of the biological terrain. (9, 76, 98)

dietary supplement: A product taken to supplement one's regular diet because of its richness in nutrients. Vitamins, minerals, trace elements, flower and bee pollen, brewer's yeast, seaweed and kelp, wheat germ, and spirulina are some of the many dietary supplements available. (100)

disassimilation: The passage of toxins through the intestinal mucous membranes (600 square meters or 1968 square feet of surface). The intestines, like all the excretory organs, filter the blood that passes through their tissues to remove the wastes. These wastes are then eliminated with fecal matter. (85)

diuretics: Medicinal plants that stimulate the kidneys to work. When proper doses are utilized, the volume of urine will increase and possibly double. The urine will also contain a greater amount of wastes; consequently, it will assume a deeper color and thicker consistency. (88)

drainers: Products that encourage the drainage of toxins from the body by stimulating the function of the excretory organs. These are medicinal plants or other products that have hepatic, laxative, diuretic, or similar properties. (20, 83, 93)

drainage: Drainage is a process that intentionally triggers the elimination of toxins from the body. The purpose is to reestablish normal elimination if it has been insufficient, and even to increase it for a while in order to compensate for the previous period of insufficiency.

The excretory organs are the essential vehicles for drainage. During this period, the work performed by the liver, intestines, kidneys, skin, and lungs is stimulated through a variety of techniques and cleanses. These can include medicinal plants, juice or food that has detoxifying properties, inducement of heavy sweating, poultices, intestinal enemas, and the like.

Depending on the strength of the individual patient, a drainage can be performed through one or several excretory organs. (19)

elimination: Evacuation through the excretory organs (liver, kidneys, and so on) of toxins burdening the biological terrain and becoming the source of disease. The elimination of toxins is encouraged by diet, exercise, and drainage. Health is regained through correction of the biological terrain. (18)

excretory organs: The excretory organs, or emunctories, are responsible for filtering all the metabolic residue and waste out of the blood so it can be expelled from the body. They are, therefore, not only "doors" that can be opened to allow the passage of toxins, but organs that actively cleanse the blood for the purpose of purifying it.

These organs include the liver (evacuates waste in bile), intestines (stool), kidneys (urine), lungs (exhalation), sweat glands (perspiration), and the sebaceous glands (sebum).

When they are functioning properly, the excretory organs eliminate all the wastes that are ingested or produced by a normal lifestyle. Their capacities can be exceeded by an excess production of wastes, which happens, for example, when a sedentary lifestyle is combined with overeating: toxins are not evacuated, the biological terrain deteriorates, and disease appears. (6, 19)

extracellular fluid: *See* Intracellular and extracellular fluids.

fast: A period of time during which a person abstains from any nutritional intake other than water. No food of any kind is consumed. This regimen aims at forcing the body to survive through breaking down and digesting toxins and sick tissues (autolysis), which eliminates them from the biological terrain and brings about a return to health. (21, 94)

fever: Fever is not a disease per se but a reflection of the body's attempt to defend itself from a biological terrain overloaded with toxins. Depending on the individual case, it may occur in tandem with a bacterial infection. The acceleration of immune defenses, blood circulation, respiration, and cellular exchanges produces heat and thereby increases body temperature. Fever is, therefore, a manifestation of the body defending itself, which is why it is a common symptom of so many different maladies.

If fever did not occur naturally it would need to be devised; it is a brilliant way of enabling the body to incinerate and eliminate a large amount of toxins in a short space of time. Unless the patient's temperature climbs so high that it poses risks to the body, breaking a fever amounts to obstructing the body's defense system. (31)

filling the deficiencies: This is the action of supplying missing nutrients to the body to alleviate deficiencies. In this expression, deficiencies are viewed as holes to be plugged by filling them with the missing nutrients. (98)

healing: Healing represents the return to health after an illness. A true healing takes place when the symptoms of the disease, as well as the deficiencies of the biological terrain that engendered them, have vanished. This new state of health is stable and lasting because the primary causes of the disease have been eliminated.

Healings obtained locally by treatments targeting only the symptoms are fictitious, as these treatments are satisfied with burying the toxins in the depths of the body without correcting the biological terrain. Although seeming to be cured, the patient's biological terrain remains in a degraded state. (23)

health: Health is not the absence of detectable disease symptoms, but corresponds to a state of the biological terrain in which the composition of the bodily fluids ensures and provides the conditions favorable to the cells' unhampered normal activity. Health is determined by the state of the body's internal cellular environment. If this biological terrain is healthy, then the body is healthy; if it is unhealthy, the body is ill, even if there are no apparent symptoms.

Because the biological terrain is dependent on our health and lifestyle decisions, health is an unstable equilibrium that is constantly menaced by overloads and deficiencies. The balance represented by good health is not acquired once and for all, but requires constant vigilance to maintain. (5)

health assessment: An analysis of the patient's diet, eliminatory capacity, and self-care to determine what has degraded the biological terrain and caused the manifestation of specific localized disorders. The health assessment does not determine which anti-symptom remedies are required, but suggests measures for draining toxins out of the body, filling its deficiencies, giving support to under-performing organs, and reforming the patient's self-care and awareness as necessary. These measures correct the biological terrain, thereby bringing about the elimination of the symptoms of disease. (23)

hepatic: A person suffering from liver ailments. Also, a product or substance that stimulates the elimination of waste by the liver. Through the taking of hepatic plants (dandelion, boldo, rosemary), the liver filters more waste out of the bloodstream, which leads to an increased production of bile. A hepatic reaction can also be obtained with a hot water bottle. (70, 84)

hygiene: All the methods (diet, exercise, rest, and so on) taken together that can be implemented for restoring or preserving health. A method based on hygiene seeks to adapt the lifestyle to the body's capacity, whereas an anti-symptom therapy too often consists only of adapting the physical capacities to the lifestyle. (11)

iatrogenic: This designates a health problem resulting from the medication prescribed to heal the patient, sometimes described as side effects. This type of event is extremely rare in naturopathy, but much more common with the use of anti-symptom remedies in allopathic medicine. (24)

immune response: The body's ability to defend itself not only when confronted by germs, but also when faced with various toxins that clog the biological terrain. (16)

internal cellular environment: *See* Biological terrain.

intracellular and extracellular fluids: Fluids found both inside (intra) and outside (extra) the cells. This is the cellular serum, a pale white liquid. It has almost the same composition as blood, but without blood's red corpuscles.

The extracellular fluid, which represents 15 percent of the weight of the body, constitutes the external environment of the cells. This substance carries oxygen and nutrients to the cells, and carries away wastes they expel, toward the excretory organs.

Intracellular fluid represents 50 percent of the weight of the body. It fills the cells, gives the body shape and tone, and allows the exchanges that need to take place between organs. (4)

intrinsic illness: The constricted state of the body's internal cellular environment caused by toxins in the biological terrain that exceed the body's capacity for restoring its own balance. (6)

laxative: Any product or substance that stimulates the elimination of intestinal waste. A laxative effect is induced with plants such as alder buckthorn and mallow, or through enemas, abdominal massage, and so on. A laxative gently stimulates intestinal peristalsis, encouraging regular evacuation of stools. The term *purgative* is reserved for products that powerfully stimulate the intestines and bring about the rapid and complete emptying of their contents. (21, 86)

laws of health: These are the physiological imperatives to which the body is subject and from which it cannot escape, and which compel us to act in a specific manner in order to stay healthy. Eating enough raw food to cover the body's nutrient needs, for example, is one law of health, because the body inevitably will fall ill if it does not get them. Drinking enough water on a daily basis, getting sufficient physical exercise, regularly eliminating toxins produced by the body, and so on are all laws of health. (108)

metabolism: Metabolism refers to all the biochemical transformations that take place in the body tissue during digestion, assimilation, energy production, catabolism, exchanges, and so forth. Waste and residue, called toxins, are the result of these transformations and need to be eliminated through the excretory organs. (9–10)

mono diets: During the course of a mono diet, only one (mono) food is consumed. Each meal consists exclusively of the food in question, eaten either raw or cooked, or as juice when possible. The most common mono diets use grapes, carrots, or rice. (21, 94)

naturopathy: Naturopathy is a therapeutic method that treats disease using natural methods and takes action to improve the biological terrain rather than to diminish symptoms. In supporting the body's own healing power, it addresses the deep roots of illness rather than the effects, and employs a variety of natural techniques as listed below. (1, 3, 7)

Nutrition

- Healthy diet: organic foods; unrefined, whole grain foods without additives
- Restrictive and dietetic diets: fasts, mono diets, food-combining diets, natural foods diets
- Nutritional diets to make up for deficiencies
- Natural food supplements

Water Therapies

- Cold and hot hydrotherapy
- Balneotherapy, thermal and mud baths
- Enemas

Exercise

- Moderate exercise, gentle gymnastics, body building, martial arts, sports

Plant Therapies

- Medicinal plants in their various forms: infusions, decoctions, mother tinctures, essential oils
- Fruits and vegetables with healing properties

Massage

- Different types of massage: whole body, specific region, sports, deep tissue, French, Swedish, Chinese, Thai; chiropractic; osteopathy

Reflexology

- Stimulation of the reflex zones of the feet, hands, ears, nose, or back

Light Therapies

- Beneficial effects of the sun (heliotherapy), influence of the moon and stars
- Colors and their properties

Air

- Breathing techniques
- Oxygenation
- Aromatherapy

Energetic Techniques

- Therapeutic magnets
- Revitalization through the magnetism of precious and semi-precious stones and their benefits
- Earth energies

Mental Attitude

- Importance of thoughts and attitudes, mental health
- Stress management
- Relaxation, self-suggestion, visualization
- Sleep

nutrients: Substances necessary for the construction and functioning of the body that are normally provided by food. These include proteins, carbohydrates, fats, minerals, trace elements, and vitamins. (37)

opening the excretory organs: Increasing the elimination of toxins through the body's excretory organs. This is recommended when these organs are working too slowly or are "closed," or clearly functioning below normal. (83)

overloads: Wastes, toxins, and toxic by-products, including fats but not exclusively, that dangerously burden the biological terrain when they collect in overly large quantities; in other words, they overload it. This has nothing to with being over-weight, but rather having an excess of all kinds of toxins. (8)

pH: Measuring unit for the degree of acidity or alkalinity of a substance; pH is shorthand for the substance's potential (p) or power to free hydrogen (H) ions. The measuring scale goes from 0 to 14: 0 is absolute acidity, 14 absolute alkalinity, and 7 is the middle position known as neutral pH. The optimal pH of the blood and the biological terrain is slightly alkaline: 7.39. (43, 67)

plurality of disease: The concept that each disease is unique by nature and has causes specific to it and dissimilar from those of other illnesses. There are, therefore, no common elements among disparate diseases. This concept in allopathic medicine leads practitioners to treat every disease with a specific remedy (therapeutic plurality).

This concept is diametrically opposed to the single cause, or unity of disease that is the foundation of naturopathy. (3)

purify: To purify is to make clean. In naturopathy, this word refers to all the efforts deployed to rid the blood and the biological terrain of toxins. (21)

relapse: When an illness, bronchitis for example, has been cleared up using only an anti-symptom treatment, the biological terrain will not have been corrected and the vital force will make renewed attempts to purify the internal cellular environment. Each of these attempts may manifest at another excretory organ (*see* transfer of disease) or on the same organ. In the latter case, the illness is referred to as a relapse. The toxins that have been pushed into the body's depths by the anti-symptom treatment find their way back to the excretory organ used initially. One case of bronchitis is soon followed by another case of bronchitis. It is sometimes believed that this is the appearance of a new case of illness, but in fact it is the same healing crisis that was momentarily interrupted, but is triggered anew as soon as circumstances permit. (26)

remedy: Product containing active substances for treating illness. In naturopathy, remedies are not used to cause the arbitrary disappearance of symptoms without taking any action on the biological terrain. To the contrary, they aim to support elimination via the excretory organs in order to correct the body's internal cellular environment, where the root of the problem is located. This correction will automatically bring about the disappearance of the symptoms. (14)

restrictive diet: A diet characterized by a reduced quantity of foods (low calorie, low salt, and so forth) or by a reduction in the scope of foods permitted (meatless, salt-free, fat-free, and so on). Such diets aim to bring relief to the body and trigger the process of autolysis to eliminate toxins. (94)

sedentary lifestyle: A state in which the motor capacities of the body are underutilized either because of a job that requires the worker to remain seated, the use of motor vehicles to travel rather than walk even for short distances, the absence of physical activity during leisure times, or all of the above. A sedentary lifestyle weakens the muscles and organs, causes under-oxygenation, slowed metabolism of food intake, and poor elimination of toxins. (62)

self-healing: Remedies alone are incapable of healing a patient. They can only restore, support, or reinforce the healing process implemented by the vital force that animates and guides the body. In this sense, healing does not come from the outside but from within the body. The vital force corresponds with what the ancients called the medicalizing nature, which we know as the immune response.

The body is, therefore, capable of working alone to effect its own healing, in other words, self-healing. "It is nature that heals disease, and medicine is the art of imitating the healing procedures of nature," wrote Hippocrates. Somewhat later in time, the famous French surgeon Ambroise Paré (1509–1590) would say: "I dress wounds; it is nature that heals them." (16)

self-poisoning: This kind of poisoning comes from toxins not outside, but within the body. It begins in the intestines when they are unable to empty properly or well. The poisons, toxins, and wastes that result from fermentation and putrefaction, and are not rapidly evacuated in stools, are absorbed into the intestinal walls and then enter the bloodstream. From there they are conducted all over the body, initiating self-poisoning. (38)

sudorific: Any product or substance that stimulates the elimination of toxins through the sudoriferous (sweat) glands. Saunas, hot baths, and exercise have a sweat-inducing effect, as do medicinal plants such as linden and elder flowers. All of these cause the glands to expel a greater quantity of sweat, which will have a higher content of toxins. (89, 104)

supplies: Everything taken in by the body that allows it to function—food, vitamins, water, oxygen, and so on. (4, 11)

symptoms: Symptoms are the surface manifestations of the deep-rooted illness of the deteriorated biological terrain. All the symptoms of a disease, such as the inflamed and painful joints of rheumatism, are often considered to be the intrinsic disease. In reality, the true disease is the degraded biological terrain that has allowed these symptoms to manifest. (2)

toxins: Toxins are the wastes and residues created by the metabolic process. The largest quantity of toxins comes from the breaking down of food substances by the body. For example, used proteins create urea, uric acid, and creatine; the combustion of glucose produces lactic acid; poorly transformed fats turn into ketonic acid, and so forth.

Another portion of bodily toxins is produced by wear and tear on the tissues. This includes the debris of dead cells, vestiges of red corpuscles, exhausted minerals, and so on.

Other toxins are poisons that come into the body from the outside and are not part of the normal biological cycle: heavy metals from pollution (mercury, cadmium), insecticides, herbicides, preservatives, food additives, and the list goes on. To be precise, the word *toxin* should be applied only to wastes produced by the body; however, the toxic substances described here are also commonly referred to as toxins. (4, 9)

transfer of disease: The vital force of the body constantly seeks to rid the biological terrain of excess toxins, which, in addition to normal eliminations, can be revealed by more consequential evacuations from the skin (pimples, eczema), lungs (coughing), and so on. When this effort is countered by an anti-symptom treatment, the vital force does not abandon its efforts, but may transfer the excess toxins to another excretory organ. For example, wastes present in the skin will be redirected to the lungs to be eliminated from the body. This is how eczema "turns into" a cough. (26)

unity of disease: This concept of disease, which is distinctive to natural medicine, believes all health disorders are the expression of a single illness: the degradation of the biological terrain. Diseases are, therefore, only various surface manifestations of a unique, deeply rooted health problem. Hence the fundamental naturopathic aphorism, "There are no local diseases; there are only general diseases."

As the degradation of the biological terrain is always the origin for any disease, and thereby necessarily precedes the appearance of any local health problems, therapy is always essentially the same (therapeutic uniqueness): correct this internal cellular environment by ridding it of any overloads and by filling its deficiencies.

Hippocrates, the father of medicine, said in this regard: "The nature of all illness is the same. It differs only in its seat. I think it only reveals itself in such diversity because of the multiplicity of places where the illness is established. In fact, its essence is one, and the cause producing it is also one." (7, 18)

vital force: The vital force organizes living matter and orchestrates, synchronizes, and harmonizes all its organic functions. It is intangible and therefore cannot be identified with any single organ of the body. Its existence is revealed only by its effects. All of its efforts are aimed at maintaining the body in the optimum state of health. It is this force that enlivens the organs and governs the processes of respiration, circulation, digestion, exchanges, and elimination. It also triggers the reactions of the body's defense system; it scars wounds, neutralizes poisons, and prompts healing crises.

It is an intelligent force that acts wisely for the good of the organism. Hippocrates believed the medical practitioner should be "the interpreter and minister" of this medicalizing force; in other words, the therapy should reflect and mimic this force. (14)

warning signals: Minor health problems that warn us when the biological terrain is out of balance and beginning to break down. It could be not feeling well, fatigue, nervous tension, or even a few pimples or minor digestive disorder. The overload rate is still low, but correction of the lifestyle must be quickly implemented to avoid continued deterioration of the biological terrain. (29)

waste: A combination of toxins and toxic substances that degrade the biological terrain. (5)

Bibliography

꽃

Cabot, Sandra, and Marie-France Muller. *Régénérez votre foie!* St.-Julien-en-Genevois, France: Editions Jouvence, 2004.

Carton, Paul. *The Ten Commandments of Health and Happiness.* New York: Deronda Publishing Company, 1929.

Davis, Adele. *Let's Eat Right to Keep Fit.* New York: Signet, 1970.

Lust, Benedict. *Zone Therapy: Relieving Pain and Sickness by Nerve Pressure.* Chicago: Kessinger, 2003.

Lust, Benedict, and Louis Kuhne. *Neo Naturopathy: The New Science of Healing or the Unity of Diseases.* Chicago: Kessinger, 2003.

Mignot, Josiane. *Hydrotherapie du colon.* St.-Julien-en-Genevois, France: Editions Jouvence, 2005.

Valnet, Jean. *The Practice of Aromatherapy: A Classic Compendium of Plant Medicines and Their Healing Properties.* Edited by Robert Tisserand. Rochester, Vt.: Healing Arts Press, 1982, 1990.

Vasey, Christopher. *The Acid–Alkaline Diet for Optimum Health: Restore Your Health by Creating pH Balance in Your Diet.* Rochester, Vt.: Healing Arts Press, 2002. Second edition, 2006.

———. *Les compléments alimentaires naturels.* St.-Julien-en-Genevois, France: Editions Jouvence, 2003.

———. *The Detox Mono Diet.* Rochester, Vt.: Healing Arts Press, 2006.

———. *The Water Prescription.* Rochester, Vt.: Healing Arts Press, 2006.

———. *The Whey Prescription.* Rochester, Vt.: Healing Arts Press, 2006.

Resources

လာ

To find a local naturopathic physician, visit the website of the American Association of Naturopathic Physicians: **www .naturopathic.org.**

In Canada, use the search function provided by the Canadian Association of Naturopathic Doctors: **www.cand.ca.**

ALKALINE SUPPLEMENTS

pHion Nutrition
14201 N. Hayden Road, Suite A4
Scottsdale, AZ 85260
888-744-8589
www.phionbalance.com

pHion Nutrition manufactures and distributes pH test strips, alkalizing supplements, and other products geared toward detoxifying and augmenting healthy body chemistry.

AUTHOR'S WEBSITE

www.christophervasey.ch
The author presents his different books and provides for each the table of contents and a general introduction to the subject of the book. The website also contains biographical information, a calendar of conferences, and contact information.

Index

❧

acid-alkaline balance, 43, 67–70, 80, 101–6, 110
acidifying foods, 102–3
acidosis, 110
acids, 40
acne, 15, 29, 59
acute illnesses, 30–32, 110
adrenalin, 73
agitation, 73
AIDS, 22, 29, 34
air, 121
alcoholic beverages, 50–51, 80
alkalizing foods, 102, 103–4
allopathic medicine, 3, 22–23, 111
almonds, 68, 103
anaerobic phase, 42
animals, 12, 52
anti-vitamins, 66
artichoke, 89
asthma, 17
autolysis, 94, 111
avocados, 104

bacteria, 17
balneotherapy, 21, 120
bananas, 68, 103
baths, 90–91
bee pollen, 22, 100
beverages, 11

bile, 57
biological terrain. *See* internal cellular environment
black olives, 103–4
black radish, 85
blackstrap molasses, 100
blood, 3
blood circulation, 6
blood pressure, 47–48
bodily fluids, 4, 4–5, 7, 26. *See also* specific fluids
bone marrow, 16–17
bowel movements, 58
brazil nuts, 103
bread, 103
brewer's yeast, 22, 100
bronchitis, 32, 60
buckthorn, 86
butter, 45–46

cancer, vii, 29, 54–55
carbohydrates, 11, 42–43, 77
carcinogens, 54–55
Carrel, Alexis, 9
Carton, Paul, 16
castor oil, 87
catalytic minerals, 66
cells, 3, 5, 34
cerebrospinal fluid, 3
cheese, 102

BOOKS OF RELATED INTEREST

The Acid–Alkaline Diet for Optimum Health
Restore Your Health by Creating pH Balance in Your Diet
by Christopher Vasey, N.D.

The Detox Mono Diet
The Miracle Grape Cure and Other Cleansing Diets
by Christopher Vasey, N.D.

The Whey Prescription
The Healing Miracle in Milk
by Christopher Vasey, N.D.

The Water Prescription
For Health, Vitality, and Rejuvenation
by Christopher Vasey, N.D.

Traditional Foods Are Your Best Medicine
Improving Health and Longevity with Native Nutrition
by Ronald F. Schmid, N.D.

Optimal Digestive Health: A Complete Guide
*Edited by Trent W. Nichols, M.D.,
and Nancy Faass, MSW, MPH*

The Seasonal Detox Diet
Remedies from the Ancient Cookfire
by Carrie L'Esperance

Food Allergies and Food Intolerance
The Complete Guide to Their Identification and Treatment
by Jonathan Brostoff, M.D., and Linda Gamlin

INNER TRADITIONS • BEAR & COMPANY
P.O. Box 388
Rochester, VT 05767
1-800-246-8648
www.InnerTraditions.com
Or contact your local bookseller